A PRACTICAL GUIDE TO

Teaching and Assessing the ACGME Core Competencies

SECOND EDITION

ELIZABETH A. RIDER, MSW, MD, FAAP • RUTH H. NAWOTNIAK, MS, C-TAGME

 HCPro

A Practical Guide to Teaching and Assessing the ACGME Core Competencies, Second Edition is published by HCPro, Inc.

ISBN: 978-1-60146-740-9

Elizabeth A. Rider, MSW, MD, FAAP, Author
Ruth H. Nawotniak, MS, C-TAGME, Author
Julie A. McCoy, Editor
Erin E. Callahan, Group Publisher
Mike Mirabello, Senior Graphic Artist
Audrey Doyle, Copyeditor
Amy Cohen, Proofreader
Matt Sharpe, Production Supervisor
Susan Darbyshire, Art Director
Jean St. Pierre, Director of Operations

HCPro, Inc.
75 Sylvan Street, Suite A-101
Danvers, MA 01923
Telephone: 800/650-6787 or 781/639-1872
Fax: 781/639-2982
E-mail: *customerservice@hcpro.com*

Visit HCPro at: *www.hcpro.com* and *www.hcmarketplace.com*

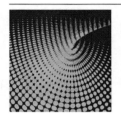

Contents

Contents

Chapter 3: Patient Care

Chapter 4: Practice-Based Learning and Improvement

Chapter 5: Systems-Based Practice

Chapter 6: Professionalism

Chapter 7: Competencies, Organizational Coherence, and the Hidden Curriculum of Medical Education

Concluding Comments

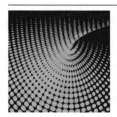

About the Authors

Elizabeth A. Rider, MSW, MD, FAAP

Elizabeth A. Rider, MSW, MD, FAAP, is director of academic programs at the Institute for Professionalism and Ethical Practice, Children's Hospital Boston, where she creates and implements local and national courses to enhance relational learning and communication skills for medical education leaders, faculty, residents, and practicing clinicians. She is also director of programs for communication skills at the John D. Stoeckle Center for Primary Care Innovation, Massachusetts General Hospital, a center dedicated to revitalizing and redesigning primary care and to enhancing patients' and families' experience of care. She is an assistant professor of pediatrics at Harvard Medical School (HMS).

A graduate of HMS, she completed her pediatric residency at Children's Hospital Boston and fellowship in general academic pediatrics at Massachusetts General Hospital. She also holds a master's degree in clinical social work from Smith College. A former child and family therapist, she is board certified in both pediatrics and clinical social work (LICSW, BCD), and is a Fellow of the American Academy of Pediatrics, the American Academy on Communication in Healthcare, and the National Academies of Practice.

She directs the international Harvard faculty development course "Difficult Conversations in Healthcare: Pedagogy and Practice" and the Difficult Conversations Program for Residents at Children's Hospital Boston. She also codirects the year-long psychosocial pediatrics course "Emotional and Psychosocial Issues in Children and Families: Pediatrics for the New Millennium."

She designs and leads educational programs at three Harvard-affiliated hospitals and did similar work at HMS. She was a member of the Kalamazoo Consensus Statement Group on Physician–Patient Communication in Medical Education, and brought the Kalamazoo framework to HMS, where she and colleagues implemented assessment in communication competencies across all four years and a communication skills curricular model in the core medicine clerkships. At HMS, Rider was also coordinator of faculty development for the resident as teacher programs, and taught for a number of years in the Patient-Doctor III course. She currently serves as faculty for the Harvard Macy Institute Program for Educators in Health Professions.

A winner of various teaching awards, Dr. Rider teaches and consults nationally and internationally on communication skills, relationship-centered care, reflective practice, and medical education program development. In 2007, she was invited by the Education Ministry of Taiwan to teach 125 medical education leaders from Taiwan's 11 medical schools about teaching, assessing, and integrating communication skills into medical education curricula.

She was elected to the Medicine Academy of the National Academies of Practice as a Distinguished Scholar and Practitioner, and was appointed co-chair of the Medicine Academy in 2006. The National Academies of Practice, comprised of Academies of 10 healthcare professions, serves as a distinguished policy forum to advise U.S. governmental bodies on interprofessional approaches to healthcare.

She serves on the National Board of Medical Examiners' Communication Skills Task Force. She is section editor (Reflective Practice) for the international journal *Patient Education and Counseling* and an associate editor for *Medical Encounter*. She practices pediatrics part-time at Roslindale Pediatric Associates in Boston, and was selected by her peers for inclusion in *Best Doctors*.

Ruth H. Nawotniak, MS, C-TAGME

Ruth H. Nawotniak, MS, C-TAGME, is a co-founder of the National Board for Certification of Training Administrators of Graduate Medical Education Programs (TAGME) and its first president. She spearheaded the creation of TAGME to establish standards for the profession, to acknowledge the expertise needed to successfully manage graduate medical education programs, and to recognize those training program administrators who have achieved competence in all fields related to their profession. She worked on certification development for several years before becoming chair of the communications committee. Nawotniak also serves as the training program administrator for the general surgery residency program at the University at Buffalo-SUNY and is the training program administrator liaison to the Graduate Medical Education Committee.

In addition, she has presented at teaching hospitals and academic centers across the country. Her topics include the professional coordinator, coordinator certification, new program coordinators, developing goals and objectives, and various activities and tasks of a program administrator.

She has authored and/or co-authored many publications on various facets of graduate medical education, with particular emphasis on aspects of managing residency training programs. She also holds a master's degree in English education.

About the Contributors

Judith L. Bowen, MD, FACP

Judith L. Bowen, MD, FACP, is adjunct professor of medicine at the Oregon Health and Science University (OHSU) School of Medicine in Portland, Oregon. A graduate of Williams College and Dartmouth Medical School, she completed categorical internal medicine residency training at Virginia Mason Hospital in Seattle, where she later served as residency director. She has advanced training in healthcare ethics (1991) and medical education (2006), both from the University of Washington.

She has received numerous teaching awards including the regional Society of General Internal Medicine (SGIM) Clinician-Teacher Award of Excellence (2002) and the national SGIM award, *Scholarship in Educational Methods and Teaching* (2003). In 2009, Dr. Bowen received the distinguished Dema C. Daley Founder's Award from the Association of Program Directors in Internal Medicine.

From 1998 to 2009, Bowen served as chief of the Division of General Internal Medicine & Geriatrics in the Department of Medicine at OHSU. She also served as the associate residency program director for primary care internal medicine. In that role, she developed and implemented several innovative curricula, including a nationally recognized program in chronic care and quality improvement.

Currently, she serves as the co-chair of the SGIM's Task Force on the Patient-centered Medical Home (PCMH) and the director of the PCMH Education Summit. In 2001, Dr. Bowen was elected to serve on the Research in Medical Education (RIME) conference committee for the Association of American Medical Colleges (AAMC) and subsequently selected to serve as Conference Chair in 2005.

William T. Branch, Jr., MD

William T. Branch, Jr., MD, is Carter Smith, Sr., professor of medicine and director of the Division of General Internal Medicine at Emory University School of Medicine. He founded the primary care residency at the Brigham and Women's Hospital in 1974, among the first primary care residency programs. He was a key leader of the New

Pathway project at Harvard Medical School, serving as coordinator of the required first-year Patient Doctor Course in 1988 and director of the required third-year Patient Doctor Course from 1989 to 1995.

He attended the formative meeting of the SGIM thirty-two years ago. Dr. Branch served as a member of the SGIM Council and later as secretary. He was the first leader of the Clinician-Educator Initiative and co-edited the JGIM Supplement on the Clinician-Educator. He was the second recipient of SGIM's National Award for Career Achievements in Medical Education. He is a facilitator in the American Academy on Communication on Healthcare (AACH) and currently is immediate past President of the AACH.

At Emory University, he served as director of the Division of Internal General Medicine. He more than tripled the size of the division, and founded a primary care residency program and a faculty development program for young faculty members. He planned and implemented a required end-of-life course for Emory medical students, and is one of three co-directors of Emory's four-year "Being a Doctor" course.

Eugene C. Corbett, Jr., MD, FACP

Eugene C. Corbett, Jr., MD, FACP, is a general internist with a clinical education background in surgery, internal medicine, and public health. Following 11 years of rural general practice experience, he serves full time in an academic career at the University of Virginia School of Medicine as a clinician, teacher, and educator since 1985. His medical education interests include clinical skills education, physical examination, and curriculum and faculty development in both undergraduate and graduate education.

He has also been involved with the AAMC as chair of its Clinical Skills Task Force. This national consensus effort is focused upon advancing clinical performance education in the undergraduate medical curriculum. The Task Force published a number of monographs containing recommendations regarding the design and content of clinical skills education curricula. These include a model that specifies the generic set of patient care competencies required of all physicians.

He has received many recognitions and awards for his work in medical education. Most recently, he received the Robert J. Glaser Distinguished Teacher Award, co-sponsored by the national honorary society, Alpha Omega Alpha, and the AAMC.

Richard L. Cruess, MD

Richard L. Cruess, MD, graduated with a Bachelor of Arts from Princeton in 1951 and a medical degree from Columbia University in 1955. He is professor of orthopedic surgery and a member of the Centre for Medical Education at McGill University. An orthopedic surgeon, he served as chair of orthopedics (1976–1981), directing a basic science laboratory and publishing extensively in the field. He was dean of the faculty of medicine at McGill University from 1981 to 1995. He was president of the Canadian Orthopedic Association (1977–1978), the American Orthopedic Research Society (1975–1976), and the Association of Canadian Medical Colleges (1992–1994). He is an officer of The Order of Canada and of *L'Ordre National du Québec*. Since 1995, with his wife Sylvia Cruess, MD, he has taught and carried out independent research on professionalism in medicine. They have published widely on the subject and been invited speakers at universities, hospitals, and professional organizations throughout the world.

Sylvia R. Cruess, MD

Sylvia R. Cruess, MD, graduated from Vassar College with a Bachelor of Arts in 1951 and a medical degree from Columbia University in 1955. She is an endocrinologist, professor of medicine, and a member of the Centre for Medical Education at McGill University. She previously served as director of the metabolic Day Centre (1968–1978) and as medical director of the Royal Victoria Hospital (1978–1995) in Montreal. She was a member of the Deschamps Commission on Conduct of Research on Humans in Establishments. Since 1995, with her husband Richard Cruess, MD, she has taught and carried out research on professionalism in medicine. They have published extensively on the subject and been invited speakers at universities, hospitals, and professional organizations throughout the world.

F. Daniel Duffy, MD, MACP, FAACH

F. Daniel Duffy, MD, MACP, FAACH, is dean of the University of Oklahoma School of Community Medicine in Tulsa. He and colleagues are leading development of a four-year medical school program that integrates clinical medicine with the principles and practices of trans-disciplinary health and care for whole communities.

Previously, he was executive vice president for the American Board of Internal Medicine (ABIM) where he introduced the practice of quality improvement into the maintenance of certification programs for practicing physicians in the ABIM Practice Improvement Modules. While at the ABIM, he also held an adjunct professorship at the University of Pennsylvania in internal medicine where he taught principles of medical education. Prior to his service to the certification movement, he was chair of the Department of Medicine at the University of Oklahoma in Tulsa, where he was honored with the Stanton L. Young Master Teacher Award in 1989.

He served as a director of the American Board of Medical Specialties, regent for the American College of Physicians, and Oklahoma governor for the College. He is a founding member of the American Academy on Communications in Healthcare where he served as chair of the Board of Directors. He also served on and chaired the ACGME's Residency Review Committee for Internal Medicine.

He received a bachelor's degree from the University of Pittsburgh and medical degree from Temple University Medical School. He completed residency training in internal medicine and fellowship training in pulmonary disease at the University of Oklahoma Health Sciences Center. Though his board certification in internal medicine is time-unlimited, Dr. Duffy voluntarily renewed his certificate in 2006.

Frederic W. Hafferty, PhD

Frederic W. Hafferty, PhD, is professor of behavioral sciences at the University of Minnesota School of Medicine-Duluth. He received his undergraduate degree in social relations from Harvard University in 1969 and his PhD in medical sociology from Yale in 1976. He is the author of *Into the Valley: Death and the Socialization of Medical Students* (Yale University Press); *The Changing Medical Profession: An International Perspective* (Oxford University Press), with John McKinlay; and the recently published *The Sociology of Complexity: A New Field of Study* with Brian Castellani (Springer).

He is currently working on a volume tracing the hidden curriculum in medical education. He is past chair of the Medical Sociology Section of the American Sociological Association and associate editor of the *Journal of Health and Social Behavior*, and currently sits on the AAMC's Council of Academic Societies. Research focuses on the evolution of medicine's professionalism movement, mapping social networks within medical education, the application of complexity theory to medical training, issues of medical socialization, and disability studies.

Stacy M. Higgins, MD, FACP

Stacy M. Higgins, MD, FACP, is the associate program director for ambulatory education and the director of the primary care track internal medicine residency program at Emory University School of Medicine in Atlanta.

After graduating from Dartmouth College in 1989, she received her medical degree from Cornell University Medical College in New York in 1995. She completed residency training in internal medicine at Columbia University's Presbyterian Hospital, followed by a year as chief medical resident. She joined the faculty of Emory

University's School of Medicine in 1999, and is clinically based at Grady Hospital. She also works in immigrant health at the International Medical Clinic, as well as women's health in the Women's Clinic.

David C. Leach, MD

David C. Leach, MD, is the retired CEO of the ACGME. He was born in Elmira, New York, received a Bachelor of Arts from St. Michael's College of the University of Toronto in 1965, and a medical degree from the University of Rochester School of Medicine and Dentistry in 1969. He completed residency training in internal medicine and endocrinology at the Henry Ford Health System (HFHS) in Detroit, and he is certified in those disciplines. He also had additional training in pediatric endocrinology. He was awarded the A Good Samaritan Award by Governor John Engler for his work of over 25 years at a free clinic in Detroit.

He was assistant dean at the University of Michigan for several years, primarily directing the HFHS experiences for students. He was a residency program director and designated institutional official at HFHS. He is interested in how physicians acquire competence and are enabled to be authentic practitioners of the art, science, and craft of medicine. He received grant support for innovative curricula for both medical students and residents from the Robert Wood Johnson Foundation and the Pew Charitable Trust. He is interested in Achaordic organizations, the teaching of improvement skills, aligning accreditation with emerging healthcare practices, and the use of educational outcome measures as an accreditation tool. He has received honorary degrees from five medical schools.

He is interested in honoring program directors through the Parker J. Palmer Courage to Teach award. He is a member of the Gold Humanism Honorary Society and is deeply interested in the use of values as well as rules in guiding the behavior of physicians and teachers. He believes that we teach who we are as well as what we are. He is the 2007 recipient of the Abraham Flexner Award for Distinguished Service to Medical Education.

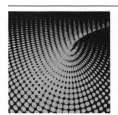

Foreword

David C. Leach, MD

It is a privilege to be asked to write this foreword to *A Practical Guide to Teaching and Assessing the ACGME Core Competencies*, Second Edition. As the competency movement developed and the accompanying ACGME requirements were deployed, many program directors, faculty, and educational coordinators said, "Look, we are busy people; just tell us what to do." This book fulfills that need, but it also does much more.

Career pathways began to open up for those who took education seriously; grants became available, and publications resulted. The importance of resident physician training became evident. This book also serves the needs of those who want to dive deeper into the phenomenon of physician competence. In this foreword, I have decided to share my observations on the competency movement and my journey toward understanding the movement.

I am an endocrinologist who was primarily interested in medical student education until 1983 when I was asked to become a program director for a transitional-year residency at my institution. Thinking about how my 20 residents were learning and moving toward competence changed my life. I then became a designated institutional official and had stewardship over about 50 residency programs that housed 800 residents. In 1997, after 14 years of experience with residents, I was asked to serve as the executive director of the ACGME and did so for 10 years. I retired in 2008 and am now free to speak my mind (the little that's left of it), and would like to encourage those who take education seriously—it is a terrific vocation.

In September 1997, the ACGME committed to the use of educational outcomes as an accreditation tool. We began a process designed to help us understand what that meant. Research identified key publications on physician competence, and we settled on about 84 frequently mentioned aspects of competence thought to be important. Susan Swing, PhD, ACGME's director of research, surveyed several different constituents including deans, hospital CEOs, patients, program directors, faculty, residents, public health officials, and policy leaders who helped us rank the various competencies by their importance and the feasibility of measuring competence in them. Paul Batalden, MD, a program director from Dartmouth Medical School, whose importance in the competency movement cannot be overstated, chaired an advisory committee of experts in education and assessment. Over the course of a year and a half, the advisory committee created a recommendation to the ACGME board which in turn adopted the six competencies.

We settled on six for two main reasons. First, we knew that most people could remember six or seven things but not more, and we wanted to avoid the necessity of going to a manual whenever discussions about competency arose. We also wanted the competencies to foster conversations across the various specialties and to be general enough to include all physicians, not just particular specialties.

We decided to create a timeline gentle enough to give the field time to get the movement right. Phase One, a one-year phase, was an invitational phase. In essence, we said to the GME community, "We invite you to respond to the challenge of teaching and assessing these competencies." We wanted the experience of early adopters to inform our next steps. Phase Two was titled "Clarifying the meaning and sharpening the focus of the competencies." This four-year phase was designed to get real about the meaning and assessment of each competency and to be clear about how they would be used in the accreditation of programs. Phase Three, another four-year phase, was designed to link measured improvement in competency teaching and assessment with improvements in patient care and the accreditation system. Phase Four consisted of ongoing improvement in the teaching and assessment of resident physician competence.

Several lessons were learned over the following few years. I would like to highlight these few:

1. Once the basic vocabulary, knowledge, and rules of a discipline are mastered, competence can be thought of as the demonstrated habit of reflective practice. It seems to me that this definition contains all the crucial elements: To become competent you have to have experience; to reflect on the experience you must have a system in place that can document those facts. Stages before competence (novice and advanced beginner, per the Dreyfus brothers1) involve learning the vocabulary and rules, and stages after (proficient, expert, and master) involve an ever-deepening practical wisdom. Competence is at the nexus of these two worlds: that is, between passing a multiple-choice exam and actually being useful to patients. Context assumes a more important role and the rules. Although still fundamental, rules become interpreted in the light of context. Medicine is both a science (generalizable science-based knowledge) and an art (particular patients and the contexts of their reality). Competence is generated where rules meet contexts and accountability for decisions is made. Once the rules of a given skill are mastered, the emergence of competence depends on practice and reflection on the experiences of practice. Reflection, in turn, requires solitude and community: solitude to organize and clarify one's own thinking about experience, and community to see if one's observations and conclusions hold up under scrutiny.

Competence and community are interdependent. The six competencies identified by the ACGME and widely adopted by other organizations are designed to, in the words of the late Marvin Dunn, "enable conversations about the work of medicine." They help organize reflections on experience and conversations in community on reflected experiences. This second edition of *A Practical Guide to Teaching and Assessing the ACGME Core Competencies* continues the conversation and offers additional clarity about just how one might teach and assess these competencies.

2.   If you are interested in teaching and assessing competence, you'd better get comfortable with paradox. Paradoxes are encountered whenever competency is taken seriously; and it is necessary to honor both arms of all paradoxes to move to a higher level of competence. For example, a competent accrediting body must honor both arms of the lumper/splitter paradox. Naming the competencies requires lumping; measuring them requires splitting. The ACGME sets standards for and accredits more than 120 specialties and sub-specialties, each requiring very different skills, yet we wanted to foster conversations that cut across specialty lines and invite input from all physicians. We wanted this to be a professionwide conversation, not simply 120-plus different conversations. We wanted the conversation to belong to everyone. Yet measuring competence requires that representative particular behaviors be examined in fine detail, behaviors that are quite different across the various specialties. We had to aggressively lump and aggressively split the phenomena to take competence seriously.

Consider the following example. Many are familiar with the "genius" resident who scores near perfect on every objective exam but cannot seem to tolerate the ambiguities associated with discerning the truth in the case of real patients. Likewise, some residents are gifted in social and conversational skills but lack the discipline and skill to be of real service to patients. Neither of these residents is competent. Competence requires that both arms of the art/science continuum be honored. Measurement tends to reward the first resident and punish the second, but instead, measurement should be used to inform a learning path forward for each.

3.   Competence reduces fear and opens up space for joy. Fear is pervasive in healthcare. Patients and their families are understandably afraid; healthcare workers must overcome a natural tendency to turn and run away from human suffering. They must stand and directly face suffering and human vulnerability to be effective. Likewise, learners are terrified of either hurting patients or doing something that would make them appear incompetent. Fear taints all conversations in hospitals and other healthcare settings. It is toxic. Truth and truth telling about competence reduces fear. Thomas Merton once said, "We exhaust ourselves supporting our illusions."[2] Doing the work of patient care is hard enough; it is truly exhausting to both do the work and maintain false illusions/delusions of competence. My life changed when I began to tell patients

that, "Hospitals can be dangerous places; bad things occasionally happen. Everyone has to be vigilant. I will try to be vigilant, but I also need you to be vigilant. Please let me know if you see anything out of the ordinary." Each time I rounded I would ask them how they were doing, as well as how we were doing. It opened up a partnership that both enhanced safety and enabled guarded territory to see sunlight. Properly done, the work of healthcare is noble work. Helping each other in our weakness is as good as humans get. When done well, caring for patients enables joy to emerge even in the dreariest of places and circumstances. I believe that the ultimate measure of success in the competency movement is better patient care and that better patient care nourishes and permits a deep satisfaction to emerge in both patients and their caregivers. When we get it right, joy will return to the workplace.

4.   It's best to work with, not against, human nature. All humans come equipped with three faculties useful in the work of medicine: the intellect, the will, and the imagination. The object of the intellect is truth; that of the will is goodness; and that of the imagination is beauty or harmony. In the case of healthcare, this translates into three reflections. At the end of every day, we should all ask ourselves (and occasionally others): "How good a job did I do discerning and telling the truth?" "How good a job did I do putting what is good for the patient above my own interest?" "How good a job did I do harmonizing the best science and art—harmonizing the best scientific knowledge with a deep understanding of the patient in ways that informed and made my clinical decisions creative and marked by the practical wisdom inherent in good medicine?" Disciplined reflection on these three questions opens a path to competence.

These four lessons also apply to those who teach, assess, and lead educational programs. Individual and communal reflection on experience, tolerance of paradox, overcoming fear of change by truth telling, and working with the intellect, will, and imagination all foster the emergence of competent institutions and educational communities.

I close by congratulating the authors of the chapters in this book. They have taken competence seriously and have provided a solid framework for ongoing community conversations about competence. Community leads to clarity and clarity leads to courage, the courage needed to carry the movement to the next level.

References

1.   Dreyfus, H. On the Internet, Routledge Press, 2001. Hubert and Stuart Dreyfus are brothers (Hubert is a philosopher and Stuart a mathematician) both at UC Berkley. This book summarizes their elegant and extremely practical approach to the acquisition of skills by humans. Chapter 2, pp. 28–49, is especially relevant but the entire book is well worth while.

2   Merton, Thomas. Lectures to Novices, Credence cassettes. Credence cassettes has published an extensive series of audiotapes recording the voice of Thomas Merton lecturing the novices at Gethsemani when he was novice master. The tapes were never intended to be distributed beyond the walls of the monastery but contain many rich observations useful to lay people.

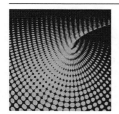

Preface

Welcome to the second edition of *A Practical Guide to Teaching and Assessing the ACGME Core Competencies.* In order to receive accreditation from the Accreditation Council for Graduate Medical Education (ACGME), residency programs must assess and document resident performance in the core competencies: interpersonal and communication skills, medical knowledge, patient care, practice-based learning and improvement, systems-based practice, and professionalism.

This book is intended for a wide audience as medical organizations and regulatory bodies worldwide use the same or similar competencies for physicians at all levels. In the United States, many medical schools, specialty and licensing boards, and medical accreditation organizations, including the American Board of Medical Specialties, the Federation of State Medical Boards, The Joint Commission, and others, have adopted these competencies.

A Practical Guide to Teaching and Assessing the ACGME Core Competencies, Second Edition, provides the research background, evidence-base, curricular models, teaching methods, assessment strategies, and faculty development suggestions for all six core competencies. In addition, you will find a number of assessment tools, many studied and validated, for evaluation and documentation. Many are also available online via the link included in this book.

We have substantially revised and updated the entire book to keep pace with changes in medical education and competency requirements. All chapters contain new perspectives, information, and resources. Some chapters have new or additional authors, all well-respected experts in medical education and in their chapter content. With growing recognition of the learning environment and its significant effect on medical education and organizational culture, we've added a new chapter on the hidden curriculum written by Fred Hafferty, PhD.

This second edition includes new curricular models, innovative teaching strategies, and new or updated assessment methods and tools for each competency. David C. Leach, MD, former executive director of the ACGME, provides a lively and wise perspective in the Foreword for this edition.

We would like to thank Gary Smith, EdD, for his two chapters in the first edition. They have laid the foundation for the second edition chapters on those topics. We appreciate the new chapter authors who graciously and expeditiously gave of their time and expertise. A special thank you to Julie McCoy, our editor for the second edition, for her patience, good nature, and skillful editing.

Our "hidden curriculum" for the book is to promote relationship-centered teaching and learning, reflection, compassion, strong values, and careful consideration of how we can help develop reflective physicians who have a strong foundation of knowledge along with excellent clinical reasoning capabilities, lifelong learning skills, and the capacity to engage in mindful and caring relationships with their patients and colleagues. We hope this book will provide inspiration, guidance, and practical advice as you develop educational opportunities for your learners and faculty alike.

> "Never doubt that a small group of thoughtful, committed people
> can change the world. Indeed, it's the only thing that ever has."
> —Margaret Mead

Elizabeth A. Rider, MSW, MD, FAAP

Ruth H. Nawotniak, MS, C-TAGME

INTRODUCTION

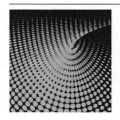

Graduate Medical Education: Making the Implicit Explicit

Sylvia R. Cruess, MD
Richard L. Cruess, MD

"The challenge for professional education is how to teach the complex ensemble of analytic thinking, skillful practice, and wise judgment upon which each profession rests."[1]

The relationship between medicine and society has undergone a profound transformation during the past decades. As one observer has noted, "the professionals' autonomy is severely restricted by budgets, bureaucracy, guidelines and peer review" while, at the same time, "a better informed community is asking for accountability, transparency, and sound professional standards."[2]

There is evidence that neither physicians nor society is entirely content with the current situation. Surveys of physicians have indicated substantial dissatisfaction with the contemporary practice of medicine.[3, 4, 5] Patients' satisfaction with their individual physicians remains high, but trust in the profession as a whole has diminished.[6, 7]

Although many factors have led to the current situation, a few require special attention in a discussion of the graduate education of physicians. First, the effectiveness of modern healthcare has made it essential to the well-being of citizens if they are to lead healthy and productive lives.[8] For this reason, the education and training of the modern medical workforce has become important to contemporary society.

Second, the impact of technology and the related subspecialization of medicine have threatened to turn physicians into technocrats rather than the healers who have served society for millennia. Neither society nor the medical profession wishes for this to occur.[9, 10]

Third, there is a belief that organized medicine and individual physicians have failed to meet some of the obligations expected of them as professionals.[1, 11] They are perceived as pursuing their own self-interest rather than demonstrating altruism, and it is believed that their commitment to self-regulation has been flawed. Thus, there is now a need for more explicit guidelines in teaching what is expected of a physician in today's world.

Finally, the structure of contemporary healthcare systems throughout the world has posed threats to the value system of medicine everywhere.[9] As either governments or commercial organizations became the principal third-party payers, they have tended to regard medicine as a commodity rather than a moral endeavor. Again, medical educators have concluded that if the values that have been the foundation of the practice of medicine for generations are to survive, they must be taught explicitly and reinforced throughout the continuum of medical education.[12, 13, 14]

As a result of these pressures, medicine's institutions—including licensing and certifying bodies, as well as educational and training establishments—have determined that it is necessary to address the aspects of medicine that are under their direct control. As a part of this process, there has been a serious reexamination of undergraduate medical education, graduate education and training, and the credentialing of physicians, including licensure, certification, and maintenance of competence. In graduate education, this has led to an analysis of the component parts of being a physician, which have been called "competencies," and to an effort to address each component during the course of training.[15]

Competencies: Definition and History

Many organizations within the healthcare field began efforts to better define competency in the 1970s, and at that time there were attempts to base educational programs on this concept.[16, 17] Although these activities certainly had an impact, it was not until they were applied at the graduate level that their potential became apparent. Virtually every organization concerned with graduate education in medicine expressed dissatisfaction with the methods used,[18] and a consensus developed that the practice of medicine needed to be divided into its component parts and that each component should be explicitly taught and the results evaluated.

If one looks at the evolution of medical education over the past 250 years, this seems to be a next logical step. Medical education in the eighteenth and early nineteenth centuries took place in apprenticeship-like settings.[18, 19] The development of structured curricula based on science represented an early and important step in addressing the increasing complexity of medicine.[20] However, graduate medical education continued to resemble an apprenticeship until a few decades ago, when attempts were made to improve its educational content. The development of the concept of competencies continues this trend, making the objectives and standards more explicit.

As is true of so many aspects of the practice of medicine, dictionary definitions do not completely describe the meaning that medicine ascribes to competency. Epstein and Hundert have defined competence in medicine as "the habitual and judicious use of communication, knowledge, technical skills, clinical reasoning, emotions, values, and reflection in daily practice for the benefit of the individuals and communities being served."[21] This accurately describes the aspects of the practice of medicine that are the subject of this book.

The history of the concept of medicine as constituting a group of competencies is instructive. In one major initiative, it started, appropriately, with an analysis of what patients wish to find in their physicians. In the 1980s, a study was carried out in Ontario, Canada, titled "Educating Future Physicians for Ontario" (EFPO).[22] An important component to this study was a series of focus groups involving patients who outlined what they expected from their physicians. The Royal College of Physicians and Surgeons of Canada (the organization responsible for certifying all specialists in medicine in Canada) took the results and developed the concept of "competencies" at the postgraduate level. They proposed that the object of graduate training is to turn out a medical expert (the central role) who will demonstrate the following competencies: communicator, collaborator, health advocate, manager, scholar, and professional.[23] Since 1996, graduate medical education in Canada has been structured around this framework, and this model (CanMEDS) has been used by several countries, including Australia and the Netherlands.

The Accreditation Council for Graduate Medical Education (ACGME) adopted the principle of competency-based graduate medical education and developed its own list of general competencies which form the basis of this book: patient care, medical knowledge, practice-based learning and improvement, interpersonal and communication skills, professionalism, and systems-based practice. These were implemented in 2001, and at the time of this writing all accredited residency programs in the United States must ensure that each competency is actively taught and that its residents are evaluated in each.[15, 22]

Although the ACGME only has jurisdiction over residency education, the impact of this concept has affected other educational levels as well. The Joint Commission, which provides accreditation to U.S. hospitals and other facilities, has adapted the core competencies as evaluation and recertification standards for medical staff members. Additionally, there was a movement toward competency-based undergraduate education[16, 17] which recently has been given added impetus. Two major studies, one in the United States[25] and the other in Canada[26], have strongly recommended that a competency-based curriculum serve as the model for undergraduate medical education. Many faculties of medicine have already moved in this direction, and it can be anticipated that more will follow.

Challenges

Osler described medicine as "a calling in which your heart will be exercised equally with your head."[27] The challenge for medical education is to address both the head and the heart. Without question, this is true of attempting to teach the competencies.

Reaching the head requires that students master the cognitive base of each competency. For this to occur, shared learning objectives must be developed for each competency, and these must be understood by both teachers and learners. It seems to us that a structured program that ensures that all of the material is actually covered is the best way to achieve this.

However, if one reaches only the head, it is unlikely that much of what has been acquired will actually be put into practice. Professional identity arises "from a long-term combination of experience and reflection on experience."[28] A major objective of medical education should be to provide stage-appropriate education and training opportunities for both gaining experience in each competency and reflecting on it. The knowledge gained becomes part of a larger body of knowledge described as "tacit": that which one knows but has difficulty in telling.[29] Although tacit knowledge is difficult to teach, it can be learned, and situated learning,[30] which encourages self-reflection and promotes "mindfulness"[31] or "reflective practice,"[32] facilitates this process.

One can reach neither the head nor the heart unless the environment in which learning takes place is supportive. Hafferty has pointed out that the curriculum is more complex than it appears.[33, 34] There is the "formal curriculum" that is outlined in mission statements and course objectives, detailing what the faculty believe they are teaching. There is also a powerful "informal curriculum" at work, consisting of unscripted, unplanned, and highly interpersonal forms of teaching and learning that take place among and between faculty and students. Role models at several levels, from peers to senior physicians, function in the informal curriculum and can have a profound effect for good or ill.[35]

Finally, there is a set of influences that are largely hidden, functioning at the level of the organizational culture and structure. The influence of this "hidden curriculum" on teaching and learning can, like role models, be either positive or negative. Without question, the hidden and informal curricula form the background against which competency-based teaching and learning takes place. If these curricula are not supportive of the program, it is difficult to meet the desired objectives.[34]

Evaluation of the results of teaching the competencies presents a challenge, partly because competency-based education is a relatively new concept. There are tested tools for evaluating knowledge and skills, and these must be used.[36] However, attitudes and values cannot be evaluated in a reliable and valid fashion. Only observable behaviors that reflect these attitudes and values can be evaluated, and at the time of this writing very few evaluation tools are available to accomplish this.[21, 37] Therefore, the challenge is to develop reliable and reproducible evaluation methods as quickly as possible. Finally, the neglected field of remediation for underperforming students, residents, or practitioners must receive some attention.[38] At the present time, methods are available for remediation of gaps in knowledge and skills, but not for behaviors.

In addition, programs of competency-based graduate medical education must themselves be evaluated in a rigorous fashion. As a self-regulating profession, medicine enjoys the privilege of setting and maintaining standards for education and practice.[39, 40] Therefore, it has a societal obligation to ensure that physicians leaving their residency programs meet "sound professional standards." This will require long-term follow-up of residents in their practice.

Role Models and Faculty Development

For generations, respected role models were the principal means of transmitting knowledge, skills, and, most importantly, the values of the profession. Role models were and are capable of reaching both the head and the heart. Although the restructuring of graduate medical education represents recognition that role models alone are not sufficient to reliably produce a contemporary physician, they remain absolutely essential to the process.

Role models are the most potent means of transmitting those intangibles that have been called the art of medicine.[41, 42, 43, 45] They facilitate the development of a sense of collegiality in which students and residents acquire a sense of "belonging."[46] Conversely, negative role models can be extremely destructive, impeding professional development. Their negative influence posed difficulties before competency-based education was developed, and will certainly continue to do so unless the issue is addressed explicitly. Faculty development can assist in cultivating more effective role models, in part by ensuring that all faculty members understand the competencies and "speak the same language."[47] Removing physicians who constitute a negative influence on students, residents, and peers is also essential.

Some caveats must be mentioned. The first relates to professionalism, a competency which is fundamental to medical practice and which serves as the basis of medicine's social contract with society.[11] Legitimate doubts have been raised as to whether professionalism is a competency which is more than mere expertise. It has been suggested that professionalism represents medicine's moral base, not just expertise, and there are questions as to whether morality can be taught.[48] Without question, this is one reason teaching and assessing professionalism has posed special problems that have not yet been completely solved, particularly at the postgraduate level.

Second, medicine's competencies overlap with those found in other health professions, and the current need for team medicine appears to dictate that some attention must be paid to integrating medical education with the education of other health professionals.[49, 50] Third, and linked to the preceding point, the competency movement stresses, as it must, the development of competencies in individual physicians. The future will certainly see an increased emphasis on team performance rather than individual performance. This will require the use of educational methods that encourage collective competence through "distributed knowing" and knowledge-building communities.[51]

A final point must be made. Competency-based graduate education divides the practice of medicine and the medical act into a series of separate domains. However, this does not reflect what physicians do in the presence of their patients. These domains must be reintegrated into a seamless whole, and this can be done only by individual physicians as they gain experiential knowledge. Postgraduate programs, in addition to teaching the competencies explicitly and providing opportunities for experiential learning, are responsible for ensuring that this reintegration takes place. It appears to us that assisting in this essential task may represent the most important function of the role models of the future.

References

1. Sullivan W. *Work and Integrity: The Crisis and Promise of Professionalism in North America*. 2nd. ed. San Francisco, CA: Jossey-Bass; 2005.

2. Dunning AJ. Status of the doctor – present and future. *Lancet*. 1999;354(sup):SIV 18.

3. Feldman DS, Novack DH, Graceley E. Effects of managed care on physician-patient relationships, quality of care, and the ethical practice of medicine. *Arch Int Med*. 1998;158:1626–1633.

4. Horton R. Doctors in the NHS: the restless many and the squabbling few. *Lancet*. 2000;355:2010–2012.

5. Blendon RJ, Schoen C, Des Roches C, Osborn R. Confronting competing demands to improve quality: a five country survey. *Health Affairs*. 2004;23:119–131.

6. Hall MA, Dugan E, Zheug B, Mishra AK. Trust in physicians and medical institutions: what is it, can it be measured and does it matter? *Milbank Quarterly*. 2000;79:613–639.

7. Schlesinger M. A loss of faith: the sources of reduced political legitimacy for the American medical profession. *Milbank Quarterly*. 2002;80:185–235.

8. Rawls JA. *Theory of Justice*. Cambridge, MA: Harvard University Press; 1999.

9. Stevens R. Public roles for the medical profession in the United States: beyond theories of decline and fall. *Milbank Quarterly*. 2001;79:327–353.

10. Stevens R. Specialization, specialty organizations, and the quality of health care. In: Mechanic D, Rogut LB, Colby DC, Knickman JR, eds. *Policy Challenges in Modern Health Care*. New Brunswick, NJ: Rutgers University Press; 2006:206–224.

11. Cruess RL, Cruess SR. Expectations and obligations: professionalism and medicine's social contract with society. *Pers Biol Med*. 2008;51:579–598.

12. Cruess SR, Cruess RL. Professionalism must be taught. *BMJ*. 1997;315:1674–1677.

13. Ludmerer KM. Instilling professionalism in medical education. *JAMA*. 1999;282:881–882.

14. Cruess R, Cruess S. Teaching professionalism: general principles. *Med Teach*. 2006;28:205–208.

15. Bataldan P, Leach D, Swing S, Dreyfus H, Dreyfus S. General competencies and accreditation in graduate medical education. *Health Affairs*. 2002;21:103–110.

16. Carraccio C, Wolfsthal SD, Englander R, Ferentz K, Martin C. Shifting paradigms: from Flexner to competencies. *Acad Med*. 2002;77:361–367.

17. Whitcomb, ME. More on competency-based education. *Acad Med*. 2004;79:493–494.

18. Ludmerer KM. *Learning to Heal: The Development of American Medical Education*. New York, NY: Basic Books; 1985.

19.   Bonner TN. *On Becoming a Physician: Medical Education in Great Britain, France, Germany, and the United States.* New York, NY: Basic Books; 1995.

20.   Flexner A. Medical education in the United States and Canada: a report to the Carnegie Foundation for the Advancement of Teaching. Washington, D.C. Science and Health Publication, 1910.

21.   Epstein RM, Hundert E. Defining and assessing professional competence. *JAMA.* 2002:287;226–235.

22.   Neufeld VR, Maudsley RF, Pickering RJ, et al. Educating future physicians for Ontario. *Acad Med.* 1998;73:1133–1148.

23.   Royal College of Physicians and Surgeons of Canada. The CanMeds roles framework. 2005. *http://rcpsc.medil.org. canmeds/index.php.* Accessed February 5, 2007.

24.   Leach DC. Competence is a habit. *JAMA.* 2002;287:243–244.

25.   Irby DM, Cooke M, O'Brien BC. Calls for reform of medical education by the Carnegie Foundation for the Advancement of Teaching: 1910 and 2010. *Acad Med.* 2010;85:220–227.

26.   Busing N, Slade S, Rosenfeld J, Gold I, Maskill S. In the spirit of Flexner: working toward a collective vision for the future of medical education in Canada. *Acad Med.* 2010;85:340–348.

27.   Osler W. *Aequanimitas, with Other Addresses to Medical Students, Nurses and Practitioners of Medicine.* 3rd. ed. Philadelphia, PA: P. Blakiston; 1932.

28.   Hilton SR, Slotnick HB. Proto-professionalism: how professionalization occurs across the continuum of medical education. *Med Educ.* 2005;39:58–65.

29.   Polanyi M. *Personal Knowledge: Towards a Post-Critical Philosophy.* Chicago, IL: University of Chicago Press; 1958.

30.   Brown JS, Collins A, Duguid P. Situated cognition and the culture of learning. *Ed Researcher.* 1989;18:32–42.

31.   Epstein RM. Mindful practice. *JAMA.* 1999;282:833–839.

32.   Schon DA. *Educating the Reflective Practitioner: Toward a New Design for Teaching and Learning in the Professions.* San Francisco, CA: Jossey-Bass; 1987.

33.   Hafferty FW, Franks R. The hidden curriculum, ethics teaching, and the structure of medical education. *Acad Med.* 1994;69:861–871.

34.   Hafferty FW. Beyond curriculum reform: confronting medicine's hidden curriculum. *Acad Med.* 1998;73:(4).

35.   Inui TS. *A Flag in the Wind: Educating for Professionalism in Medicine.* Washington, DC: Association of American Medical Colleges; 2003.

36.   Epstein RM. Assessment in medical education. *NEJM.* 2007;356:387–396.

37.   Arnold L. Assessing professional behaviors: yesterday, today, and tomorrow. *Acad Med.* 2002;77:502–515.

38. Sullivan, Arnold. Assessment and remediation in programs of teaching professionalism. In: Cruess RL, Cruess SR, Steinert Y, eds. *Teaching Medical Professionalism*. Cambridge University Press; 2009:124–150.

39. Freidson E. *Professionalism: The Third Logic*. Chicago, IL: University of Chicago Press; 2001.

40. Durning SJ, Artino AR, Holmboe E. On regulation and medical education: sociology, learning, and accountability. *Acad Med*. 2009;84:545–547.

41. Wright SM, Kern D, Kolodner K, Howard D, Brancati FL. Attributes of excellent attending-physician role models. *NEJM*. 1998;339:1986–1993.

42. Wright SM, Carrese JA. What values do attending physicians try to pass on to house officers. *Med Educ*. 2001;35:941–945.

43. Hafferty FW. Reconfiguring the sociology of medical education: emerging topics and pressing issues. In: Bird CE, Conrad P, Fremont AM, eds. *Handbook of Medical Sociology*. 5th ed. Upper Saddle River, NJ: Prentice Hall; 2003:238–257.

44. Kenny NP, Mann KV, MacLeod HM. Role modeling in physician's professional formation: reconsidering an essential but untapped educational strategy. *Acad Med*. 2003;78:1203–1210.

45. Cruess SR, Cruess RL, Steinert Y. Role modeling: making the most of a powerful teaching strategy. *BMJ*. 2008;336:718–721.

46. Ihara CK. Collegiality as a professional virtue. In: Flores A, ed. *Professional Ideals*. Belmont, CA: Wadsworth; 1988:56–65.

47. Steinert Y, Cruess SR, Cruess RL, Snell L. Faculty development for teaching and evaluating professionalism: from program design to curricular change. *Med Educ*. 2005;39:127–136.

48. Huddle TS. Teaching professionalism: is medical morality a competency? *Acad Med*. 2005;80:885–891.

49. Graham MJ, Naqvi Z, Encandela JA, et al. What indicates competency in systems based practice? An analysis of perspective consistency among health care team members. *Adv Health Sci Educ*. 2009;14:187–203.

50. Reeves S, Fox A, Hodges BD. The competency movement in the health professions: ensuring consistent standards or reproducing conventional domains or practice? *Adv Health Sci Educ*. 2009;14:451–453.

51. Lingard L. What we see and don't see when we look at "competence": notes on a god term. *Adv Health Sci Educ*. 2009;14:625–628.

DOWNLOAD YOUR MATERIALS NOW

Download PDFs or customizable versions of many of the teaching and assessment tools included in this book. Just visit the website listed below.

www.hcpro.com/downloads/8535

Thank you for purchasing this product!

⊢CPro

CHAPTER 1

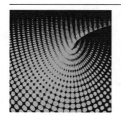

Interpersonal and Communication Skills

Elizabeth A. Rider, MSW, MD, FAAP

The treatment of a disease may be entirely impersonal; the care of a patient must be completely personal. The significance of the intimate personal relationship between physician and patient cannot be too strongly emphasized, for in an extraordinarily large number of cases both diagnosis and treatment are directly dependent on it, and the failure of the young physician to establish this relationship accounts for much of his ineffectiveness in the care of patients.

—Francis W. Peabody, MD, 1927[1]

Introduction

Most physicians would agree that good communication with their patients is a desirable goal. In contrast, teaching and assessing communication skills often receives short shrift in the crowded medical training curriculum; however, many medical schools and residency training programs are working to improve in this area. We now know that physicians do not acquire good interpersonal and communication skills from birth, nor via osmosis, and that communication skills must be learned and practiced, just like other clinical skills.

The medical interview is the most commonly performed task in clinical medicine. The average physician performs between 160,000 and 200,000 interviews in a 40-year career.[2]

Physicians' interpersonal and communication skills correlate with improved patient health outcomes and

healthcare quality and have a significant impact on patient care. Numerous evidence-based studies, including the Institute of Medicine's (IOM) 2001 report *Crossing the Quality Chasm*,[3] support the central premise that communication is a critical factor in providing quality patient care.

Medical organizations and regulatory bodies worldwide require competency in communication skills at all levels of medical training (Figure 1.1).

In 1999, the ACGME implemented six general competencies for which residents must demonstrate proficiency. Interpersonal and communication skills is one of these competencies.[4] The American Board of Medical Specialties (ABMS) and the Federation of State Medical Boards have adopted the same competencies for practicing physicians.[5] The Joint Commission identified six general competencies that closely align with the ACGME competencies, including interpersonal and communication skills, as a frame of reference for considering proficiency of medical staff members.[6]

Medical school guidelines also reflect increasing international recognition of the importance of teaching and assessing communication skills during undergraduate medical training. Since 2004, U.S. medical students and international medical school graduates applying to train or practice in the United States must demonstrate competence in clinical, interpersonal, and communication skills on the United States Medical Licensing Examination (USMLE) Step 2 Clinical Skills Exam.[7] Additionally, consensus statements—Kalamazoo,[8] Toronto,[9] International,[10] and, more recently, the UK[11] and Basel[12] consensus statements and others[13]—identify essential interpersonal and communication competencies for medical education at all levels.

Figure 1.1	**Selected International Organizations and Groups with Requirements for Teaching and/or Assessment of Interpersonal and Communication Skills**

Training level	Organization
Undergraduate	• American Association of Medical Colleges (AAMC)[14] • Association of Faculties of Medicine of Canada (AFMC)[15] • Basel Consensus Statement[12] • Committee on Accreditation of Canadian Medical Schools (CACMS)[16] • Dundee Learning Outcomes[17] • General Medical Council (GMC)[18] • Institute for International Medical Education (IIME)[19] • Liaison Committee on Medical Education (LCME)[20] • The Tuning Project (Europe)[21] • UK Consensus Statement[11] • United States Medical Licensing Examination (USMLE) Step 2 Clinical Skills Exam
Graduate	• Accreditation Council for Graduate Medical Education (ACGME) • Confederation of Postgraduate Medical Education Councils (CPMEC)—Australia[22] • Educational Commission for Foreign Medical Graduates (ECFMG)[23] • General Medical Council—UK[24] • Royal College of Physicians and Surgeons of Canada (CanMEDS)[25, 26]
Postgraduate	• American Board of Medical Specialties (ABMS)[27] • Royal Australian College of General Practitioners (RACGP)[22] • Royal College of General Practitioners (RCGP)[28] • Royal College of Physicians and Surgeons of Canada (CanMEDS)[25, 26]

Communication in healthcare: How are we doing?

Communication problems in healthcare are common.[29] They usually involve communication issues rather than competency issues,[30] and they may negatively affect patient management and outcomes. Studies show that physicians:

- Fail to elicit 54% of patients' complaints and 45% of their concerns[31]

- Often pursue a "doctor-centered" approach that discourages patients from telling their story[32]

- Use jargon that patients do not understand[33]

Failure to elicit the patient's agenda is associated with a 24% reduction in physician understanding.[34] In 1984, Beckman and Frankel[35] found that physicians interrupted patients within 18 seconds—so quickly that patients did not disclose significant concerns. When patients were allowed to state their concerns, none took more than 150 seconds.

By 1999, little had changed. Marvel et al.[36] found that physicians redirected their patients an average of 23 seconds after they began to tell their stories. When not interrupted, patients took only six more seconds to share their concerns. The study also showed that when physicians gave patients time to complete their opening statements, they were less likely to voice concerns late in the interview. Instead, they stated them earlier in the conversation. The authors concluded that by asking for the patient's agenda, physicians can save time, improve interview efficiency, and obtain more data.

Ineffective communication skills and a lack of focus on the physician–patient relationship correlate with malpractice claims, lawsuits, and medical error.[37, 38] Beckman et al.[39] found four communication problems present in 71% of malpractice depositions. The communication issues cited in these cases include:

- Deserting the patient in 32% of the cases

- Devaluing patient and/or family views in 29% of the cases

- Delivering information poorly in 26% of the cases

- Failing to understand the patient and/or the family perspective in 13% of the cases

The evidence remains clear. We can no longer minimize the need to develop and implement quality curricula to enhance interpersonal and communication skills and the physician–patient relationship.

Can communication skills be learned?

"The idea of communication as bedside manner or history taking has given way to a reconceptualization of communication as a measurable clinical skill."[40]

It is incorrect to assume that doctors will acquire the ability to communicate empathically with their patients as a matter of course during their medical training.[41] Numerous studies show that interpersonal and communication competencies involve a series of skills that can be learned and taught.[42, 43, 44, 45, 46] Training produces measurable changes in physicians' communication skills, and physicians sustain the changes five years after completing such training.[47]

Many educators assume they can teach residents communication skills by osmosis, lectures, workshops, Web modules alone, or other minimal instruction. Along with the effects of the hidden curriculum in medical education, it is likely that this assumption may contribute to the failure of some physicians to develop good communication skills.

Why teach interpersonal and communication skills?

Surprisingly, some question the necessity for teaching and learning communication skills. Evidence-based studies show that good communication and patient-centered care can lead to better health outcomes.[48, 49, 50] Good communication correlates directly with improved quality of care, increased patient satisfaction[51] and adherence to treatment plans,[52] greater symptom improvement,[53, 54, 55] better management of chronic conditions,[56] and fewer medication errors[57] and malpractice claims.[58] A physician's caring and openness to communication are significant factors in a patient's decision to continue a relationship with that physician.[59] In addition, a patient's positive perception of communication with his or her physician is associated with improved efficiency of care, including a significant reduction in diagnostic testing and referrals.[60] Effective interpersonal and communication skills correlate with greater physician satisfaction[61] and may decrease physician burnout. For example, in oncology, effective communication is associated with improved patient quality

of life and coping, decreased distress, and reduced clinician fatigue and emotional exhaustion.[62, 63]

Despite extraordinary scientific and technological advances in medicine, the sine qua non for the delivery of quality healthcare remains that of skillful communication and the development and maintenance of therapeutic and caring relationships with patients and their families.[64]

Definitions of Interpersonal and Communication Competencies

Medicine has traditionally defined communication skills as the performance of specific tasks or behaviors. Alone, these behaviors can neither create nor sustain a therapeutic relationship. Although they are components of the same competency, communication and interpersonal skills are different. As we build curricula for teaching and learning these competencies, we must attend to both.

Interpersonal skills are relational and process-oriented and include a focus on humanistic qualities and the effects of communication on others. The Kalamazoo II Report[65] lists the following important elements of interpersonal skills:

- Respecting and treating others as one would like to be treated

- Being present in the moment and aware of the importance of the relationship

- Paying attention to the patient with open nonverbal, verbal, and intuitive communication channels [66]

- Possessing a caring intent to relieve suffering, and showing curiosity and interest in the patient's ideas, concerns, and values

- Having flexibility, including the ability to adjust interpersonal skills as necessary in real time[67]

Dyche[68] outlines an "interpersonal skill set" of understanding, empathy, and relational versatility. Each of these three skills arises from a core humanistic attitude that encompasses curiosity, caring, and respect. It is how one thinks, feels, and behaves (cognitive, affective, and behavioral domains) in his or her orientation to the relationship with the patient. Understanding involves respectful curiosity, a desire to learn about the patient's perspective, and a sincere interest in the human experience. When the physician has the courage and openness to explore the patient's life, an understanding occurs, and the patient recognizes that the physician knows him or her as a person with individual concerns, hopes, and perspectives.

The second interpersonal skill, empathy, has both cognitive (accurate understanding of the patient's feelings) and affective (caring) aspects. Caring is the basis of empathy, and it is central to relationship-centered care. The empathic physician has a caring and emotionally responsive attitude toward the feelings of others and an awareness and self-understanding of his or her own reactions to patients. Dyche notes, "Developing universal caring involves being able to find a commonality with people of very different backgrounds and values and being able to join together around shared human values."(p. 1037) [68]

Relational versatility involves the physician's ability to vary his or her interpersonal approach to the needs of different patients.[68] We can also call this "the differential use of self"—that is, how we use ourselves in different ways in our relationships with different patients and families. Each relationship between a patient and a physician is unique. Relational versatility requires the ability to be self-aware, observe ourselves the way others experience us, be "present," and attend to the patient in a way that allows for flexibility in the interactions and relationship with the patient.

Communication with colleagues is an additional component of the interpersonal and communication skills competencies. The IOM[37] reports that healthcare team communication failures cause mistakes that endanger patient safety. The ability of healthcare professionals to work effectively together is a key component of quality healthcare, yet physicians usually learn interprofessional communication through a hidden curriculum of experiences, or not at all.[69]

In 1999, the ACGME listed interpersonal and communication skills as one of the six competencies in which residents must become proficient.[70] The organization updated the ACGME Common Program Requirements in 2007.[71]

Using an expert consensus group process, Rider and Keefer[13] and an international group of medical education leaders, further defined and expanded the original ACGME interpersonal and communication skills competencies, added 20 subcompetencies, and connected these competencies to teaching strategies for all levels of medical education (undergraduate, graduate, and postgraduate). The expanded competencies apply globally across different settings and specialties and are sensitive to different definitions of healthcare.

Figure 1.2 shows the original ACGME communication competencies and the expanded competencies and subcompetencies.

Figure 1.2	**Expanded Definitions for the Interpersonal and Communication Skills Competencies**
Original ACGME language	**Expanded competencies and subcompetencies**
Residents must be able to demonstrate interpersonal and communication skills that result in effective information exchange and teaming with patients, their patients' families, and professional associates. Residents are expected to: 1. Create and sustain a therapeutic and ethically sound relationship with patients	1. **Create and sustain a relationship that is therapeutic for patients and supportive of their families** • Be "present," paying attention to the patient, caring for the patient, and working collaboratively and from strengths. • Accept and explore the patient's feelings, including negative feelings. • Provide a sustainable relationship that allows for repair when mistakes are made and includes authenticity, honesty, admission of, and sorrow for, mistakes. • Communicate with the patient's family honestly and supportively. In some cases (e.g., pediatrics and geriatrics), the doctor-patient relationship is imbedded in and extends to the family; in other circumstances, the doctor's relationship with the family may be separate from that with the patient.
2. Use effective listening skills and elicit and provide information using effective nonverbal, explanatory, questioning, and writing skills	2. **Use effective listening skills to facilitate relationship. Elicit and provide information using effective nonverbal, explanatory, questioning, and writing skills. Respond promptly to patients' queries and requests.** • Demonstrate effective listening by hearing and understanding in a way that the patient feels heard and understood. Use nonverbal cues such as nodding, pausing, and maintaining eye contact, and verbal skills including backtracking, reflecting, and mirroring. • Recognize the patient's preferred (or current) mode of communication and selectively choose the most effective mode of communication for the situation. Assess patient's understanding of problem and desire for more information; explain using words that are easy for the patient to understand. • Understand the patient's perspective, including the patient's individual concerns, beliefs, and expectations; respect the patient's cultural and ethnic beliefs, practices, and language.

Figure 1.2	**Expanded Definitions for the Interpersonal and Communication Skills Competencies (cont.)**

	<ul><li>Create an atmosphere of mutuality and respect through patient participation and involvement in decision-making.<ul><li>– Include patient in choices and decisions to the extent he or she desires</li><li>– Collaboratively set agenda for encounters</li><li>– Negotiate mutually acceptable plans in partnership with patient</li></ul></li></ul>
3. Work effectively with others as a member or leader of a healthcare team or other professional group	3. Work effectively with others as a member or leader of the healthcare team or other professional group. In all areas of communication and interaction, show respect and empathy toward colleagues and learners.<ul><li>Demonstrate excellent collaboration and cooperation with other members of the healthcare team involved in the patient's care<ul><li>– Be specific with questions asked of, and answers given to, colleagues; ensure that the communication is clearly understood</li><li>– Include adequate and complete information in all documentation and written communication about a patient's care</li><li>– Resolve conflict and give constructive feedback on mistakes</li></ul></li><li>Communicate clearly in the role of teacher<ul><li>– Assess the educational needs of learners</li><li>– Collaboratively set realistic learning expectations with learners</li><li>– Identify and eliminate barriers in team teaching; maintain an appropriate balance between patient care and teaching</li><li>– Offer, seek, and accept honest, constructive, and timely feedback</li></ul></li></ul>

Reprinted from: Rider, EA; Keefer, CH. "Communication skills competencies: definitions and a teaching toolbox." Medical Education 2006; 40:624–629. © Blackwell Publishing Ltd 2006. Used with permission.

Building a Curriculum for Interpersonal and Communication Skills

"MEDICINE HAS USED THE SKILLS OF THE HEAD AND
HANDS, BUT ADDING THE SKILLS OF THE HEART ADDS UP
TO GOOD PATIENT CARE. … IT TURNS OUT THAT
PATIENT CARE IS BETTER WHEN THE WHOLE DOCTOR
SHOWS UP, NOT JUST THE INTELLECT."

—DAVID C. LEACH, MD,
FORMER EXECUTIVE DIRECTOR, ACGME[72]

How do we create a curriculum in interpersonal and communication skills that will develop physicians who use both their intellect and the "skills of the heart"? First, building a successful curriculum for these competencies requires an understanding of relationship-centered care and how it differs from patient-centered care, of communication competency and relationships, and of the importance of the learner–teacher relationship. Second, we must determine the knowledge, skills, attitudes, and values learners need in order to attain competency in interpersonal and communication skills. Third, we must explore ways to integrate interpersonal and communication skills throughout the medical education curriculum. Finally, attention to the big picture—the hidden curriculum, learning environment, and organizational culture–remains essential.

Patient-centered and relationship-centered care

In 2001, the IOM published "Crossing the Quality Chasm: A New Health System for the 21st Century"[3] and listed "continuous healing relationships" as the first principle for improving the quality of patient care.

The IOM outlined six primary aims, including patient-centered care, for organizing fundamental changes to improve healthcare.

Patient-centered care focuses on the patient's disease and illness experience and is respectful of, and responsive to, individual patient needs, perspectives, and values. The physician acknowledges each patient as a unique individual, and considers the patient's and family's culture, personality, and related factors relevant to the process of healthcare. Both patient-centered care and relationship-centered care include cultural competence.

Relationship-centered care takes patient-centered care a step further and enhances patient-centered care. The premise is that relationships are the medium of care, relationships are therapeutic, and both patients and physicians are active participants. What the physician brings to the relationship is important. The focus on the patient expands to include ways in which both the physician and the patient relate to each other and the ways in which clinicians relate to each other and to the community. According to C. Tresolini and the Pew-Fetzer Task Force, "The phrase 'relationship-centered care' captures the importance of the interaction among people as the foundation of any therapeutic or healing activity."(p. 11) [73]

Beach, Inui, and colleagues[74] note that relationship-centered care is founded upon four principles:

1. Relationships should include the personhood of the participant

2. Affect and emotion are essential elements of these relationships

3. All healthcare relationships occur in the context of reciprocal influence

4. The formation and maintenance of true, genuine relationships is morally indispensable. (p. S3) 74

The relationship-centered physician understands that his or her interactions with patients shape the course and outcome of care. Hence, the clinician's capacity for self-awareness and reflection becomes an important component of relationship-centered care.

Educating for relational competency: Communication and relationships

> "... THE REWARD IS TO BE FOUND IN THAT PERSONAL BOND WHICH FORMS THE GREATEST SATISFACTION OF THE PRACTICE OF MEDICINE. ONE OF THE ESSENTIAL QUALITIES OF THE CLINICIAN IS INTEREST IN HUMANITY, FOR THE SECRET OF THE CARE OF THE PATIENT IS IN CARING FOR THE PATIENT."
>
> —FRANCIS PEABODY, MD, 1927[1]

Interpersonal and communication skills are more than just behaviors. Zoppi and Epstein note, "... skills-focused training is not always directed toward fostering a genuine, strong, compassionate, caring relationship between physician and patient."[75] The stakes are high. All physicians are called upon to share bad news and difficult information with patients and families. Such interactions are stressful for both patients and physicians, and residents report a lack of confidence in their skills in giving bad news.[44] Research shows that if bad news is communicated poorly or insensitively, it may have a lasting impact on patients' and families' ability to adjust and adapt and may cause confusion and resentment.[76] Communicating bad news well can help patients and families understand, adjust, and accept.

The learner–teacher relationship

> "PHYSICIANS MAY BE FULLY INFORMED ABOUT PNEUMONIA BUT, WHEN A PARTICULAR PATIENT HAS PNEUMONIA, TREATMENT OF THAT PATIENT IS AN ART. ACHIEVING THIS HARMONY REQUIRES A RELATIONSHIP WITH THE PATIENT, AND TEACHING THIS HARMONY REQUIRES A CLOSE RELATIONSHIP BETWEEN TEACHER AND STUDENT."
>
> —DAVID C. LEACH, MD[77]

To be effective, communication skills instruction and learning must take place within respectful learner–teacher relationships. With such relationships, learners are more attentive and more willing to disclose their lack of understanding, and they become more actively engaged and ask more questions.[78] Weston and Brown[79] recommend showing the same caring and humanism to the learner that we expect the learner to use with patients because learners' experiences with their teachers help them to understand relationships with patients. Skiles states:

> "There is an undeniable parallel between educational process and clinical behavior . ... [T]he way you treat me as a student will set the tone for how I treat patients. So if you want me to take a personal interest in my patients and to treat patients as partners, the most powerful thing you can do as a teacher is to treat me the same way."(p. 67) 80

Just as the relationship between physician and patient is primary in quality healthcare, educational models that do not support and nourish the relationship between learner and teacher can disrupt both relationships.

What knowledge, skills, and values do learners need for relational competency?

With the increasingly recognized need to enhance the quality of healthcare from both patient and practitioner perspectives, the Pew-Fetzer Task Force formed to develop an agenda for encouraging an integrated biomedical–psychosocial perspective in health professions' educational programs.[73]

The Task Force, serving in an advisory capacity to the Pew Health Professions Commission at the University of California San Francisco Center for the Health Professions and to the Fetzer Institute, determined that "… a primary focus on ways to enhance and enrich the relationships that are relevant to health care through both education and practice is of critical importance."[(p. 10) 73]

Their comprehensive report described the concept of relationship-centered care and provided principles for curricular and programming activities in health professions education.

The Pew-Fetzer Task Force defined knowledge, skills, and values in four areas that practitioners must develop in order to provide effective relationship-centered care. Figure 1.3 provides guidance as we develop curricula in interpersonal and communication skills.

Figure 1.3	Areas of Knowledge, Skills, and Values for the Patient-Practitioner Relationship		
Area	**Knowledge**	**Skills**	**Values**
Self-awareness	• Knowledge of self • Understanding self as a resource to others	• Reflect on self and work	• Importance of self-awareness, self-care, self-growth
Patient experience of health and illness	• Role of family, culture, community in development • Multiple components of health • Multiple threats and contributors to health as dimensions of one reality	• Recognize patient's life story and its meaning • View health and illness as part of human development	• Appreciation of the patient as a whole person • Appreciation of the patient's life story and the meaning of the health-illness condition
Developing and maintaining caring relationships	• Understanding of threats to integrity of the relationship (e.g., power inequalities) • Understanding of potential for conflict and abuse	• Attend fully to the patient • Accept and respond to distress in patient and self • Respond to moral and ethical challenges • Facilitate hope, trust, and faith	• Respect for patient's dignity, uniqueness, and integrity (mind-body-spirit unity) • Respect for self-determination • Respect for person's own power and self-healing processes
Effective communication	• Elements of effective communication	• Listen • Impart information • Learn • Facilitate the learning of others • Promote and accept patient's emotions	• Importance of being open and nonjudgmental

Reprinted from: Tresolini CP and the Pew-Fetzer Task Force. Health Professions Education and Relationship-Centered Care. San Francisco, CA: Pew Health Professions Commission, 1994, p. 30. © The Fetzer Institute. Used with permission.

Integrate interpersonal and communication skills teaching and assessment into the overall curriculum

Until more recently, most graduate training programs have not focused on or consistently taught and assessed interpersonal and communication competencies and the physician-patient relationship. Accreditation and licensing requirements for competence in clinical skills, including communication skills, drive curricular change to teach and assess these competencies in a more organized and comprehensive manner. Training institutions must lay the groundwork for a focus on interpersonal and communication skills throughout the curriculum.

Silverman[81] argues for extensive integration of communication teaching and assessment throughout the medical education curriculum to enable it to become "a mainstream activity, valued by the institution and learners alike."[(p. 363)] He recommends the following approaches:

- Build a curriculum, not just a one-off course. Learners' communication skills do not benefit from just one course. Instead, educators need

to develop a curriculum for communication skills. Teaching needs to be well timed, increasingly complex, and distributed throughout the curriculum.

- Curricula should revisit skills taught in the past. A linear curriculum is not as beneficial as those that provide opportunities throughout training for learners to build upon and refine existing skills while learning new and more complex skills.

- Communication curricula should be integrated with the rest of the medical curriculum. Communication is relevant to all clinical encounters and applicable to all specialties and disciplines, not a separate entity or an "inessential frill."[81]

Curricula in interpersonal and communication skills mature over time, from stand-alone courses to fully integrated curricula that include teaching and assessment. Figure 1.4 shows Silverman's pyramid of increasing maturity of communication curricula. He notes that investing in faculty development is the most efficient method to hasten the curricular maturation process.[81]

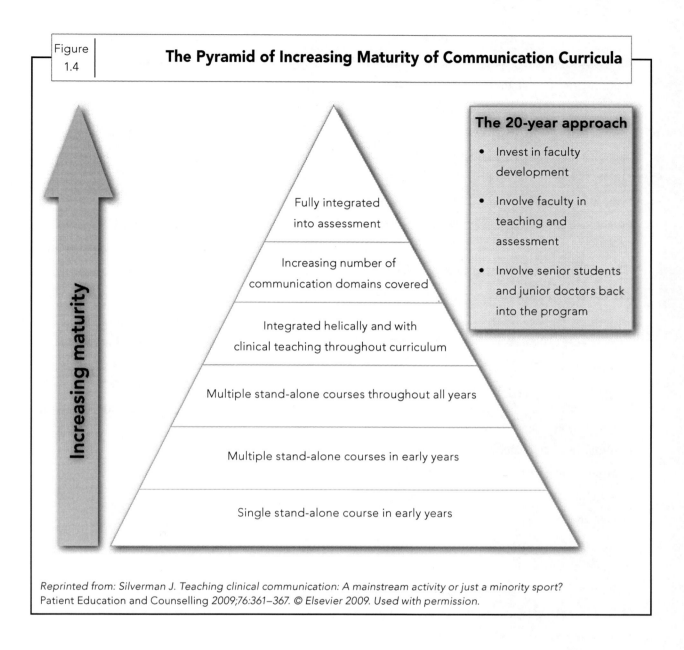

| Figure 1.4 | **The Pyramid of Increasing Maturity of Communication Curricula** |

The 20-year approach

- Invest in faculty development

- Involve faculty in teaching and assessment

- Involve senior students and junior doctors back into the program

Increasing maturity

Fully integrated into assessment

Increasing number of communication domains covered

Integrated helically and with clinical teaching throughout curriculum

Multiple stand-alone courses throughout all years

Multiple stand-alone courses in early years

Single stand-alone course in early years

Reprinted from: Silverman J. Teaching clinical communication: A mainstream activity or just a minority sport? Patient Education and Counselling 2009;76:361–367. © Elsevier 2009. Used with permission.

Barriers to improving the teaching and learning of communication skills persist.[82] The business of medicine, emphasis on the technological aspects of care, and increasing demands on faculty time pose significant barriers to developing attitudes in learners that value the relational and interpersonal aspects of care.[83] Overcoming these obstacles requires attention to the hidden curriculum and the learning environment as well as to the organizational culture.

The hidden curriculum and the culture of learning

"WHAT YOU DO SPEAKS SO LOUDLY THAT I CANNOT HEAR WHAT YOU SAY."

—RALPH WALDO EMERSON

The hidden curriculum[84] presents a significant challenge to medical education. Our learners learn more powerfully from the environment in which they are educated than from formal curricular content and readings.

The hidden curriculum in medical education refers to tacit (implicit) learning, which includes "… all those aspects of the curriculum and the socialization process that instill professional values and a sense of professional identity, but do so without explicitly articulating those issues."[(p. 600) 85] While the hidden curriculum has the potential for positive influence, the tacit learning of the hidden curriculum often proves harmful. Coulehan and Williams note:

"The explicit curriculum stresses empathy and associated listening and responding skills, the relief of suffering, the importance of trust and fidelity, and a primary focus on the patient's best interest. Tacit learning, on the other hand, stresses objectivity, detachment, wariness, and distrust of emotions [and] patients . ..."[(p. 600) 85]

The hidden curriculum affects learning, professional interactions, clinical practice, and the emotional and moral development of learners. We know that relational abilities may diminish during the course of medical training.[86, 87] Studies show that empathy scores of internal medicine residents decrease during their training,[88, 89] and medical students experience a significant decline in empathy during the third year of medical school.[90] Collier and colleagues[91] found that 61% of medical residents report becoming cynical during their postgraduate training.

The hidden curriculum in medical education pressures residents to conform and focus on pleasing superiors, sometimes at the patients' expense.[92] Inui suggests, "Noting the difference between what we say and what we do, students learn that medicine is a profession in which you say one thing and do another, a profession of cynics."[93]

Aspects of the hidden curriculum, including negative role modeling, undermine the attitudinal messages of the formal curriculum. Learners internalize and perpetuate attitudes and behaviors of their role models[94] and feel caught between their moral principles and pressures to suppress those principles to fit in with team members.[95] It is not surprising, then, that communication skills and empathy decline during medical education.

Role models are the greatest influence on the hidden curriculum. They also have a profound effect on the way the hidden curriculum impacts students and residents.[93] Karnieli-Miller and colleagues[96] studied 272 medical students' reflective narratives in order to enhance understanding of the informal and hidden curricula at the Indiana University School of Medicine. They found that both their role models' positive and negative behaviors shaped students' perceptions of medicine and its values, and that "… interactions that manifest respect and other qualities of good communication with patients, families, and colleagues taught powerfully."[(p. 124) 96]

The most common theme in the students' narratives involves respect or disrespect in clinical interactions with patients, families, colleagues, and coworkers. The recent UK Consensus Statement on the content of communication curricula in undergraduate medical education places respect for others as the central component, underlying all others, of effective clinical communication.[11]

Pololi and colleagues[97] studied the impact of the medical school culture on medical faculty at five disparate U.S. medical schools and found that the relational aspects were central. Faculty felt disrespected, not valued, and not recognized as people beyond their work roles. The authors concluded that problems in the organizational culture may affect faculty professionalism, vitality,

productivity, and retention.[97] These issues also impact the learners in those institutions.

The learning environment

Attention to the learning environment, which includes the hidden curriculum, is important, and its potential negative influence is increasingly recognized. The Liaison Committee on Medical Education (LCME) recently developed new accreditation criteria that include the following standard:

> "MEDICAL SCHOOLS MUST ENSURE THAT THE LEARNING ENVIRONMENT FOR MEDICAL STUDENTS PROMOTES THE DEVELOPMENT OF EXPLICIT AND APPROPRIATE PROFESSIONAL ATTRIBUTES (ATTITUDES, BEHAVIORS, AND IDENTITY) IN THEIR MEDICAL STUDENTS."
> —LCME, STANDARD MD-31 A: EFFECTIVE JULY 1, 2008[98]

The LCME notes that the learning environment includes formal learning activities as well as "… attitudes, values, and informal 'lessons' conveyed by individuals with whom the student comes in contact."[98] The LCME identifies a shared responsibility for creating an appropriate learning environment among faculty, students, residents, staff members, and clinical teaching sites. This responsibility includes regular assessment of the learning environment to identify and mitigate negative influences and to enhance positive influences.

Strategies for addressing the hidden curriculum include creating culturally safe ways to identify and make the hidden curriculum explicit, and positive mentoring and role modeling. As we consider the learning environment and the hidden curriculum, it is important to help all stakeholders, especially faculty, become aware that they serve as role models at all times, "24/7."

What does a relationship-centered learning environment look like? Branch and colleagues[99, 100] note that the humanistic learning environment treats learners with respect, engenders an atmosphere of trust and collaborative learning among teachers and learners, and pays attention to the human needs of learners. Such an environment equally values, respects, and seeks to understand the perspectives of patients and their families.

Organizational interventions for fostering communication and relationship-centered learning and care

Medical education occurs in environments with strong organizational and cultural forces. The organizational culture of institutions can support or subvert how much value residents and faculty see in interpersonal and communication skills and caring. The culture also affects whether residents and faculty members demonstrate competent interpersonal and communication skills and caring. Educational leaders and faculty must work together to influence organizational culture and to address the hidden curriculum in order to foster communication and relationship-centered care and learning.

How do we create an organizational culture that truly values, not just espouses, the quality of relationships with patients and among colleagues and the connection between the intellect and the "skills of the heart"? Even excellent formal curricula can be undermined if disrespect, cynicism, and depersonalization are part of the organizational cultures of institutions where trainees learn.[93] Suchman[101] suggests that if an institution is

truly serious about promoting a humanistic approach among its learners and graduates, it will:

- Promote faculty development programs that teach and spread methods to create caring and collaborative learning environments

- Select trainees based on relational and humanistic capabilities, not just academic performance

- Create systems of leadership education, feedback, and accountability to ensure that leaders create positive work settings for all

- Present institutional committees with opportunities to reflect on values and ethics implied in and transmitted by their policies and courses of action[(p. 1630) 101]

Organizational culture change starts with recruiting learners with desired personal and interpersonal attributes during the medical school, residency, and fellowship recruitment and selection process. Medical schools are designing innovative methods to measure the noncognitive attributes—personal and interpersonal qualities—of their candidates, including mini interviews, objective structured clinical examinations (OSCE), and simulation.[102, 103, 104] The Association of Faculties of Medicine of Canada's report *The Future of Medical Education in Canada*[15] recommends enhancing the admissions process by including "... the assessment of key values and personal characteristics of physicians—such as communication, interpersonal and collaborative skills, and a range of professional interests—as well as cognitive abilities."[(p. 5) 15]

Additionally, healthcare organizations have successfully changed organizational culture using the appreciative inquiry and positive deviance processes.[105] Both methods propose that solutions already exist within the community of the organization, and members only need to discover them. The Indiana University School of Medicine is one organization that changed the culture of the learning environment using appreciative inquiry.[94, 106, 107]

Appreciative inquiry is a process that identifies the attributes in an organization that work rather than those that do not work.[108] It builds on the organization's values, assets, innovative ideas, and strategic opportunities by aligning practices and systems within the organization's positive and generative core. Appreciative inquiry invites us to learn from moments of exceptional performance at the system or individual level.

Positive deviance, a similar approach to organizational change, more specifically defines "positive deviants" as individuals whose successful strategies or behaviors have enabled them to find better solutions to problems. From this wisdom in the community, the organization focuses on learning from the innovations of these individuals and replicating the successful process of creating solutions.[109]

Although many models of organizational change exist, the strength-based approaches of appreciative inquiry and positive deviance have proven promising. Faculty, educators, and organizational leaders can use these models to promote relationship-centered learning, care, and reflection on the hidden curriculum's effect on education. The goal is to encourage organizational change that supports the enhancement of interpersonal and communication skills and a relationship-centered focus throughout the organization.

Teaching Interpersonal and Communication Competencies

Enhancing self-awareness and reflection

> "… THE MOST PRACTICAL THING WE CAN ACHIEVE IN ANY KIND OF WORK IS INSIGHT INTO WHAT IS HAPPENING INSIDE US AS WE DO IT."[(p. 5)]
> —PARKER J. PALMER, PhD, THE COURAGE TO TEACH[110]

An important component of teaching interpersonal and communication skills includes the concurrent learning of self-awareness and reflection. We know that the physician's self-awareness and ability to reflect are essential for effective communication, for a good physician–patient relationship, for accurate gathering of clinical information,[111, 112] and for mastery of patient-centered interviewing.[113]

Physicians' feelings and attitudes about many issues (e.g., death, bad news, pain, anger, and others) influence how they communicate with patients. Unrecognized feelings and attitudes can hinder a physician's ability to feel and be empathetic,[114] to have sensitive conversations with patients about hard topics, to avoid under- or overinvolvement with patients,[115] and to obtain the data needed to make the right diagnosis and come to an agreement with the patient about treatment plans. Smith and colleagues[116] found that residents' persistent poor interviewing performance was frequently due to unrecognized feelings about components of the physician–patient relationship. Without acknowledgment and discussion of these feelings, interactions and the relationship between physician and patient will suffer, patients may not have the opportunity to talk about what is important to them, and physicians may lose the opportunity to provide support and comfort.[117]

The ability to inspire and enable self-reflection in learners is an important skill for clinical teachers. The ACGME recognizes reflective learning as a foundation for competency and for the development of reflective practitioners.[118] Reflection is not intuitive,[119] and reflective skills can be taught. Developing curricula for enhancing these capacities begins with the selection and training of faculty who are respectful of learners' needs, are personally aware themselves, are able to reflect, and have experience with interviewing and interacting with learners.

Dobie[120] offers questions teachers can ask learners to promote self-awareness and to ensure that personal growth is a focus for learning:

- What do you believe?

- What were your assumptions?

- What were your expectations?

- What do you/did you need from this encounter?

- What did you learn about yourself?

- What were you feeling during the encounter?

- What gift did you receive from this relationship, or what did you take away from this relationship and into your personal life?(p. 425) [120]

Bringing patient and family perspectives into learning remains essential. Branch[100] suggests helping learners see things through the patient's eyes by asking questions such as "What was it like for this patient?" followed by reflection on the relationship between doctor and patient ("What did you convey to help the patient make a decision?" "What made it work?"), and then taking learning forward ("Is there something you can take away to help you in similar circumstances?").[100]

Humanistic medical education and practice

The concept of humanism provides another way of thinking about relationship-centered care and reflection. Humanism, essential to medical practice and to interpersonal and communication skills, is rarely explicitly taught, although it is increasingly recognized as an important component of medical education.[99, 121] Branch and colleagues define humanism in medicine as "… the physician's attitudes and actions that demonstrate interest in and respect for the patient and that address the patient's concerns and values."(p. 1067) [99] They note that specific teaching strategies, including taking advantage of seminal events, role modeling, and using active learning skills that engage learners in acting, discussing, and reflecting, can positively influence the hidden curriculum.[99]

Gracey and colleagues[122] identify educational methods that promote teaching of humanistic care, including integrating psychosocial issues into the teaching intervention to enhance the learner's understanding and awareness (e.g., asking about the patient's understanding of his or her illness, family supports, cultural issues), reflecting with the learner on the learning experience, facilitating openness and self-assessment, and role modeling humanistic care.

Miller and Schmidt[123] offer a framework to inculcate humanism into every patient encounter and into the medical culture as a whole. Their "habit of humanism" includes:

- Identifying the multiple perspectives in each encounter (patient, support person, physician)

- Reflecting on possible conflicts that could aid or hinder forming a relationship with a patient

- Choosing to act altruistically, that is, supporting the patient's perspective above all, even if it conflicts with the physician's agenda or interest

Educating for relational competency: Teaching strategies

> "THE GOAL IS NOT THE POLITICALLY CORRECT INTERVIEW THAT CONTAINS A REQUISITE NUMBER OF OPEN-ENDED QUESTIONS AND EMPATHIC-SOUNDING RESPONSES."
>
> —RONALD EPSTEIN, MD[124]

The ability to form deeper relationships and connections with patients and families goes beyond acquiring a set of communication behaviors. As noted earlier in this chapter, patient-centered and relationship-centered care integrate the patient's perspective and experience of illness, values, and the psychosocial context, and attend to what the clinician brings to the relationship. Personal self-reflection is an essential component of quality healthcare because it allows the physician to

listen to the patient's distress, make evidence-based decisions, identify errors, and focus values so that the physician can act with insight, compassion, and competence.[37]

Relationship-centered skills and capacities are complex. How do we teach and assess a resident's ability to "be present" and to develop a sustainable relationship that allows for repair when mistakes are made?[13] How do we teach and assess a "way of being" rather than just a set of behaviors and tasks?

There are numerous reports of communication skills programs, ranging from one-session workshops to multifaceted courses, clinical rotations, longitudinal clinical experiences, and other methods. Learning opportunities for self-reflection can occur individually, in one-on-one learning situations with a trusted teacher, and in small groups. Smith and colleagues[125] describe curricula for teaching self-awareness to medical students and residents. Stewart et al.[126] suggest using small group discussions with real patients and videotaping and then reviewing residents' interactions with standardized patients to promote mindful reflection. Additional teaching methods include questioning to promote reflection, thinking out loud,[127] giving immediate feedback (from trained faculty and simulated patients),[128] and conducting self-awareness groups.[129, 130]

Educators have successfully built trainees' reflective skills by incorporating reflective writing and narrative into medical training.[131, 132, 133, 134, 135, 136] Reis and colleagues[137] recently developed a framework and guide called the Brown Educational Guide to Analysis of Narrative (BEGAN) for crafting faculty feedback on medical students' reflective writing. Educators have also integrated the arts with medical education to enhance communication skills and self-reflection.[138, 139, 140]

Rider and Keefer[13] and an international group of medical education leaders applied an expert consensus group model to expand the ACGME interpersonal and communication competencies and to create a "teaching toolbox" that connects these competencies to teaching strategies for all levels of medical education (undergraduate, graduate, and postgraduate). Various settings and specialties can use the toolbox.

Rider and Keefer and colleagues found that, at each education level and for each competency, the teaching strategy recommended by the expert consensus group most frequently was observation—in real time or on videotape—followed by feedback.

The second most popular strategy was reflection and self-assessment, including reflective writing, such as keeping learning journals and narrative work. Role play and role modeling were also frequently recommended.[13] Figure 1.5 shows the teaching toolbox.

    A Practical Guide to Teaching and Assessing the ACGME Core Competencies, Second Edition

Figure 1.5	**Interpersonal and Communication Skills: A Teaching Toolbox**

Interpersonal and communication competencies	Teaching strategies* by level of training
1. Create and sustain a relationship that is therapeutic for patients and supportive of their families	UME†: observation (in real time) with feedback; role modeling; videotape with standardized patient; workshops. Also mentioned: problem-based learning (PBL); narrative (reading and writing); mentoring; feedback from standardized patient; role play; personal self-reflection in small group; lecture; mini-lecture; setting a corporate culture
	GME‡: observation in real time with feedback; role modeling; reflection/self-assessment; videotape Also mentioned: workshops; small group discussion of cases; simulated patient; Web-based module
	CME§: narrative (reading and writing); reflection/self-assessment; videotape Also mentioned: workshops; role play; Balint group; simulation
2. Use effective listening skills to facilitate relationship. Elicit and provide information using effective nonverbal explanatory, questioning, and writing skills. Respond promptly to patients' queries and requests.	UME, GME, CME: observation with feedback in small group or PBL; role play; bedside teaching; narrative (reading and writing); keeping journals; microskills; group OSCE; web-based learning Content complexity and difficulty increase from UME to GME to CME, while the strategies remain the same.
3. Work effectively with others as a member or leader of the healthcare team or other professional group. In all areas of communication and interaction, show respect and empathy toward colleagues and learners.	UME: observation and feedback with standardized learner and colleagues; observation and feedback (real time); role play Also mentioned: videotape; microteaching; workshops; role modeling; keeping journals; reflection/self-assessment.
	GME: role modeling (on rounds, in clinic); mentoring; observation with feedback; workshops Also mentioned: reflection/self-assessment; videotape; 360-degree observation of the team by the team used as data for a workshop
	CME: workshops; reflection/self-assessment Also mentioned: 360-degree evaluation; case discussion

*Teaching strategies are listed in order of most strongly recommended. † UME = undergraduate medical education (medical students); ‡ GME = graduate medical education (interns, residents, fellows); § CME = continuing medical education (practicing physicians, faculty).

Adapted and reprinted from: Rider EA; Keefer CH. Communication skills competencies: definitions and a teaching toolbox. Medical Education 2006;40:624–629. © Blackwell Publishing Ltd 2006. Used with permission.

Additional teaching approaches and conceptual frameworks

Many methods exist to effectively teach interpersonal and communication skills and self-reflection, and various institutions and groups have developed unique teaching strategies.[13, 99, 101, 122, 142, 143, 144, 145, 146, 147, 148] Several innovative approaches as well as a variety of well-established communication frameworks/models and assessment instruments are presented in the last section of this chapter.

An important caveat

Educators must consider the ways we use communication skills frameworks or models for teaching and assessment. Although behavioral checklists may be useful as students begin their work with patients and may satisfy curricular requirements, we must encourage trainees to move beyond prescribed "scripts"[149] in order to fully appreciate their patients' stories and to integrate and engage their own authenticity and deeper relationship capacities in the physician–patient encounter. As expected by the authors of most communication skills frameworks/models, using these frameworks includes integration with trainees' individual experiences and learning, their "personhood," and the opportunity for ongoing discussion, respectful feedback, and reflection. One of the most important capacities for physicians and other clinicians to develop is the "differential use of self," or relational diversity, discussed previously in this chapter.

In summary, the acquisition of skills and behaviors alone remains insufficient. The physician's relational and humanistic capacities, including the ability to reflect, self-awareness, being "present" for self and others, compassion, respect for the patient and family, trustworthiness, and attention to one's own behavior, are essential capacities significantly associated with patients' perceptions of the quality of care.[44]

Assessment of Interpersonal and Communication Competencies

> "WE CAN MEASURE EVERYTHING EXCEPT THOSE
> THINGS THAT ARE WORTH MEASURING."
>
> —ROBERT KENNEDY

Assessment of interpersonal and communication skills remains a challenge; there is no gold standard, and all assessment methods have strengths and weaknesses. The ACGME provides a list of considerations for selecting assessment instruments, including validity, reliability, feasibility, and the ability to provide valuable information.[150] The ACGME recommends assessment consistent with curricular and program objectives, the use of multiple assessment approaches and instruments, multiple observations, multiple observers and raters, prespecified criteria and standards, and fairness in assessment. The ACGME highly recommends the following tools for assessing interpersonal and communication skills competencies:

- Observer ratings (direct or video observation of interactions with real or simulated patients)

- Patient ratings (by simulated or real patients)

- 360-degree evaluations by patients, faculty, peers, colleagues, and oneself[151]

The Kalamazoo II conference reported on the state of the art in teaching and assessing competence in interpersonal and communication skills. This expert group recommended the following:

> "... at a minimum, evaluation of competence in communication skills should be based on direct observation by persons who competently perform these skills ... . For the evaluation of interpersonal skills, however, patients or evaluators simulating patients may be necessary to assess accurately the interpersonal skills that create the therapeutic relationship."(p. 500) 65

Various authors note that the patient's experience may be a more relevant measure of the patient–physician relationship than observations by impartial coders.[152, 153] An evaluator personally involved in the interaction—such as a real patient, simulated patient, professional actor, or standardized patient—may be able to more accurately measure the experience of the therapeutic relationship.[75]

Use a uniform framework to guide both teaching and assessment

> "WHATEVER WE MEASURE, WE TEND TO IMPROVE."
> —DAVID C. LEACH, MD,
> FORMER EXECUTIVE DIRECTOR, ACGME[154]

Applying a conceptual framework or model to organize communication skills teaching and assessment proves advantageous. Continuous reinforcement and longitudinal development of skills remain critical for retaining and expanding those skills. Uniform frameworks for teaching and assessment (formative and summative) enable learners to reinforce basic skills and learn more complex communication competencies when given repeated opportunities to receive feedback and respectful debriefing on directly observed interviews.

In 1999, an Association of American Medical Colleges (AAMC) study found that less than one-third (32%) of medical schools reported using a specific framework for teaching or assessing communication skills. Only 23% reported using such a framework for both teaching and assessment. Makoul notes that "the reliability and effectiveness of observation and feedback, regardless of the particular method, are likely to be compromised unless they are grounded in a coherent conceptual framework."[40]

Institutions and medical education leaders developing interpersonal and communication skills programs do not need to develop their own frameworks or models for curriculum development. Well-established frameworks/models exist to choose from, and these can be adapted to the needs of each institution and its learners. The majority of the models for teaching and assessing communication skills are evidence-based and include specific communication behaviors associated with improved health outcomes. A number of these frameworks, along with their assessment instruments, are presented in the last section of this chapter. As the models stem from the same research literature, overlap in concepts and skills are present. No consensus exists on best models and assessment tools.

Assessment instruments may be used in a variety of ways

The goals of any curriculum should encourage reflection and continuous self-directed learning, not only in technical skills, but also in relational skills and self-awareness. Promote these goals by using assessment tools for formative evaluation and feedback, and for self-assessment.

The New York University School of Medicine uses a version of the Macy Initiative in Health Communication Model Checklist in a Comprehensive Clinical Skills Exam (CCSE), which is a high-stakes, multistation standardized patient exam that all rising fourth-year students participate in. Kalet[155] reports that each student receives a CCSE report card that presents his or her individual scores displayed as a point on a curve representing the scores of his or her classmates for each of four competencies (communication, history taking, physical exam, and clinical reasoning skills). Students who score in the lowest decile on two of the four competencies or on communication skills alone participate in required remediation. This remediation includes a detailed review of CCSE scores, feedback from standardized patients, a review of a videotaped interview, and a repeat three-station exam focused on communication skills only.[155]

Rider and colleagues[156] implemented a uniform, longitudinal approach to the assessment of communication competencies across the Harvard Medical School curriculum. They adopted the Kalamazoo Consensus Statement framework, and adapted the Kalamazoo Essential Elements Communication Checklist.[157]

To reinforce the skills, faculty and/or standardized patients evaluate students on the Kalamazoo core communication competencies in several formative assessment exercises during the first three years of medical school and in a summative exercise (nine-station OSCE, a requirement for graduation) at the beginning of the fourth year. Depending on the exercise, faculty and/or standardized patient evaluators complete the adapted Kalamazoo communication checklist. Students receive feedback on their scores as a means of informing them of their strengths and weaknesses.

Recertification of practicing physicians, also called Maintenance of Certification, is a major activity of the ABMS.[158] The American Board of Internal Medicine (ABIM) offers Practice Improvement Modules (PIM), including the Patient and Physician Peer Assessment and additional communication surveys, as tools for self-evaluation of communication and interpersonal skills.[159, 160] Patient and peer ratings provide feedback intended to stimulate physicians to self-reflect and to improve the quality of healthcare they provide.[161]

Which instruments to use

"THE PRACTICE OF MEDICINE IS AN ART, NOT A TRADE; A CALLING, NOT A BUSINESS; A CALLING IN WHICH YOUR HEART WILL BE EXERCISED EQUALLY WITH YOUR HEAD."
—SIR WILLIAM OSLER, MD, 1932[162]

How do we measure the physician's use of both "heart and head"? The framework or model you implement or adapt for teaching and assessment should focus on both interpersonal and communication competencies, and pay particular attention to the physician–patient relationship, understanding the patient's perspective, and patient-centered and relationship-centered care.

Evaluate more than communication skills and tasks. Assess the learners' ability to show compassion and empathy and to develop and sustain relationships with patients, colleagues, and those they teach. The assessment process should promote and enhance reflection, values, respect for the physician–patient relationship, and relationships between the physician and colleagues, learners, the medical team, and society.

Schirmer and colleagues[163] examined which communication assessment instruments measure the essential elements of physician–patient communication. They rated 15 instruments on the Kalamazoo Consensus Statement elements, the instruments' psychometric properties, interview efficiency, exploration of family issues, and usability/practicality. The authors found that the instruments varied considerably in their content, psychometric qualities, and usability. They delineated between checklists (e.g., presence/absence of behaviors) and rating scales with assigned weights for each competency (e.g., Likert scales), and made the general suggestion that checklists (e.g., the original Kalamazoo, Macy, SEGUE) may be useful for less experienced faculty evaluators, whereas rating scales (e.g., Common Ground, Four Habits, Calgary-Cambridge) may be useful when a faculty member has more communication expertise.[163]

Hullman and Daily[164] replicated and extended the work of Schirmer and colleagues, and noted that communication assessment instruments assess different communication skills. They recommended incorporating the evaluation of physician flexibility and adaptability in communication, and family interviewing skills into the Kalamazoo Consensus Statement instrument and other instruments lacking these measures.

Although some assessment instruments were designed originally for medical students in undergraduate interviewing/communication programs, graduate and postgraduate training programs have successfully implemented many of them as well. Suzanne Kurtz, PhD, describes learning interpersonal and communication skills as similar to learning to play basketball. While one learns the same initial skills in the first grade, these skills are practiced, refined, and deepened as training continues, and the student learns to apply them in increasingly more complex situations. The skills/competencies evaluated at each level are generally the same, yet they are taught and assessed at different levels of mastery and refinement.[165]

A unique assessment model: Gap analysis

The medical field has increasingly incorporated multirater and 360-degree assessments into its evaluations.[166, 167] The 360-degree evaluation originated in the business world, and medical educators have adapted it for use in training physicians. The ACGME recommends 360-degree evaluations as a tool for assessment.

The 360-degree and multirater assessments position the trainee in the center of a web of relationships that includes not only the preceptor and other faculty members, but also interdisciplinary team members, peers, supervisees, and patients and their families, all of whom may be solicited for feedback.[168, 169] A multirater approach provides a number of advantages, including an interdisciplinary component and the opportunity for use of the patient and/or family as a gold standard.

Calhoun, Rider, and colleagues[169] expanded the Kalamazoo Consensus Statement instrument and developed a multirater methodology with gap analysis. Gap analysis enhances the effectiveness of 360-degree and multirater evaluation and provides important additional information about the differences in the learner's self-perception and the perceptions of others. Gap analysis involves the systematic examination and interpretation of the differences between the ratings from multiple observers and the learner's self-ratings. Educators can use it to draw inferences about the learner's self-awareness and self-insight.[168, 169]

Gap analysis methodology provides unique opportunities for formative feedback and for enhancing self-insight and reflection in learners. Multirater assessment with gap analysis methodology and the expanded Kalamazoo assessment tool are included in detail in the Appendix section.

Nine Take-Home Points on the Assessment of Interpersonal and Communication Skills

1. Choose or adapt a uniform interpersonal and communication skills conceptual framework/model to guide both teaching and assessment. Adapt the framework to your institution, its settings, and the level of trainees. Repeated and widespread use of a coherent framework reinforces the skills/competencies, as well as faculty and learner expectations.

2. The framework you use for teaching and assessment should focus on both interpersonal and communication skills and pay particular attention to the physician-patient relationship, understanding the patient's perspective, relationship-centered care, and the enhancement of self-awareness and reflection in the learner. A large research base supports the association of these components with improved health outcomes.

3. The competency is more than simply a set of communication tasks and behaviors. Evaluate the learners' ability to show compassion and empathy and to develop and sustain good relationships with patients and families, colleagues, and those they teach. The assessment process should enhance values and teach respect for the physician-patient relationship and the relationships between the physician and colleagues, learners, the medical team, and society.

4. Bring patients' perspectives—the patients' voice—into the evaluation of learners, particularly to assess the quality of the physician-patient relationship. Demonstration of interpersonal and relational capacities requires observation and ratings by real or trained simulated patients (i.e., professional actors or standardized patients) during real or simulated clinical encounters.

Nine Take-Home Points on the Assessment of Interpersonal and Communication Skills (cont.)

5. Use your assessment methods and tools in a variety of ways for both formative and summative evaluation and for teaching:

   - Formative evaluations: Assess learning needs, create learning opportunities, guide feedback and coaching, promote reflection, and shape values[170]

   - Summative evaluations: Judge competence in high-stakes evaluations for promotion, licensing, and certification

6. The most effective approach includes a program with multiple methods of evaluation. When practical, use multiple assessment approaches and instruments, multiple observations, and multiple trained observers and raters. Consider inclusion of the following:

   - Observation by faculty followed by respectful feedback and reflection. If you use a checklist or rating form, also include narrative comments and discuss these with the learner.

   - Evaluation and feedback by real or simulated patients.

   - 360-degree or multirater evaluations. Consider including evaluations from interdisciplinary team members, peers, supervisees, and patients and their families.

   - The addition of gap analysis methodology[169] to provide information about the learner's self-insight and to enhance feedback and reflection, when using 360-degree and multirater evaluations.

   - Self-assessment by learners to promote reflection and self-awareness.

7. Selection of assessment methods by a given educational program depends upon available resources and the level of validity and reliability required. High-stakes examinations require higher levels of validity and reliability.

8. Use evaluation criteria that are developmentally appropriate for the learning objectives and expectations for each year of training.

9. Faculty development is key to promoting uniformity of assessment and the development and enhancement of effective role models. Use experts to train faculty to teach and assess interpersonal and communication skills. Provide ongoing training and support for faculty to continue to develop and maintain their expertise.

The Importance of Faculty Development

"Not surprisingly, communication teaching is often the blind leading the partially sighted, as there were whole generations of doctors like me who received no communication skills training and yet now facilitate learners who have had more teaching than themselves."(p. 365)

—Jonathan D. Silverman, FRCGP, University of Cambridge, UK[81]

Faculty members are often unprepared to teach and assess interpersonal and communication skills,[171] and they have varying experience and approaches.[172] Faculty who are good communicators may be unfamiliar with conceptual frameworks, making it difficult to describe what they do and even more difficult for them to teach others. Those who are more than several years out of training may be unfamiliar with evidence-based or experiential teaching methods for communication skills.

Some institutions do not regularly use the interactive teaching methods—observation and feedback, demonstration of desired skills, ongoing practice and reinforcement, and attention to developing self-awareness and the ability to reflect—needed for communication skills learning. Implementation of new and ongoing curricula in interpersonal and communication competencies requires a strong faculty development program.

We know that students can learn communication skills, and that faculty and other role models determine whether students hone or lose these over time.[47, 86] As noted earlier in this chapter, we cannot overlook the powerful effects of the hidden curriculum and the organizational culture on medical education. Although institutions espouse good communication and interactions with patients, learners regularly observe poor interpersonal and relationship skills. Faculty development programs that emphasize role modeling can promote learner exposure to appropriate values, attitudes, and behaviors, and develop a critical mass of faculty members who model and support good communication and relationships with patients and colleagues.

Faculty development can create enthusiasm in junior faculty by orienting them to the mission and importance of teaching and assessing communication skills. Faculty development also can address the needs of more senior faculty, prevent stagnation and burnout, improve the curriculum, and promote positive changes in the organizational culture. Faculty development strategies include:

- Initial and periodic training of faculty by outside or local experts in the teaching and assessment of interpersonal and communication competencies

- Ongoing faculty development sessions, workshops, and retreats

- Longitudinal meetings and support

- Adjunct use of Web-based learning modules[173, 174]

Include participation in faculty development as one expectation for academic promotion. Tailor faculty training for different departments and divisions based on their needs, and identify exemplary role models and champions.

Finally, faculty development in the assessment of the competencies remains essential. Use experts to train faculty to assess interpersonal and communication competencies. Continued periodic training, along with regular opportunities for faculty to meet and share experiences and perspectives, can help to maintain and enhance faculty competence in assessment.

Unique Faculty Development Programs: Developing Faculty for Relationship-Centered Care

"GOOD TEACHERS, LIKE 'REFLECTIVE PRACTITIONERS' IN OTHER PROFESSIONS, CONSTANTLY TEST, ADJUST, AND REFRAME THEIR MODELS OF PRACTICE ON THE BASIS OF EXPERIENCE AND REFLECTION."
—THEODORE J. MARCHESE, PHD, FORMER VICE PRESIDENT, AMERICAN ASSOCIATION FOR HIGHER EDUCATION[175]

A number of methods exist to train faculty to teach interpersonal and communication skills and to enhance reflection. Various institutions and groups have developed unique faculty development programs.

A faculty development program to enhance humanistic teaching

Branch and colleagues[176] designed and created a longitudinal faculty development program for enhancing humanistic teaching and reflective exploration of values at five medical schools. All programs incorporated reflective and experiential learning to enhance humanistic teaching, and provided a supportive group process. Various learning methods and topics were employed, including narrative writing and other reflective activities such as Balint groups, as well as discussions about renewal and meaning in faculty

members' professional lives; appreciative inquiry; role modeling; use of reflection in clinical teaching; teaching caring attitudes; and giving feedback. The results were striking: Learners perceived faculty participants at all five schools as superior humanistic teachers and role models, as well as more humane and caring physicians, compared to the control group.[176]

Indiana University School of Medicine's professional formation initiative

The goal of Indiana University School of Medicine's (IUSM) "professional formation initiative" is to remake the educational environment and to begin broad curricular revisions.[106] IUSM used an appreciative inquiry process to initiate organizational change.[94] In addition to traditional faculty development offerings, IUSM offers faculty nontraditional programs. These programs provide various personal formation approaches for faculty, and include "… activities intended to invite their whole selves and values to be expressed in their work—with the assumption that such activities restore integrity and vitality to their daily work and enhance their ability to serve others."(p. 314) [106]

Faculty development efforts have included the introduction of processes such as appreciative inquiry activities, small group work, "checking in" at the beginning of meetings, and appreciative debriefing of meetings. More formal programs have included a Courage to Lead Retreat series modeled after the work of Parker Palmer,[110] retreats on humanities and the arts, team-building activities, a "change agent" program to develop faculty skills in conflict resolution and relational small group leadership, a "generosity of spirit" conference, and others.[106] The professional transformation initiative at IUSM has been associated with increased faculty and student satisfaction, notably increased medical school applications, and increased faculty vitality.[177]

Difficult Conversations in Healthcare: Pedagogy and Practice

Difficult Conversations in Healthcare: Pedagogy and Practice is an international faculty development course for physicians and other healthcare professionals who teach interpersonal and communication skills and relationship-centered care.[178] Participants learn about a range of educational methods, and develop strategies to implement relationship-centered teaching and learning in their home institutions.

In addition to narratives for reflection, evocative trigger tapes, appreciative inquiry, small and large group learning, and facilitated reflection, participants engage in a learning model known as the Program to Enhance Relational and Communication Skills (PERCS). PERCS was developed by senior clinicians and educators from Children's Hospital, Harvard Medical School, and the Education Development Center, and serves as the pedagogical model[141] for courses developed by the Institute for Professionalism & Ethical Practice (IPEP) at Children's Hospital in Boston.[179]

IPEP's interdisciplinary learning model includes physician, psychosocial, and family faculty (i.e., patients/parents), as well as professional actors, who reenact real-life scenarios that delve into difficult conversations and how practitioners, patients, and family members experience those conversations. Respectful debriefing

and reflection follow the enactments. Difficult Conversations in Healthcare: Pedagogy and Practice incorporates the learning principles of the PERCS model,[141] including:

- Integrity of learning space

- Interdisciplinary involvement

- Whole-person learning (cognitive, emotional, and spiritual)

- Patient and family perspective

- Suspension of hierarchy

- Multiple perspectives

- Attention to everyday ethics

Between 2006 and the beginning of 2010, 138 medical education leaders (64% physicians) have participated in the faculty development program, and 99% of the participants reported that the program enhanced their ability to guide and teach others about communication and relationship skills with patients and families. Ninety-seven percent reported feeling an improved sense of preparation and 96% noted an improved sense of confidence to teach difficult conversations.[180]

Conclusion

Physicians must develop proficient interpersonal and communication skills to effectively practice medicine. A large amount of evidence-based literature confirms that physicians' competency with these skills is directly associated with improved health outcomes, including

A Practical Guide to Teaching and Assessing the ACGME Core Competencies, Second Edition

improved symptom resolution, better patient adherence to treatment plans, greater patient and physician satisfaction, and fewer behaviors associated with malpractice claims and medical error. In addition, the ability to inspire reflection and self-awareness in the learner is emerging as an important skill for clinical teachers. Reflective skills are associated with the ability to develop insight into one's self, to direct one's learning, and to ensure that the physician can ultimately practice well autonomously.

The goal of this chapter is to provide the knowledge, values, and resources necessary to enable those responsible for medical education at all levels to create an effective curriculum in the interpersonal and communication competencies, considered by many to be the heart and soul of medicine.

> "YOU MUST BE THE CHANGE YOU
> WISH TO SEE IN THE WORLD."
> —MAHATMA GANDHI

The Bottom Line: How to Integrate Interpersonal and Communication Skills Teaching and Assessment into Your Already Crowded Curriculum

1. Choose or adapt a communication skills framework/model and use it for both teaching and assessment in multiple settings in your institution. Repeated and widespread use reinforces the skills/competencies, as well as faculty and learner expectations.

2. Adapt the framework to your institution, its settings, and the level of your trainees.

3. Emphasize teaching and assessment of both interpersonal and communication competencies throughout the curriculum. Consider ways to mature your curriculum in this area.[81]

4. Provide trainees with multiple opportunities for the following:

   - Learning and practicing the skills

   - Observation followed by respectful feedback and reflection on the skills

   - Enhancing self-awareness and reflection

   - Assessment of the skills

5. Go beyond a focus on communication tasks and behaviors. Teach about relationship-centered care, and assess the learners' ability to develop and sustain relationships with patients, colleagues, and those they teach.

6. Carefully consider the learning environments in your institution. Address the hidden curriculum head-on. Explicitly assert and model appropriate values, attitudes, and behaviors as standards. Work organizationally to enhance the culture of teaching and learning and create culturally safe ways to identify and make explicit the hidden curriculum.

The Bottom Line: How to Integrate Interpersonal and Communication Skills Teaching and Assessment into Your Already Crowded Curriculum (cont.)

7. The learner–teacher relationship sets the stage for the physician–patient relationship. Understanding the importance of the relationship between learners and teachers is essential. Remove poor role models from teaching roles.

8. Explicitly articulate, teach, and expect good values and the demonstration of respect for patients and colleagues. Articulate and enhance learners' understanding of the importance of, and evidence for, developing excellent interpersonal and communication skills and engaging in relationship-centered care.

9. Faculty development is key to promoting uniformity in teaching and assessment and the development and enhancement of effective role models. Use experts to train your faculty to teach and assess interpersonal and communication skills, and then provide ongoing faculty development. Provide opportunities for faculty self-reflection.

10. Document your teaching programs and methods of evaluation, and the individual growth and evaluation of your learners over time.

11. Appoint and support a designated interpersonal and communication skills curriculum director or expert group to ensure that the teaching and assessment of these competencies are included throughout the larger curriculum and institutional training programs. Integrating these competencies into the ongoing training curriculum will not occur without specific planning and intent.[181]

Acknowledgments

I want to thank my colleagues who contributed their conceptual frameworks, assessment tools, comments, and inspiration to this chapter. I appreciate their time and generosity. My gratitude to Bill Branch, MD; Judy Belle Brown, PhD; David Browning, MSW, BCD; Aaron Calhoun, MD; Greg Carroll, PhD; Bill Clark, MD; Kathy Cole-Kelly, MS, MSW; Meg Comeau, MHA; Sylvia Cruess, MD; Richard Cruess, MD; Dan Duffy, MD; Larry Dyche, ACSW; Ron Epstein, MD; Daniel Federman, MD; Rich Frankel, PhD; Michael Goldstein, MD; Geoff Gordon, MD; Paul Haidet, MD; Barbara Joyce, PhD; Adina Kalet, MD; Constance Keefer, MD; Howard King, MD, MPH; Sanae Kishimoto, MHS, MPH; Ed Krupat, PhD; Suzanne Kurtz, PhD; Forrest Lang, MD; David Leach, MD; Brook Longmaid, MD; Greg Makoul, PhD; Elaine Meyer, PhD, RN; Dennis Novack, MD; David Robinson, EdD; Bridget Ryan, MSc, PhD; Julia Swartz MSW, LICSW; Jonathan Silverman, MD; Bob Smith, MD, MS; Terry Stein, MD; John Stoeckle, MD; Bob Truog, MD; and Wayne Weston, MD.

Thank you all for your commitment to improving the physician–patient relationship and communication in healthcare.

Innovative Approaches, Models, and Assessment Tools for Teaching and Assessing the Interpersonal and Communication Competencies

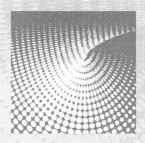

CONTENTS

CONTENTS

Introduction

This section contains several diverse, innovative approaches for teaching along with a number of well-established conceptual frameworks or models for teaching and assessing interpersonal and communication competencies. Current assessment instruments follow each framework description. In addition, several recently developed instruments are provided:

- An expanded Kalamazoo Essential Elements Communication Checklist modified for multirater assessment with gap analysis

- Communication Assessment Tool (CAT) for individuals and teams

- The C3 (Communication, Curriculum, and Culture) Instrument, a unique tool used to characterize the patient-centeredness of the hidden curriculum

The framework or model you choose or adapt for teaching and assessment should focus on both interpersonal and communication competencies and pay particular attention to the physician–patient relationship, understanding the patient's perspective, and relationship-centered learning and care.

Remember the caveat stated earlier in this chapter: The acquisition of skills and behaviors alone is not enough. The physician's relational and humanistic capacities, including being "present" for self and others, compassion, respect for the patient and family, trustworthiness, the ability to reflect, self-awareness, and attention to one's own behavior, are essential capacities significantly associated with patients' perceptions of the quality of care.[44]

A Note About Assessment Instruments

This section includes evaluation instruments to help medical educators interested in using and/or adapting frequently used and validated assessment tools. Ideally, an assessment instrument is selected as part of a uniform framework for teaching and assessing the interpersonal and communication competencies.

Some instruments are designed for use by faculty or other observers/raters with content expertise, others are designed for patient (real or simulated) raters, and still others have been used by both groups or for learner self-assessment. Most instruments are also used for teaching, formative feedback, and enhancing learner reflection.

For all instruments, please contact the person listed for permission to use. Contact information for each instrument is provided. Some of these assessment tools come with a guide or training manual and additional educational materials, and these are available from the contact person or website listed.

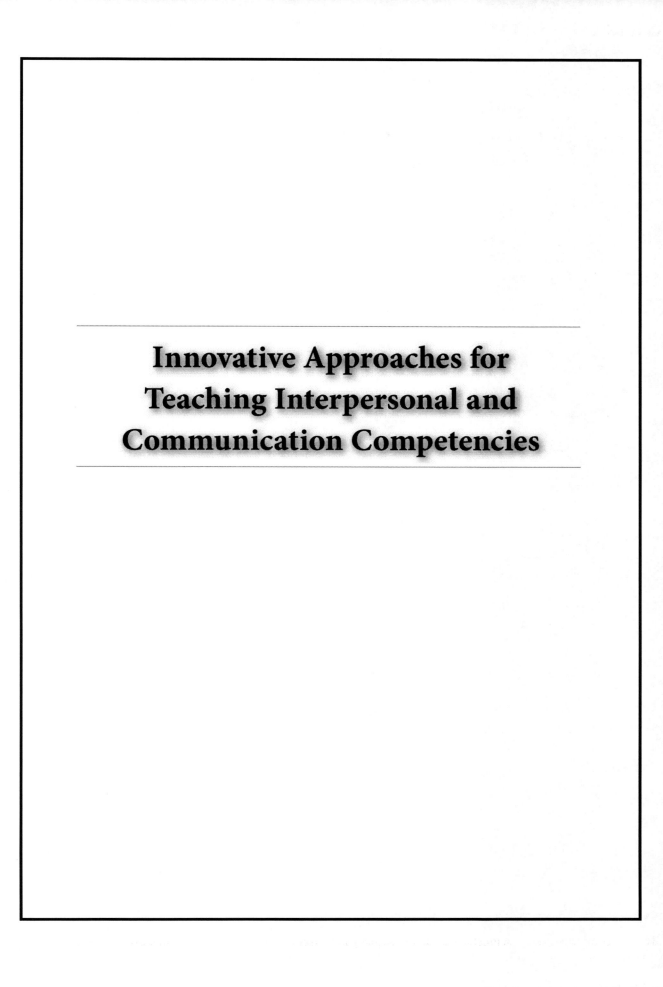

Innovative Approaches for Teaching Interpersonal and Communication Competencies

Creating Synergy: Linking Interpersonal and Communication Skills with Quality and Safety Initiatives

Rich opportunities exist to design curricula linking ACGME accreditation mandates with national quality and safety initiatives in the area of interpersonal and communication skills. The Office of Graduate Medical Education and Department of Quality and Safety at the Henry Ford Health System (HFHS) in Detroit created an innovative and standardized institutional curriculum in interpersonal and communication skills for residency training programs. The program was created for all 20 core residency programs at HFHS, and all incoming first-year residents participate.[182]

Curriculum and assessment

HFHS created a multidisciplinary committee that developed curricular models for four areas: informed consent, disclosure of error, sharing bad news, and handoffs.

Residency program directors or faculty champions lead small group discussions focusing on each of the four chosen topic areas. Each small group discussion centers on specific communication skill sets, the quality or safety initiative, and specialty-specific cases.

For the handoff module, residents engage in a cognitive simulation in which they hand off simulated cases to a peer following a specific protocol.

After each small group discussion, residents complete a three-station objective structured clinical examination (OSCE) related to the topic area. Following each OSCE, standardized patients complete an assessment of residents' performance and residents complete a self-assessment, both using the Kalamazoo Essential Elements Communication Checklist – Adapted (KEECC-A).[157]

Each resident's faculty mentor reviews the assessments. The resident and faculty member then meet to discuss the resident's performance and areas where improvements can be made. Reviewing the resident's videotape of his or her OSCEs gives the faculty member essential insight into the resident's communication skills early in the resident's first year. In the handoff module, peers evaluate residents' skills in handing off patients.

Faculty development

Faculty members attend educational sessions that give them a deeper understanding of the initiative and the Kalamazoo assessment tool (KEECC-A). Faculty members receive a curricular packet containing specialty-specific guides for facilitating group discussions and for debriefing residents about their performance. Faculty members report that these guides are useful and helpful.

Program evaluation and improvement

HFHS uses a mixed-method approach for course evaluation and improvement. Residents complete a course evaluation after each module. Faculty focus groups provide qualitative data about how the curriculum resonates with both teachers and learners.

In addition, rapid prototyping of curricular materials and educational Plan-Do-Study-Act (PDSA) continuous quality improvement cycles are used to improve curricula. Using course evaluation data and faculty feedback in an educational PDSA cycle allows rapid change of curriculum content based on the feedback.[182]

Contact: Barbara Joyce, PhD, Henry Ford Hospital and Health Network, Detroit: *BJOYCE2@hfhs.org.*

Additional resource: Joyce, B. "Building bridges: linking GME with quality and safety – an institutional perspective." *ACGME Bulletin.* January 2009:7–9. ACGME website. *www.acgme.org/acWebsite/bulletin/bulletin0109.pdf.* Accessed March 23, 2010.

Psychosocial Pediatrics: An Innovative Approach to Enhancing Physician–Patient Communication

Through an innovative approach to teaching and enhancing physician–patient communication, Children's Emotional HealthLink (CEHL) at Newton-Wellesley Hospital in Newton, MA, designed and implemented a training model in "psychosocial pediatrics." The year-long, longitudinal, continuing medical education program is called Emotional and Psychosocial Issues in Children and Families: Pediatrics for the New Millennium. CEHL leaders developed this program for experienced pediatricians, family practitioners, and medicine-pediatrics physicians in primary care practice. Residency and clerkship program directors and several pediatric nurse practitioners also participate in each program.

Program goals include:

- Enhancing participants' abilities to create and sustain therapeutic relationships

- Identifying and addressing psychosocial, behavioral, and emotional issues commonly seen in pediatric practice with children, adolescents, and their families

Competencies addressed by the program include:

- Being "present"

- Understanding the patient/family perspective

- Using reflective listening skills

- Assessing the patient's and family's concerns and discussing them in an empathic and constructive fashion

- Understanding how family history may influence the current social-emotional conditions of family members

- Understanding the impact of the clinician's own family history on communication and interactions with patients

The CEHL training program utilizes a variety of teaching methods and focuses on collaborative learning with and from one's peers. The program consists of 12 monthly interactive sessions, in-depth case presentations, individual meetings with a course leader, readings, self and patient evaluations, and online discussions and reflections about case presentations and course topics on a secure website. Attendees also participate in a seven-hour training program titled "Difficult Conversations in Primary Care Pediatrics" that includes realistic enactments with professional actors and was designed by faculty from the Institute for Professionalism and Ethical Practice at Children's Hospital in Boston.[180]

Case presentations include a "process recording" of an extended interview with a patient/family from the course participant's practice and a biopsychosocial assessment. These are prepared with the consultation of two program leaders and are shared with the group. The process recording comes from the clinical social work tradition of expanding interview skills and self-awareness by recording, from memory, the entire interactional process of an interview between patient and practitioner. This exercise provides course participants with the opportunity to review and reflect on an interview with a patient and/or family. Participants meet with a program leader for a consultation to enhance interviewing skills through reflective questions and suggestions about interviewing techniques. The participant then presents the interview to the group for further discussion and reflection.

The overriding theme of the monthly session topics is relationship-centered care and the examination of what practitioners and patients bring to each clinical encounter. Monthly session topics include:

- Role of family systems in pediatric practice

- Art of the therapy referral

- Reflective listening and empathic interviewing skills

- Use of narrative to enhance reflection

- Professional boundaries

- Role of shame in the clinical encounter

- Conducting a psychosocial interview

A team that includes two pediatricians trained in psychosocial pediatrics, a clinical social worker, and an educational psychologist teach Emotional and Psychosocial Issues in Children and Families: Pediatrics for the New Millennium. The program encourages practitioners to be active and innovative, to focus on developing trust, and to promote relationships with patients and parents where important issues in the life of the family can surface and be discussed. The CEHL team is carrying out a randomized trial to examine the effectiveness of its training.

Contact: Howard S. King, MD, MPH, Children's Emotional HealthLink, Newton-Wellesley Hospital, Newton, MA: *HowieKing@aol.com.*

Websites: *www.cehl.org* and *www.cehl.org/ppctp.shtml.*

Additional resource: King, HS. "Shifting from traditional to biopsychosocial pediatrics: modifying the pediatrician–parent relationship to promote normal childhood development." *Permanente J.* 2005; 9:60–63. *http://xnet.kp.org/permanentejournal/fall05/shifting.html.* Accessed March 23, 2010.

Teaching the Skills of Relationship-Centered Medicine: Elements of a "Hidden" Curriculum

Interpersonal skills development is most sensitive to "process" or "hidden" aspects of curricula, including the contexts of teaching, role modeling, parallel processing, and self-reflection. Lawrence Dyche, ACSW, and Deborah Swiderski, MD, developed and wrote the following outline of ways to structure and deliver a curriculum in order to nurture humanism and promote relationship-centered learning. Their approach selects three humanistic attitudes for consideration: curiosity, caring, and respect, or how one thinks, feels, and behaves in approaching relationships.

Stimulate Curiosity

Interpersonal curiosity, a desire to see the world as another sees it, is the cognitive impulse that drives relationships and shapes the collaborative process. Becoming an "understanding" physician requires curiosity—a genuine interest in the human experience, recognition of life's complexity, and a joy in surprise.

Discover and use students' curiosity

Educators best deliver curricula by starting with the cases and themes that most intrigue or concern learners. Many of the lessons about relational matters in medicine will emerge from the students.

Deconstruct certainty and expertise

Certainty is the enemy of curiosity, and medicine fosters the need to assume an attitude of expertise. One strategy for countering the cultural push toward these tendencies in student physicians is for faculty to model the opposite.

Faculty can share their own uncertainty about aspects of particular cases or decisions and ask students to be their consultants in complicated situations. By reversing the learner–teacher roles, we provide a model for physicians to allow their patients to be their teachers when needed.

Examine the dialectics of medical practice

Medicine is typically taught as if there is "one right answer." But in the relational matters of medical practice, and often in biomedical aspects, more than one right answer often exists. The physician must be open to various possibilities and make thoughtful choices about finding a balance. Challenging balances include:

- Thoroughness versus efficiency

- Intimacy versus formality in the patient–physician relationship

- Patient education versus biomedical intervention

Demonstrate the power of the individual case versus statistical probabilities

As Sir William Osler noted, "It is much more important to know what sort of a patient has a disease than what sort of a disease a patient has."[183] A patient's personal capacities, relationships, and resources influence outcomes.

However, clinical epidemiology, which often reduces treatment choices to learning bytes, typically excludes these unique patient aspects from the case discussion. Allow the time and space to address these matters.

Explore the literature of medicine and medicine as literature

We can access the humanity of both patient and physician through writing and literature. Narrative is the primary way that human beings create meaning. Bringing relevant literature into class discussion and asking learners to engage in reflective writing about their personal experiences as healers facilitates the introduction of aesthetic perspectives. The appreciation of paradox, irony, and humor can help to extract meaning from the complexity and contradiction of the lived experience.

Make home visits

Visiting clinic or hospital patients in their homes almost always yields a revelation. People's stories and their lives emerge from the pictures and mementos (or lack thereof) in their homes. Walking patients' streets or climbing their steps can elicit deeper empathy for the patients. Conducting an encounter on the patient's turf gives physicians a new appreciation of the patient's perspective.

Nurture Caring

Caring is the heart of relationship-centered medicine and the basis of empathy. Faculty must model caring and ensure that they reflect it in the contexts of teaching. Maintaining caring requires that faculty help learners develop an understanding of, and respect for, their own personal needs.

Make the doctor's emotional experience a legitimate subject for discussion

The concept of reciprocity in relationship-centered care means that physician satisfaction becomes a significant variable. Altruism is not a limitless virtue; the physician as well as the patient must be nurtured. Faculty can demonstrate nurturance through their interest and concern for learners' well-being.

Becoming a physician necessitates a "trial by fire," but caring for patients also requires being cared for. Educators should teach learners the principles of physician self-care, including recognizing personal limits and preferences, setting reasonable expectations, and accepting that one's life extends beyond the office.

Give student physicians a safe place to love and to hate

Bringing the physician's affective experience into the sphere of learning means recognizing and accepting the emotional intensity that caring for patients can evoke. Strong attachment to patients enhances the joy of practice and the potential loss of needed objectivity. Negative reactions to patients and situations are an inevitable part of the practice of medicine. Students need to learn from mentors that these are understandable and manageable feelings.

Learn to connect with unsympathetic patients

Empathy sometimes means being able to care for some people who do not readily awaken our sympathy. Many patients are likeable and easy to care about; others who come from different life experiences and backgrounds than our own may present challenges.

Empathy may be best measured by the quality of our care for the patients we find most undesirable. Learning the relational dimension in medicine requires ongoing self-examination and reflection to better understand our own personal and cultural biases, to resist premature assumptions, and to restrain our critical impulses.

Learn to say 'no' to patients

The empathic physician is not always solicitous or permissive. Educators should discuss with students professional boundaries, the rights of the physician, and appropriate times to set limits with patients. When these matters are not considered in a reflective atmosphere, student physicians may handle them reactively or unconsciously.

Teach Respect for Diversity in Interpersonal Styles

Respect involves honoring interpersonal differences. Relationship-centered medicine, by its nature, recognizes that relationships are made up of unique individuals who form a unique pairing. Learners must come to understand other people's needs and preferences as well as their own style. Students must question the common idea that only one "doctor–patient relationship" exists.

Instead, they should recognize that every doctor–patient relationship is unique. Physicians can develop a meta-perspective on their interactions with patients and work to expand their own communication and interpersonal repertoire.

Observe yourself and others in practice

An emphasis on uniformity and exactness sometimes subverts individual style and interpersonal flexibility in medical practice. Reviewing videotaped interviews with patients is a common practice in medical training.

However, these exercises may focus on a critique of how well the student followed the "script," rather than what was unique about the interaction between patient and physician. By watching the videos in a small group and suggesting that the teacher and students simply observe the conversation, learners have the opportunity to appreciate the individuality of participants in the encounter.

Write narrative descriptions of the doctor–patient encounter

Help learners take a meta-perspective by asking them to take alternative points of view of their relational behavior. Narratives are one way to work on this level of understanding.

For example, a faculty member can ask the learner questions, such as "How might the patient describe this visit to a close friend?" or "What would a 'fly on the wall' observe during this visit?"

Examine and share your reflections and narratives

Although narratives are constructions, faculty and students can glean much from the degree of coherence, balance, and complexity they contain. It is not likely that we could develop a story in which we make ourselves a three-dimensional character without undertaking some level of self-examination. Narratives can be particularly useful when used in small groups and in conjunction with video review exercises.

Contact: Lawrence Dyche, ACSW, Montefiore Medical Center/Albert Einstein College of Medicine, Bronx, NY: *ldyche@montefiore.org.*

Additional resources: Dyche, L. "Interpersonal skill in medicine: the essential partner of verbal communication." *J Gen Intern Med.* 2007; 22:1035–1039.

Dyche L. "The significance of self-awareness, curiosity, and caring in physician communication. *Medical Encounter.* 2005;19(2): 20–22.

doc.com: An Interactive Resource for Healthcare Communication

Quality Web-based learning modules can be a useful adjunct to communication skills teaching programs, although they should not comprise the entire teaching program for these competencies. The American Academy on Communication in Healthcare and Drexel University College of Medicine publish a comprehensive and interactive Web-based resource, *doc.com*,[174] that provides knowledge, skills review, opportunities for reflection, and faculty resources. This online resource is used internationally to enhance communication skills of medical students, residents, fellows, and practicing physicians.

doc.com includes 41 learning modules and more than 400 videos that delineate and demonstrate core and advanced communication competencies that the IOM, ACGME, and AAMC consider essential. Each module presents key principles, evidence-based recommendations, a skills checklist, videos, and commentary.

Education platform

Interactive features of *doc.com* include functionality for assessment tests, feedback, learning group formation, giving assignments, and accessing test results. Learners' free-text responses to reflection questions and their scores on the assessment test included in each module, combined with the ability for faculty to communicate online with students, give faculty additional flexibility for their learning sessions. For documentation and portfolio development, learners and/or programs can easily authenticate and record learner accomplishments on assessment tests and reflection questions using *doc.com*'s interactive Learning Management System.

Additional faculty resources

doc.com provides sample curricula at the course and session levels, as well as sections on using role play, giving feedback, and other teaching strategies. For experienced and new faculty, the *doc.com* editors also developed Facilitator Guides and accompanying Learner Handouts that offer specific instructions for organizing and conducting 50-minute sessions on the learning modules.

The Facilitator Guides are available for 12 learning modules, including Breaking Bad News, Communicating Across Cultures, Managing Strong Emotions (anger, fear, sadness), Patient Perspective, Professional Boundaries, Drug Abuse, and Tobacco Cessation. Each Facilitator Guide includes suggestions for activities related to engaging learner interest, setting goals and developing skills, and a timed agenda. Accompanying Learner Handouts present goals and principles, rationale for the session, pre- and post-session surveys, and questions for session evaluation and feedback. A Japanese translation of the initial 12 modules with Japanese subtitles for videos is also available.[184]

Websites: *www.aachonline.org/?page=doccomoverview* and *http://webcampus.drexelmed.edu/doccom/user*.
Japan: *www.igakueizou.co.jp/product/system/doccom/about_doccom.html*.

Additional resource: Spagnoletti CL, Bui T, Fischer G, Gonzaga AMR, Rubio DM, Arnold RM. Implementation and evaluation of a web-based communication skills learning tool for training internal medicine interns in patient-doctor communication. *Journal of Communication in Healthcare.* 2009;2:159–172.

Models and Assessment Tools for Teaching and Assessing Interpersonal and Communication Competencies

The Four Habits Model

Education leaders at Kaiser Permanente created the Four Habits Model[185, 186] based on a blend of clinical experience and empirical literature. The model organizes communication tasks into four interrelated families of skills, provides techniques for enacting these habits, and explains the benefits of each. A "habit" denotes integrated and organized ways of thinking and acting in the clinical encounter. The four habits and their accompanying skills are:

1. Invest in the beginning. Create rapport quickly, elicit the full spectrum of the patient's concerns, and plan for the visit.

2. Elicit the patient's perspective. Ask for the patient's ideas, seek to identify the patient's expectations and requests, and explore the impact of the illness on the patient's life.

3. Demonstrate empathy. Be open to the patient's emotions, and convey empathy to the patient both verbally and nonverbally.

4. Invest in the end. Give information, provide education, involve the patient in making decisions, and plan future steps.[186]

Kaiser Permanente has successfully implemented the Four Habits Model throughout its system nationwide, and thousands of Kaiser physicians have learned the model. The model covers a wide range of communication issues, from culturally sensitive care to communication between physicians. Various residency programs have taught the model, and it has been adapted for use internationally.

Medical schools also teach this model in their curricula, and some have found other unique uses. For example, the Indiana University School of Medicine admissions committee uses the Four Habits Model. Faculty interviewers receive training on the model and use it to identify and explore applicants' competencies in several key areas (communication skills, moral and ethical reasoning, professionalism, and personal awareness) as a basis for admission to the medical school.

Figure 1.6			The Four Habits Model

Habit	Skills	Techniques and examples	Payoff
Invest in the beginning	Create rapport quickly	• Introduce self to everyone in the room • Refer to patient by last name and Mr. or Ms. until a relationship has been established • Acknowledge wait • Make a social comment or ask a non-medical question to put patient at ease • Convey knowledge of patient's history by commenting on prior visit or problem • Consider patient's cultural background and use appropriate eye contact and body language	• Establishes a welcoming atmosphere • Allows faster access to real reason for visit • Increases diagnostic accuracy • Requires less work • Minimizes "Oh by the way ..." at the end of the visit • Facilitates negotiating an agenda • Decreases potential for conflict
	Elicit the patient's concerns	• Start with open-ended questions: "What would you like help with today?" or "I understand that you're here for ... Could you tell me more about that?" • Speak directly with the patient when using an interpreter	
	Plan the visit with the patient	• Repeat concerns back to check understanding • Let patient know what to expect: "How about if we start with talking more about ..., then I'll do an exam, and then we'll go over possible tests/ways to treat this. Sound okay?" • Prioritize when necessary: "Let's make sure we talk about X and Y. It sounds like you also want to make sure we cover Z. If we can't get to the other concerns, let's ..."	

Figure 1.6		**The Four Habits Model (cont.)**	

Habit	Skills	Techniques and examples	Payoff
Elicit the patient's perspective	Ask for the patient's ideas	• Assess patient's point of view: "What do you think might be causing your problem?"; "What worries or concerns you most about this problem?"; "What have you done to treat your illness so far?"	• Respects diversity • Uncovers hidden concerns and diagnostic clues • Reveals use of alternative treatments or requests for tests • Improves diagnosis of depression and anxiety
	Elicit specific request	• Ask about ideas from loved ones or from community	
	Explore the impact on the patient's life	• Determine patient's goal in seeking care: "How were you hoping I could help?" • Check context: "How has the illness affected your daily activities/ work/family?"	
Demonstrate empathy	Be open to the patient's emotions	• Respond in a culturally appropriate manner to changes in body language and voice tone	• Adds depth and meaning • Builds trust, leading to better diagnostic information and outcomes • Makes limit-setting or saying "no" easier
	Make an empathetic statement	• Look for opportunities to use brief empathetic comments: "You seem really worried." • Compliment patient on efforts to address problem	
	Convey empathy nonverbally	• Use a pause, touch, or facial expression	
Invest in the end	Deliver diagnostic information Provide education	• Frame diagnosis in terms of patient's original concerns • Explain rationale for tests and treatments • Review possible side effects and expected course of recovery • Discuss options that are consistent with patient's lifestyle, cultural values, and beliefs • Provide resources (e.g., written materials) in patient's preferred language when possible	• Increases potential for collaboration • Influences health outcomes • Improves adherence • Reduces return calls and visits • Encourages self care

| | | **Figure 1.6** | **The Four Habits Model (cont.)** |

Habit	Skills	Techniques and examples	Payoff
Invest in the end *(cont.)*	Involve the patient in making decisions	• Discuss treatment goals; express respect toward alternative healing practices. • Assess patient's ability and motivation to carry out plan. • Explore barriers: "What do you think we could do to help overcome any problems you might have with the treatment plan?" • Test comprehension by asking patient to repeat instructions. • Set limits respectfully: "I can understand how getting that test makes sense to you. From my point of view, since the results won't help us diagnose or treat your symptoms, I suggest we consider this instead."	
	Complete the visit	• Summarize visit and review next steps • Ask for additional questions: "What questions do you have?" • Assess satisfaction: "Did you get what you needed?" • Close visit in a positive way: "It's been nice meeting you. Thanks for coming in."	

Reprinted from: Stein, T. "A decade of experience with a multiday residential communication skills intensive: has the outcome been worth the investment?" Permanente J. 2007; 11:30–40. © 2004, 2007 The Permanente Medical Group, Inc. Reprinted with permission.

The Four Habits Model Coding Scheme and The Four Habits Patient Questionnaire

The Four Habits Coding Sheet and Coding Scheme, derived directly from the Four Habits Model, is a validated instrument used successfully for assessing practicing physicians at Kaiser Permanente, residents in various programs, medical students at Indiana University School of Medicine, and in other settings. To assess patient perceptions of physician behavior, patients can complete a related assessment tool, the Four Habits Patient Questionnaire. These tools are provided here.

Contact: Ed Krupat, PhD, Harvard Medical School, Boston: *ed_krupat@hms.harvard.edu.*

Additional resources: Frankel, R; Stein, T. "Getting the most out of the clinical encounter: the Four Habits Model." *Permanente J.* 1999; 3:79–88. *http://xnet.kp.org/permanentejournal/fall99pj/habits.html.* Accessed March 14, 2010.

Stein, T. "A decade of experience with a multiday residential communication skills intensive: has the outcome been worth the investment?" *Permanente J.* 2007;11:30–40. *http://xnet.kp.org/permanentejournal/Fall07/communication_skills.html.* Accessed March 28, 2010.

Stein, T; Frankel, RM; Krupat E. "Enhancing clinician communication skills in a large healthcare organization: a longitudinal case study." *Patient Educ Couns.* 2005; 58:4–12.

Figure 1.7	**The Four Habits Coding Sheet**

Note: *The Four Habits Coding Scheme should be used to determine ratings. This is a coding worksheet that can be used to list ratings from the Four Habits Coding Scheme if desired.*

Code each of the items below using the categories 1, 3, or 5. If you feel strongly that the behavior being coded is directly in between categories, you may use the categories 2 or 4.

	Highly Effective				Not Very Effective

1. Invest in the Beginning

A. Shows familiarity with patient	1	(2)	3	(4)	5
B. Greets patient warmly	1	(2)	3	(4)	5
C. Makes small talk	1	(2)	3	(4)	5
D. Tries to identify the problem	1	(2)	3	(4)	5
E. Encourages expansion of patient's concerns	1	(2)	3	(4)	5
F. Elicits the full range of concerns	1	(2)	3	(4)	5

2. Elicit the Patient's Perspective

A. Interested in patient's understanding of problem	1	(2)	3	(4)	5
B. Asks about patient's goals for visit	1	(2)	3	(4)	5
C. Shows interest in impact on patient's life	1	(2)	3	(4)	5

3. Demonstrate Empathy

A. Encourages expression of emotion	1	(2)	3	(4)	5
B. Accepts/validates patient's feelings	1	(2)	3	(4)	5
C. Helps to identify/label feelings	1	(2)	3	(4)	5
D. Displays effective nonverbal behavior	1	(2)	3	(4)	5

4. Invest in End

A. Frames information using patient's perspective	1	(2)	3	(4)	5
B. Allows time for information to be absorbed	1	(2)	3	(4)	5
C. Explains clearly/uses little jargon	1	(2)	3	(4)	5
D. Explains rationale for tests and treatments	1	(2)	3	(4)	5
E. Effectively tests for comprehension	1	(2)	3	(4)	5
F. Encourages involvement in decision-making	1	(2)	3	(4)	5
G. Explores acceptability of treatment plan	1	(2)	3	(4)	5
H. Explores barriers to implementation	1	(2)	3	(4)	5
I. Encourages additional questions	1	(2)	3	(4)	5
J. Makes clear plans for follow-up	1	(2)	3	(4)	5

© The Permanente Medical Group, Inc. Used with permission.

| Figure 1.8 | **The Four Habits Coding Scheme** |

Habit 1. Invest in the Beginning

A1. Clinician indicates clear familiarity with patient's history/chart (e.g., mentions recent tests performed or visit information based on previous chart notes)

3. Clinician makes some reference to past visits or history, but familiarity with these does not seem strong

5. Clinician needs to refer to chart continually to familiarize self with case or does not relate current visit with patient's history or chart (or doesn't even have chart)

B1. Patient is greeted in manner that is personal and warm (e.g., clinician asks patient how s/he likes to be addressed, uses patient's name)

3. Patient is greeted in manner that recognizes patient, but without great warmth or personalization

5. Greeting of patient is cursory, impersonal, or non-existent

C1. Clinician makes non-medical comments, using these to put the patient at ease

3. Clinician makes cursory attempt at small talk (shows no great interest, keeps discussion brief before moving on)

5. The clinician gets right down to business without any attempt at small talk (or cuts patient off curtly and abruptly, or if later in visit, shows only passing interest)

D1. The clinician tries to identify the problem(s) using primarily open-ended questions (asks questions in a way that allows patient to tell own story with minimum of interruptions or closed-ended questions)

3. The clinician tries to identify the problem(s) using a combination of open- and closed-ended questions (possibly begins with open-ended but quickly reverts to closed-ended)

5. The clinician tries to identify the problem(s) using primarily closed-ended questions (staccato style)

E1. The clinician encourages the patient to expand in discussing his/her concerns (e.g., using various continuers such as "Aha," "Tell me more," "Go on").

3. Clinician neither cuts the patient off nor expresses great interest in learning more (listens, but does not encourage expansion or further discussion)

5. The clinician interrupts or cuts the patient off in his/her attempt to expand (is clearly not very interested)

Figure 1.8	**The Four Habits Coding Scheme (cont.)**

F1. The clinician attempts to elicit the full range of the patient's concerns by generating an agenda early in the visit (clinician does other than simply pursue first stated complaint)

3. The clinician makes some reference to other possible complaints, or asks briefly about them before pursuing the patient's first complaint, or generates an agenda as the visit progresses

5. The clinician immediately pursues the patient's first concern without an attempt to discover other possible concerns of the patient's

Habit 2. Elicit the Patient's Perspective

A1. Clinician shows great interest in exploring the patient's understanding of the problem (e.g., asks the patient what the symptoms mean to him/her)

3. Clinician shows brief or superficial interest in understanding the patient's understanding of the problem

5. Clinician makes no attempt/shows no interest in understanding the patient's perspective

B1. Clinician asks (or responds with interest) about what the patient hopes to get out of the visit (e.g., can be general expectations or specific requests such as meds, referrals)

3. Clinician shows interest in getting a brief sense of what the patient hopes to get out of the visit, but moves on quickly

5. Clinician makes no attempt to determine (shows no interest in) what the patient hopes to get out of the visit

C1. Clinician attempts to determine in detail/shows great interest in how the problem is affecting patient's lifestyle (work, family, daily activities)

3. Clinician attempts to determine briefly/shows only some interest in how the problem is affecting patient's lifestyle

5. Clinician makes no attempt to determine/shows no interest in how the problem is affecting patient's lifestyle

Figure 1.8	**The Four Habits Coding Scheme (cont.)**

Habit 3. Demonstrate Empathy

A1. Clinician openly encourages/is receptive to the expression of emotion (e.g., through use of continuers or appropriate pauses (signals verbally or nonverbally that it is okay to express feelings)

3. Clinician shows relatively little interest or encouragement for the patient's expression of emotion; or allows emotions to be shown but actively or subtly encourages patient to move on

5. Clinician shows no interest in patient's emotional state and/or discourages or cuts off the expression of emotion by the patient (signals verbally or nonverbally that it is not okay to express emotions)

B1. Clinician makes comments clearly indicating acceptance/validation of patient's feelings (e.g., "I'd feel the same way," "I can see how that would worry you")

3. Clinician briefly acknowledges patient's feelings but makes no effort to indicate acceptance/validation

5. Clinician makes no attempt to respond to/validate the patient's feelings, or possibly belittles or challenges them (e.g., "It's ridiculous to be so concerned about ...")

C1. Clinician makes clear attempt to explore patient's feelings by identifying or labeling them (e.g., "So how does that make you feel?" "It seems to me that you are feeling quite anxious about ...")

3. Clinician makes brief reference to patient's feelings, but does little to explore them by identification or labeling

5. Clinician makes no attempt to identify patient's feelings

D1. Clinician displays nonverbal behaviors that express great interest, concern, and connection (e.g., eye contact, tone of voice, and body orientation) throughout the visit

3. Clinician's nonverbal behavior shows neither great interest or disinterest (or behaviors over course of visit are inconsistent)

5. Clinician's nonverbal behavior displays lack of interest and/or concern and/or connection (e.g., little or no eye contact, body orientation, or use of space inappropriate, bored voice)

| Figure 1.8 | **The Four Habits Coding Scheme (cont.)** |

Habit 4. Invest in the End

A1. Clinician frames diagnostic and other relevant information in ways that reflect patient's initial presentation of concerns

3. Clinician makes cursory attempt to frame diagnosis and information in terms of patient's concerns

5. Clinician frames diagnosis and information in terms that fit physician's frame of reference rather than incorporating those of the patient

B1. Clinician pauses after giving information with intent of allowing patient to react to and absorb it

3. Clinician pauses briefly for patient reaction, but then quickly moves on (leaving the impression that the patient may not have fully absorbed the information)

5. Clinician gives information and continues on quickly without giving the patient an opportunity to react (impression is that this information will not be remembered properly or fully appreciated by the patient)

C1. Information is stated clearly and with little or no use of jargon

3. Information contains some jargon and is somewhat difficult to understand

5. Information is stated in ways that are technical or above patient's head (indicating that the patient has probably not understood it fully or properly)

D1. Clinician fully/clearly explains the rationale behind current, past, or future tests and treatments so that patient can understand the significance of these to diagnosis and treatment

3. Clinician only briefly explains the rationale for tests and treatments

5. Clinician offers/orders tests and treatments, giving little or any rationale for these

E1. Clinician effectively tests for the patient's comprehension

3. Clinician briefly or ineffectively tests for the patient's comprehension

5. Clinician makes no effort to determine whether the patient has understood what has been said

| Figure 1.8 | **The Four Habits Coding Scheme (cont.)** |

F1. Clinician clearly encourages and invites patient's input into the decision-making process

3. Clinician shows little interest in inviting the patient's involvement in the decision-making process, or responds to the patient's attempts to be involved with relatively little enthusiasm

5. Provider shows no interest in having patient's involvement or actively discourages/ignores patient's efforts to be part of decision-making process

G1. Clinician explores acceptability of treatment plan, expressing willingness to negotiate if necessary

3. Clinician makes brief attempt to determine acceptability of treatment plan, and moves on quickly

5. Clinician offers recommendations for treatment with little or no attempts to elicit patient's acceptance of (willingness or likelihood of following) the plan

H1. Clinician fully explores barriers to implementation of treatment plan

3. Clinician briefly explores barriers to implementation of treatment plan

5. Clinician does not address whether barriers exist for implementation of treatment plan

I1. Clinician openly encourages and asks for additional questions from patient (and responds to them in at least some detail)

3. Clinician allows for additional questions from patient, but does not encourage question

   asking nor respond to them in much detail

5. Clinician makes no attempt to solicit additional questions from patient or largely ignores them if made unsolicited

J1. Clinician makes clear and specific plans for follow-up to the visit

3. Clinician makes references to follow-up, but does not make specific plans

5. Clinician makes no reference to follow-up plans

© The Permanente Medical Group, Inc. Used with permission.

| Figure 1.9 | **The Four Habits Patient Questionnaire** |

How did your doctor communicate with you?

We now explore how physicians communicate with their patients. In order to do so, we need to hear the experience of patients. That is why we need your help. Please fill in this questionnaire as soon as possible after the consultation. When you're finished, put it in the attached envelope and mail it to us.

The numerical code on top of the paper is to identify your physician. We will not know who you are. Your physician will not get to know what you answered personally. Your future healthcare will not depend on whether you respond to this questionnaire, but we hope to start a process in which all physicians will improve in the long run.

Your date of birth: _____

Sex: _____

Date of consultation with the physician: _____

Please tick the box that best fits your experience. **If there are questions that do not fit this consultation, please go to the next question.**

      A Practical Guide to Teaching and Assessing the ACGME Core Competencies, Second Edition

Figure 1.9	**The Four Habits Patient Questionnaire (cont.)**

	Definitely yes	Somewhat yes	Somewhat no	Definitely no
Did the doctor seem to know the important information about your medical history?	❏	❏	❏	❏
At the beginning of the visit, did the doctor meet you in a way that helped put you at ease?	❏	❏	❏	❏
In exploring your health concerns, did the doctor give you a good chance to express yourself in your own words?	❏	❏	❏	❏
Did the doctor encourage you to fully describe your health concerns?	❏	❏	❏	❏
Did the doctor ask about all of your health concerns rather than just focusing on the first one you mentioned?	❏	❏	❏	❏
Did the doctor seem interested in finding out how you thought about the health concerns?	❏	❏	❏	❏
Did the doctor ask about your expectations for the visit?	❏	❏	❏	❏
Did the doctor seem interested in finding out how your current health problems are affecting your daily life?	❏	❏	❏	❏
Did you get good eye contact with the doctor?	❏	❏	❏	❏
Did the doctor seem sensitive to your feelings?	❏	❏	❏	❏
Did you feel that the doctor was interested in you as a person?	❏	❏	❏	❏
Did the doctor encourage you to express any emotions that you felt?	❏	❏	❏	❏
Did the doctor do anything to help you feel okay about whatever emotions you were feeling?	❏	❏	❏	❏

Figure 1.9	**The Four Habits Patient Questionnaire (cont.)**

	Definitely yes	Somewhat yes	Somewhat no	Definitely no
Did the doctor help you to understand your feelings better?	❑	❑	❑	❑
Did the doctor give you information that directly addressed the concerns you had expressed?	❑	❑	❑	❑
When the doctor gave you information, did s/he give you as much time as you needed to understand it and absorb it?	❑	❑	❑	❑
When the doctor gave you information, was it clear and in words you could easily understand?	❑	❑	❑	❑
After the doctor gave you information, did s/he make sure to find out how well you understood the information?	❑	❑	❑	❑
Did the doctor encourage you to be as much involved as you would like in the decisions about your healthcare?	❑	❑	❑	❑
Did the doctor check to see whether the treatment plan was okay with you?	❑	❑	❑	❑
Did the doctor make sure whether you would be able to carry out the treatment plan?	❑	❑	❑	❑
Toward the end of the visit, did the doctor encourage you to ask any questions?	❑	❑	❑	❑
Toward the end of the visit, did the doctor make clear and specific plans about what you should do as a follow-up?	❑	❑	❑	❑

Using any number from 0 to 10, where 0 is the worst medical care possible and 10 is the best medical care possible, what number would you use to rate the medical care you received during this visit with the doctor?

Write number here _____

The Kalamazoo Consensus Statement Framework

The Kalamazoo Consensus Statement[8] identifies seven evidence-based "essential elements," or tasks, of effective physician–patient communication and provides skill competencies for each element. Twenty-one medical education leaders and communication experts from the United States and Canada developed the Kalamazoo Consensus Statement in 1999 and then met in subsequent years to develop an assessment tool and other resources.

The group included representatives from various specialties and from major medical education and professional organizations in North America, including the AAMC, CanMEDS 2000 Project, ACGME, ABIM, Educational Commission for Foreign Medical Graduates, National Board of Medical Examiners, Macy Health Communication Initiative, and the American Medical Association. The Fetzer Institute and the Bayer Institute for Health Care Communication (now the Institute for Healthcare Communication) jointly sponsored the meetings.

Architects of five physician–patient communication models were included in the Kalamazoo Consensus Statement group. The group examined each model and its research base, underlying assumptions, and applications. The five models included:

- Calgary-Cambridge Guides

- Patient-Centered Clinical Method

- Three Function Model/Brown Interview Checklist

- Institute for Health Care Communication 4E Model

- SEGUE framework and instrument

The group also highlighted skills and tasks in existing consensus statements and guidelines, and organization representatives provided information on their efforts to develop criteria for teaching and assessing communication skills.

The Kalamazoo Consensus Statement group's aim was to delineate a set of essential elements in physician–patient communication in order to identify and articulate ways to facilitate teaching and assessment of communication skills at all levels of medical education. The framework considers building a relationship with a patient to be an ongoing task that physicians perform during each interaction with the patient. Another tenet of the framework is that the therapeutic relationship depends on the use of good communication skills. Gordon[187] notes that the Kalamazoo Consensus Statement outlines four key communication skills for building a therapeutic relationship with a patient:

1. Establish and maintain a personal connection with the patient

2. Elicit the patient's perspective on his or her chief complaint

3. Demonstrate empathy in response to patient cues

4. Express a desire to work with the patient toward better health

Medical schools as well as graduate and postgraduate training programs around the world use the Kalamazoo Consensus Statement for teaching communication.

Figure 1.10 shows a comparison of the competencies presented in the Kalamazoo Consensus Statement framework and the Four Habits Model.

Figure 1.10	A Comparison of the Communication and Relationship Competencies of the Four Habits Model and the Kalamazoo Consensus Statement Framework

The Four Habits Model[186]	Kalamazoo Consensus Statement Framework [8, 157]

Habit 1. Invest in the beginning
 	
• Create rapport quickly
 	
• Elicit the patient's concerns
 	
• Plan the visit with the patient
	1. Build a relationship (throughout interview)
	
	  • Greet and show interest in patient as a person
	
	  • Use words that show care and concern throughout the interview
	
	  • Use tone, pace, eye contact, and posture that show care and concern
	
	2. Open the discussion
	
	3. Gather information

Habit 2. Elicit the patient's perspective
 	
• Ask for the patient's ideas
 	
• Elicit specific request
 	
• Explore impact on the patient's life
	4. Understand the patient's perspective
	
	  • Ask about life events, circumstances, other people who might affect health
	
	  • Elicit patient's beliefs, concerns, and expectations about illness and treatment
	
	  • Respond explicitly to patient statements about ideas, feelings, and values

Habit 3. Demonstrate empathy • Be open to the patient's emotions • Make an empathic statement • Convey empathy nonverbally	*Incorporated in 1. Build a relationship 4. Understand the patient's perspective
Habit 4. Invest in the end • Deliver diagnostic information • Provide education • Involve patient in making decisions • Complete the visit	**5. Share information** **6. Reach agreement** **7. Provide closure**

* A specific competency, Demonstrates Empathy, is included in the modified Kalamazoo instrument,[169] Gap–Kalamazoo Communication Skills Assessment Form.

Adapted and reprinted from: Rider, EA. "Communicating with children and families." In: Rudolph, C; Lister, G; Gershon, A; First, L; Rudolph, A; eds. Rudolph's Pediatrics, 22nd edition. NY: McGraw-Hill. In press. Used with permission.

The Kalamazoo Consensus Statement Framework Assessment Tools

The Kalamazoo Consensus Statement Group developed an assessment tool, "Essential Elements: The Communication Checklist," that is applicable to all levels of medical training and various settings.[157] It includes seven core communication competencies and 24 subcompetencies. Educators can rate learners' performance on the competencies and subcompetencies in four categories:

- Done well

- Needs improvement

- Not done

- Not applicable

At Harvard Medical School, Rider and colleagues[156] adapted the Kalamazoo Essential Elements Communication Checklist by using global ratings for the seven competencies and a Likert scale (1 = poor to 5 = excellent). Faculty members and/or standardized patients use the adapted Kalamazoo assessment tool to evaluate communication skills in schoolwide formative and summative assessment exercises. Educators also use the checklist as a teaching tool for the core medicine clerkships.[156]

Calhoun, Rider, and colleagues recently expanded the use of the Kalamazoo Essential Elements Communication Checklist by adapting it for use as a multirater evaluation with gap analysis methodology.[169]

Contact: Elizabeth Rider, MSW, MD (member, Kalamazoo Consensus Statement Group), Harvard Medical School, Boston: *elizabeth_rider@hms.harvard.edu*

Additional resources: Bayer-Fetzer Conference on Physician–Patient Communication in Medical Education. Essential elements of communication in medical encounters: the Consensus Statement. *Acad Med.* 2001;76:390–393.

Rider EA, Hinrichs MM, Lown BA. A model for communication skills assessment across the undergraduate curriculum. *Med Teach.* 2006;28:e127–e134.

Figure 1.11	**Kalamazoo Essential Elements Communication Checklist**

Date: _____ Setting: _____

Learner: _____

Observer: _____

	Done well	Needs improvement	Not done	Not applicable
Build a Relationship				
Greets and shows interest in patient as a person	❏	❏	❏	❏
Uses words that show care and concern throughout the interview	❏	❏	❏	❏
Uses tone, pace, eye contact, and posture that show care and concern	❏	❏	❏	❏
Open the Discussion				
Allows patient to complete opening statement without interruption	❏	❏	❏	❏
Asks "Is there anything else?" to elicit full set of concerns	❏	❏	❏	❏
Explains and/or negotiates an agenda for the visit	❏	❏	❏	❏
Gather Information				
Begins with patient's story using open-ended questions ("Tell me about …")	❏	❏	❏	❏
Clarifies details as necessary with more specific or "yes/no" questions	❏	❏	❏	❏
Summarizes and gives patient opportunity to correct or add information	❏	❏	❏	❏
Transitions effectively to additional questions	❏	❏	❏	❏
Understand the Patient's Perspective				
Asks about life events, circumstances, other people that might affect health	❏	❏	❏	❏
Elicits patient's beliefs, concerns, and expectations about illness and treatment	❏	❏	❏	❏
Responds explicitly to patient statements about ideas, feelings, and values	❏	❏	❏	❏
Share Information				
Assesses patient's understanding of problem and desire for more information	❏	❏	❏	❏
Explains using words that are easy for patient to understand	❏	❏	❏	❏
Checks for mutual understanding of diagnostic and/or treatment plans	❏	❏	❏	❏
Asks whether patient has any questions	❏	❏	❏	❏

| Figure 1.11 | **Kalamazoo Essential Elements Communication Checklist (cont.)** |

	Done well	Needs improvement	Not done	Not applicable
Reach Agreement (if new/changed plan)				
Includes patient in choices and decisions to the extent s/he desires	❑	❑	❑	❑
Asks about patient's ability to follow diagnostic and/or treatment plans	❑	❑	❑	❑
Identifies additional resources as appropriate	❑	❑	❑	❑
Provide Closure				
Asks whether the patient has questions, concerns, or other issues	❑	❑	❑	❑
Summarizes	❑	❑	❑	❑
Clarifies follow-up or contact arrangements	❑	❑	❑	❑
Acknowledges patient and closes interview	❑	❑	❑	❑

Comments:

_____

_____

_____

_____

_____

_____

Source: © Bayer-Fetzer Group on Physician-Patient Communication in Medical Education, May 2001. Reference: The Bayer-Fetzer Conference on Physician-Patient Communication in Medical Education. Essential Elements of Communication in Medical Encounters: The Kalamazoo Consensus Statement. Academic Medicine 2001; 76:390–393. Used with permission.

    A Practical Guide to Teaching and Assessing the ACGME Core Competencies, Second Edition

Figure
1.12

Kalamazoo Essential Elements Communication Checklist—Adapted

How well does the learner do the following:

	1 Poor	2 Fair	3 Good	4 Very Good	5 Excellent
A. Builds a Relationship (includes the following):	○	○	○	○	○

- Greets and shows interest in patient as a person
- Uses words that show care and concern throughout the interview
- Uses tone, pace, eye contact, and posture that show care and concern

	1 Poor	2 Fair	3 Good	4 Very Good	5 Excellent
B. Opens the Discussion (includes the following):	○	○	○	○	○

- Allows patient to complete opening statement without interruption
- Asks "Is there anything else?" to elicit full set of concerns
- Explains and/or negotiates an agenda for the visit

	1 Poor	2 Fair	3 Good	4 Very Good	5 Excellent
C. Gathers Information (includes the following):	○	○	○	○	○

- Begins with patient's story using open-ended questions (e.g."tell me about…")
- Clarifies details as necessary with more specific or "yes/no" questions
- Summarizes and gives patient opportunity to correct or add information
- Transitions effectively to additional questions

	1 Poor	2 Fair	3 Good	4 Very Good	5 Excellent
D. Understands the Patient's Perspective (includes the following):	○	○	○	○	○

- Asks about life events, circumstances, other people that might affect health
- Elicits patient's beliefs, concerns, and expectations about illness and treatment
- Responds explicitly to patient's statements about ideas and feelings

	1 Poor	2 Fair	3 Good	4 Very Good	5 Excellent
E. Shares Information (includes the following):	○	○	○	○	○

- Assesses patient's understanding of problem and desire for more information
- Explains using words that patient can understand
- Checks for mutual understanding of treatment plan
- Asks if patient has any questions

	1 Poor	2 Fair	3 Good	4 Very Good	5 Excellent
F. Reaches Agreement (if new/changed plan) (includes the following):	○	○	○	○	○

- Includes patient in choices and decisions to the extent s/he desires
- Asks about patients ability to follow diagnostic and/or treatment plans
- Identifies additional resources as appropriate

	1 Poor	2 Fair	3 Good	4 Very Good	5 Excellent
G. Provides Closure (includes the following):	○	○	○	○	○

- Asks if patient has questions, concerns or other issues
- Summarizes / asks patient to summarize plans until next visit
- Clarifies follow-up or contact arrangements
- Acknowledges patient and closes interview

*Adapted from Essential Elements: The Communication Checklist, ©Bayer-Fetzer Group on Physician-Patient Communication in Medical Education, May 2001, and from: The Bayer-Fetzer Conference on Physician-Patient Communication in Medical Education. Essential Elements of Communication in Medical Encounters: The Kalamazoo Consensus Statement. *Academic Medicine* 2001; 76:390-393.

Contact: Elizabeth A. Rider, MSW, MD – elizabeth_rider@hms.harvard.edu (member, Kalamazoo Consensus Group)

The Kalamazoo Consensus Statement Framework: Multirater Assessment with Gap Analysis

An innovative development related to the Kalamazoo Essential Elements Communication Tool is an expansion and use for multirater assessment with gap analysis. This provides a potentially powerful methodology for assessing communication skills and self-insight, and for encouraging self-reflection.

Calhoun, Rider, and colleagues[169] used the Kalamazoo Consensus Statement framework and 360-degree assessment models to develop a multirater methodology with gap analysis. They used this methodology for individual and team assessments in interdisciplinary, simulation-based communication skills programs.

Gap analysis consists of a systematic comparison between the mean scores obtained from a rater group and the self-score of the participant or team being assessed. The gap itself is calculated by subtracting the learner's or team's self-assessment score on a given communication dimension or competency from the mean assessment of that dimension by the rater group.

Positive values or gaps correspond to self-underappraisal, and negative gaps correspond to self-overappraisal. By enabling the quantitative assessment of self-insight and appraisal, gap analysis empowers faculty members to specifically reinforce learners' strengths and to focus on areas where poor self-insight is shown, potentially enhancing learning and reflection.

This assessment tool includes the original seven dimensions of the Kalamazoo Consensus Statement framework (builds a relationship, opens the conversation, gathers information, understands the patient's/family's perspective, shares information, reaches agreement, and provides closure).[8] It also includes two additional dimensions: demonstrates empathy and communicates accurate information, which improve the tool's ability to assess difficult conversations.[169]

The tool contains Likert-scale, forced-choice, and free-text fields, enabling it to provide absolute and relative scores for each aspect of communication and specific comments regarding strengths and areas needing improvement. A similar version of the instrument, which includes language written at a sixth grade reading level, was created for actual or simulated patient/family use.

The tool has high measures of internal consistency, with a Cronbach's alpha of 0.84 for the original seven Kalamazoo dimensions, and 0.87 for the nine dimensions of the expanded instrument. Factor analysis indicated that all nine dimensions of the expanded instrument contributed to a single measured construct.[169]

These statistics strongly support both the unity and consistency of the expanded tool's contents and confirm that an overall score averaged across all dimensions can function as a marker of general communication competence.

Multirater assessment with gap analysis methodology is not specific to the communication skills model, and many of the existing assessment tools relying on these models could be suitably altered for multirater assessment and gap analysis with little effort.

Using 360-degree and multirater assessments[168, 188] and analyzing the gaps between the perceptions of the learner or team and those of interdisciplinary observer groups can generate formative feedback and potentially enhance learner self-insight and reflection regarding interpersonal and communication skills.

Contact: Aaron W. Calhoun, MD, University of Louisville School of Medicine, Louisville, KY: *aaron.calhoun@louisville.edu.*

Additional resources: Calhoun, AW; Rider, EA; Meyer, EC; Lamiani, G; Truog, RD. "Assessment of communication skills and self-appraisal in the simulated environment: feasibility of multirater feedback with gap analysis." *Simul Healthc.* 2009; 4(1):22–29.

Calhoun, AW; Rider, EA. "Engagement and listening skills: identifying learner needs." *Med Educ.* 2008; 42:1134–1135.

| Figure 1.13 | **Gap–Kalamazoo Communication Skills Assessment Form: Clinician*** |

Subject identifier _____. Rater title: MD ☐, RN ☐, SW ☐, SELF ☐, _____,

Family meeting: __1 __2 __3 __Sim

How well does the clinician do the following:

	1 Poor	2 Fair	3 Good	4 Very good	5 Excellent
A. Builds a relationship (includes the following):	○	○	○	○	○

- Greets and shows interest in the patient and patient's family
- Uses words that show care and concern throughout the interview
- Uses tone, pace, eye contact, and posture that show care and concern
- Responds explicitly to patient and family statements about ideas and feelings

	1 Poor	2 Fair	3 Good	4 Very good	5 Excellent
B. Opens the discussion (includes the following):	○	○	○	○	○

- Allows patient and family to complete opening statements without interruption
- Asks "Is there anything else?" to elicit full set of concerns
- Explains and/or negotiates an agenda for the visit

	1 Poor	2 Fair	3 Good	4 Very good	5 Excellent
C. Gathers information (includes the following):	○	○	○	○	○

- Addresses patient and family statements using open-ended questions
- Clarifies details as necessary with more specific or "yes/no" questions
- Summarizes and gives family opportunity to correct or add information
- Transitions effectively to additional questions

Figure 1.13	Gap–Kalamazoo Communication Skills Assessment Form: Clinician* (cont.)

	1	2	3	4	5
	Poor	Fair	Good	Very good	Excellent

D. Understands the patient's and family's perspective (includes the following):

- Asks about life events, circumstances, other people that might affect health
- Elicits patient's and family's beliefs, concerns, and expectations about illness and treatment

	1	2	3	4	5
	Poor	Fair	Good	Very good	Excellent

E. Shares information (includes the following):

- Assesses patient's and family's understanding of problems and desire for more information
- Explains using words that family can understand
- Asks whether family has any questions

	1	2	3	4	5
	Poor	Fair	Good	Very good	Excellent

F. Reaches agreement (if new/changed plan) (includes the following):

- Includes family in choices and decisions to the extent they desire
- Checks for mutual understanding of diagnostic and/or treatment plans
- Asks about acceptability of diagnostic and/or treatment plans
- Identifies additional resources as appropriate

	1	2	3	4	5
	Poor	Fair	Good	Very good	Excellent

G. Provides closure (includes the following):

- Asks whether patient and family have questions, concerns, or other issues
- Summarizes
- Clarifies future time when progress will again be discussed
- Provides appropriate contact information if interim questions arise
- Acknowledges patient and family, and closes interview

Figure 1.13	**Gap–Kalamazoo Communication Skills Assessment Form: Clinician* (cont.)**

	1	2	3	4	5
	Poor	Fair	Good	Very good	Excellent

H. Demonstrates empathy

(includes the following):
- Clinician's demeanor is appropriate to the nature of the conversation
- Shows compassion and concern
- Identifies/labels/validates patient's and family's emotional responses
- Responds appropriately to patient and family's emotional cues

	1	2	3	4	5
	Poor	Fair	Good	Very good	Excellent

I. Communicates accurate information

(includes the following):
- Accurately conveys the relative seriousness of patient's condition
- Took other participating clinician's input into account
- Clearly conveys expected disease course
- Clearly presents and explains options for future care
- Gives enough clear information to empower decision-making

What did this clinician do the best at?   (Please pick three choices.)

❑ Builds a relationship
❑ Opens the discussion
❑ Gathers information
❑ Understands the patient's and family's perspective
❑ Shares information
❑ Reaches agreement
❑ Provides closure
❑ Demonstrates empathy
❑ Communicates accurate information

Figure 1.13	**Gap–Kalamazoo Communication Skills Assessment Form: Clinician* (cont.)**

Why did you choose those particular answers?

_____
_____
_____
_____
_____
_____
_____
_____
_____

What could this clinician improve on? (Please pick three choices.)

❑ Builds a relationship
❑ Opens the discussion
❑ Gathers information
❑ Understands the patient's and family's perspective
❑ Shares information
❑ Reaches agreement
❑ Provides closure
❑ Demonstrates empathy
❑ Communicates accurate information

What could they have done better?

_____
_____
_____
_____
_____
_____
_____
_____

*Adapted from: Essential Elements: The Communication Checklist, ©Bayer-Fetzer Group on Physician-Patient Communication in Medical Education, May 2001, and from: The Bayer-Fetzer Conference on Physician-Patient Communication in Medical Education. Essential Elements of Communication in Medical Encounters: The Kalamazoo Consensus Statement. Academic Medicine 2001; 76:390–393. Contacts: Elizabeth Rider, MSW, MD - elizabeth_rider@hms.harvard.edu (member, Kalamazoo Consensus Statement Group) and Aaron Calhoun, MD - aaron.calhoun@louisville.edu.

Figure 1.14	**Gap–Kalamazoo Communication Skills Assessment Form: Parent/Family***

Clinician identifier _____. Family meeting: __1 __2 __3 __Sim

How well did your child's doctor do at ...

	1	2	3	4	5
	Poor	Fair	Good	Very good	Excellent

A. Builds a relationship:
- The doctor was really interested in my family
- The doctor's words showed that he/she cared for my child
- The doctor seemed to care about our feeling and what we wanted
- The doctor's body language showed that he/she cared for my child

	1	2	3	4	5
	Poor	Fair	Good	Very good	Excellent

B. Opens the discussion:
- The doctor let us finish things we had to say without interrupting
- The doctor asked us about other things that might be worrying us
- The doctor clearly explained why we were meeting

	1	2	3	4	5
	Poor	Fair	Good	Very good	Excellent

C. Gathers information:
- The doctor didn't try to force the conversation with his/her questions
- The doctor asked us for more detail about things that we said
- The doctor would occasionally repeat back what we had said as a summary
- The doctor did not seem to interrupt us as he/she asked their own questions

Figure 1.14	**Gap–Kalamazoo Communication Skills Assessment Form: Parent/Family* (cont.)**

	1	2	3	4	5
	Poor	Fair	Good	Very good	Excellent

D. Understands the patient's and family's perspective:
- The doctor asked about parts of our lives and personal histories that would affect health
- The doctor showed interest in our personal beliefs and concerns
- The doctor asked what we thought about the treatments and tests being done

	1	2	3	4	5
	Poor	Fair	Good	Very good	Excellent

E. Shares information:
- The doctor asked what we understood about our child's illness
- We understood the words our doctor used to describe our child's illness
- The doctor would check to see whether we had any questions after each explanation
- The doctor gave us enough time to think about what he/she had said before moving on

	1	2	3	4	5
	Poor	Fair	Good	Very good	Excellent

F. Reaches agreement:
- The doctor included us in all the decisions that were being made
- The doctor made sure that we understood what the next step would involve
- The doctor asked what our feelings were about those plans before making any decisions
- The doctor brought in outside help when we needed it (social work, pastor)

Figure 1.14	Gap–Kalamazoo Communication Skills Assessment Form: Parent/Family* (cont.)

	1	2	3	4	5
	Poor	Fair	Good	Very good	Excellent
G. Provides closure:	○	○	○	○	○

- The doctor made sure that we had no more questions before leaving
- The doctor gave a summary at the end of what we had talked about
- The doctor set a time to meet again
- The doctor told us who to call if we had more questions
- The doctor showed a real interest in our family as people as he/she ended the meeting

	1	2	3	4	5
	Poor	Fair	Good	Very good	Excellent
H. Demonstrates empathy:	○	○	○	○	○

- The doctor showed compassion for our family
- The doctor seemed to understand how we were feeling
- The doctor responded to how we felt in a way that made sense to us

	1	2	3	4	5
	Poor	Fair	Good	Very good	Excellent
I. Communicates accurate information:	○	○	○	○	○

- The doctor clearly explained our child's condition
- The doctor clearly explained what our options were
- The explanations our doctor gave were good enough for us to make important decisions

| Figure 1.14 | **Gap–Kalamazoo Communication Skills Assessment Form: Parent/Family* (cont.)** |

What did this doctor do the best at? (Please pick three choices.)

❑ Builds a relationship
❑ Opens the discussion
❑ Gathers information
❑ Understands the patient's and family's perspective
❑ Shares information
❑ Reaches agreement
❑ Provides closure
❑ Demonstrates empathy
❑ Communicates accurate information

Why did you choose those particular answers?
_____
_____
_____
_____
_____
_____
_____

What could this doctor improve on? (Please pick three choices.)

❑ Builds a relationship
❑ Opens the discussion
❑ Gathers information
❑ Understands the patient's and family's perspective
❑ Shares information
❑ Reaches agreement
❑ Provides closure
❑ Demonstrates empathy
❑ Communicates accurate information

What could they have done better?
_____
_____
_____
_____
_____
_____
_____
_____

Adapted from: Essential Elements: The Communication Checklist, ©Bayer-Fetzer Group on Physician-Patient Communication in Medical Education, May 2001, and from: The Bayer-Fetzer Conference on Physician-Patient Communication in Medical Education. Essential Elements of Communication in Medical Encounters: The Kalamazoo Consensus Statement. Academic Medicine 2001; 76:390–393. Contacts: Elizabeth Rider, MSW, MD - elizabeth_rider@hms.harvard.edu (member, Kalamazoo Consensus Statement Group) and Aaron Calhoun, MD - aaron.calhoun@louisville.edu.

Common Ground Assessment Instrument (CGAI)

The Kalamazoo and Toronto consensus statements are the foundation of the The Common Ground Assessment Instrument (CGAI). The CGAI provides a reliable and valid assessment consistent with these frameworks. This criteria-based instrument evaluates skills in conducting a patient-centered/relationship-centered medical interview. The instrument combines elements of both checklist and global assessment ratings. The CGAI is rated highly on its focus on patient-centered communication, and educators effectively use it with medical students at all levels and with incoming and current residents.

The CGAI is an assessment instrument generally completed by faculty members or trained raters in real time as they observe an interview with real or standardized patients (as in an OSCE). Raters identify frequencies of patient-centered or non-patient-centered behaviors and record a global rating in seven categories by comparing interview performance with objective global criteria.

Additional rating forms and scoring instructions are available for family interviews and patient comments, along with feedback and recommendation forms for interviewing skills with patients and families.

Contact: Forrest Lang, MD, Quillen College of Medicine, East Tennessee State University, Johnson City, TN: *LANG@etsu.edu.*

Additional resources: Lang, F; Harvill, L; McCord, R; Anderson, D. "Communication assessment using the Common Ground Instrument: psychometric properties." *Fam Med.* 2004; 36(3):189–198.

Family Medicine Interview Study Group. "Guidelines for using common ground assessment instrument." East Tennessee State University. 2008.

Figure 1.15	**Common Ground Assessment Instrument (CGAI)**

Interviewer _____ Faculty/rater _____ Patient _____ Date _____

1. Rapport

(Number of Occurrences)

No	1	2	3	4	5	
O	O	O	O			Initial introduction/preference
O	O	O	O	O	O	Social conversation
O	O	O	O	O	O	Explicit "Positive Speak"
O	O	O	O	O	O	Explicit caring/commitment
O	O	O	O	O	O	Verbal interruption
O	O	O	O	O	O	Negative talk (implied or explicit)

Nonverbal Rating scale	-2 Strong negative	-1 Negative	0 Neutral	+1 Positive	+2 Strong positive
Body position and eye contact	O	O	O	O	O
Voice qualities	O	O	O	O	O

(Rating scale)

1	2	3	4	5	NA	**Overall rapport**
O	O	O	O	O	O	

2. Eliciting all agenda items

(Number of occurrences)

No	1	2	3	
O	O	O	O	Agenda setting effort "What brings you in?"
O	O			Early (1–2 min.) full exploration i.e., "That's it."
O	O	O		Checks for additional agenda later.

(Rating scale)

1	2	3	4	5	NA	**Overall agenda**
O	O	O	O	O	O	

3. Information management

O _____

C _____

(Number of occurrences)

0–1	2–3	4–5	6–7	8–10	
O	O	O	O	O	For the first 10 questions, record the open-ended questions.

0	1	2	3	4	
O	O	O	O	O	Performs summary (3 or more items), segues, organizing directives.

(Rating scale)

1	2	3	4	5	NA	**Overall information management**
O	O	O	O	O	O	

4. Active listening for full understanding of ideas, concerns, and expectations

No	Yes	N/A	PT's clues or statements needing follow-up.
O	O	O	#1
O	O	O	#2
O	O	O	#3
O	O	O	#4

(Number of occurrences)

0	1	2	3	4	
O	O	O	O	O	Asks (or affirms) about patients' ideas, concerns, expectations.

(Rating scale)

1	2	3	4	5	NA	**Overall active listening**
O	O	O	O	O	O	

5. Addressing feelings with patient

No	Yes	N/A	PT's stated or implied feelings needing follow-up.
O	O	O	#1 -
O	O	O	#2 -
O	O	O	#3-
O	O	O	#4

(Number of occurrences)

0	1	2	3	4	
O	O	O	O	O	Explore or address other feelings.

(Rating scale)

1	2	3	4	5	NA	**Overall deals with feelings**
O	O	O	O	O	O	

Figure 1.15	**Common Ground Assessment Instrument (CGAI) (cont.)**

6. Closing the interview

(Rating scale)

No 1 2 3 N/A

O O O O O Identifies **patient's perspective** (knowledge, concerns, expectations) and builds plan accordingly:

No = Little or not at all; 1= Partially, 2 = Adequately; 3 = Notably

O O O O O Explains **impressions** (Dx, Tx, options):

No = Strikingly ineffective,

1= Somewhat ineffective,

2 = Effective, 3 = Notably effective

O O O   O Checks for **agreement/feasibility**

No = None, 1 = Minimal, 2 = Effective

O O O   O Checks for **understanding**

No = None, 1 = Yes/No, 2 = Teach back

O O O   O Establishes **mutual responsibility**

No = None, 1 = Partial, 2 = Thorough

7. Reaching common-ground—uses:

(Number of occurrences)

0 1 2 3   **Informational strategies**

O O O O   Provides information, explanations,

4 5 6   and recommendations

O O O

_____

_____

_____

_____

0 1 2 3   **Patient engaging strategies** ➔

O O O O

4 5 6   _____

O O O   _____

_____

_____

_____

0 1 2 3   **Less effective strategies**

O O O O   Direction, repetition of position, using

4 5 6   morbidity/mortality data (fear); clinician

O O O   centered recommendations, personal

appeal or authority

(Rating scale)

1 2 3 4 5 NA   **Overall reaching common ground**

O O O O O O

8. Global interview performance

(Rating scale)

1 2 3 4 5 NA   **Overall global interview**

O O O O O O

Observations and comments:

Patient engaging strategies

___ **P**t centered (ideas, concerns, expectations)

___ **R**eadiness to change

___ **I**nformation – Ask, Tell, Ask

___ **D**ecision analysis (1–4 elements)

___ **E**mpathic connection

___ **A**mbivalence

___ **B**rainstorming

___ **C**riteria

___ **D**octor's recommendation

___ **E**mpathic response

___ **F**amily involvement

___ **F**raming differently (reframing)

___ **F**ollow-up

Source: © 2005/2008 Family Medicine Interview Study Group, East Tennessee State University. Reprinted with permission.

Figure 1.16	**Common Ground Assessment Instrument— Global Rating of Core, Common Ground Interview Skills**

Rapport building: Global criteria

5. Demonstrates rapport-building skills such that most patients would subsequently go out of their way to tell friend or family about this interviewer with extraordinary interpersonal skills. Usually include two or more elements of "positive speak" and expressions of nonverbal interest that are exceptionally warm.

4. Notably warm and makes effective connection via identifiable elements of both verbal and nonverbal connection.

3. Clearly professional, respectful, and interested but minimal or ineffective specific verbal or nonverbal efforts to make a more personal connection.

2. For the most part, professional and respectful. Absent of specific effective efforts at rapport building. Present are some comments, expressions, or nonverbal behaviors, which might have a negative reception by a least some patients.

1. Absent are positive elements of relationship building. Present are clearly negative comments or expressions, which would leave many patients with negative feelings about the interviewer.

Agenda setting: Global criteria

5. Explores complete agenda at the beginning (first two minutes after rapport building) till the point that the patient says, "Nothing else." Explicitly plans agenda and, if several agenda, prioritize amongst them. Explores for additional agenda later or at the end.

4. Explores complete agenda early till "Nothing else," but does not summarize or prioritize or explore for more agenda at end.

3. Explores for agenda partially with at least two efforts at agenda setting. One can be at beginning and one at end.

2. Asks only once at the beginning e.g., "What brings you in today?" or "How can I be of help?" or, at the end, "Is there anything else?"

1. Doesn't explore for agenda but begins addressing an established problem. Identical in chart. Doesn't return to agenda at any point.

Information management: Global criteria

5. Begin interview with effective open-ended question and non-directed facilitation. Continue in this mode (with occasional closed-ended points of clarification) till most/all of patient's information about the condition has been expressed. Notably effective information flow with explicit summary(s), directives and/or segues. Asks appropriate focused (closed) questions toward the end.

4. Begins with a majority of effective open-ended questions/facilitations. Appropriate mixes of open- and closed-ended questions. (Required) Effectively manages info flow. Uses some form of summary, directives, or segues.

Figure 1.16	**Common Ground Assessment Instrument— Global Rating of Core, Common Ground Interview Skills (cont.)**

3. Uses some open-ended and closed-ended questions from the beginning. Doesn't use summaries, directives, or segues. Organization adequate.

2. Mostly closed-ended questions. Info flow weak, repetitive, or disorganized.

1. Mostly closed-ended questions. Uses numbers of flawed, leading, or repeated questions. Disorganized, confusing, misleading info flow.

Active listening to understand the patient's perspective on illness: Global criteria

5. Very effective at identifying the patients perspective on illness PPI (i.e., what the patient thinks may be going on; the greatest concern about the problem; and the expectations for the visit). The PPI is repeatedly explored using active listening to understand the meaning behind the patients "clues." Once the PPI is disclosed, these elements are acknowledged, normalized, and used as part of a plan to address the medical diagnosis and the PPI.

4. Demonstrates genuine interest in the PPI by using active listening at least part of the time. Does explore the clues initially, but not always fully. Once identified, PPI will be partially addressed with some elements of acknowledgment, normalization, and building a plan based on the PPI.

3. Demonstrates some interest in the PPI through occasional exploration of clues (efforts may not be effective). May not pick up on clues but rather asks about the patient's ideas.

2. Fails to demonstrate effective interest in what the patient thinks may be going on; his/her greatest concern about the problem; and the expectations for the visit.

1. Actively discourages or devalues the PPI.

Addressing feelings: Global criteria

5. Responds to all opportunities to address feelings. When feelings surface, these are effectively addressed and then incorporated into the visit. Also effectively seeks out the "potential feelings" when situations with high likelihood of feelings surface in the interview.

4. Acknowledges feeling when expressed. Does not fully address/incorporate into visit. Does not fully address "potential" feeling situations.

3. Acknowledges expressed feelings but does not attempt to integrate into visit.

2. May not acknowledge any of the feelings of the case or does so ineffectively.

1. Comments or responds in a way which demeans, criticizes, or devalues patients' feelings.

| Figure 1.16 | **Common Ground Assessment Instrument—Global Rating of Core, Common Ground Interview Skills (cont.)** |

Reaching common ground—closing the interview: Global criteria.

5. Plan linked explicitly to a thorough understanding of the patient's knowledge and perspective. Discusses feasibility and decision-making and matches plan to patient's apparent or explicit preference. Explains the diagnosis and treatment clearly and concisely, checks effectively for understanding (tell-back required) and feasibility.

4. Plan begins with a considerable understanding of patient's knowledge and perspective. Explains clearly with only occasional use of jargon. Checks for understanding and feasibility explicitly. Supports patient's decision-making preference.

3. Partial or minimal understanding of patient's knowledge and perspective. Provides information with general clarity. May include some jargon. Some effort to determine understanding and/or feasibility. (Often with a single closed-ended question.)

2. Minimal or absent understanding of patient's knowledge and perspective. Information provided is somewhat confusing. Minimal effort to check understanding and feasibility.

1. No patient baseline assessment. Explanations confusing/disorganized/misleading. Minimal or absent attempt to check understanding or feasibility.

Reaching common ground (differences in expectations apparent): Global criteria

Note: Rating is based on what the interviewer does, not how the patient responds.

5. Works very effectively at bridging differences between the interviewer and the patient. Performs a full exploration of the PPI and uses the PPI to reach common ground. Uses a number of the more effective skills in reaching common ground (e.g. decision analysis, ask/tell/ask approach, reframing, patient-centered suggestions, criteria setting, brainstorming, compromise, etc.). Avoids less effective methods (e.g., use of authority, personal appeal, repetition of serious complications, or chance of death). Would likely facilitate a desirable change in behavior toward health.

4. Demonstrates clear skills in reaching common ground. Does obtain most of the PPI and attempts to use at least some (but not all) of its elements in a plan. Uses a mix of strategies to reach the plan. Heavier use of the more effective skills.

3. While does not connect the plan with PPI, uses a balanced mix of skills to reach common ground that includes at least one of the more effective strategies.

2. Does not use the patient's issues to help to solve the difference. Uses more of the less effective strategies in trying to create a plan (e.g., use of authority, personal appeal, and repetition of serious complications). For most patients, this plan would not significantly affect the long-term behavior in question.

1. Uses less effective strategies almost exclusively. In missing the patient's issues and in using authority or threat, the patient would be unlikely to change long-term behavior and would probably leave upset with the interviewer's approach to problem solving.

Figure 1.16	**Common Ground Assessment Instrument— Global Rating of Core, Common Ground Interview Skills (cont.)**

Overall interview: Global criteria

5. At the level of an experienced clinician who is expert in using all communications skills effectively. Skills demonstrated such that a patient would likely note such skills to friends and family.

4. Uses all communication skills effectively; minor suggestions for change are noted which are unlikely to have measurable importance on encounter.

3. Uses most communication skills effectively; some interview behaviors present which, if modified, could lead to an even more effective impact on a real encounter.

2. Uses some communication skills effectively and others ineffectively; certain areas of communication might cause clinical problems. (Patient dissatisfaction or confusion.)

1. Inadequate communication skills; likely to create significant clinical problems. (Patient dissatisfaction or confusion.)

In general, the numbers above translate into the following:

5 = Exemplary   **4** = Very Effective   **3** = Competent/Adequate   **2** = Marginal   **1** = Needs Improvement

Source: © 2004/2008 Family Medicine Interview Study Group, East Tennessee State University. Reprinted with permission.

Calgary-Cambridge Guides

The Calgary-Cambridge Guides, developed by Kurtz, Silverman, and Draper,[142, 145] identify 70 evidence-based core communication process skills within a framework of tasks and objectives. The Calgary-Cambridge framework brings together communication process skills (i.e., how to communicate) and content skills (i.e., what to communicate, including the traditional medical history), incorporating the patient's perspective, the biomedical history, and the physical examination.

Two companion books[142, 145] present the comprehensive research evidence, theoretical concepts, and experience that validate the Calgary-Cambridge Guides and their approach to teaching and learning communication skills in medicine. In 2003, the authors enhanced and updated the Calgary-Cambridge Guides by designing diagrams that visually and conceptually enhance communication skills teaching. They also place the communication process within a comprehensive clinical method of medical interviewing that incorporates the process of communication skills with history-taking and physical examination.[189]

The Calgary-Cambridge Guides consist of three guides:

- Guide 1: Interviewing the Patient

- Guide 2: Explanation and Planning

- Guide 3: Content Guide

Appropriate items are selected from the process guides (Guides 1 and 2) for each communication scenario assessed. The guides differentiate process and content, and educators can separate them within the assessment instruments.

The guides are widely used internationally by practicing physicians across specialties and at all levels of medical training. More than 60% of medical schools in the United Kingdom use the Calgary-Cambridge Guides.

Contacts: Suzanne Kurtz, PhD, College of Veterinary Medicine, Washington State University, Pullman, WA: *smkurtz@vetmed.wsu.edu.*

Dr. Jonathan Silverman, FRCGP, University of Cambridge School of Clinical Medicine, Cambridge, UK: *js355@medschl.cam.ac.uk.*

Website: *www.skillscascade.com.*

Additional resources: Kurtz, S; Silverman, J; Benson, J; Draper, J. "Marrying content and process in clinical method teaching: enhancing the Calgary-Cambridge Guides." *Acad Med.* 2003; 78:802–809.

Kurtz, S; Silverman, J; Draper, J. *Teaching and Learning Communication Skills in Medicine.* 2nd ed. Abingdon, Oxon, UK: Radcliffe Medical Press; 2005.

Silverman, J; Kurtz, S; Draper J. *Skills for Communicating with Patients.* 2nd ed. Abingdon, Oxon, UK: Radcliffe Medical Press; 2005.

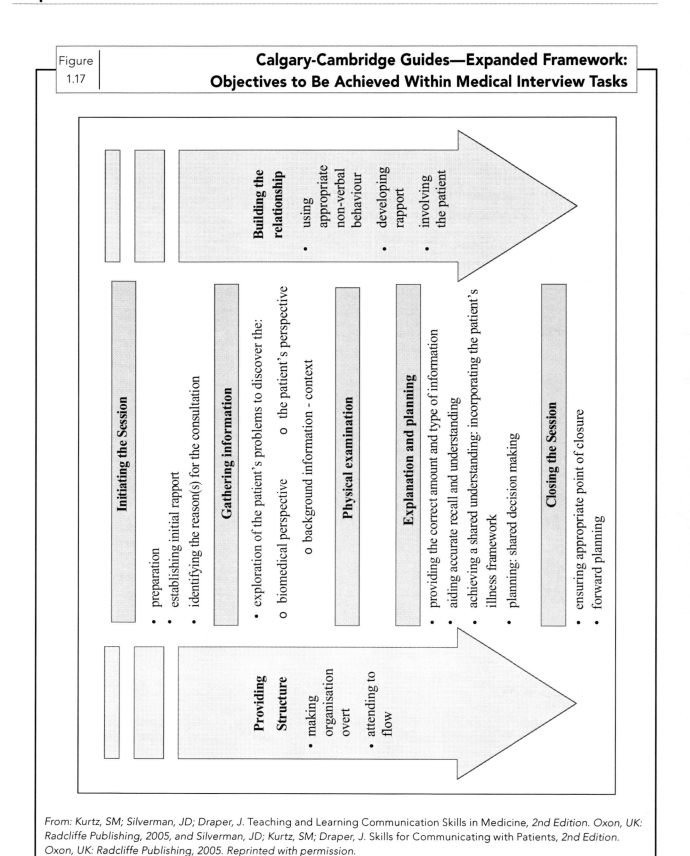

**Calgary-Cambridge Guides—Expanded Framework:
Objectives to Be Achieved Within Medical Interview Tasks**

Building the relationship
- using appropriate non-verbal behaviour
- developing rapport
- involving the patient

Initiating the Session
- preparation
- establishing initial rapport
- identifying the reason(s) for the consultation

Gathering information
- exploration of the patient's problems to discover the:
  - o biomedical perspective
  - o the patient's perspective
  - o background information - context

Physical examination

Explanation and planning
- providing the correct amount and type of information
- aiding accurate recall and understanding
- achieving a shared understanding: incorporating the patient's illness framework
- planning: shared decision making

Closing the Session
- ensuring appropriate point of closure
- forward planning

Providing Structure
- making organisation overt
- attending to flow

From: Kurtz, SM; Silverman, JD; Draper, J. Teaching and Learning Communication Skills in Medicine, *2nd Edition. Oxon, UK: Radcliffe Publishing, 2005, and Silverman, JD; Kurtz, SM; Draper, J.* Skills for Communicating with Patients, *2nd Edition. Oxon, UK: Radcliffe Publishing, 2005. Reprinted with permission.*

Figure 1.18	**Calgary-Cambridge Guides—Expanded Framework: Example of the Interrelationship Between Content and Process (Gathering Information)**

Gathering Information

Process Skills for Exploration of the Patient's Problems

- Patient's narrative
- Question style: open to closed cone
- Attentive listening
- Facilitative response
- Picking up cues

- Clarification
- Time-framing
- Internal summary
- Appropriate use of language
- Additional skills for understanding patient's perspective

Content to Be Discovered

The bio-medical perspective—disease

- Sequence of events
- Symptom analysis
- Relevant systems review

The patient's perspective—illness

- Ideas and beliefs
- Concerns
- Expectations
- Effects on life
- Feelings

Background information—context

- Past medical history
- Drug and allergy history
- Family history
- Personal and social history
- Review of systems

From: Kurtz, SM; Silverman, JD; Draper J. Teaching and Learning Communication Skills in Medicine, 2nd Edition. Oxon, UK: Radcliffe Publishing, 2005, and Silverman, JD; Kurtz, SM; Draper J. Skills for Communicating with Patients, 2nd Edition. Oxon, UK: Radcliffe Publishing, 2005. Reprinted with permission.

| Figure 1.19 | **Calgary-Cambridge Guides:** **Gathering Information/Explanation and Planning Sample Forms** |

The following three OSCE mark sheets demonstrate how process and content can be distinctly separated within assessment instruments. The differentiation of content and process skills enables examiners to appreciate more clearly the skills that they are marking and allows marks for content and process to be weighted differently for each individual station.

Note that each mark sheet has been derived by selecting appropriate items from the Calgary-Cambridge process guides for each communication process challenge being assessed. Process items are then combined with case-specific content items for each scenario.

Source: Appendix 4: Sample OSCE mark sheets. In: Kurtz, S; Silverman, J; Draper, J. Teaching and Learning Communication Skills in Medicine. 2nd Ed. Abingdon, Oxon, UK: Radcliffe Medical Press, 2005. Reprinted with permission.

| Figure 1.19 | **Calgary-Cambridge Guides: Gathering Information/Explanation and Planning Sample Forms (cont.)** |

School of Clinical Medicine, University of Cambridge
OSCE STATION – GATHERING INFORMATION: MATURITY ONSET DIABETES

Process grid	Good Yes (2)	Adequate Yes but (1)	Not done/inadequate No (0)
1. **Greets** patient and obtains patient's name			
2. **Introduces** self, role and nature of interview; obtains consent			
3. Demonstrates interest and **respect**, attends to patient's physical comfort			
4. Uses appropriate **opening question** (e.g. "What problems brought you to hospital today?")			
5. **Listens** attentively, allowing patient to complete statements without interruption and leaving space for patient to think before answering or go on after pausing			
6. Checks and **screens** for further problems (e.g. "so that's headaches and tiredness, what other problems have you noticed?")			
7. Encourages patient to **tell the story** of the problem(s) from when first started to the present in own words			
8. Uses **open and closed questions**, appropriately moving from open to closed			
9. **Facilitates** patient's responses verbally and non-verbally e.g. use of encouragement, silence, repetition, paraphrasing, interpretation			
10. Picks up verbal and non-verbal **cues** (body language, speech, facial expression, affect); checks out and acknowledges as appropriate			
11.**Clarifies** statements which are vague or need amplification (e.g. "Could you explain what you mean by light headed")			
12. Periodically **summarises** to verify own understanding of what the patient has said; invites patient to correct interpretation or provide further information.			
13. Uses clear, easily understood **language**, avoids jargon			
14. Actively **determines** patient's perspective (ideas, concerns, expectations, feelings, effects on life)			
15. Appropriately and sensitively **responds to and further explores patient's perspective**			
16. Demonstrates appropriate **non-verbal behaviour** e.g. eye contact, posture & position, movement, facial expression, use of voice			
17. **Acknowledges** patient's views and feelings; is not judgmental			
18. Uses **empathy** to communicate appreciation of the patient's feelings or predicament			
19. Provides **support**: expresses concern, understanding, willingness to help			
20. Progresses from one section to another using **signposting**; includes rationale for next section			
21. Structures interview in logical **sequence**, attends to **timing**, keeps interview on task			

Content grid	Yes (1)	No (0)
Symptoms		
1. tired, few months		
2. septic spots		
3. rash		
4. thirst		
5. polyuria		
6. weight loss		
Other symptoms		
7. joint aches		
8. blurred vision		
Relevant functional enquiry		
9. no loss of appetite		
Ideas and thoughts		
10. diabetes		
11. hep C		
Concerns		
12. amputations or blindness		
Expectations		
13. tests		
Feelings		
14. to be taken seriously		
Past medical history		
15. migraine		
16. hepatitis		
17. asthma		
18. vitiligo		
Drugs		
19. atenolol		
20. two inhalers		
21. steroids intermittently		

Notes to student on performance:

Source: Appendix 4: Sample OSCE mark sheets. In: Kurtz S, Silverman J, Draper J. Teaching and Learning Communication Skills in Medicine. 2nd Ed. Abingdon, Oxon, UK: Radcliffe Medical Press, 2005. Reprinted with permission.

| Figure 1.19 | **Calgary-Cambridge Guides:** **Gathering Information/Explanation and Planning Sample Forms (cont.)** |

School of Clinical Medicine, University of Cambridge

OSCE STATION: DEALING WITH A DISTRESSED PATIENT OR RELATIVE

Process grid

	Good Yes (2)	Adequate Yes but (1)	Not done/ inadequate No (0)
1. **Greets** patient and obtains patient's name			
2. **Introduces** self, role			
3. Demonstrates interest and **respect**, attends to patient's physical comfort			
4. **Listens** attentively, allowing patient to complete statements without interruption and leaving space for patient to think before answering or go on after pausing			
5. **Facilitates** patient's responses verbally and non–verbally e.g. use of encouragement, silence, repetition, paraphrasing, interpretation			
6. Picks up verbal and non–verbal **cues** (body language, speech, facial expression, affect); checks out and acknowledges as appropriate			
7. Actively and sensitively explores **patient's feelings** (2 if explores effectively once stated)			
8. Actively and sensitively explores **patient's concerns** (2 if explores effectively once stated)			
9. Demonstrates appropriate **non–verbal behaviour** e.g. eye contact, posture & position, movement, facial expression, use of voice			
10. **Acknowledges** patient's views and feelings; is not judgmental			
11. Uses **empathy** to communicate appreciation of the patient's feelings or predicament (2 if verbal and nonverbal empathy)			
12. Avoids **platitudes or false reassurance**			
13. Provides **support**: expresses concern, understanding, willingness to help			

Notes to student on performance:

Content grid

		Yes (1)	No (0)
1	worried re kids		
2	father was sent home from hospital and had fatal MI		
3	wish husband was at home		
4	husband's vasectomy		

Source: Appendix 4: Sample OSCE mark sheets. In: Kurtz S, Silverman J, Draper J. Teaching and Learning Communication Skills in Medicine. 2nd Ed. Abingdon, Oxon, UK: Radcliffe Medical Press, 2005. Reprinted with permission.

| Figure 1.19 | Calgary-Cambridge Guides: Gathering Information/Explanation and Planning Sample Forms (cont.) |

School of Clinical Medicine, University of Cambridge

OSCE STATION: EXPLANATION AND PLANNING RE CHEST PAIN INVESTIGATIONS

PROCESS GRID

	Good Yes (2)	Adequate Yes but (1)	Not done/inadequate No (0)
BUILDING A RELATIONSHIP			
1. Demonstrates interest and **respect** for patient as a person			
2. Demonstrates appropriate **non-verbal behaviour** e.g. eye contact, posture and position, movement, facial expression, use of voice			
3. Uses **empathy** to communicate appreciation of the patient's feelings or predicament (2 if verbal and non-verbal empathy)			
PROVIDING THE CORRECT AMOUNT/TYPE OF INFO FOR THE INDIVIDUAL PATIENT			
4. **Chunks and checks**, using patient's response to guide next steps			
5. Assesses the **patient's starting point** (2 if carefully tailors explanation)			
6. Discovers what **other information** would help patient, seeks and addresses patient's info needs			
AIDING ACCURATE RECALL AND UNDERSTANDING			
7. **Organises** explanation (2 if uses signposting/summarising)			
8. Checks **patient's understanding** (2 if asks patient to restate information given)			
9. Uses clear **language**, avoids jargon and confusing language			
ACHIEVING A SHARED UNDERSTANDING: INCORPORATING THE PATIENT'S PERSPECTIVE			
10. Relates explanations to patient's **illness framework**			
11. **Encourages** patient to contribute reactions, feelings and own ideas (2 if responds well)			
12. Picks up and responds to patient's **non-verbal and covert verbal cues**			
PLANNING: SHARED DECISION MAKING			
13. Explores management **options** with patient (2 if signposts pos^n of equipoise or own preferences)			
14. **Involves** patient in decision making (2 if establishes level of involvement patent wishes)			
15. Appropriately **negotiates** mutually acceptable action plan			

CONTENT GRID

	Yes (1)	No (0)
1. Appropriate gravity of explanations		
2. Discusses driving		
3. Discusses smoking		

Notes to student on performance:

Source: Appendix 4: Sample OSCE mark sheets. In: Kurtz S, Silverman J, Draper J. Teaching and Learning Communication Skills in Medicine. 2nd Ed. Abingdon, Oxon, UK: Radcliffe Medical Press, 2005. Reprinted with permission.

Patient-Centered Clinical Method

Because disease and illness are intertwined, the patient-centered clinical method seeks both a diagnosis and an understanding of the patient's experience of illness. Levenstein developed the original concept of the patient-centered clinical method based on the observation of a large number of patients in his practice.[190] Educational leaders at the University of Western Ontario in Canada further developed this model.[191] The patient-centered clinical method includes six interwoven components, rather than discrete tasks, and skilled practitioners move back and forth among the components as they follow the patient's cues.[192] Patient-centered care includes:

- Exploring dimensions of illness (e.g., feelings, ideas, and impact on the patient's function and expectations)

- Understanding the whole person (e.g., life history, family, social supports, culture, community, and others)

- Coming toward a common ground with issues and goals

- Paying explicit attention to enhancing the patient–physician relationship via the physician's use of self-awareness and effective relationship tools (e.g., empathy, genuineness)

- Incorporating health promotion and prevention

- Being realistic with time, teamwork, resources, and care of self

Educators can use the patient-centered method to teach and assess medical students, residents, fellows, faculty members, and community physicians. The following figure illustrates how the components of the patient-centered method interconnect.

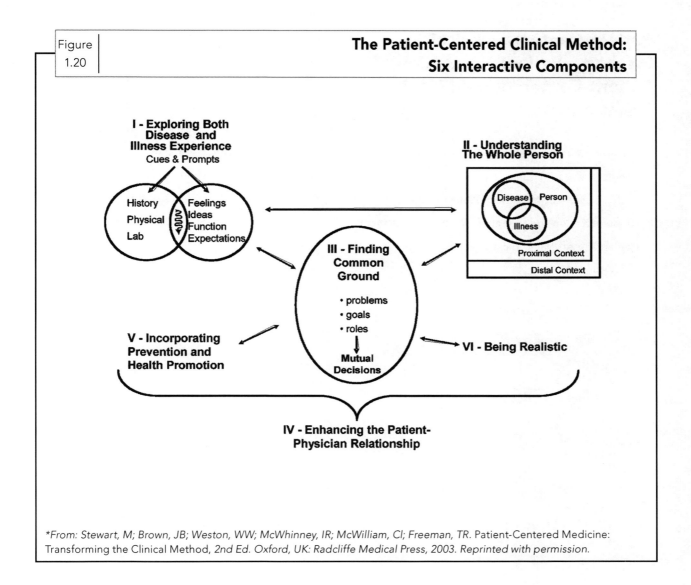

The Patient-Centered Clinical Method: Six Interactive Components

Figure
1.20

From: Stewart, M; Brown, JB; Weston, WW; McWhinney, IR; McWilliam, CJ; Freeman, TR. Patient-Centered Medicine: Transforming the Clinical Method, 2nd Ed. Oxford, UK: Radcliffe Medical Press, 2003. Reprinted with permission.

Patient-Centered Clinical Method—Patient Perception of Patient-Centeredness (PPPC) Questionnaire

The group at the University of Western Ontario, London, Canada, designed two measures of patient-centeredness—the Measure of Patient-Centered Communication and the Patient Perception of Patient-Centeredness (PPPC). The nine-item version of the PPPC, for use with patients and physicians, is provided on the following pages.

These two forms were developed for educational purposes to provide feedback to residents and practicing physicians regarding their own and their patients' perceptions over a series of encounters. The PPPC forms are used with medical students, residents, fellows, faculty members, and community physicians.

Contact: *www.uwo.ca/fammed/csfm/publications/working_papers.html.*

Additional resources: Brown, JB; Stewart, M; Ryan, BL. "Assessing communication between patients and physicians: the measure of patient-centered communication." Working Paper Series #95-2 (2nd ed). Center for Studies in Family Medicine. The University of Western Ontario, London, Ontario, Canada; 2001.

Brown, JB; Stewart, M; Weston, WW. *Challenges and Solutions in Patient-Centered Care: A Case Book.* Oxford, UK: Radcliffe Publishing; 2002.

Stewart, M; Brown, JB; Weston, WW; McWhinney, IR; McWilliam CL; Freeman TR. *Patient-Centered Medicine: Transforming the Clinical Method.* Oxford, UK: Radcliffe Medical Press; 2003.

Stewart, M; Meredith, L; Ryan, BL; Brown, JB. "The patient perception of patient-centeredness questionnaire (PPPC)." Working Paper Series #04-1. Center for Studies in Family Medicine. The University of Western Ontario, London, Ontario, Canada; 2004.

Figure 1.21	**PPPC Patient Form**

A SELF-ASSESSMENT AND FEEDBACK ON
COMMUNICATION WITH PATIENTS – PATIENT ASSESSMENT – PPPC

Please check (✔) the box that best represents your response.

1. **To what extent was your main problem(s) discussed today?**

   ❏ Completely ❏ Mostly ❏ A little ❏ Not at all

2. **How satisfied were you with the discussion of your problem?**

   ❏ Very satisfied ❏ Satisfied ❏ Somewhat satisfied ❏ Not satisfied

3. **To what extent did the doctor listen to what you had to say?**

   ❏ Completely ❏ Mostly ❏ A little ❏ Not at all

4. **To what extent did the doctor explain this problem to you?**

   ❏ Completely ❏ Mostly ❏ A little ❏ Not at all

5. **To what extent did you and the doctor discuss your respective roles? (Who is responsible for making decisions and who is responsible for what aspects of your care?)**

   ❏ Completely ❏ Mostly ❏ A little ❏ Not discussed

6. **To what extent did the doctor explain treatment?**

   ❏ Very well ❏ Well ❏ Somewhat ❏ Not at all

7. **To what extent did the doctor explore how manageable this (treatment) would be for you? He/she explored this ...**

   ❏ Completely ❏ Mostly ❏ A little ❏ Not at all

8. **How well do you think your doctor understood you today?**

   ❏ Very well ❏ Well ❏ Somewhat ❏ Not at all

9. **To what extent did the doctor discuss personal or family issues that might affect your health?**

   ❏ Completely ❏ Mostly ❏ A little ❏ Not at all

Source: Stewart, M; Brown, JB; Weston, WW; McWhinney, IR; McWilliam, CL; Freeman, TR. Patient-Centered Medicine: Transforming the Clinical Method, 2nd Ed. Oxford, UK: Radcliffe Medical Press, 2003. Reprinted with permission..

Figure
1.22

PPPC Physician Form

A SELF-ASSESSMENT AND FEEDBACK ON
COMMUNICATION WITH PATIENTS – PHYSICIAN ASSESSMENT – PPPC

Please check (✔) the box that best represents your response.

1. **To what extent was your patient's main problem(s) discussed today?**

    ❑ Completely   ❑ Mostly   ❑ A little   ❑ Not at all

2. **How satisfied were you with the discussion of your patient's problem?**

    ❑ Very satisfied   ❑ Satisfied   ❑ Somewhat satisfied   ❑ Not satisfied

3. **To what extent did you listen to what your patient had to say?**

    ❑ Completely   ❑ Mostly   ❑ A little   ❑ Not at all

4. **To what extent did you explain the problem to the patient?**

    ❑ Completely   ❑ Mostly   ❑ A little   ❑ Not at all

5. **To what extent did you and the patient discuss your respective roles? (Who is responsible for making decisions and who is responsible for what aspects of your care?)**

    ❑ Completely   ❑ Mostly   ❑ A little   ❑ Not discussed

6. **To what extent did you explain treatment?**

    ❑ Very well   ❑ Well   ❑ Somewhat   ❑ Not at all

7. **To what extent did you and the patient explore how manageable this (treatment*) would be for the patient? We explored this ...**

    ❑ Completely   ❑ Mostly   ❑ A little   ❑ Not at all

8. **How well do you think you understood the patient today?**

    ❑ Very well   ❑ Well   ❑ Somewhat   ❑ Not at all

9. **Regarding today's problem, to what extent did you discuss personal or family issues that might be affecting your patient's health?**

    ❑ Completely   ❑ Mostly   ❑ A little   ❑ Not at all

Source: Stewart, M; Brown, JB; Weston, WW; McWhinney, IR; McWilliam, CL; Freeman, TR. Patient-Centered Medicine: Transforming the Clinical Method, 2nd Ed. Oxford, UK: Radcliffe Medical Press, 2003. Reprinted with permission.

The Communication Assessment Tool (CAT)

The Communication Assessment Tool (CAT) is a brief, reliable, and valid instrument designed to elicit patient perspectives on the interpersonal and communication skills of physicians.

A systematic scale development process produced a psychometrically sound 15-item instrument. The CAT is written at the fourth grade reading level and employs a five-point response scale (1 = poor to 5 = excellent). Fourteen items focus on the physician and one rates the staff. Pilot-testing established that the CAT differentiates between physicians who rated high and low on a separate satisfaction scale.

Physicians from a variety of specialties and from around the United States and their patients participated in a field test to assess the feasibility of using the CAT in everyday practice. The CAT has been used in both outpatient and inpatient settings, and is available in English and Spanish.

Studies in the emergency room setting led to the development of the Communication Assessment Tool – Team (CAT-T), which gauges patient perceptions of communication with the medical team.

The group that developed the CAT tested a number of different response scales for the items (e.g., no/yes; strongly disagree/strongly agree; poor/excellent), and found that "excellent" maps onto "yes" while everything else (poor, fair, good, very good) maps onto "no." They suggest reporting the proportion of "excellent" ratings given by patients, which is tangible and more useful than summarizing scores via means which can be highly skewed.[193]

The CAT can be used for both collecting information and providing feedback about interpersonal and communication skills.[193]

Contact: Gregory Makoul, PhD, Saint Francis Hospital and Medical Center, Hartford, CT: *gmakoul@stfranciscare.org*.

Additional resources: Makoul, G; Krupat, E; Chang, CH. "Measuring patient views of physician communication skills: development and testing of the Communication Assessment Tool." *Patient Educ Couns.* 2007; 67:333–342.

Mercer, LM; Tanabe, P; Pang, PS et al. "Patient perspectives on communication with the medical team: pilot study using the Communication Assessment Tool – Team (CAT-T)." *Patient Educ Couns.* 2008; 73:220–223.

Myerholtz, L; Simons, L; Felix, S et al. "Using the Communication Assessment Tool (CAT) in family medicine residency programs." *Fam Med.* In press.

Wayne, DB; Cohen, E; Makoul, G; McGaghie, WC. "The impact of judge selection on standard setting for a patient survey of physician communication skills." *Acad Med.* 2008; 83:S17–S20.

| Figure 1.23 | **Communication Assessment Tool (CAT)** |

Communication with patients is a very important part of quality medical care. We would like to know how you feel about the way your doctor communicated with you. **Your answers are completely confidential, so please be as open and honest as you can.**

Your participation is completely voluntary and will not affect your medical treatment in any way.

Please rate the doctor's communication with you. Circle your answer for each item below.
Thank you very much.

The doctor ...	Poor	Fair	Good	Very good	Excellent
1. Greeted me in a way that made me feel comfortable	1	2	3	4	5
2. Treated me with respect	1	2	3	4	5
3. Showed interest in my ideas about my health	1	2	3	4	5
4. Understood my main health concerns	1	2	3	4	5
5. Paid attention to me (looked at me, listened carefully)	1	2	3	4	5
6. Let me talk without interruptions	1	2	3	4	5
7. Gave me as much information as I wanted	1	2	3	4	5
8. Talked in terms I could understand	1	2	3	4	5
9. Checked to be sure I understood everything	1	2	3	4	5
10. Encouraged me to ask questions	1	2	3	4	5
11. Involved me in decisions as much as I wanted	1	2	3	4	5
12. Discussed next steps, including any follow-up plans	1	2	3	4	5
13. Showed care and concern	1	2	3	4	5
14. Spent the right amount of time with me	1	2	3	4	5
Your care					
15. How would you rate the care provided by your doctor?	1	2	3	4	5

Figure
1.23

Communication Assessment Tool (CAT) (cont.)

Comments:

This set of questions **about the patient** is for statistical purposes. Your own responses are completely confidential. Please mark one answer for each question.

1. How old are you?

    ❏ 1 24 or younger   ❏ 4 65–84

    ❏ 2 25–44   ❏ 5 85 or older

    ❏ 3 45–64

2. Are you male or female?

    ❏ 1 Male

    ❏ 2 Female

3. Have you seen this doctor before?

    ❏ 1 No

    ❏ 2 Yes, but only once

    ❏ 3 Yes, more than once

4. How would you describe
    your race or ethnicity?

    ❏ 1 American Indian or Alaska Native

    ❏ 2 Asian or Asian-American

    ❏ 3 Black or African-American

    ❏ 4 Hispanic or Latino

    ❏ 5 Native Hawaiian or Pacific Islander

    ❏ 6 White or Caucasian

    ❏ 7 Other _____

5. Were you the patient today?

    ❏ 1 Yes

    ❏ 2 No, I was with the patient today

Thank you very much.

Figure 1.24	**Communication Assessment Tool (CAT)—Team**

Communication with patients is a very important part of quality medical care. We would like to know how you feel about the way your medical team communicated with you. **Your answers are completely confidential, so please be as open and honest as you can.**

Your participation is completely voluntary and will not affect your medical treatment in any way.

Please rate the medical team's communication with you. Circle your answer for each item below. Thank you very much.

The medical team ...	Poor	Fair	Good	Very good	Excellent
1. Greeted me in a way that made me feel comfortable	1	2	3	4	5
2. Treated me with respect	1	2	3	4	5
3. Showed interest in my ideas about my health	1	2	3	4	5
4. Understood my main health concerns	1	2	3	4	5
5. Paid attention to me (looked at me, listened carefully)	1	2	3	4	5
6. Let me talk without interruptions	1	2	3	4	5
7. Gave me as much information as I wanted	1	2	3	4	5
8. Talked in terms I could understand	1	2	3	4	5
9. Checked to be sure I understood everything	1	2	3	4	5
10. Encouraged me to ask questions	1	2	3	4	5
11. Involved me in decisions as much as I wanted	1	2	3	4	5
12. Discussed next steps, including any follow-up plans	1	2	3	4	5
13. Showed care and concern	1	2	3	4	5
14. Spent the right amount of time with me	1	2	3	4	5
The front desk staff ...					
15. Treated me with respect	1	2	3	4	5
Your care					
16. How would you rate the care provided by your medical team?	1	2	3	4	5

Figure 1.24	Communication Assessment Tool (CAT)—Team (cont.)

Comments:

This set of questions **about the patient** is for statistical purposes. Your own responses are completely confidential. Please mark one answer for each question.

1. How old are you?
   - ❏ 1 24 or younger
   - ❏ 2 25–44
   - ❏ 3 45–64
   - ❏ 4 65–84
   - ❏ 5 85 or older

2. Are you male or female?
   - ❏ 1 Male
   - ❏ 2 Female

3. Have you seen this doctor before?
   - ❏ 1 No
   - ❏ 2 Yes, but only once
   - ❏ 3 Yes, more than once

4. How would you describe your race or ethnicity?
   - ❏ 1 American Indian or Alaska Native
   - ❏ 2 Asian or Asian-American
   - ❏ 3 Black or African-American
   - ❏ 4 Hispanic or Latino
   - ❏ 5 Native Hawaiian or Pacific Islander
   - ❏ 6 White or Caucasian
   - ❏ 7 Other _____

5. Were you the patient today?
   - ❏ 1 Yes
   - ❏ 2 No, I was with the patient today

Thank you very much.

Macy Initiative in Health Communication Model

In 2003, the Josiah Macy Foundation funded a collaboration among three medical schools—New York University School of Medicine, Case School of Medicine, and University of Massachusetts Medical School—to develop, establish, and evaluate a comprehensive communication skills curriculum. This collaboration resulted in the Macy Model, which is derived from many established communication models but includes some unique features of its own. The group organized communication competencies into three domains:

- Communicating with patients

- Communicating about patients

- Communicating about medicine and science[146]

The creators subdivided each domain into the three functions of the medical interview: gathering data, building relationships, and educating.[146] Each school developed its own curriculum and faculty development training, and all worked from a single evidence-based document summarizing the core communication skills competencies.[194] Faculty members derived evaluation checklists from the Macy Model, which outlines the structure and sequence of effective physician–patient communication.[195]

From this model, the schools developed assessment tools and use them in a variety of settings. In a controlled study, the three schools showed that a comprehensive clinical clerkship communication skills curriculum could significantly improve the communication skills of medical students.[196]

Macy Initiative in Health Communication Model: Macy Communication Checklist

The New York University School of Medicine administers a version of the Macy Communication Checklist in a high-stakes, multistation standardized patient exam, called the Comprehensive Clinical Skills Exam (CCSE), for all rising fourth-year students.[197]

In addition, a number of residency programs incorporate the Macy Communication Checklist into their OSCEs.[198] The checklist serves as an outcome measure in various curriculum evaluation studies.[199, 200] Performance-based assessments for medical students, residents, and fellows include the same 17 core communication skills on the Macy Checklist. Poor student performance on the communication skills competency of the CCSE can predict poor performance on the USMLE II Clinical Skills Exam.

Educators score the Macy Checklist by calculating the percentage of checklist items identified by standardized patients as "well done," averaged across cases for each student. Performance is determined by either tallying one overall communication score based on all 17 items, or dividing the scores into three subgroups:

1. Information-gathering skills (items 1–6)

2. Relationship development skills (items 7–11)

3. Education and counseling (items 12–14)[155]

With three hours of rater training (in addition to case portrayal and physical exam training), rater reliabilities measured as Cronbach's alpha were 0.7–0.9 for the subsets of items and the overall Macy Communication Checklist. Students receive their overall communication score unless they do poorly. In those cases, subscores and individual item scores are reviewed, with the caveat that this kind of analysis lacks the reliability of the overall scores.[155]

Contact: Adina Kalet, MD, MPH, New York University School of Medicine, New York: *adina.kalet@nyumc.org*.

Additional resources: Kalet, AL; Pugnaire, MP; Cole-Kelly, K et al. "Teaching communication in clinical clerkships: models from the Macy Initiative in Health Communications." *Acad Med.* 2004; 79:511–520.

Stevens, D; King, D; Laponis, R et al. "Medical students retain pain assessment and management skills long after an experiential curriculum: a controlled study." *Pain.* 2009; 145(3):319–324.

Zabar, S; Hanley, K; Kachur, E et al. " 'Oh! She doesn't speak English!' Assessing resident competence in managing linguistic and cultural barriers." *J Gen Intern Med.* 2006; 21(5):510–513.

Figure 1.25	**Comprehensive Clinical Skills Exam (CCSE) Communication Checklist— NYU Version of the Macy Model Checklist**

COMMUNICATION				Comments
Opening				
Introduced self	Did not introduce self	Introduced self only by name and student status	Gave name, student status, and purpose of interview	
Information Gathering				
Started with **open-ended** questions	Started with closed, yes/no questions	Began with open-ended questions but stopped prematurely	Started with open-ended questions and continued using them as appropriate	
Asked you **what you thought** was the matter	Did not specifically ask	Asked but did not give you enough time to share your views	Asked so that you fully shared your views	
Managed the **narrative flow** of your story	Not able to elicit your story because questions not organized logically	Elicited main elements of story, but illogical order of questions disrupted flow	Elicited full story by asking questions that facilitated natural flow of story	
Elicited your story using **appropriate questions**	Impeded story by asking leading questions or more than one question at a time	Used some leading questions and/or asked more than one question at a time, but still able to share most of your story	Facilitated the telling of your story by asking questions one at a time without leading you in your responses	
Clarified information by repeating to make sure he/she understood you on an ongoing basis	Did not clarify (did not repeat info you provided)	Repeated the information but didn't give you chance to indicate whether accurate	Repeated information and directly invited you to indicate whether accurate	
Allowed you to talk **without interrupting**	Interrupted you	Did not interrupt you directly but cut your responses short by not giving you enough time	Did not interrupt and allowed time to express thoughts fully	

Figure 1.25	**Comprehensive Clinical Skills Exam (CCSE) Communication Checklist— NYU Version of the Macy Model Checklist (cont.)**

COMMUNICATION				Comments
Relationship Development				
Communicated **concern** or intention to help	Did not communicate intention to help/concern via words or actions	Words OR actions conveyed intention to help/concern	Actions AND words conveyed intention to help/concern	
Nonverbal behavior enriched communication (e.g., eye contact, posture)	Nonverbal behavior was negative or interfered with communication	Nonverbal behavior demonstrated attentiveness	Nonverbal behavior facilitated effective communication	
Acknowledged your emotions appropriately	Did not acknowledge your emotions	Attempted to acknowledge emotions	Responded to your emotions in ways that made you feel better	
Was **accepting/ non-judgmental**	Expressed judgment	Did not express judgment but did not demonstrate respect either	Demonstrated respect toward you	
Used words you understood and/or explained **jargon**	Jargon made it difficult to understand	Used jargon occasionally but did not significantly interfere with understanding	Provided no opportunity for misunderstanding by avoiding or spontaneously explaining jargon	
Education and Counseling				
Asked questions to see what you understood about his/her diagnosis/ treatment strategy	Did not check to see what you understood	Asked whether you had any questions	Asked whether you had questions AND made sure you understood the situation by checking your understanding through additional questioning	
Provided **clear explanations** concerning diagnosis/treatment	Gave confusing or no explanations which made it impossible to understand possible diagnosis	Explanations were somewhat clear but still led to some difficulty in understanding possible diagnosis	Provided small bits of information at a time and repeated and summarized to ensure that you understood	
Collaborated with you in identifying possible **next steps** in diagnosis/treatment	Did not give you opportunity to weigh in on next steps (told you what would happen next) OR didn't discuss next steps at all	Told you next steps and then asked you about your views	Elicited your views on next steps, shared her/his ideas, and then mutually you and the student developed plan of action	

Figure 1.25	**Comprehensive Clinical Skills Exam (CCSE) Communication Checklist— NYU Version of the Macy Model Checklist (cont.)**

COMMUNICATION				Comments
Organization				
Paced encounter well	Poorly paced the encounter: At 10-minute knock the student had failed to systematically obtain majority of information and/or perform physical exam procedures	Paced encounter passably: At 10-minute knock the student had covered a large amount of information but had to rush to cover additional material (including physical exam procedures) in the final minutes	Interview well paced: At 10-minute knock the student had covered a majority of the material (including physical exam procedures) and used the remaining minutes to gather additional information	
Brought encounter to a **close**	No closure	Acknowledged the end of the visit	Acknowledged the end of the visit and summarized and/or clarified next steps	

Would you recommend this doctor to a friend?

Not Recommend	Recommend with Reservation	Recommend	Highly Recommend

Source: New York University School of Medicine Communication Checklist. Used with permission.

Five-Step Patient-Centered Interviewing Model

Smith[144] synthesized the literature on patient-centered interviewing into a unified, step-by-step interview, developed the Five-Step Patient-Centered Interviewing Model, and studied the model in a randomized control trial. With residents trained in the model, Smith and colleagues found significant improvement in attitudes, knowledge, self-confidence, and skills in interviewing patients, dealing with relationships, managing and communicating with somatizing patients, and educating patients.[201] The method was subsequently taught, in separate studies, to family medicine faculty members and to nurse practitioners as part of an intervention for patients with medically unexplained symptoms. Each study saw prominent increases in patient satisfaction with the clinician–patient relationship and improvement in mental and physical health status on a number of measures. These studies thus linked the Five-Step method with patient health outcomes.[202, 203]

The Five-Step method, including step-by-step instruction on specific behaviors, guided residents' training. The training was experiential and skills-oriented, and fostered positive attitudes toward patient-centered interviewing. Faculty members used a learner-centered approach that attended to the teacher–resident relationship and the development of the resident's self-awareness.[204] Directly observed resident–patient interviews, followed by open-ended inquiries about residents' emotional responses, feedback, discussion, and group work, promoted residents' self-awareness of thoughts, emotions, and attitudes that could interfere with communication and relationships with patients.

Smith notes that becoming facile with the NURS emotion-handling skills (see Step 4 of the evaluation tool for a definition of the NURS skills) is the "single most important thing to learn … and it is the focus of teaching for difficult learners and for short, one- or two-hour teaching sessions."[205] All faculty members received training in psychosocial medicine and met regularly to discuss residents' progress and issues.

Faculty members use the Five-Step Patient-Centered Interviewing Model as the foundation of interviewing courses at all levels of medical education (undergraduate, graduate, and postgraduate) in the United States and other countries.

Five-Step Patient-Centered Interviewing Evaluation Tool

The Five-Step Patient-Centered Interviewing Evaluation Tool consists of a summary of the five steps and 21 substeps. Raters mark whether learners complete each of the 21 substeps. The key part of the evaluation is to determine whether the student demonstrated the physical, personal, emotional, and NURS components in step 4 of the assessment.

The Five-Step Patient-Centered Interviewing Evaluation Tool is applicable to a variety of learners including students, residents, faculty members, and practicing physicians. Teaching typically occurs in groups, and noninterviewing group members and faculty members perform the ratings.

The evaluation tool also lends itself to self-critique. A separate research assessment form is available upon request.

Contact: Robert C. Smith, MD, MS, Michigan State University College of Human Medicine, East Lansing, MI: *Robert.Smith@HT.MSU.edu.*

Additional resources: Smith, RC. *Patient Centered Interviewing: An Evidence Based Method.* 2nd ed. Philadelphia, PA: Lippincott Williams & Wilkins; 2002.

Smith, RC; Lyles, JS; Gardiner, JC et al. "Primary care clinicians treat patients with medically unexplained symptoms – a randomized controlled trial." *J Gen Intern Med.* 2006; 21:671–677.

Smith, R; Gardiner, J; Luo, Z; Schooley, S; Lamerato, L. "Primary care physicians treat somatization." *J Gen Intern Med.* 2009; 24:829–832.

| Figure 1.26 | **Five-Step Patient-Centered Interviewing Method** |

STEP 1. Set the stage

1.   Welcome the patient

2.   Use the patient's name

3.   Introduce self and identify specific role

4.   Ensure patient readiness and privacy

5.   Remove barriers to communication

6.   Ensure comfort and put the patient at ease

STEP 2. Establish chief complaint and agenda

1.   Indicate time available

2.   Indicate own needs

3.   Obtain list of all issues patient wants to discuss

4.   Summarize and finalize the agenda; negotiate specifics if too many agenda items

STEP 3. Opening the History of the Present Illness (HPI)

1.   Open-ended beginning question

2.   Nonfocusing open-ended skills (silence, neutral utterances, nonverbal encouragement)

3.   Obtain additional data from nonverbal sources: nonverbal cues, physical characteristics, autonomic changes, accouterments, and environment

STEP 4. Continuing the HPI

PHYSICAL SYMPTOM STORY

1.   Obtain description of physical symptoms (focusing open-ended skills)

PERSONAL STORY

2.   Develop the more general personal/psychosocial context of the physical symptoms (focusing open-ended skills)

| Figure 1.26 | **Five-Step Patient-Centered Interviewing Method (cont.)** |

EMOTIONAL STORY

3. Develop an emotional focus (emotion-seeking skills)

4. Address emotion (emotion-handling skills – NURS)

    a. **N**aming – labeling ("You sound sad.")

    b. **U**nderstanding – legitimize ("I can understand why …")

    c. **R**especting – praising ("You have been very resourceful.")

    d. **S**upporting – partnership ("I am here to help you however I can.")

EXPAND STORY

5. Expand the story to new chapters (focusing open-ended skills, emotion-seeking skills, emotion-handling skills)

STEP 5. Transition to second (doctor-centered) phase of the interview

1. Brief summary and final use of emotion-handling skills

2. Check accuracy

3. Indicate that content and style of inquiry are about to change if the patient is ready ("I'm going to switch gears now and ask you some questions to better understand what might be going on.")

Adapted from: Smith, RC. Patient Centered Interviewing: An Evidence Based Method, 2nd ed. Philadelphia: Lippincott Williams & Wilkins, 2002.

American Board of Internal Medicine (ABIM) Patient Assessment for Continuous Professional Development

- Communication–Primary Care

- Communication–Subspecialists

- Communication with Referring Physicians

The American Board of Internal Medicine (ABIM) introduced the Patient and Physician Peer Assessment module into its recertification program following concerns that written examinations do not assess the full spectrum of clinical competence, including interpersonal and communication skills, humanistic qualities, and professionalism.[161]

The Patient and Physician Peer Assessment module includes patient ratings, physician peer ratings, and physician self-ratings. Residency programs and specialty organizations have used and/or modified these assessment forms, and they have been adapted for use in Canada.

As part of its Maintenance of Certification program, the ABIM developed additional modules, known as Practice Improvement Modules (PIM), as an option for self-evaluation of communication and interpersonal skills. PIMs addressing these competencies include:

Physicians use PIMs to obtain feedback from patients regarding their communication and interpersonal skills, and they bring together this feedback with a self-assessment of the practice systems that support access and coordination of care for the patient. Additionally, the Communication with Referring Physicians module solicits feedback from physician peers about the communication skills of consultants and ties the feedback with the systems of care in the consultant's practice. PIMs have proven to be popular selections in ABIM's Maintenance of Certification program and have emphasized the importance of using feedback in the self-assessment and quality improvement of communication skills in practice.[159]

The "Using Patient Assessment for Continuous Professional Development" form is provided on the following pages. Information about the additional PIM modules is available at the websites listed below.

Contact: Eric Holmboe, MD, American Board of Internal Medicine, Philadelphia: *eholmboe@abim.org.*

Websites: *www.acgme.org/outcome/downloads/IandC_1.pdf, www.abim.org/moc/earning-points.aspx,* and *www.abim.org/program-directors-administrators/PIMs-training-programs.aspx.*

Additional resource: Lipner, RS; Blank, LL; Leas, BF; Fortna, GS. "The value of patient and peer ratings in recertification." *Acad Med.* 2002; 77(10 Suppl): S64–S66.

Figure 1.27	**Using Patient Assessment for Continuous Professional Development**

AMERICAN BOARD OF INTERNAL MEDICINE
Using Patient Assessment for Continuous Professional Development

RATING SCALE

HOW IS THIS DOCTOR AT...	Poor	Fair	Good	Very Good	Excellent	Unable to Evaluate
1. Telling you everything; being truthful, upfront and frank; not keeping things from you that you should know	1	2	3	4	5	#
2. Greeting you warmly; calling you by the name you prefer; being friendly, never crabby or rude	1	2	3	4	5	#
3. Treating you like you're on the same level; never "talking down" to you or treating you like a child	1	2	3	4	5	#
4. Letting you tell your story; listening carefully; asking thoughtful questions; not interrupting you while you're talking	1	2	3	4	5	#
5. Showing interest in you as a person; not acting bored or ignoring what you have to say	1	2	3	4	5	#
6. Warning you during the physical exam about what he/she is going to do and why; telling you what he/she finds	1	2	3	4	5	#
7. Discussing options with you; asking your opinion; offering choices and letting you help decide what to do; asking what you think before telling you what to do	1	2	3	4	5	#
8. Encouraging you to ask questions; answering them clearly; never avoiding your questions or lecturing you	1	2	3	4	5	#
9. Explaining what you need to know about your problems, how and why they occurred, and what to expect next	1	2	3	4	5	#
10. Using words you can understand when explaining your problems and treatment; explaining any technical medical terms in plain language	1	2	3	4	5	#

| Figure 1.27 | **Using Patient Assessment for Continuous Professional Development (cont.)** |

The following questions are asked for statistical purposes. Your responses are confidential.

11.   Please enter your age: _____

12.   Please enter your gender:
   1 Male
   2 Female

13.   In general, how is your health:

   1 Poor
   2 Fair
   3 Good
   4 Very Good
   5 Excellent

14.   Is this doctor your primary care doctor whom you see for general care or a consultant or specialist whom you see for a particular health-related problem?

   1 Primary Care Doctor
   2 Consultant

15.   How long have you been under this doctor's care?

   1 This was my 1st visit
   2 Less than 6 months
   3 6 months to 1 year
   4 More than 1 year

16.   How many visits did you make to this doctor in the past 12 months?

   1 1-3
   2 4-7
   3 More than 7

17.   Would you recommend this physician to a friend or relative?
   1 Yes
   2 No

18.   Please enter your telephone number including your area code:
   (_ _ _) - _ _ _ - _ _ _ _

*Thank you for completing your assessment of this doctor
as part of the ABIM Continuous Professional Development Program.*

Note 1: Reprinted with permission from the American Board of Internal Medicine®. All rights reserved.
Note 2: Examples of supporting references are below. McLeod, PJ; Tamblyn, R; Benaroya, S et al. "Faculty ratings of resident humanism predict patient satisfaction ratings in ambulatory medical clinics." *J Gen.Intern Med*. 1994; 9:321–26. Tamblyn, R; Benaroya, S; Snell, L et al. "The feasibility and value of using patient satisfaction ratings to evaluate internal medicine residents." *J Gen Intern Med*. 1994; 9:146–152.

SEGUE Framework and Instrument

The SEGUE Framework for Teaching and Assessing Communication Skills, developed and tested at Northwestern University Feinberg School of Medicine by Makoul,[206] focuses on specific communication tasks and evaluation of whether the physician achieves the tasks during the medical interview. The SEGUE checklist consists of 25 communication tasks grouped into five sections:

- Setting the stage

- Eliciting information

- Giving information

- Understanding the patient's perspective

- Ending the encounter

SEGUE is a research-based checklist of communication tasks that focuses on observable behavior rather than attitudes. Makoul recommends reinforcing that SEGUE is a flexible framework, rather than a step-by-step formulation. The task approach encourages physicians-in-training and physicians-in-practice to develop a repertoire of skills and strategies to accomplish tasks in a way that fits their style, the patient, and the situation. When they are used for assessment, Makoul suggests evaluators also include space for narrative comments, to provide detail not captured by a checklist.[186]

Contact: Gregory Makoul, PhD, Saint Francis Hospital and Medical Center, Hartford, CT: *gmakoul@stfranciscare.org.*

Additional resource: Makoul, G. "The SEGUE Framework for teaching and assessing communication skills." *Patient Educ Couns.* 2001; 45:23–34.

Figure 1.28	The SEGUE Framework

The SEGUE Framework   Patient: _____   Physician or Student: _____

Set the Stage

		Yes	No
1.	Greet patient appropriately		
2.	Establish reason for visit: _____		
3.	Outline agenda for visit (e.g., "anything else?", issues, sequence)		
4.	Make a personal connection during visit (e.g., go beyond medical issues at hand)		
→ 5.	Maintain patient's privacy (e.g., close door)		

Elicit Information

		n/a	Yes	No
6.	Elicit patient's view of health problem and/or progress			
7.	Explore physical/physiological factors			
8.	Explore psychosocial/emotional factors (e.g., living situation, family relations, stress)			
9.	Discuss antecedent treatments (e.g., self-care, last visit, other medical care)			
10.	Discuss how health problem affects patient's life (e.g., quality-of-life)			
11.	Discuss lifestyle issues/prevention strategies (e.g., health risks)			
→ 12.	Avoid directive/leading questions			
→ 13.	Give patient opportunity/time to talk (e.g., don't interrupt)			
→ 14.	Listen. Give patient undivided attention (e.g., face patient, verbal acknowledgement, nv feedback)			
→ 15.	Check/clarify information (e.g., recap, ask "how much")			

Give Information

		n/a	Yes	No
16.	Explain rationale for diagnostic procedures (e.g., exam, tests)			
17.	Teach patient about his/her own body & situation (e.g., provide feedback from exam/tests, explain rationale)			
18.	Encourage patient to ask questions / Check understanding			
→ 19.	Adapt to patient's level of understanding (e.g., avoid/explain jargon)			

- Items without an arrow focus on *content*; mark "Yes" if done *at least one time* during the encounter.
- Items with an arrow (→) focus on *process* and should be maintained throughout the encounter; mark "No" if at least one relevant instance when not done (e.g., just one use of jargon).

Figure 1.28	The SEGUE Framework (cont.)

Understand the Patient's Perspective

		n/a	Yes	No
20.	Acknowledge patient's accomplishments/progress/challenges			
21.	Acknowledge waiting time			
→ 22.	Express caring, concern, empathy			
→ 23.	Maintain a respectful tone			

End the Encounter

		Yes	No
24.	Ask if there is anything else patient would like to discuss		
25.	Review next steps with patient		

If suggested a new or modified treatment/prevention plan:

		n/a	Yes	No
26.	Discuss patient's expectation/goal for treatment/prevention			
27.	Involve patient in deciding upon a plan (e.g., options, rationale, values, preferences, concerns)			
28.	Explain likely benefits of the option(s) discussed			
29.	Explain likely side-effects and risks of the option(s) discussed			
30.	Provide complete instructions for plan			
31.	Discuss patient's ability to follow plan			
32.	Discuss importance of patient's role in treatment/prevention			

Comments:

Institute for Healthcare Communication "4E" Model

The creators of the 4E Model for physician–patient communication derived the model from an extensive literature review. It has been useful for coaching and teaching physicians with different levels of experience in a wide variety of specialties and practice settings.

Developed by Keller and Carroll[207] at the Institute for Healthcare Communication, the 4E Model has been used to train thousands of practicing physicians.

The 4E Model lists the following communication skills needed for effective patient interviews:

- **Engagement:** skills that support the development of rapport with patients

- **Empathy:** skills that help clinicians reflect concern for the patient's condition

- **Education:** skills needed for discovering and developing the patient's understanding of his or her condition

- **Enlistment:** skills that help in motivating and changing behavior[208]

Website: *www.healthcarecomm.org.*

Additional resources: Keller, V; Carroll, JG. "A new model for physician–patient communication." *Patient Educ Couns.* 1994; 23:131–140.

Keller, VF; Goldstein, MG; Runkle, C. "Strangers in crisis: communication skills for the emergency department clinician and hospitalist." *J Clin Outcomes Manag.* 2002; 9:439–444.

C3 Instrument: Characterizing the Patient-Centeredness of the Hidden Curriculum

The C3 (Communication, Curriculum, and Culture) Study Group developed the C3 Instrument, a unique survey tool that measures the patient-centeredness of a medical school's hidden curriculum.[209] Although the group developed the C3 Instrument for medical students with some clinical experience during medical school, the instrument has also been used with residents and fellows.

The 29-item instrument includes five dimensions that are organized into three general content areas:

- Role modeling: measures the frequency with which learners observe teachers modeling patient-centered behaviors in the course of clinical work

- Students' experiences: presents learners with several vignettes that portray varying levels of patient-centered activities and measures how often learners find themselves in similar scenarios, giving a rough measure of the patient-centeredness of the micro-environments of the hospital ward services

- Support for students' behaviors: measures how much encouragement learners receive when they engage in patient-centered activities

The authors of the C3 Instrument note that, by organizing the patient-centered learning environment into three separate areas, medical educators can develop effective interventions to create a learning environment that is supportive of curricula designed to teach the skills and attitudes of patient-centered care.

The instrument provided on the following pages was adapted by adding ratings for attending physicians in Content Area 1: Role Modeling. For the original validated C3 Instrument, see the first article listed below.

Contact: Paul Haidet, MD, MPH, Pennsylvania State University College of Medicine, Hershey, PA: *phaidet@hmc.psu.edu.*

Additional resources: Haidet, P; Kelly, PA; Chou, C et al. "Characterizing the patient-centeredness of hidden curricula in medical schools: development and validation of a new measure." *Acad Med.* 2005; 80:44–50.

Haidet, P; Kelly, PA; Bentley S et al. "Not the same everywhere: patient-centered learning environments at nine medical schools." *J Gen Intern Med.* 2006; 21(5):405–409.

Figure 1.29	**The C3 Instrument for Characterizing the Patient-Centeredness of a Medical School's Hidden Curriculum**

Scoring instructions: Using the scoring guidelines for the content areas below, calculate three content area scores as the mean of the item scores in each content area.

Content area 1: Role Modeling

Instructions: Please indicate how often you observed the individuals in the following positions engaged in the following kinds of behaviors. Rate each group: attendings, chief residents, senior residents, and interns. For chief residents, only answer in regard to chief residents who were involved in direct patient care.

Scoring scale:

Always: 7	Less than half of the time: 3
Almost always: 6	Rarely: 2
More than half of the time: 5	Never: 1
About half of the time: 4	

Items

1. How often did you observe the individuals in the following positions communicate concern and interest in patients as unique persons?

	7 Always	6 Almost always	5 More than half of the time	4 About half of the time	3 Less than half of the time	2 Rarely	1 Never
Attendings							
Chief residents							
Senior residents							
Interns							

2. How often did you observe the individuals in the following positions encourage patients' participation in their own care?

	7 Always	6 Almost always	5 More than half of the time	4 About half of the time	3 Less than half of the time	2 Rarely	1 Never
Attendings							
Chief residents							
Senior residents							
Interns							

| Figure 1.29 | **The C3 Instrument for Characterizing the Patient-Centeredness of a Medical School's Hidden Curriculum (cont.)** |

3. How often did you observe the individuals in the following positions take seriously patients' concerns about their conditions or care?

	7 Always	6 Almost always	5 More than half of the time	4 About half of the time	3 Less than half of the time	2 Rarely	1 Never
Attendings							
Chief residents							
Senior residents							
Interns							

4. How often did you observe the individuals in the following positions develop good rapport with patients?

	7 Always	6 Almost always	5 More than half of the time	4 About half of the time	3 Less than half of the time	2 Rarely	1 Never
Attendings							
Chief residents							
Senior residents							
Interns							

5. How often did you observe individuals in the following positions explore emotional aspects of patients' illnesses?

	7 Always	6 Almost always	5 More than half of the time	4 About half of the time	3 Less than half of the time	2 Rarely	1 Never
Attendings							
Chief residents							
Senior residents							
Interns							

Figure 1.29	**The C3 Instrument for Characterizing the Patient-Centeredness of a Medical School's Hidden Curriculum (cont.)**

Content area 2: Students' Experiences

Instructions: For each vignette, rate how often you have experienced a similar situation. Please consider how often you have experienced similar situations across all of your experiences during medical school.

Score scale:

Very often: 1   Fairly often: 2   Occasionally: 3   Rarely: 4   Never: 5

Patients-as-objects dimension

Items

1. You overhear an attending physician discussing a patient's case history with another attending or house officer. During the course of the conversation, the patient is referred to as a diagnosis (e.g., "I had a great pancreatitis on my team the other day").

1	2	3	4	5
Very often	Fairly often	Occasionally	Rarely	Never

2. When you describe social history information about a patient (e.g., career, hobbies) during ward rounds, you notice that the rest of the team is not paying attention.

1	2	3	4	5
Very often	Fairly often	Occasionally	Rarely	Never

3. During rounds, your attending is paged to his office. His secretary has a patient present, and wants to know when the attending will return. The attending replies, "Tell the patient to wait. I'll get there when I get there."

1	2	3	4	5
Very often	Fairly often	Occasionally	Rarely	Never

4. You hear students telling stories about patients. These stories tend to portray patients as diagnoses rather than unique human beings.

1	2	3	4	5
Very often	Fairly often	Occasionally	Rarely	Never

5. Your ward team is rounding on a patient in his room when one of the consulting services arrives for this patient. Your attending and the consulting attending proceed to talk about the patient's case as if the patient weren't there.

1	2	3	4	5
Very often	Fairly often	Occasionally	Rarely	Never

Figure 1.29	**The C3 Instrument for Characterizing the Patient-Centeredness of a Medical School's Hidden Curriculum (cont.)**

Learning relationships dimension (these items are reverse-scored):

Items

1. You hear students telling stories about patients. These stories tend to portray how the relationship with the patient affected the student(s) personally.

1	2	3	4	5
Very often	Fairly often	Occasionally	Rarely	Never

2. During your third or fourth year of medical school, an attending or house officer observes you while you interview a patient and provides you with feedback on your bedside manner.

1	2	3	4	5
Very often	Fairly often	Occasionally	Rarely	Never

3. During your third or fourth year of medical school, you are asked to interview a patient (either "real" or "standardized") and you are provided with feedback on how well you listened to the patient (either from the patient or an observer).

1	2	3	4	5
Very often	Fairly often	Occasionally	Rarely	Never

4. You are given advice from students in the classes ahead of you on what you need to do to succeed in medical school. This advice emphasizes the importance of good communication skills with patients.

1	2	3	4	5
Very often	Fairly often	Occasionally	Rarely	Never

Bad news for patients and students dimension:

Items

1. During a rotation in the outpatient clinic, you have to convey bad news to a patient without any teaching or discussion about how to break the news in a caring manner.

1	2	3	4	5
Very often	Fairly often	Occasionally	Rarely	Never

2. You and your ward team have to convey bad news to a patient. Sometime after the bad news is conveyed, you find yourself having to answer many of the patient's questions about the news without any teaching about how to talk to patients after they have been given bad news.

1	2	3	4	5
Very often	Fairly often	Occasionally	Rarely	Never

Figure 1.29	**The C3 Instrument for Characterizing the Patient-Centeredness of a Medical School's Hidden Curriculum (cont.)**

Content area 3: Support for Students Own Patient-Centered Behaviors

Instructions: Please rate the response that you received from your instructors when you exhibited efforts to engage in each of the following behaviors. (fill in the blank)

Scoring scale:

Completely encouraged: 5

Mostly encouraged: 4

Slightly encouraged: 3

Neither encouraged or discouraged: 2

Discouraged: 1

Items

1. In general, when I made an effort to develop rapport with patients, my instructors _____ _____ me.

5	4	3	2	1
Completely encouraged	Mostly encouraged	Slightly encouraged	Neither encouraged or discouraged	Discouraged

2. In general, when I made an effort to get to know patients as unique persons, my instructors _____ _____ me.

5	4	3	2	1
Completely encouraged	Mostly encouraged	Slightly encouraged	Neither encouraged or discouraged	Discouraged

3. In general, when I made an effort to legitimize patients' concerns about their condition or care, my instructors _____ me.

5	4	3	2	1
Completely encouraged	Mostly encouraged	Slightly encouraged	Neither encouraged or discouraged	Discouraged

Source: Adapted from Haidet P, Kelly PA, Chou C, and The Communication, Curriculum, and Culture Study Group.

References

1. Peabody FW. The care of the patient. *JAMA*. 1927;88:877–882.

2. Lipkin M Jr. Preface. In: Lipkin M Jr, Putman SM, Lazare A, eds. *The Medical Interview: Clinical Care, Education, and Research*. New York, NY: Springer-Verlag; 1995:ix–xi.

3. Committee on Quality of Health Care in America. *Crossing the Quality Chasm: A New Health System for the 21st Century*. Institute of Medicine, Washington, DC: National Academies Press; 2001. *http://books.nap.edu/openbook.php?record_id=10027*. Accessed February 2010.

4. Accreditation Council for Graduate Medical Education. General competencies: ACGME outcome project 2001. *www.acgme.org/outcome/comp/compMin.asp*. Accessed April 5, 2010.

5. Special Committee on Maintenance of Licensure. Draft report on maintenance of licensure. Federation of State Medical Boards. July 2008. *www.fsmb.org/pdf/Special_Committee_MOL_Draft_Report_February2008.pdf*. Accessed March 21, 2010.

6. Medical Staff Standard. Behaviors that undermine a culture of safety. The Joint Commission, July 9, 2008. *www.jointcommission.org*. Accessed March 2010.

7. Klass D, De Champlian A, Fletcher E, King A, Macmillan M. Development of a performance-based test of clinical skills for the United States Licensing Examination. *Federal Bulletin*. 1998;85:177–185.

8. Bayer-Fetzer Conference on Physician-Patient Communication in Medical Education. Essential elements of communication in medical encounters: the Kalamazoo Consensus Statement. *Acad Med*. 2001;76:390–393.

9. Simpson M, Buckman R, Stewart M, et al. Doctor–patient communication: the Toronto consensus statement. *BMJ*. 1991;202:1384–1387.

10. Makoul G, Schofield T. Communication teaching and assessment in medical education: an international consensus statement. *Patient Educ Couns*. 1999;137:191–195.

11. von Fragstein M, Silverman J, Cushing A, Quilligan S, Salisbury H, Wiskin C, on behalf of the UK Council for Clinical Communication Skills Teaching in Undergraduate Medical Education. UK consensus statement on the content of communication curricula in undergraduate medical education. *Med Educ*. 2008;42:1100-1107.

12. Kiessling C, Dieterich A, Fabry G, et al., on behalf of the Committee "Communication and Social Competencies" of the Association for Medical Education (Gesellschaft für Medizinische Ausbildung, GMA) and the Basel Workshop Participants. Communication and social competencies in medical education in German-speaking countries: The Basel Consensus Statement. Results of a Delphi Survey. *Patient Educ Couns*. March 9, 2010. [Epub ahead of print.]

13. Rider EA, Keefer CH. Communication skills competencies: definitions and a teaching toolbox. *Med Educ*. 2006;40:624–629.

14. Association of American Medical Colleges. Medical School Objectives Project, Report III. *Contemporary Issues in Medicine: Communication in Medicine*. Washington, DC: Association of American Medical Colleges; 1999.

15. Association of Faculties of Medicine of Canada. *The Future of Medical Education in Canada (FMEC): A Collective Vision for MD Education*. Ottawa, ON, Canada: The Association of Faculties of Medicine of Canada (AFMC); 2010. *www.afmc.ca/fmec/*. Accessed March 14, 2010.

16. Frank JR. *The CanMEDS 2005 physician competency framework. Better standards. Better physicians. Better care*. Ottawa: The Royal College of Physicians and Surgeons of Canada; 2005. *http://rcpsc.medical.org/canmeds/CanMEDS2005/CanMEDS2005_e.pdf*. Accessed March 14, 2010.

17. Shumway JM, Harden RM. AMEE Medical Education Guide No 25: the assessment of learning outcomes for the competent and reflective physician. *Med Teach.* 2003;25:569–584.

18. General Medical Council. Tomorrow's doctors: outcomes and standards for undergraduate medical education. England, Wales, and Scotland; September 2009. *www.gmc-uk.org/education/undergraduate/ tomorrows_doctors_2009.asp.* Accessed April 3, 2010.

19. Institute for International Medical Education. Global minimum essential requirements in medical education. *Med Teach.* 2002;24:130–135.

20. Liaison Committee on Medical Education. *Functions and Structure of a Medical School.* Washington DC: Liaison Committee on Medical Education; 1998.

21. Cumming AD, Ross MT. The Tuning Project (medicine)–learning outcomes/competences for undergraduate medical education in Europe. Edinburgh: The University of Edinburgh; 2008. *www.tuning-medicine.com/.* Accessed March 14, 2010.

22. Confederation of Postgraduate Medical Education. Australian Curriculum Framework for Junior Doctors (version 2.2), 2009. *www.cpmec.org.au/Page/acfjd-project.* Accessed March 14, 2010.

23. Whelan GP. Educational Commission for Foreign Medical Graduates: clinical skills assessment prototype. *Med Teach.* 1999;21:156–160.

24. General Medical Council. The new doctor: guidance on foundation training. September 2009. *www.gmc-uk.org/ New_Doctor09_FINAL.pdf_27493417.pdf.* Accessed March 14, 2010.

25. The Royal College of Physicians and Surgeons of Canada (RCPSC). The CanMEDS Physician Competency Framework. 2005. *http://rcpsc.medical.org/canmeds/.* Accessed March 14, 2010.

26. Frank JR, Danoff D. The CanMEDS initiative: implementing an outcomes-based framework of physician competencies. *Med Teach.* 2007;29:642–647.

27. American Board of Medical Specialties. MOC competencies and criteria. *www.abms.org/Maintenance_ of_Certification/MOC_competencies.aspx.* Accessed April 3, 2010.

28. Royal College of General Practitioners (RCGP). Good medical practice for general practitioners. *www.rcgp. org.uk/pdf/PDS_Good_Medical_Practice_for_GPs_ July_2008.pdf.* Accessed March 14, 2010.

29. Tates K, Elbers E, Meeuwesen L, Bensing J. Doctor-parent-child relationships: a 'pas de trois'. *Patient Educ Couns.* 2002;48:5–14.

30. Richards T. Chasms in communication. *BMJ.* 1991;303:1385–1387.

31. Stewart MA, McWhinney IR, Buck CW. The doctor/patient relationship and its effect upon outcome. *J R Coll Gen Pract.* 1979;29:77–81.

32. Byrne PS, Long BEL. *Doctors Talking to Patients.* London: RCGP Publications; 1976.

33. Hadlow J, Pitts M. The understanding of common health terms by doctors, nurses and patients. *Soc Sci Med.* 1991;32:193–196.

34. Dyche L, Swiderski D. The effect of physician solicitation approaches on ability to identify patient concerns. *J Gen Intern Med.* 2005;20:267–270.

35. Beckman HB, Frankel RM. The effect of physician behavior on the collection of data. *Annals Int Med.* 1984;101:692–696.

36. Marvel MK, Epstein RM, Flowers K, Beckman HB. Soliciting the patient's agenda: have we improved? *JAMA.* 1999;281:283–287.

37. Kohn LT, Corrigan JM, Donaldson MS, eds. *To Err Is Human: Building a Safer System.* Committee on Quality Health Care in America, Institute of Medicine. Washington, DC: National Academies Press; 2000. *www.nap.edu/openbook.php?record_id=9728.* Accessed April 5, 2010.

38. Shapiro RS, Simpson DE, Lawrence SL, Talsky AM, Sobocinski KA, Scheidermayer DL. A survey of sued and nonsued physicians and suing patients. *Arch Int Med*. 1989;149:2190–2196.

39. Beckman HB, Markakis KM, Suchman AL, Frankel RM. The doctor-patient relationship and malpractice: lessons from plaintiff depositions. *Arch Int Med*. 1994;154:1365–1370.

40. Makoul G. Communication skills education in medical school and beyond. *JAMA*. 2003;289:93.

41. Sanson-Fisher RW, Poole AD. Training medical students to empathize: an experimental study. *Med J Aust*. 1978;1(9):473–476.

42. Aspegren K. Teaching and learning communication skills in medicine: a review with quality grading of articles. Best Evidence in Medical Education Guide No. 2. Dundee, Scotland, UK: Association for Medical Education in Europe; 1999. [Also published in *Med Teach*. 1999:21:563–570.]

43. Hulsman RL, Ros WJG, Winnubst JAM, Bensing JM. Teaching clinically experienced physicians communication skills. A review of evaluation studies. *Med Educ*. 1999;33:655–668.

44. Rider EA, Volkan K, Hafler JP. Pediatric residents' perceptions of communication competencies: implications for teaching. *Med Teach*. 2008;30:e208-e217. *http://informahealthcare.com/doi/full/10.1080/01421590802208842*. Accessed April 5, 2010.

45. Maguire P, Pitceathly C. Key communication skills and how to acquire them. *BMJ*. 2002;325:697–700.

46. Simpson M, Buckman R, Stewart M, et al. Doctor-patient communication: the Toronto consensus statement. *BMJ*. 1991;303:1385–1387.

47. Maguire P, Fairbairn S, Fletcher C. Consultation skills of young doctors: I. Benefits of feedback training in interviewing as students persist. *BMJ*. 1986;292:1573–1576.

48. Heisler M, Bouknight RR, Hayward RA, Smith DM, Kerr EA. The relative importance of physician communication, participatory decision making, and patient understanding in diabetes self-management. *J Gen Intern Med*. 2002;17:243–252.

49. Cabana MD, Slish KK, Evans D, et al. Impact of physician asthma care education on patient outcomes. *Pediatrics*. 2006;117:2149–2157.

50. Gascon JJ, Sanchez-Ortuno M, Llor B, Skidmore D, Saturno PJ, for the Treatment Compliance in Hypertension Study Group. Why hypertensive patients do not comply with treatment: results from a qualitative study. *Fam Pract*. 2004;21:125–130.

51. DiMatteo MR, Taranta A, Friedman HS, Prince LM. Predicting patient satisfaction from physicians' nonverbal communication skills. *Med Care*. 1980;18:376–387.

52. DiMatteo MR. The role of effective communication with children and their families in fostering adherence to pediatric regimens. *Patient Educ Couns*. 2004;55:339–344.

53. Brody DS, Miller SM, Lerman CE, Smith DG, Caputo GC. Patient perception of involvement in medical care: relationship to illness attitudes and outcomes. *J Gen Intern Med*. 1989;4:506–511.

54. Mumford E, Schlesinger HJ, Glass GV. The effects of psychological intervention on recovery from surgery and heart attacks: an analysis of the literature. *Am J Public Health*. 1982;72:141–151.

55. Egbert LD, Battit GE, Welch CE, Bartlett MK. Reduction of post-operative pain by encouragement and instruction of patients: a study of doctor-patient rapport. *NEJM*. 1964;270:825–827.

56. Greenfield S, Kaplan SH, Ware JE Jr, Yano EM, Frank HJL. Patients' participation in medical care: effects on blood sugar control and quality of life in diabetes. *J Gen Intern Med*. 1988;3:448–457.

57. Wartman SA, Morlock LL, Malitz FE, Palm EA. Patient understanding and satisfaction as predictors of compliance. *Med Care*. 1983;21:886–891.

58. Shapiro RS, Simpson DE, Lawrence SL, Talsky AM, Sobocinski KA, Scheidermayer DL. A survey of sued and nonsued physicians and suing patients. *Arch Int Med.* 1989;149:2190–2196.

59. DiMatteo RM, Prince LM, Taranta A. Patients' perceptions of physicians' behavior: determinants of patient commitment to the therapeutic relationship. *Journal of Community Health.* 1979;4:280–290.

60. Stewart M, Brown JB, Donner A, et al. The impact of patient-centered care on outcomes. *J Fam Pract.* 2000;49:796–804.

61. Daghio MM, Ciardullo AV, Cadioli T, et al. GPs' satisfaction with the doctor-patient encounter: findings from a community-based survey. *Fam Pract.* 2003; 20: 283–288.

62. Fallowfield LJ, Hall A, Maguire GP, Baum L. Psychological outcomes of different treatment policies in women with early breast cancer outside a clinical trial. *BMJ.* 1990;301:575–580.

63. Maguire P. Improving communication with cancer patients. Eur J Cancer. 1999;35:1415–1422.

64. Rider EA. Communicating with children and families. In: Rudolph C, Lister G, Gershon A, First L, Rudolph A, eds. *Rudolph's Pediatrics.* 22nd ed. New York, NY: McGraw-Hill; in press.

65. Duffy FD, Gordon GH, Whelan G, Cole-Kelly K, Frankel R, and all participants in the American Academy on Physician and Patient's Conference on Education and Evaluation of Competence in Communication and Interpersonal Skills. Assessing competence in communication and interpersonal skills: The Kalamazoo II Report. *Acad Med.* 2004;79:495–507.

66. Janisse T, Vuckovic N. Can some clinicians read their patients' minds? Or do they just really like people? A communication and relationship study. *Permanente J.* 2002;6:35–40.

67. Epstein RM. Mindful practice. *JAMA.* 1999; 282: 833–839.

68. Dyche L. Interpersonal skill in medicine: the essential partner of verbal communication. *J Gen Intern Med.* 2007;22:1035–1039.

69. Hundert EM, Douglas-Steele D, Bickel J. Context in medical education: the informal ethics curriculum. *Med Educ.* 1996;5:353–364.

70. Accreditation Council for Graduate Medical Education. General competencies: ACGME outcome project 2001. *www.acgme.org/outcome/comp/compFull.asp#4.* Accessed April 5, 2010.

71. Accreditation Council for Graduate Medical Education. Common Program Requirements. *www.acgme.org/ outcome/comp/compCPRL.asp.* Accessed March 3, 2010.

72. Sedway M, Dann M. The heart of vocation. In: Fetzer Institute. *Stories of Hope and Transformation.* Kalamazoo, MI: Fetzer Institute; 2006.

73. Tresolini CP, and the Pew-Fetzer Task Force. *Health Professions Education and Relationship-Centered Care.* San Francisco, CA: Pew Health Professions Commission; 1994. *http://jerrykaiser.com/html/Pew-Fetzer Report.pdf.* Accessed March 2010.

74. Beach MC, Inui T, and the Relationship-Centered Care Research Network. Relationship-centered care. A constructive reframing. *J Gen Intern Med.* 2006;21 (1 Suppl):S3–S8.

75. Zoppi K, Epstein RM. Is communication a skill? Communication behaviors and being in relation. *Fam Med.* 2002;34(5):319–324.

76. Fallowfield L, Jenkins V. Communicating sad, bad, and difficult news in medicine. *Lancet.* 2004;363: 312–319.

77. Leach DC. Changing education to improve patient care. *Qual Health Care.* 2001;10(2 Suppl):1154–1158.

78. Tiberius RG. The why of teacher/student relationships. Essays on teaching excellence. The Professional and Organizational Development Network in Higher Education. 1993-1994 Essay Series. *www.podnetwork.org.* Accessed March 2010.

79. Weston WW, Brown JB. Teaching the patient-centered method: the human dimensions of medical education. In: Stewart M, Brown JB, Weston WW, McWhinney IR, McWilliam CL, Freeman TR. *Patient-Centered Medicine: Transforming the Clinical Method.* Thousand Oaks, CA: Sage Publications; 1995.

80. Skiles J. Teaching professionalism: a medical student's opinion. *Clin Teach.* 2005;2:66–71.

81. Silverman J. Teaching clinical communication: a mainstream activity or just a minority sport? *Patient Educ Couns.* 2009;76:361–367.

82. Cuff PA, Vanselow NA, eds. *Improving Medical Education: Enhancing the Behavioral and Social Science Content of Medical School Curricula.* Committee on Behavioral and Social Sciences in Medical School Curricula and Board on Neuroscience and Behavioral Health. Institute of Medicine of the National Academies. Washington, DC: The National Academies Press; 2004. *www.nap.edu/openbook.php?isbn=030909142X&page=R1.* Accessed April 5, 2010.

83. Ludmerer KM. *Time to Heal: American Medical Education from the Turn of the Century to the Era of Managed Care.* Oxford, UK: Oxford University Press; 1999.

84. Hafferty FW. Beyond curriculum reform: confronting medicine's hidden curriculum. *Acad Med.* 1998;73: 403–407.

85. Coulehan J, Williams PC. Vanquishing virtue: the impact of medical education. *Acad Med.* 2001;76(6): 598–605.

86. Pfeiffer C, Madray H, Ardolino A, Willms J. The rise and fall of students' skill in obtaining a medical history. *Med Educ.* 1998;32:283–288.

87. Bellini LM, Shea JA. Mood change and empathy decline persist during three years of internal medicine training. *Acad Med.* 2005;80:164–167.

88. Bellini LM, Shea JA. Mood change and empathy decline persist during three years of internal medicine training. *Acad Med.* 2005;80:164–167.

89. Mangione S, Kane CK, Caruso JW, Gonnella JS, Nasca TJ, Hojat M. Assessment of empathy in different years of internal medicine training. *Med Teach.* 2002;24:370–373.

90. Hojat M, Vergare MJ, Maxwell K, et al. The devil is in the third year: a longitudinal study of erosion of empathy in medical school. *Acad Med.* 2009;84(9): 1182–1191.

91. Collier VU, Macue JD, Markus A, Smith L. Stress in medical residency: status quo after a decade or reform? *Annals Int Med.* 2002;136:384–390.

92. Reisman AB. Outing the hidden curriculum. Hastings Center Report. July-August 2006:9.

93. Inui TS. *A Flag in the Wind: Educating for Professionalism in Medicine.* Washington, DC: Association of American Medical Colleges; February 2003. *www.regenstrief.org/Members/tinui/bio.* Accessed February 2010.

94. Suchman AL, Williamson PR, Litzelman DK, et al. Toward an informal curriculum that teaches professionalism: transforming the social environment of a medical school. *J Gen Intern Med.* 2004;19:501–504.

95. Branch WT. Supporting the moral development of medical students. *J Gen Intern Med.* 2000;15: 503–508.

96. Karnieli-Miller O, Vu TR, Holtman MC, Clyman SG, Inui TS. Medical students' professionalism narratives: a window on the informal and hidden curriculum. *Acad Med.* 2010;85(1):124–133.

97. Pololi L, Conrad P, Knight S, Carr P. A study of the relational aspects of the culture of academic medicine. *Acad Med.* 2009;84(1):106–114.

98. Liaison Committee on Medical Education. New standard on the learning environment. *www.lcme.org/standard.htm#learningenvironment.* Accessed February 2010.

99. Branch WT Jr, Kern D, Haidet P, et al. Teaching the human dimensions of care in clinical settings. *JAMA.* 2001;286:1067–1074.

100. Branch WT. Viewpoint: teaching respect for patients. *Acad Med.* 2006;81:463–467.

101. Suchman AL. Advancing humanism in medical education. *J Gen Intern Med.* 2007;22:1630–1631.

102. Eva KW, Rosenfeld J, Reiter HI, Norman GR. An admissions OSCE: the multiple mini-interview. *Med Educ.* 2004;38:314–326.

103. Harris S, Owen C. Discerning quality: using the multiple mini-interview in student selection for the Australian National University Medical School. *Med Educ.* 2007;41:234–241.

104. Ziv A, Rubin O, Moshinsky A, et al. MOR: a simulation-based assessment centre for evaluating the personal and interpersonal qualities of medical school candidates. *Med Educ.* 2008;42(10):991–998.

105. Marsh DR, Schroeder DG, Dearden KA, Sternin J, Sternin M. The power of positive deviance. *BMJ.* 2004;329:1177–1179.

106. Rabow MW, Remen RN, Parmelee DX, Inui TS. Professional formation: extending medicine's lineage of service into the next century. *Acad Med.* 2010;85:310–317.

107. Cottingham AH, Suchman AL, Litzelman DK, et al. Enhancing the informal curriculum of a medical school: a case study in organizational culture change. *J Gen Intern Med.* 2008;23:715–722.

108. Hammond SA. *The Thin Book of Appreciative Inquiry.* Bend, OR: Thin Book Publishing Co.; 1998.

109. Sternin J. Practice positive deviance for extraordinary social and organizational change. In: Ulrich D, Goldsmith M, Carter L, Bolt J, Smallwood N, eds. *The Change Champion's Fieldguide: Strategies and Tools for Leading Change in Your Organization.* Best Practice Publications, LLC; 2003. *www.positivedeviance.org/resources/books.html.* Accessed March 2010.

110. Palmer PJ. *The Courage to Teach: Exploring the Inner Landscape of a Teacher's Life.* San Francisco, CA: Jossey-Bass Inc. Publishers; 1998.

111. Suchman AL, Matthews DA. What makes the patient-doctor relationship therapeutic? Exploring the connexional dimension of medical care. *Annals Int Med.* 1988;108:125–130.

112. Smith RC, Zimny GH. Physicians' emotional reactions to patients. *Psychosomatics.* 1988;29:392–397.

113. Lyles JS, Dwamena FC, Lein C, Smith RC. Evidence-based patient-centered interviewing. *J Com.* 2001;8:28–34.

114. Suchman AL, Markakis K, Beckman HB, Frankel R. A model of empathic communication in the medical interview. *JAMA.* 1997;277:678–682.

115. Marshall AA, Smith RC. Physicians' emotional reactions to patients: recognizing and managing countertransference. *Am J Gastroenterol.* 1995;90:4-8.

116. Smith RC, Dorsey AM, Lyles JS, Frankel. Teaching self-awareness enhances learning about patient-centered interviewing. *Acad Med.* 1999;74:1242–1248.

117. Lyles JS, Dwamena FC, Lein C, Smith RC. Evidence-based patient-centered interviewing. *J Com.* 2001;8:28–34.

118. Carraccio C, Englander R. Evaluating competence using a portfolio: a literature review and web-based application to the ACGME competencies. *Teach Learn Med.* 2004;16:381–387.

119. Driessen E, van Tartuijk J, Dornan T. The self-critical doctor: helping students become more reflective. *BMJ.* 2008;336:827–830.

120. Dobie S. Viewpoint: reflections on a well-traveled path: self-awareness, mindful practice, and relationship-centered care as foundations for medical education. *Acad Med.* 2007;82(4):422–427.

121. Rider EA, Konopasek L. et al. Relationship-centered medical education and practice: a tool kit of resources for humanistic care. Version 1.5. Unpublished manuscript.

122. Gracey CF, Haidet P, Branch WT, et al. Precepting humanism: strategies for fostering the human dimensions of care in ambulatory settings. *Acad Med.* 2005;80:21–28.

123. Miller SZ, Schmidt HJ. The habit of humanism: a framework for making humanistic care a reflexive clinical skill. *Acad Med.* 1999;74:800–803.

124. Epstein R. The science of patient-centered care. *J Fam Pract.* 2000;49(9). *www.jfponline.com/Pages. asp?AID=2593&UID.* Accessed April 5, 2010.

125. Smith RC, Dwamena FC, Fortin AH. Teaching personal awareness. *J Gen Intern Med.* 2005;20:201-207. Appendix includes specific curricula. *www.blackwellpublishing. com/products/journals/suppmat/jgi/jgi40212/jgi40212. htm.* Accessed February 4, 2007.

126. Stewart M, Brown JB, Donner A, et al. The impact of patient-centered care on outcomes. *J Fam Pract.* 2000;49:796–804.

127. Epstein RM. Mindful practice in action (I): technical competence, evidence-based medicine, and relationship-centered care. *Fam Syst Health.* 2003;21:1–9.

128. Levenkron JC, Greenland P, Bowley N. Teaching risk-factor counseling skills: a comparison of two instructional methods. *Am J Prev Med.* 1990;6:29–34.

129. Novack DH, Suchman AL, Clark W, Epstein RM, Najberg E, Kaplan C. Calibrating the physician: personal awareness and effective patient care. *JAMA.* 1997;278:502–509.

130. Novack DH, Kaplan C, Epstein RM, et al. Personal awareness and professional growth: a proposed curriculum. *Medical Encounter.* 1997;13:2–7.

131. Wald HS, Davis SW, Reis SP, Monroe AD, Borkan JM. Reflecting on reflections: enhancement of medical education curriculum with structured field notes and guided feedback. *Acad Med.* 2009;84(7):830–837.

132. Charon R. Narrative and medicine. *NEJM.* 2004;350: 862–864.

133. DasGupta S, Charon R. Personal illness narratives: using reflective writing to teach empathy. *Acad Med.* 2004;79:351–356.

134. Brady DW, Corbie-Smith G, Branch WT. "What's important to you?" The use of narratives to promote self-reflection and to understand the experiences of medical residents. *Annals Int Med.* 2002;137:220–223.

135. Branch W, Pels R, Lawrence RS, Arky RA. Becoming a doctor: "critical-incident" reports from third-year medical students. *NEJM.* 1993;329:1130–1132.

136. Hatem D, Rider EA. Sharing stories: narrative medicine in an evidence-based world. *Patient Educ Couns.* 2004;54:251–253.

137. Reis SP, Wald HS, Monroe AD, Borkan JM. Begin the BEGAN (The Brown Educational Guide to the Analysis of Narrative) - a framework for enhancing educational impact of faculty feedback to students' reflective writing. *Patient Educ Couns.* 2010 Jan 5. [Epub ahead of print]

138. Sklar D, Doezema D, McLaughlin S, Helitzer D. Teaching communications and professionalism through writing and humanities: reflections of ten years of experience. *Acad Emerg Med.* 2002;9:1360–1364.

139. Bertman S, Pretorius R. Webinar: Integrating the arts into medical education. Society for the Arts in Healthcare. *www.thesah.org/template/page.cfm?page_id=582.* Accessed March 14, 2010.

140. The Literature, Arts & Medicine Database. New York University School of Medicine. *http://litmed.med.nyu.edu.* Accessed March 14, 2010.

141. Browning DM, Meyer EC, Truog RD, Solomon MZ. Difficult conversations in health care: cultivating relational learning to address the hidden curriculum. *Acad Med.* 2007;82:905–913.

142. Kurtz SM, Silverman JD, Draper J. *Teaching and Learning Communication Skills in Medicine.* 2nd ed. Abingdon, Oxon, UK: Radcliffe Medical Press; 2005.

143. Stewart M, Belle Brown J, Weston WW, McWhinney IR, McWilliam CL, Freeman TR. *Patient-Centered Medicine: Transforming the Clinical Method.* Thousand Oaks, CA: Sage Publications; 1995.

144. Smith, RC. *Patient Centered Interviewing: An Evidence Based Method.* 2nd ed. Philadelphia, PA: Lippincott Williams & Wilkins; 2002.

145. Silverman J, Kurtz S, Draper J. *Skills for Communicating with Patients.* 2nd ed. Abingdon, Oxon, UK: Radcliffe Medical Press; 2005.

146. Kalet AL, Pugnaire MP, Cole-Kelly K, et al. Teaching communication in clinical clerkships: models from the Macy Initiative in Health Communications. *Acad Med.* 2004;79:511–520.

147. Meyer EC, Sellers DE, Browning DM, McGuffie K, Solomon MZ, Truog RD. Difficult conversations: improving communication skills and relational abilities in health care. *Ped Crit Care Med.* 2009;10(3):352–359.

148. Accreditation Council for Graduate Medical Education. Advancing education in interpersonal and communication skills: an educational resource from the ACGME Outcome Project. Chicago, IL: ACGME; 2005. *www.acgme.org/outcome/implement/interpercomskills.pdf.* Accessed March 14, 2010.

149. Brody B. The script. [Becoming a Physician] *NEJM.* 2006:355:979–981.

150. Accreditation Council for Graduate Medical Education. Outcome Project: key considerations for selecting assessment instruments and implementing assessment systems. Chicago, IL: ACGME; 2001. *www.acgme.org/outcome/assess/keyConsider.asp.* Accessed April 5, 2010.

151. Accreditation Council for Graduate Medical Education. Toolbox of assessment methods. Version 1.1. Chicago, IL: ACGME; 2001. *www.acgme.org/outcome/assess/toolbox.asp.* Accessed April 5, 2010.

152. Street RL. Analyzing communication in medical consultations: do behavioral measures correspond to patients' perceptions. *Med Care.* 1992:30:976–988.

153. Janisse T, Vuckovic N. Can some clinicians read their patients' minds? Or do they just really like people? A communication and relationship study. *Permanente J.* 2002;6:35–40.

154. Joyce B. Developing an assessment system facilitator's guide. ACGME Outcome Project, 2006. *www.acgme.org/outcome/e-learn/FacManual_module3.pdf.* Accessed March 2010.

155. Adina Kalet, MD. Personal communication. March 2010.

156. Rider EA, Hinrichs MM, Lown BA. A model for communication skills assessment across the undergraduate curriculum. *Med Teach.* 2006;28: e127–e134.

157. Rider EA. Competency 1: Interpersonal and communication skills. In: Rider EA, Nawotniak RH, Smith G, eds. *A Practical Guide to Teaching and Assessing the ACGME Core Competencies.* Marblehead, MA: HCPro, Inc.; 2007.

158. Holmboe ES, Lynn L, Duffy FD. Improving the quality of care via maintenance of certification and the Web: an early status report. *Pers Biol Med.* 2008;51(1):71–83.

159. Daniel Duffy, MD. Personal communication. March 2010.

160. American Board of Internal Medicine. Sample modules. *www.abim.org/moc/earning-points/productinfo-demo-ordering.aspx.* Accessed March 2010.

161. Lipner RS, Blank LL, Leas BF, Fortna GS. The value of patient and peer ratings in recertification. *Acad Med.* 2002;77(10 suppl):S64–S66.

162. Osler W. The master words in medicine. In: *Aequanimitas: With Other Addresses to Medical Students, Nurses and Practitioners of Medicine.* Philadelphia, PA: P. Blackiston's Son; 1932:368.

163. Schirmer JM, Mauksch L, Lang F, et al. Assessing communication competence: a review of current tools. *Fam Med.* 2005;37:184–192.

164. Hullman GA, Daily M. Evaluating physician communication competence scales: a replication and extension. *Comm Research Reports.* 2008;25:316–322.

165. Suzanne Kurtz, PhD. Personal communication. 2007.

166. Lockyer J, Violato C, Fidler H. Likelihood of change: a study assessing surgeon use of multisource feedback data. *Teach Learn Med.* 2003;15(3):168–174.

167. Violato C, Marini A, Toews J, Lockyer J, Fidler H. Feasibility and psychometric properties of using peers, consulting physicians, co-workers, and patients to assess physicians. *Acad Med.* 1997;72(10 Suppl 1): S82–S84.

168. Lockyer J. Multisource feedback in the assessment of physician competencies. *J Contin Educ Health Prof.* 2003;23(1):4–12.

169. Calhoun AW, Rider EA, Meyer EC, Lamiani G, Truog RD. Assessment of communication skills and self-appraisal in the simulated environment: feasibility of multirater feedback with gap analysis. *Simul Healthc.* 2009;4(1):22–29.

170. Epstein RM. Assessment in medical education. *NEJM.* 2007;356:387–396.

171. Novack DH, Volk G, Drossman DA, Lipkin M Jr. Medical interviewing and interpersonal skills teaching in US medical schools: progress, problems, and promise. *JAMA.* 1993;269:2101–2105.

172. Lang F, Everett K, McGowen R, Bennard B. Faculty development in communication skills instruction: insights from a longitudinal program with 'real time feedback'. *Acad Med.* 2000;75:1222–1228.

173. Rider EA, Hinrichs MM. Teaching communication skills: assessment and reflective feedback. MyCourses Web-based faculty development teaching module, Harvard Medical School, 2003. *http://mycourses.med.harvard. edu* and *http://ecommons.med.harvard.edu ->* CommSkills.

174. Novack DH, Clark W, Saizow R, Daetwyler C, eds. doc.com: an interactive learning resource for healthcare communication. *www.aachonline.org/ ?page=doccomoverview.* Accessed April 5, 2010.

175. Marchese TJ. The new conversations about learning: insights from neuroscience and anthropology, cognitive science and workplace studies. New Horizons for Learning; 1998. *www.newhorizons.org/lifelong/ higher_ed/marchese.htm.* Accessed March 2010.

176. Branch WT Jr, Frankel R, Gracey CF, et al. A good clinician and a caring person: longitudinal faculty development and the enhancement of the human dimensions of care. *Acad Med.* 2009;84(1):117–125.

177. Brater C. Infusing professionalism into a school of medicine: perspectives from the dean. *Acad Med.* 2007;82:1094–1097.

178. National/International Initiatives. Difficult conversations in healthcare: pedagogy and practice. Institute for Professionalism and Ethical Practice, Children's Hospital Boston. *www.ipepweb.org/courses. html#DifficultConversHealthcrPedagogyPract.* Accessed April 3, 2010.

179. A relational revolution: difficult conversations and everyday ethics. *Ped Views.* October 2007:1,6. *www.childrenshospital.org/views/october07/index.html.* Accessed April 3, 2010.

180. Elizabeth A. Rider, MSW, MD. Personal communication; 2010.

181. Kurtz SM, Laidlaw T, Makoul G, Schnabl G. Medical education initiatives in communication skills. *Cancer Prev Control.* 1999;3:37–45.

182. Barbara Joyce, PhD. Personal communication; March 2010.

183. Gyles C. On the cusp of a paradigm shift in medicine. *Can Vet J.* 2009;50:1221–1222.

184. William Clark, MD. Personal communication; March 2010.

185. Stein S, Frankel RM, Krupat E. Enhancing clinician communication skills in a large healthcare organization: a longitudinal case study. *Patient Educ Couns.* 2005;58:4–12.

186. Frankl RM, Stein T. Getting the most out of the clinical encounter: the four habits model. *Permanente J.* 1999;3(3). *http://xnet.kp.org/permanentejournal/ fall99pj/habits.html.* Accessed February 8, 2007.

187. Gordon GH. Defining the skills underlying communication competence. *Sem Med Prac.* 2002;5:21–28.

188. Calhoun AW, Rider EA. Engagement and listening skills: identifying learning needs. *Med Educ.* 2008;42:1134–1135.

189. Kurtz S, Silverman J, Benson J, Draper J. Marrying content and process in clinical method teaching: enhancing the Calgary–Cambridge Guides. *Acad Med.* 2003;78:802–809.

190. Levenstein JH. The patient-centered general practice consultation. *S Africa Fam Prac.* 1984;5:276–282.

191. Stewart M, Brown JB, Weston WW, McWhinney IR, McWilliam CL, Freeman TR. *Patient-Centered Medicine: Transforming the Clinical Method.* 2nd ed. Abingdon, Oxon, UK: Radcliffe Medical Press; 2003.

192. Stewart M, Meredith L, Ryan BL, Brown JB. The patient perception of patient-centeredness questionnaire (PPPC). Working Paper Series #04-1. Center for Studies in Family Medicine. The University of Western Ontario, London, Ontario, Canada; 2004.

193. Greg Makoul, PhD. Personal communication; March 2010.

194. NYU Macy Initiative on Health Communication. Communication competencies. *http://nyumacy.med. nyu.edu/curriculum/competencies.html.* Accessed April 4, 2010.

195. NYU Macy Initiative on Health Communication. Overview of the structure and sequence of effective doctor patient communication. *http://nyumacy.med.nyu.edu/curriculum/model/m00a.html.* Accessed April 4, 2010.

196. Yedidia MJ, Gillespie CC, Kachur E, et al. Effect of communications training on medical student performance. *JAMA.* 2003;290:1157–1165.

197. Stevens D, King D, Laponis R, et al. Medical students retain pain assessment and management skills long after an experiential curriculum: a controlled study. *Pain.* 2009;145(3):319–324.

198. Zabar S, Hanley K, Kachur E, et al. "Oh! She doesn't speak English!" Assessing resident competence in managing linguistic and cultural barriers. *J Gen Intern Med.* 2006;21(5):510–513.

199. Zabar S, Ark T, Gillespie C, et al. Can Unannounced Standardized Patients (USPs) assess professionalism and communication skills in the emergency department? *Acad Emerg Med.* 2009;16(9):915–918.

200. Hochberg MS, Kalet A, Zabar S, Kachur E, Gillespie C, Berman RS. Can professionalism be taught? Encouraging evidence. *Am J Surg.* 2010;199(1):86–93.

201. Smith RC, Lyles JS, Mettler J, et al. The effectiveness of an intensive teaching experience for residents in interviewing: a randomized controlled study. *Annals Int Med.* 1998;128:118–126.

202. Smith RC, Lyles JS, Gardiner JC, et al. Primary care clinicians treat patients with medically unexplained symptoms--a randomized controlled trial. *J Gen Intern Med.* 2006;21:671–677.

203. Smith R, Gardiner J, Luo Z, Schooley S, Lamerato L. Primary care physicians treat somatization. *J Gen Intern Med.* 2009;24:829–832.

204. Smith RC, Marshall-Dorsey AA, Osborn GG, et al. Evidence-based guidelines for teaching patient-centered interviewing. *Patient Educ Couns.* 2000;39:27–36.

205. Robert Smith, MD, MS. Personal communication; 2007.

206. Makoul G. The SEGUE framework for teaching and assessing communication skills. *Patient Educ Couns.* 2001;45:23–34.

207. Keller V, Carroll JG. A new model for physician–patient communication. *Patient Educ Couns.* 1994;23:131–140.

208. Butler J, Keller V. A better office visit for doctor and patient. *Managed Care Magazine;* May 1999. *www.managedcaremag.com/archives/9905/9905.bayercomm.html.* Accessed March 30, 2010.

209. Haidet P, Kelly PA, Chou C, et al. Characterizing the patient-centeredness of hidden curricula in medical schools: development and validation of a new measure. *Acad Med.* 2005;80:44–50.

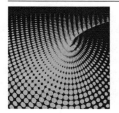

Medical Knowledge

Judith L. Bowen, MD, FACP

[Knowledge is] the fact or condition of knowing something with familiarity gained through experience or association; acquaintance with or understanding of a science, art, or technique ... knowledge applies to facts or ideas acquired by study, investigation, observation, or experience.[1]

The way medical knowledge is structured in the minds of physicians is crucial to the quality of medical diagnosis.[2]

Introduction

The medical profession is defined by its large and distinctive knowledge base, the systematic preparation of physicians, and the use of this knowledge and skills in the service of others. Medical knowledge must not simply be acquired; it must be applied thoughtfully to the care of patients and populations.

In the end, it is how a physician uses his or her knowledge that defines competency. But first, physicians must learn the knowledge in such a way that it is available for use when they are confronted with clinical problems.

This chapter reviews the different ways in which medical knowledge is acquired, stored in memory, and recalled for application in the practice of medicine. Medical educators will also find recommendations for teaching strategies designed to promote medical knowledge acquisition and application across the

medical education continuum. The chapter concludes with strategies for assessing medical knowledge.

The explosion of new discoveries and exponential advances in medical knowledge requires a new type of knowledge: the knowledge to find what one is looking for. Technology enables clinicians to have and to use resources at their fingertips rather than relying on memory alone. The disciplines of sociology, psychology, and anthropology plus the fields of management, quality improvement, and leadership influence the changing practice of medicine, with knowledge of systems, communication, teamwork, and information technology now all required for competent performance in medicine. Thus, medical knowledge can be broadly defined to encompass all of the core competencies.

For the purposes of this chapter, however, medical knowledge is more narrowly defined. To be competent in the domain of medical knowledge:

"RESIDENTS MUST DEMONSTRATE KNOWLEDGE
OF ESTABLISHED AND EVOLVING BIOMEDICAL,
CLINICAL, EPIDEMIOLOGICAL AND SOCIAL-BEHAVIORAL
SCIENCES, AS WELL AS THE APPLICATION OF
THIS KNOWLEDGE TO PATIENT CARE." [3]

Additional expectations regarding knowledge are defined by individual residency review committees of the ACGME.[3] These specific medical knowledge content areas should be the driving force for setting learning objectives and assessment components for trainees in any discipline. This chapter takes a broader view relevant to all disciplines.

How Residents Acquire Medical Knowledge

Physicians use medical knowledge to solve clinical problems. Such problems range from providing preventive health advice and optimizing management of a chronic condition to making a new diagnosis, or a treatment decision such as surgery or chemotherapy. Clinical problems range in urgency. Some require emergent, life-saving, timely decisions while others require thoughtful shared decision-making with patients contemplating the impact of their decisions on quality of life.

Assessing competence in medical knowledge, therefore, should look not only for evidence of knowledge acquisition, but also for the student's ability to use medical knowledge in a variety of decision-making circumstances and apply judgment in making those decisions. Teaching should support the acquisition of knowledge in ways that make medical knowledge accessible in memory and readily retrievable for use.

Knowledge can be acquired in many ways. The formal curriculum defines key concepts to be learned. Experiences with patients, healthcare team dynamics, institutional priorities, and faculty approaches to teaching, among other factors, determine the informal curriculum, which is highly variable. Maintaining an up-to-date, useful knowledge base is a lifelong endeavor.

The transition from the medical school curriculum

Traditionally, preclinical medical students spend most of their time in classrooms, labs, and small group discussions acquiring basic science knowledge and linking it to the pathophysiology of disease. In the absence of clinical cases or patient encounters, knowledge is organized in memory according to the course syllabus or other frameworks teachers may provide. The core knowledge-building task at this level is learning mechanisms of disease and pathophysiology to support future clinical reasoning.

In the third and fourth years of medical school, students make a long-awaited transition to learning in clinical settings where the focus is caring for patients. Much less structured, this transition can be quite abrupt. The medical knowledge that students need on a daily basis is often unknown in advance, making it difficult for them to prepare. Teachers now include residents and fellows at all levels, faculty with multiple competing responsibilities, and other health professionals.

Formal orientation to expectations for learning in these settings is often lacking, leaving transmission of survival tips to the hidden curriculum. Clinical case discussions often happen on the fly, demanding activation of knowledge at a moment's notice. Students must be more self-directed to expand their knowledge, yet commonly, they cannot accurately self-assess to determine what they need to learn.[4] When provided with reading advice, students are variably guided, from reading the latest publications in leading journals to core reading from review articles and textbooks. A structured didactic curriculum organized by discipline usually supports this clinical learning and may be loosely or tightly linked to the clinical cases students are encountering. The core knowledge-building task at this level is to revise stored pathophysiological knowledge and link it to clinical presentations.

Graduate medical education curriculum

At the graduate medical education level, resident learning is almost entirely driven by patient care problems in multiple settings. A core curriculum is often delivered via clinical case conferences, lectures, and self-study. Increasing autonomy and accountability helps residents set learning agendas as gaps in knowledge are discovered and must be addressed. Over time, clinical questions become more complex and sophisticated, requiring a deeper integration of medical knowledge, interpretation of evidence for decisions, and incorporation of patients' preferences.

The core knowledge-building tasks at this level include organizing information together into clinical syndromes. Residents begin to recognize patterns in clinical presentations they encounter frequently. Appreciating the breadth of possible presentations of common clinical

conditions one is likely to encounter is central to knowledge-building. Learning how rare and unusual clinical conditions present as similar to and different from common problems is also important for improving diagnostic accuracy.

At the practice level, little formal structure exists to encourage physicians to continually improve their medical knowledge. Physicians must rely on self-monitoring and curiosity to answer clinical questions and maintain competence. Considerable evidence exists that humans do poorly with self-assessment.[5, 6, 7] Board recertification is a significant motivator for many. The lifelong knowledge-building task at this stage is threefold:

1. Reading to stay current with advances in medicine

2. Appreciating the conflict between practice habits from residency and new knowledge that disrupts those habits and requires change in practice patterns

3. Remaining ever-vigilant in what appear to be routine, habit-filled situations to avoid missing important clinical cues that may change the outcome[8]

Over this medical education continuum, how can medical teachers most effectively promote knowledge acquisition for appropriate and timely application to clinical decisions that result in safe, effective, timely, patient-centered, efficient, and equitable care?[9] An appreciation of how medical knowledge is stored in memory and reactivated for application to solving clinical problems provides the theoretical underpinnings for the recommended teaching strategies discussed in this chapter.

Research on Memory and Reasoning

"EXPERTS MUST HAVE AVAILABLE TO THEM MORE KNOWLEDGE, OF MORE KINDS, WHICH IS BETTER ORGANIZED AND MORE ACCESSIBLE, THAN NOVICES."[10]

Early research on diagnostic reasoning focused on general problem-solving strategies. Using "think aloud" strategies with experienced clinicians, researchers postulated a hypothetico-deductive model of clinical problem-solving.[11] Because experts have more medical knowledge, it was thought that they would ask more questions, gather more information, and work through a more extensive differential diagnosis. Research did not bear this out.

Instead, experts generated better (not more) hypotheses, and the correctness of the initial suggestion strongly predicted final diagnoses.[12] Accuracy on one problem, however, did not predict accuracy on the next.[11] Diagnostic accuracy seemed strongly related to content knowledge, not to any general problem-solving strategy.

Researchers turned their attention to studying knowledge stores in memory to better understand the role of content knowledge. Research studies of chess masters and novice chess players underscored the importance of experience in building large memory stores, which can be used when facing a new opponent.[13]

Attempts to replicate these findings in medicine were mixed. Remembering an extensive catalog of examples may be helpful when the solutions are precisely defined as in chess. However, this strategy is less useful for problems in medicine, which are often ambiguous and complex. Even within the same diagnostic category (e.g., acute myocardial infarction), each patient's story is a little bit different, and the thoroughness required to remember and recall extensive details from all of these cases did not seem to result in better diagnostic abilities.[14]

"IN MEDICINE, EXPERT CLINICIANS PROBABLY HAVE MORE KNOWLEDGE AND BETTER UNDERSTANDING OF THE MECHANISMS UNDERLYING DISEASE, ... MORE KNOWLEDGE OF THE CLINICAL MANIFESTATIONS OF RARE DISEASES, BETTER INTUITIONS ABOUT PROBABILITIES AND BASE RATES, AND MUCH MORE EXPERIENCE WITH INDIVIDUAL CASES."(p. 421) [10]

Although the total amount of medical knowledge plays an important role, the kinds of medical knowledge and how the knowledge is organized in memory are likely more important. Schmidt and colleagues recognized three different types of medical knowledge associated with reasoning and proposed that clinicians move developmentally through these knowledge models or mental representations during their medical education.[15]

First, medical knowledge is stored as basic mechanisms of disease built from learning the basic science of the human body in conditions of health and illness. Second, as clinicians are exposed to clinical cases and real patients, they organize new medical knowledge around these clinical encounters.[16] Called *illness scripts*, knowledge stores of prototypical cases consistently contain three components:

1. The predisposing conditions for the illness

2. The pathophysiological malfunction leading to the illness

3. The clinical manifestations of the illness[15]

When the clinician encounters the constellation of clinical manifestations in a patient's presentation, illness scripts that best fit the story are activated from memory. Usually physicians recall more than one illness script and continue to gather focused information during the patient interview and physical examination to sort and retain the most plausible illness scripts for the clinical case. As knowledge organization begins to take the shape of illness scripts, novices' case discussions may still include extraneous detailed information and unnecessary elaborations.[17] It takes time and experience with many clinical cases to learn what information is important and what information is irrelevant.

> "PERFORMANCE IS NOT A RESULT OF GENERALLY SUPERIOR MEMORY SKILLS. RATHER IT IS A FUNCTION OF A WELL-ORGANIZED KNOWLEDGE BASE ADAPTED TO RECOGNIZE FAMILIAR CONFIGURATIONS OF STIMULI." (p. 257) [17]

Third, with more extensive clinical experience, clinicians store memories of specific patients, called *exemplars*. When faced with a new clinical case, the clinician rapidly and without conscious awareness identifies possible diagnoses through recognition of similar prior case exemplars and patterns stored in memory. The well-organized and comprehensive knowledge base of an expert accounts for increasingly smooth, adaptable, and automatic perceptions of patterns in clinical cases and situations.[17] Clinical diagnostic reasoning for many cases becomes effortless. This experience-based, informal knowledge differs from the formal, analytic knowledge stored as mechanisms of diseases or illness scripts. Both types of medical knowledge, formal and informal, are critically important. New evidence suggests that clinicians use all types of knowledge flexibly to reason clinically.[18]

Conscious processing takes place in short-term memory, also called *working memory*. In this "space," one is consciously aware of thinking, of manipulating ideas and concepts, of integrating new information, and of making sense of new situations. The capacity of working memory during thinking, however, is limited. Generally, a clinician's working memory cannot hold more than seven to 10 unique pieces of information. Clinical teachers should keep this in mind when teaching new concepts. Explaining less information well and connecting it to prior learning is probably a better strategy.

The human mind has evolved several strategies to overcome the limited capacity of working memory. Two are particularly relevant for learning medicine. First, information commonly associated together can be grouped together, and once grouped, it can be considered as one item. For example, medical students learning renal physiology and acid-base balance will initially store each electrolyte as a unique piece of information in their memory. With use in clinical contexts, they group these molecular components together and recall them as "electrolytes" in relationship to each other. One can observe students transitioning from trying to recall the last sodium, potassium, chloride, and bicarbonate levels for their patients to reporting easily on the last several values and trends of the same information from memory. This transition occurs when the pattern of information (i.e., electrolytes) takes on new meaning in the context of specific patient problems and is grouped together.

Second, repetitive and familiar tasks do not need conscious working memory to be carried out. These tasks are done unconsciously and automatically, leaving working memory to puzzle over unusual findings and new concepts—attention-demanding complex tasks.[17] Two examples are important here.

First, when initially making the transition to clinical learning during clerkships, medical students often struggle to present clinical cases in a predictable, orderly fashion. Once they master the "language" of clinical case presentations, case presentations become more fluid and automatic.

Second, as first-year residents make frequent transitions to new hospital and clinic settings, they must learn new rules of engagement that require conscious attention. Once residents learn these routines and they become more automatic, the resident can more easily care for a larger number of patients using working memory to attend to the clinical details rather than the work routine.

Knowledge-Building Teaching Strategies

Building upon theories of medical knowledge acquisition, recall, and application, there are several teaching strategies medical educators can utilize to enhance medical knowledge.[19]

Preclinical recommendations

Link basic science learning to clinical cases. The early years of medical school have historically focused on learning basic sciences relevant to medicine and the pathophysiological mechanisms of disease. It is critical to create a stronger link between the basic science and clinical years of medical school to support the building of knowledge that can be used clinically. Medical schools in North America are moving in that direction.[20] *Curricular integration* refers to interdisciplinary courses in the preclinical years of medical school that bring together basic, clinical, and social sciences into one course.[21,22]

> "... COGNITIVE THEORIES OF LEARNING SUGGEST THAT AN INTEGRATED APPROACH TO EDUCATION MAY HAVE IMPORTANT BENEFITS FOR LEARNING AND RETENTION BECAUSE IT FACILITATES CONTEXTUAL AND APPLIED LEARNING, AND CAN PROMOTE DEVELOPMENT OF THE WELL ORGANIZED-KNOWLEDGE STRUCTURES THAT UNDERLIE EFFECTIVE CLINICAL REASONING." (p. 779) [21]

Clinicians' medical knowledge is activated from memory in relationship to clinical experience. Although early, some empirical evidence supports the notion that an integrated curriculum connects basic science learning to clinically relevant circumstances.

Schmidt has demonstrated that when trained in an integrated curriculum, students arrived at more correct diagnoses.[23] To accomplish integration, clinician educators must take responsibility for co-developing and co-teaching preclinical courses, bringing relevant clinical examples to the classroom. Basic science educators must welcome these partnerships. Classrooms must use active learning methods that challenge students to manipulate and apply newly learned material to the clinical examples and expose areas of poor understanding. Both clinical and basic science teachers must be on hand to answer questions and provide further explanations.

Link instruction in the medical interview and physical exams to clinical cases. When preclinical medical students are learning the language of clinical case presentations, physical examination techniques, and relevant epidemiological and social-behavioral sciences, faculty members should organize curricula around clinical cases. The traditional de-contextualized instruction of the physical examination may explain why students have difficulty selecting relevant examination components later on. Learning these skills in relationship to real clinical cases embeds relevant history and physical examination maneuvers in the diagnostic reasoning tasks of clinical training.[24]

Yudkowsky has shown that hypothesis-driven physical examination learning results in students identifying more diagnostically meaningful and discriminating findings when examining standardized patients during their clinical skills assessment. Teaching purposeful inquiry[25] and hypothesis-driven examination supports the development of early illness scripts as students link relevant history and examination features to diagnostic hypotheses.

Select common clinical conditions as examples. Educators must wisely choose the clinical cases used at this stage of training. Clinical problems that learners commonly encounter in the local clinical setting are ideal for several reasons.

First, medical students with some clinical experience during the first two years of school will be more likely to see patients with these problems and make connections in memory with their classroom learning. Second, when transitioning to clinical learning, seeing patients with familiar clinical problems will boost students' confidence in applying their nascent clinical skills. And third, students will likely already have begun to build knowledge stored as illness scripts for clinical cases discussed recurrently in several preclinical settings.

Clinical recommendations

Guide learners in specific reading strategies. Early in clinical training, both students and first-year residents are reorganizing their medical knowledge in memory for use in clinical settings. Lists of memorized static diagnoses represent inadequate connections between knowledge in memory and patients' problems.[26]

To remedy this, learners should read regularly about their own patients. They will then store knowledge in the context from which they will retrieve it as new cases trigger memories of previous cases.

Assign purposeful case-based reading. Encourage learners to take note of their clinical questions related to their patients' illnesses and read to resolve these questions. Recommending background reading is best, using textbooks and review articles to explore concepts and questions. The goal is to strengthen core knowledge structures for use in clinical contexts. If the students' preclinical curriculum is significantly integrated with clinical cases and patients, this re-modeling should go quickly.

At any point in time, clinicians may encounter a disease or syndrome that is new to them. Background reading is also appropriate under these circumstances. Reading about the pathophysiology and clinical presentations for unusual or rare clinical problems not previously encountered, and comparing and contrasting them with common diagnostic hypotheses for similar clinical presentations, helps to build deep knowledge structures and facilitates recall of appropriate illness scripts and exemplars in the future.

Reading assignments at more advanced training levels may not need to have a direct connection to residents' active clinical cases. Educators implementing weekly reading assignments followed by a multiple-choice examination with immediate feedback on test performance and discussion of reading assign-ments demonstrated a significant improvement in resident performance on the American Board of Surgery In-Training Examination in one surgery residency program.[27]

Encourage reading to compare and contrast. Students and residents should read about two things at once. This allows them to compare and contrast two repre-sentative or prototypical problems and establish in

their memory common and distinguishing features. This strategy facilitates knowledge-building that is discriminatory rather than comprehensive and over-whelming, thereby establishing a strong basis on which to build subsequent knowledge.[26]

For diagnostic problems, instruct learners to read about the clinical presentation of the leading diagnostic hypo-thesis as compared to the second most likely diagnosis, making note of features that distinguish one diagnosis from the other. For diagnostic testing choices, it is useful for residents to read about the diagnostic utility of two competing options (e.g., CT scan versus MRI scan) for the specific clinical situation to compare risks and benefits, sensitivity and specificity for the diagnostic question, and the application of test results to the case.

For management decisions, have learners read to compare and contrast two alternative approaches (e.g., a minimally invasive surgical approach versus open laparotomy), looking for differences in risks and benefits, morbidity and mortality.

Promote reading to promote understanding over memorization. Encourage learners to read for under-standing. More advanced learners should test their understanding by explaining concepts to others. Guide early learners in this process to prevent them from passing along misunderstandings. Avoid setting expectations for learners to know everything. Less is better in the beginning. Deep reading that leads to the understanding of a few critical concepts is more likely to be stored in memory and recalled appropriately than long lists of facts unrelated to clinical cases.

"THERE IS AN INVERSE RELATIONSHIP BETWEEN THE NUMBER OF DISEASES ONE TRIES TO ASSIMILATE AND THE CREATION OF PROTOTYPES OR STRONG ANCHOR POINTS IN MEMORY." (p. 884) 26

Encourage reading to promote retention. Unfortunately, memory naturally decays, and maintaining and improving medical knowledge requires activities to improve knowledge retention. One example of a reinforcing practice is called *spaced education*.[28] Because one objective of medical education is to create long-term learning, Kerfoot and colleagues studied the use of recurring educational encounters to improve retention in long-term memory. The study authors e-mailed medical students clinical scenarios and multiple-choice questions weekly. The e-mail also contained the answers and summary points, a discussion of the answers, and a reminder of the previous week's take-home learning points. Students participating in spaced education had significantly improved medical knowledge retention as measured by year-end examinations.

Promote accountability for knowing. Two strategies for teaching efficiently in small groups in clinical settings (e.g., hospital-based teaching rounds) or one-on-one teaching (e.g., precepting in ambulatory settings) promote learner accountability and responsibility. The first, the one-minute preceptor, has been utilized in multiple settings over nearly two decades.[29] The one-minute preceptor consists of the following five steps:

1. Obtain a commitment from the learner to his or her decision about the patient's treatment

2. Ask the learner for supporting evidence

3. Teach broad rules

4. Emphasize what the learner did well

5. Provide feedback about errors

The first two microskills assist the clinical teacher in determining how the learner is thinking. The remaining three microskills are designed to structure teaching directly related to the teacher's diagnosis of the learner's thinking.

The second strategy, SNAPPS, consists of six steps. SNAPPS shows promise for promoting medical student responsibility for effective case presentations, including articulating reservations regarding their clinical reasoning.[30] SNAPPS is an acronym for:

*   **S**ummarize history and findings

*   **N**arrow the differential

*   **A**nalyze the differential

*   **P**robe preceptor about uncertainties

*   **P**lan management

*   **S**elect case-related issues for self-study

When medical students used this learner-centered method for structuring their clinical case presentations, they were more concise with their case summaries but did not leave out important information, considered more relevant diagnoses, justified their diagnostic considerations in relationship to clinical case findings more often, compared and contrasted two diagnostic possibilities more often, and expressed many more questions and uncertainties to their preceptors than students who were not taught this technique. In addition, students using SNAPPS more often identified case-related readings to pursue.[31]

Ask for a commitment. Ask learners to make a commitment to a leading diagnosis, a testing strategy, or a management decision. Accountability for a choice promotes knowledge acquisition at a higher level. Knowledge moves from knowing what (facts) to knowing how (conceptual understanding). Asking for a commitment also exposes knowledge gaps. Educators can then focus teachings and correct misunderstandings. It also provides the best opportunity to build confidence in the learner's knowledge base as he or she makes more and more correct decisions over time. To do this well, clinical teachers must create a learning environment where it is safe to be wrong.

This will be most evident to learners by watching how the teacher deals with being wrong him or herself, or how the teacher provides constructive criticism to others. Teachers using this strategy must orient learners to this expectation, especially in group learning environments. Include learners in discussions about how the team will handle situations in which a team member does or says something wrong in front of the team or patients and families.

Provide specific and timely feedback. Tell learners when their knowledge is accurate and relevant and their thinking is correct, and when it is not. Point out where the learner's understanding went astray, making specific recommendations to further correct misunderstandings. Make corrections in a timely manner.

Failure to correct mistakes reinforces incorrect knowledge structures that may cause the learner to repeat the mistakes. Check for understanding by asking learners to explain what they have learned.

Assessing Medical Knowledge

"... The public expects, in return for the privilege of self-regulation, that physicians undergo a rigorous, periodic examination of knowledge." [32]

Assessing competence of medical knowledge requires attention to two components: 1) knowledge and application of basic science and 2) investigatory and analytic thinking. The primary strategies suggested in the ACGME/American Board of Medical Specialties (ABMS) Toolbox for formally evaluating knowledge and application include multiple-choice question (MCQ) examinations and oral examinations. Primary strategies suggested for formally assessing investigatory and analytic thinking include chart stimulated recall, oral examinations, and use of simulation. Educators use simulation to assess competencies that are difficult to observe or consistently interpret in a standardized way, such as the application of knowledge in medical decision-making.[33] All of these assessment methods may be used either as high-stakes, summative assessments or for formative evaluation and feedback.

At the formative level, clinical teachers can continually assess medical knowledge through interactive case-based discussions, such as those described previously. Concerns about poor knowledge stores or poor application of knowledge at the formative level should be based on multiple observations. Because the acquisition of medical knowledge for application in clinical situations is highly contextualized, learners who have rarely or never cared for patients with specific conditions will likely have little knowledge to apply to the case. Evaluating a learner's prior experience (e.g., "Have you seen a case like this one before?") prior to making judgments about a lack of developmentally appropriate medical knowledge is important. Formal knowledge assessment should follow any concern for persistently poor demonstration of knowledge.

Chart stimulated recall

In a chart stimulated recall (CSR) examination, the residents' own patient cases are used in a standardized oral examination. Because there are often discrepancies between what a physician does and what he or she records in the chart, the CSR interview starts with the chart note and allows the trainee an opportunity to explain his or her thinking.[34] The process triggers reflection on practice decisions and gives the resident a chance to demonstrate his or her knowledge. In a formal CSR examination, a trained clinical evaluator asks the physician about the patient case, looking for the reasons the physician provided the care that he or she did.[35]

MCQs

Written or computer-based MCQ examinations are the most common assessment method to test medical knowledge and understanding.[36] MCQs test medical knowledge. Multiple-choice tests can be administered in a defined period, and can be computer-scored, making administration straightforward and standardized.[37] Commonly, each clinically based test item contains an introductory patient case and clinical

findings, displays relevant data, and is followed by question-and-answer options. Examinees select the best option.

As compared to MCQs, key feature problems (KFP) use a different format to test clinical decision-making skills. This format also begins with a clinical case, but it allows the trainee to select more than one correct answer from a long list of possible answers for each question. The sequence of questions prompts trainees to think about problem identification, diagnostic strategy, and management decisions for each clinical case. The multiple-answer format accounts for variation in training during which several approaches to the clinical case may be acceptable.[38]

The script concordance (SC) test, another alternative to the MCQ exam, consists of several patient vignettes and associated test questions. The vignettes are purposefully ambiguous to probe trainee reasoning over knowledge recall. Each question presents a situation (e.g., shortness of breath in an older man), asks the trainee to consider several possible diagnoses (e.g., heart failure, pulmonary embolus, community-acquired pneumonia), and then provides additional information (e.g., fever), and asks the trainee to measure how much the additional data increases or decreases the likelihood of each initial diagnosis.[39] Both KFPs and SC items show promise as better methods for assessing investigatory and analytic thinking.

In-training examinations

In-training examinations typically use MCQ-type test items. Generally given annually, these tests evaluate residents' knowledge of basic sciences and specialty-specific clinical problems. Using the exam results, residents and their teachers can determine strengths and weaknesses in knowledge, to measure their growth from year to year and to compare residents' performance on a national level.

In-training exams are often abbreviated versions of the exam used for certification, whereby residents are able to familiarize themselves with the specialty board examination. For some specialties, in-training examination results for an individual resident can predict reasonably well his or her chance of passing the subsequent specialty board certification exam.[40, 41]

Oral examinations

During standardized oral examinations, a trained physician examiner questions the resident about realistic patient cases. These exams typically last about 90 minutes. During this time, the examiner presents a case scenario and clinical problem. Cases represent the patients a resident or independent physician would see in his or her practice. The resident describes how he or she would manage the patient. Throughout the resident's answer, the examiner asks questions, digging into the resident's clinical reasoning. Each scenario typically takes three to five minutes.

Many of the ABMS Member Boards also use oral examinations to test physicians for initial certification. Each case is scored, and a final score is derived by combining all scores or by determining pass/fail for each case or all scenarios combined.

Residency programs also use mock orals, which are like practice sessions for the board oral exams. These get the residents familiar with the format of the board exam. Mock oral exams are difficult for residency programs to create as much expertise is needed to create and examine residents. Additionally, grading the residents objectively can be challenging. Even with faculty examiner training, results from studies exploring the relationship between trainees' communication skills and oral examination scores are mixed.[42, 43]

Simulations

Medical educators can use simulations to assess the application of medical knowledge during a clinical performance that closely resembles reality. Simulations provide a close-to-real-life scenario in which educators can observe how residents manage clinical problems and use their clinical reasoning. They are also an opportunity for residents to receive real-time feedback so that they can correct mistakes.

Increasingly, simulations are used for instruction, practice, and formative performance assessment with feedback and reflection. Rarely do simulations assess knowledge in isolation from other competencies. At best, simulations allow educators to evaluate the application of knowledge in medical decision-making. Multiple formats are available, including standardized patients, clinical team simulations, and sophisticated simulator mannequins. Trained observers assess performance using standardizing checklists that, in part, may focus on appropriate recall and application of medical knowledge in the simulation scenario.[44, 45, 46]

Conclusion

A distinctive, ever-expanding knowledge base defines the profession of medicine. Competency in medical knowledge is defined not only by what one knows, but also by how this knowledge is used in the service of patients and populations. Medical knowledge must be learned in ways that make this knowledge available in memory when needed to solve clinical problems.

Decades of research have advanced our understanding of how knowledge is acquired, recalled, and applied in clinical reasoning to make correct diagnoses and optimize management plans. Appreciation of this body of research can serve as a framework for making curricular, teaching, and assessment decisions to promote competence in medical knowledge.

Key curricular considerations include linking the preclinical curriculum to clinically relevant examples, teaching reading strategies that reinforce a knowledge base organized around the clinical context from which it will be triggered and retrieved for use, and promoting learners' accountability for knowing, explaining, reasoning, and revealing uncertainties that, when addressed, will strengthen knowledge stores and engage lifelong learning habits.

Innovative Approaches, Models, and Assessment Tools for Teaching and Assessing Medical Knowledge

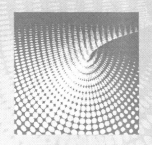

CONTENTS

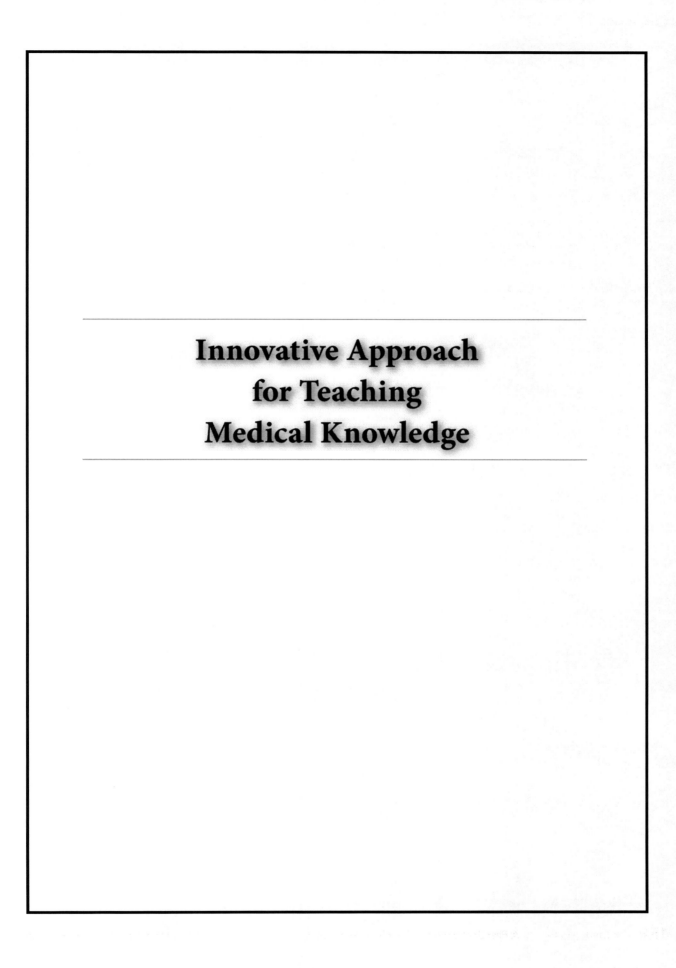

Innovative Approach
for Teaching
Medical Knowledge

Tuesday School: Redesign of Residency Program Core Curriculum

Our inpatient core curriculum was previously delivered through a traditional noon conference lecture series. Resident attendance and attention was erratic, faculty preparation was variable; learner preparation and accountability for material taught was negligible. Resident performance on the In-service Training Examination and the American Board of Internal Medicine Board Examination was flagging.

Curricular description

This year, we replaced noon conferences with "Tuesday School," a dedicated half day of curricular programming. The year is divided into three unequal trimesters:

- **Block I (June–September):** Multidisciplinary fundamentals in inpatient medicine

- **Block II (October–April):** Discipline specific blocks in sub-specialty medicine

- **Block III (May–June):** Multidisciplinary analysis of complex clinical cases

In developing the first trimester schedule, we encouraged faculty to design curriculum to address three areas:

- Specific core skill sets (i.e. interpretation of electrocardiograms, arterial blood gasses, chest X-rays, running codes, facilitating family meetings)

- Basic topics, including discipline-specific approaches to the focused history and physical

for resident-level learners (i.e. approach to anemia, managing pain, approach to the addicted patient, abdominal pain, GI bleeding, the neurologic exam, approach to chest pain, the cardiac exam, fluid and electrolyte management)

- Broad overarching conceptual frameworks for each disciplines (i.e. the lung as pump, microbes and defense, cardiac hemodynamics, the kidney's role in regulating acid-base balance).

First trimester topics will be taught on an annual repeat cycle with second and third year residents serving as co-teachers alongside subspecialist faculty.

In the second trimester, subspecialty disciplines (cardiology, infectious disease, hematology/ oncology, nephrology, rheumatology, gastroenterology, pulmonology, endocrinology, and neurology) have a dedicated one-month long block or half-block.

Each month-long "mini-course" includes a resident-led journal club session on an important contemporary article regarding the focus subspecialty discipline. This allows us to integrate our evidence-based medicine curriculum into our core didactics. Faculty members are encouraged to include sessions on cross-cutting themes related to interpersonal skills and communication as well as systems-based practice.

The hematology-oncology block included, for example, a palliative care session with role play practice on discussions of advance directives. The cardiology block included a session on our institution's approach to improving performance in the Joint Commission's core quality measures for the care of patients with acute coronary syndromes and congestive heart failure. The nephrology block included a discussion of racial disparities in the care of patients with end stage renal disease. Topics in the second trimester will be taught on a two-year repeat cycle.

In the third trimester, sessions are organized around the evaluation and management of complex cases. Cases from our own institution and from published case reports are formulated into small group exercises. After wrestling with the case independently for an hour, learners engage with a panel of subspecialty faculty who discuss the case from their own disciplinary perspectives. Two cases are discussed in each four-hour afternoon session. All three cross-cutting themes—evidence-based medicine, interpersonal skills and communication, and systems-based practice—are woven into the case formulations. Cases in the third trimester will be novel each year.

Central to the success of the curriculum is protecting time for the residents to attend the sessions. Clinical coverage for the hospital during the four-hour weekly conference is provided by our hospitalist program. Residents sign out their pagers to the hospitalists who (with the help of a physicians' assistant) cross-cover on the floors take all the new admissions during the conference.

Resident preparation for teaching sessions is expected; relevant reading material for the conferences is available electronically and linked to the residency program online calendar.

Faculty development

Faculty members were convened twice in the planning phase for the pilot year. Core educational principles were developed collaboratively and curricular ideas exchanged between disciplines. The Tuesday School curriculum director then met individually with core faculty from each discipline to outline the overall syllabus and plan individual teaching sessions.

Concentrated blocks of educational time push faculty to move beyond lecture and employ adult learning theory in their teaching plans. Faculty were encouraged to plan sessions that did not stop with the transmission of an idea, but rather invited learners to "do something" with the material. They were encouraged to design around real cases whenever possible and use a variety of teaching methods and to minimize lecture, including small group exercises, role play, games, debate, video, simulation and skill practice, patient interviews.

In this pilot year, we also convened faculty again in the spring to hear about their experience and plan for the year ahead.

Program evaluation and improvement

Resident attendance at Tuesday School is tracked weekly and compares very favorably to our previous noon conference evaluation rates. Residents evaluate each Tuesday School session for the relevance of the content, the degree of interaction among learners, and the ability to identify useful "take home points." Sessions to date have been highly evaluated with overall mean scores on a 5-point Likert scale of 4.5. Faculty teachers receive feedback from the evaluation forms within one month of their teaching. We have convened an advisory board of residents that has met quarterly for mid-course evaluation and feedback; we have solicited large group feedback and mid-course evaluation from residents at large through regularly scheduled house officer meetings. Mid-year formative feedback was solicited during the pilot year from residents and faculty by survey. The survey included measures of the perceived quality of the learning environment and commitment to self-directed learning within the residency as a whole.

Resident medical knowledge is regularly assessed (at the end of each block) using test questions from the MKSAP Board Review series. Ultimately, we hope to see improvement in resident performance on standardized tests such as the In-Training Exam and the American Board of Internal Medicine certification exam, though we recognize that any improvement in scores will be difficult to attribute directly to the impact of the intervention given the non-experimental design of the intervention.

Contact: Maren Batalden, MD MPH, associate program director, internal medicine residency program, Cambridge Health Alliance. *mbatalden@challiance.org*

Models and Assessment Tools for Teaching and Assessing Medical Knowledge

Figure
2.1

General Competency Evaluation

Bridgeport Hospital Department of Internal Medicine Resident Evaluation
*Please grade using expectations for trainees at that PGY level; Narrative comments are highly encouraged (2nd page)

Resident's General Competencies - Global Evaluations												
Resident's Name				**PGY level:**								
Period of Observation				**Rotation:**								

General Competencies	Evaluation (please circle – see scale below)											
Patient Care	**Grade**										**Comments**	
Data acquisition and organization	1	2	3	4	5	6	7	8	9	n/a		
Defines problems	1	2	3	4	5	6	7	8	9	n/a		
Develops and carries out management plans	1	2	3	4	5	6	7	8	9	n/a		
Educates patients & families	1	2	3	4	5	6	7	8	9	n/a		
Written communication: H&P, SOAP, DC summaries	1	2	3	4	5	6	7	8	9	n/a		
Verbal communication	1	2	3	4	5	6	7	8	9	n/a		
Physical examination skills	1	2	3	4	5	6	7	8	9	n/a		
Provides comprehensive, holistic care	1	2	3	4	5	6	7	8	9	n/a		
Medical Knowledge												
Systematic reasoning skills	1	2	3	4	5	6	7	8	9	n/a		
Knowledge – breadth and application	1	2	3	4	5	6	7	8	9	n/a		
Practice Based Learning and Improvement												
Uses evidence from scientific studies to guide care	1	2	3	4	5	6	7	8	9	n/a		
Uses information technology to guide care	1	2	3	4	5	6	7	8	9	n/a		
Teaching (peers) skills	1	2	3	4	5	6	7	8	9	n/a		
Interpersonal and Communication Skills												
Empathetic relationships with patients	1	2	3	4	5	6	7	8	9	n/a		
Listens carefully to patients	1	2	3	4	5	6	7	8	9	n/a		
Sensitivity to gender, culture, age and disability issues	1	2	3	4	5	6	7	8	9	n/a		
Professionalism												
Interact with other health care professionals	1	2	3	4	5	6	7	8	9	n/a		
Timeliness	1	2	3	4	5	6	7	8	9	n/a		
Respects patient autonomy and patient's rights	1	2	3	4	5	6	7	8	9	n/a		
Systems-Based Practice												
Utilizes systems resources efficiently	1	2	3	4	5	6	7	8	9	n/a		
Practices cost-effective care	1	2	3	4	5	6	7	8	9	n/a		
Patient advocate	1	2	3	4	5	6	7	8	9	n/a		
Overall Assessment	**1**	**2**	**3**	**4**	**5**	**6**	**7**	**8**	**9**			

Evaluator Name:	Date:	Evaluation Scale:
		Unsatisfactory performance or often falls short of expectations: 1-3
NOTE: It is the resident's responsibility to present these forms to their attendings on the Monday of the last week of each rotation so that they can be filled out and discussed by Friday. Completed, signed forms should then be brought by residents to Elsa Riccio in the Department of Medicine		**Usually meets expectations or always meets expectations: 4-6**
		Exceeds Expectations: 7-9
		n/a = not able to assess, didn't assess

Figure
2.1

General Competency Evaluation (cont.)

General Competencies
Minimum Program Requirements Language

The residency program must evaluate residents' competencies in the 6 areas below. Toward this end, programs must define the specific knowledge, skills, and attitudes required and provide educational experiences as needed in order for their residents to demonstrate:

Patient Care that is compassionate, appropriate, and effective for the treatment of health problems and the promotion of health

Medical Knowledge about established and evolving biomedical, clinical, and cognate (e.g. epidemiological and social-behavioral) sciences and the application of this knowledge to patient care

Practice-Based Learning and Improvement that involves investigation and evaluation of their own patient care, appraisal and assimilation of scientific evidence, and improvements in patient care

Interpersonal and Communication Skills that result in effective information exchange and teaming with patients, their families, and other health professionals

Professionalism, as manifested through a commitment to carrying out professional responsibilities, adherence to ethical principles, and sensitivity to a diverse patient population

Systems-Based Practice, as manifested by actions that demonstrate an awareness of and responsiveness to the larger context and system of health care and the ability to effectively call on system resources to provide care that is of optimal value

Additional Comments:

Evaluator (sign):	**Resident (sign):**	**Date:**

BASIC PROCEDURAL COMPETENCY					
	With Supervision	With Minimal Supervision		With Supervision	With Minimal Supervision
Comments:			**Comments:**		

Source: Bridgeport Hospital Web site: www.bridgeporthospital.org/gme. Internal Medicine program. Reprinted with permission.

     A Practical Guide to Teaching and Assessing the ACGME Core Competencies, Second Edition

Figure 2.2	**Evaluation of Medical Record-Keeping and Chart-Stimulated Recall Exercise**

Trainee: _____ **Date:** _____

1. **The trainee had addressed active patients' problems.**

    ❑ Unsatisfactory   ❑ Satisfactory   ❑ Superior

2. **The trainee had addressed inactive but substantiative chronic health problems.**

    ❑ Unsatisfactory   ❑ Satisfactory   ❑ Superior

3. **The trainee had integrated psychosocial aspects of care, including discharge planning.**

    ❑ Unsatisfactory   ❑ Satisfactory   ❑ Superior

4. **The trainee had addressed nutritional issues.**

    ❑ Unsatisfactory   ❑ Satisfactory   ❑ Superior

Source: Bridgeport Hospital website: www.bridgeporthospital.org/gme. Internal Medicine program. Reprinted with permission.

Figure 2.2	**Evaluation of Medical Record-Keeping and Chart-Stimulated Recall Exercise (cont.)**

Trainee: _____ Date: _____

1. The intern and resident were identified on the chart's spine and in the orders.

   ❑ Unsatisfactory   ❑ Satisfactory   ❑ Superior

2. The history and physical (for intern) or green sheet (for resident) was present and enumerated patients' problems, differential diagnoses, diagnostic plan and therapeutic plan.

   ❑ Unsatisfactory   ❑ Satisfactory   ❑ Superior

3. Notes were timed and dated.

   ❑ Unsatisfactory   ❑ Satisfactory   ❑ Superior
   (< 50% of notes)   (50–75% of notes)   (> 75% of notes)

4. A running problem-list was kept on the inside-cover of the chart.

   ❑ Unsatisfactory   ❑ Satisfactory   ❑ Superior

5. SOAP notes emphasized a problem-based approach to assessment/of plan:

   ❑ Unsatisfactory   ❑ Satisfactory   ❑ Superior

6. Disposition/Functional and nutritional issues were included in notes.

   ❑ Unsatisfactory   ❑ Satisfactory   ❑ Superior
   (< 25% of notes)   (25–75% of notes)   (> 75% of notes)

7. Complaints present on admission are sufficiently discussed and "dealt with" in subsequent progress notes.

   ❑ Unsatisfactory   ❑ Satisfactory   ❑ Superior

Source: Bridgeport Hospital website: www.bridgeporthospital.org/gme. Internal Medicine program. Reprinted with permission.

     A Practical Guide to Teaching and Assessing the ACGME Core Competencies, Second Edition

References

1. Merriam-Webster's Online Dictionary. *www.merriam-webster.com/dictionary/knowledge*. Accessed April 14, 2010.

2. Custers EJFM, Regehr G, Norman GR. Mental representations of medical diagnostic knowledge: a review. *Acad Med.* 1996;71:S55–61, S55.

3. ACGME. *www.acgme.org/outcome/comp/ GeneralCompetenciesStandards21307.pdf*. Accessed March 23, 2010.

4. Eva KW, Cunnington JPW, Reiter HI, Keane DR, Norman GR. How can I know what I don't know? Poor self-assessment in a well-defined domain. *Adv Health Sci Educ.* 2004;9:211–224.

5. Regehr G, Eva KW. Self-assessment, self-direction, and the self-regulating professional. *Clin Orthop.* 2006;449:34–38.

6. Eva KW, Regehr G. "I'll never play professional football" and other fallacies of self-assessment. *J Contin Educ Health Prof.* 2008;28:14–19.

7. Eva KW, Regehr G. Knowing when to look it up: a new conception of self-assessment ability. *Acad Med.* 2007;82(10 Suppl):S81–S84.

8. Moulton CA, Regehr G, Mylopoulos M, MacRae HM. Slowing down when you should: a new model of expert judgment. *Acad Med.* 2007;82:S109–S116.

9. Institute of Medicine. *Crossing the Quality Chasm: A New Health System for the Twenty-first Century*. Washington, DC: National Academies Press; 2001.

10. Norman GR. Research in clinical reasoning: past history and current trends. *Med Educ.* 2005;39:418-27, 420–421.

11. Elstein AS, Shulman LS, Sprafka SA. *Medical Problem Solving: An Analysis of Clinical Reasoning*. Cambridge, MA: Harvard University Press; 1978.

12. Barrows HS, Norman GR, Neufeld VR, Feightner JW. The clinical reasoning process of randomly selected physicians in general medical practice. *Clin Invest Med.* 1982;5:49–56.

13. Ericsson KA. Deliberate practice and the acquisitions and maintenance of expert performance in medicine and related domains. *Acad Med.* 2004;79:S1–S12.

14. Neufeld VR, Norman GR, Barrows HS, Feightner JW. Clinical problem-solving by medical students: a longitudinal and cross-sectional analysis. *Med Educ.* 1981;15:315–322.

15. Schmidt HG, Norman GR, Boshuizen HPA. A cognitive perspective on medical expertise: theory implications. *Acad Med.* 1990;65:611–621.

16. Barrows HS, Feltovich PJ. The clinical reasoning process. *Med Educ.* 2005;39:107–112.

17. Patel VL, Glaser R, Arocha JF. Cognition and expertise: acquisition of medical competence. *Clin Invest Med.* 2000;23:256–260.

18. Eva KW, Hatala RM, Leblanc VR, Brooks LR. Teaching from the clinical reasoning literature: combined reasoning strategies help novice diagnosticians overcome misleading information. *Med Educ.* 2007;41:1152–1158.

19. Bowen JL. Educational strategies to promote clinical diagnostic reasoning. *NEJM.* 2006;355:2217–2225.

20. Irby D, Wilkerson L. Educational innovations in academic medicine and environmental trends. *J Gen Intern Med.* 2003;18:370–376.

21. Muller JH, Jain S, Loeser H, Irby DM. Lessons learned about integrating a medical school curriculum: perceptions of students, faculty, and curriculum leaders. *Med Educ.* 2008;42:778–785.

22. Vidic B, Weitlauf HM. Horizontal and vertical integration of academic disciplines in the medical school curriculum. *Clin Anat.* 2002;15:233–235.

23. Schmidt HG, Machiels-Bongaerts M, Hermans H, Cate JT, Venekamp R, Boshuizen HP. The development of diagnostic competence: comparison of a problem-based, an integrated, and a conventional medical curriculum. *Acad Med.* 1996;71:658–664.

24. Yudkowsky R, Otaki J, Lowenstein T, Riddle J, Nishigori H, Bordage G. A hypothesis-driven physical examination learning and assessment procedure for medical students: initial validity evidence. *Med Educ*. 2009; 43:729–740.

25. Hasnain M, Bordage G, Connell KJ, Sinacore JM. History-taking behaviors associated with diagnostic competence of clerks: an exploratory study. *Acad Med*. 2001;76:S14–S17.

26. Bordage G. Elaborated knowledge: a key to successful diagnostic thinking. *Acad Med*. 1994;69:883–885.

27. de Virgilio C, Stabile BE, Lewis RJ, Brayack C. Significantly improved American Board of Surgery in-training examination scores associated with weekly assigned reading and preparatory examinations. *Arch Surg*. 2003;138:1195–1197.

28. Kerfoot BP, DeWolf WC, Masser BA, Church PA, Federman DD. Spaced education improves the retention of clinical knowledge by medical students: a randomized controlled trial. *Med Educ*. 2007;41:23–31.

29. Neher JO, Gordon KC, Meyer B, Stevens N. A five-step microskills model of clinical teaching. *J Am Board Fam Prac*. 1992;5:419–424.

30. Wolpaw TM, Wolpaw D, Papp KK. SNAPPS: a learner-centered model for outpatient education. *Acad Med*. 2003;78:893–898.

31. Wolpaw T, Papp KK, Bordage G. Using SNAPPS to facilitate the expression of clinical reasoning and uncertainties: a randomized comparison group trial. *Acad Med*. 2009;84:517–524.

32. Holmboe ES, Lipner R, Greiner A. Assessing quality of care: knowledge matters. *JAMA*. 2008;299:338–340.

33. Srinivasan M, Hwang JC, West D, Yellowlees PM. Assessment of clinical skills using simulator technologies. *Acad Psych*. 2006;30:505–515.

34. Tugwell P, Dok C. Medical Record Review. In: Neufeld VR, Norman GR, eds. *Assessing Clinical Competence*. New York, NY: Springer-Verlag New York, Inc.; 1985.

35. Goulet F, Jacques A, Gagnon R, Racette P, Sieber W. Assessment of family physicians' performance using patient charts. *Eval Health Prof*. 2007;30:376–392.

36. Epstein RM. Assessment in medical education. *NEJM*. 2007;356:387–396.

37. Case S, Swanson D. *Constructing Written Test Questions for the Basic and Clinical Sciences*. 3rd ed. Philadelphia, PA: National Board of Medical Examiners; 2000.

38. Farmer EA, Page G. A practical guide to assessing clinical decision-making skills using the key features approach. *Med Educ*. 2005;39:1188–1194.

39. Charlin B, Brailovsky C, Roy L, Goulet F, van der Vleuten C. The Script Concordance Test: a tool to assess the reflective clinician. *Teach Learn Med*. 2000;12:189–195.

40. Babbott SF, Beasley BW, Hinchey KT, Blotzer JW, Holmboe ES. The predictive validity of the internal medicine in-training examination. *Am J Med*. 2007;120:735–740.

41. Leigh TM, Johnson TP, Pisacano NJ. Predictive validity of the American board of family practice in-training examination. *Acad Med*. 1990;65:454–457.

42. Leigh TM, Johnson TP, Pisacano NJ. Predictive validity of the American board of family practice in-training examination. *Acad Med*. 1990;65:454–457.

43. Rowland-Morin PA, Burchard KW, Garb JL, Coe NP. Influence of effective communication by surgery students on their oral examination scores. *Acad Med*. 1991;66:169–171.

44. Issenberg SF, McGaghie WC, Petrusa ER, Gordon DL, Scalese RJ. Features and uses of high-fidelity medical simulations that lead to effective learning: a BEME systematic review. *Med Teach*. 2005;27:10–28.

45. Kneebone R. Evaluating clinical simulations for learning procedural skills: a theory-based approach. *Acad Med*. 2005;80:549–553.

46. Ogen PE, Cobbs LS, Howell MR, Sibbitt SJB, DiPette DJ. Clinical simulation: importance to the internal medicine educational mission. *Am J Med*. 2007;120:820–824.

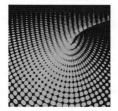

Patient Care

Ruth H. Nawotniak, MS, C-TAGME
Eugene C. Corbett, Jr., MD, FACP

One of the challenges in documenting any individual core competency is that they are all interrelated in some manner. For instance, you cannot evaluate practice-based learning without understanding the impact of systems-based practice on how the physician practices. Similarly, it is difficult to evaluate communication without evaluating professionalism and medical knowledge. The competency of patient care, then, overlaps with all other competencies. It is the lynchpin of a physician's education and the reason for training well-rounded physicians: to ensure patients are receiving the best treatment possible.

Linking UME and GME Patient Care Curricula

The foundation of residents' patient care skills is laid during their medical school experience. They carry this knowledge with them from the undergraduate medical education (UME) level to the GME level. Because UME and GME curricula are so closely linked, the competency goals for UME must set the stage for the expectations students will have to meet during residency training as set forth by the ACGME. The ACGME's six core competencies encompass a higher level of clinical development, whereas those for UME should establish a strong base for further development. Linking the UME competencies to GME competencies bridges the gap between UME and GME models for clinical competency.

The 12 general clinical competency domains

The American Association of Medical Colleges (AAMC) Taskforce on the Clinical Skills Education of Medical Students developed 12 general competencies of patient care that all students should master so that they can go on to master the ACGME competencies.[1] The 12 clinical method competencies are:

1. Professionalism

2. Patient engagement and communication

3.   Application of scientific knowledge and method

4.   History-taking

5.   Mental and physical examination

6.   Clinical testing

7.   Clinical procedures

8.   Clinical information management

9.   Diagnosis

10.   Clinical intervention

11.   Prognosis

12.   Putting care in practical context

In designing patient care experiences, educational programs should include each of these 12 competency domains in their teaching and assessment methodologies. Students receive more advanced training in each of these areas during residency. Figure 3.1 shows how the 12 AAMC competencies align with the ACGME's six core competencies.

| Figure 3.1 | UME/GME Clinical Competencies | |

UME competency	GME competency
1. Professionalism	1. Professionalism
2. Patient engagement and communication	2. Interpersonal and communication skills
3. Application of scientific knowledge and method	3. Medical knowledge
4. History-taking	4. Patient care
5. Mental and physical examination	
6. Clinical testing	
7. Clinical procedures	
8. Clinical information management	
9. Diagnosis	
10. Clinical intervention	
11. Prognosis	
12. Putting care in practical context	5. Systems-based practice
*Self-directed learning and self-assessment	6. Practice-based learning and improvement

*The AAMC lists "Self directed learning and self-assessment" as a thirteenth domain that should be integrated into each of the 12 other competencies.

Source: Recommendations for clinical skills curricula for undergraduate medical education. AAMC website. 2005. https://services.aamc.org/publications/index.cfm?fuseaction=Product.displayForm&prd_id=141&prv_id=165 (or www.aamc.org/meded/clinicalskills/). Reprinted with permission.

To facilitate the development of patient care educational activities, the AAMC grouped the 12 competencies into four subcategories and further defined each of the clinical competencies.

Competencies 1–3

At the beginning of clinical education, students typically have experience in the first three of the AAMC's competencies. Through specifically designed educational strategies, clinical education at all levels should provide opportunities for learners to continually develop and apply professionalism and evidence-based scientific and communication skills within the context of the clinical care of the patient. These strategies can include both simulated and real patient scenarios.

1. **Professionalism:** Appreciate the nature of patient care and exemplify professional and ethical behavior when providing care. Students or residents should demonstrate respect, accountability, scholarship based on evidence from the literature, integrity, selflessness, compassion, and confidentiality. The learner should also collaborate with interdisciplinary teams.

2. **Patient engagement and communication:** Develop a patient–physician relationship by drawing on interpersonal communication skills to engage the patient in order to gather information from the patient and to provide guidance, education, and support.

3. **Application of scientific knowledge and method:** Apply scientific knowledge and method to clinical problem-solving.

Competencies 4–8

Competency goals 4–8 represent discrete individual clinical activities that physicians perform in any medical encounter:

4. **History taking:** Take both a focused and a comprehensive clinical history

5. **Mental and physical examination:** Perform both types of exams

6. **Clinical testing:** Choose, justify, and interpret clinical tests and imaging

7. **Clinical procedures:** Understand and perform a variety of basic clinical procedures

8. **Clinical information management:** Record, present, research, critique, and manage clinical information

Clinical history-taking and physical examination skills are best practiced, observed, and evaluated in the real clinical setting, although medical educators can create high-fidelity clinical settings using well-trained standardized patients particularly in problem-oriented, clinical circumstances. Medical students and residents can initially learn clinical testing and procedural skills in simulated settings. For certification purposes, residents must demonstrate such skills in the actual patient care setting in order to ensure readiness for independent clinical care responsibilities. For clinical information management skills, Web-based learning and performance evaluation opportunities provide initial and ongoing adjunctive educational activities.

Competencies 9–11

Competency goals 9–11 reflect the main reasons patients seek medical care, identifying what clinical problems actually or potentially exist, what can be done to prevent or treat them, and what will happen to the patient with or without intervention. Students must integrate the first eight goals in order to meet goals 9, 10, and 11. These goals are defined as:

9. **Diagnosis:** Ascertain and explain clinical problems in terms of pathogenesis, to develop basic differential diagnoses, and to learn and demonstrate clinical reasoning and problem identification.

10. **Clinical intervention:** Understand, select, and implement clinical interventions in the natural history of disease, including basic preventive, curative, and palliative care strategies.

11. **Prognosis:** Formulate a prognosis about the future events of an individual's health and illness trajectory based upon an understanding of the patient, the natural history of disease, and known intervention alternatives. Competency in clinical prognostication is required in order to anticipate individualized healthcare outcomes and planning for future patient care needs.

Competency 12

The twelfth and final competency reflects that in providing care, the physician must also consider the individual patient's life circumstance when making clinical decisions.

12. **Put care in practical context.** The ability to provide clinical care within the context of a patient's age, gender, family, culture, and religious perspective, and personal preferences and economic circumstances. This also includes consideration of ethical, moral, and legal perspectives as well as the resources and limitations of the healthcare system.

The Competency Perspectives

There are two clinical competency domains. The first comprises the general clinical competencies that apply to all physicians, and the second involves competencies that pertain to specialty practice. For example, the clinical skill of engaging and communicating with a patient, or the skill of performing a basic physical examination, is expected of any physician and falls into the first category. On the other hand, the skill of treating schizophrenia or of performing a coronary bypass procedure is usually specialty-based. Thus, the teaching, learning, and assessment of clinical performance ability in graduate medical education (GME) must include both of these perspectives.

Because patient care is the basis of our profession, all other competencies should improve patient care. The ACGME requires residents to "provide patient care that is compassionate, appropriate and effective for the treatment of health problems and the promotion of health."[2] Some specific examples follow.

There are several program definitions of patient care. The Educational Outcomes Service Group at Bridgeport Hospital in Connecticut has assigned a simple statement to each competency that sums up the essence of that competency.[3] These statements are shown in Figure 3.2.

Figure 3.2	**Essence of the Competencies**

- Patient Care
- Medical Knowledge
- Practice-Based Learning and Improvement
- Interpersonal and Communication Skills
- Professionalism
- Systems-Based Practice

- What You Do
- What You Know
- How You Get Better
- How You Interact with Others
- How You Act
- How You Work Within the System

Source: Bridgeport Hospital. Reprinted with permission.

Additionally, an article published by the Association of Directors of Anatomic and Surgical Pathology (ADASP), titled "Curriculum content and evaluation of resident competency in anatomic pathology: a proposal," the authors define the competency of patient care for pathology residents as the following:

Residents must show diagnostic competence and that they can provide appropriate and effective consultation with pathology services.[4] In meeting the patient care competency in the context of neuropathology training programs, patient care is provided by recognizing the personal responsibility of the resident to provide clear, accurate, and timely consultations in the context of a medical team.[5]

Many surgical programs further define patient care by developing subcompetencies that residents must meet. One of these—technical and invasive procedure training—is addressed using skills labs. Dunnington at Southern Illinois University has developed a curriculum for first-, second-, and third-year residents. This curriculum prepares residents for operating room

experiences by certifying trainees in certain procedures before they perform the procedure on a patient. The program utilizes models, virtual reality training devices, cadaver parts, and animal laboratories to evaluate residents' skills.[6]

Other specialties may also create a patient care curriculum based on their particular subcompetencies. For example, pediatric-specific components of each competency have been developed by representatives of the American Board of Pediatrics (ABP), the Residency Review Committee for Pediatrics, the Association of Pediatric Program Directors, and a resident representative. The ABP website lists suggested tools to evaluate each core competency, along with a glossary of the tools (see *www.abp.org*). Check your specialty's board and/or program director associations to find out whether subcompetencies for your specialty have been developed.

The ACGME, in the *Program Director Guide to the Common Program Requirements*, discusses the progression of learning throughout the gamut of patient care—from common to nonroutine diagnoses and from uncomplicated to complex and unexpected procedures. The organization notes that throughout the learning process, the resident is aware of the needs and concerns of the patient while providing compassionate care.[7]

Building a Curriculum for Patient Care

When developing your curriculum, you will find more than adequate opportunity for not only teaching the competency of patient care, but also evaluating it. For example, every patient encounter and every case conference is a hands-on setting for teaching patient care. The patient care competency is usually the first addressed by medical educators when designing the curriculum because it is the most readily identifiable within the existing educational structure.

Patient care is closely tied to patient safety. The link between patient safety and patient care is being integrated into curricula. For example, to preserve patient safety while training new physicians, surgical educators developed a patient care subcompetency for surgical programs called *technical and invasive procedure training.*

In the surgical field, innovators develop new surgical tools at an astonishing rate, and residents and independent surgeons must become proficient in using these tools for patient care. Most notably are laparoscopic instruments that allow surgeons to enter patients and perform specific procedures through small holes rather than large incisions. Training residents on how to manipulate these instruments prior to using them on an actual patient promotes quality patient care. The ACGME requires programs to provide a skills lab for resident training, and skills lab experience is now a

part of the surgical curriculum. The American Board of Surgery now requires residents applying for initial certification to take an online course and a skills lab assessment in laparoscopic surgery.

Specific Teaching Strategies for Patient Care

The patient care competency is taught during everyday interactions between faculty members and residents in the operating room, wards, and clinics.[6] The challenge is to capture and document these interactions as teaching and learning activities.

These interactions occur with both formal and informal structures in patient and nonpatient settings. Patient settings include, but are not limited to, the following activities:

- The day-to-day bedside care of the patient

- Interactions with nursing and ancillary staff members regarding patient needs and treatment plans

- Rounds

- Outpatient practices

- Operative procedures

Nonpatient settings include, but are not limited to, the following activities:

- Skills labs

- Didactic lectures

- Case conferences

- Small group discussions

- Patient sign-out activities

- Journal clubs

- Interactions between attending and resident physicians to discuss patient treatment plans and patient care activities

Rounds and observation

One way to document resident competency in patient care is to observe residents during daily rounding activities. Bridgeport Hospital has established three types of rounds to provide opportunities for both the day-to-day management of patients and observation of residents caring for patients.[3]

- Attending work rounds provide a continuing opportunity for residents and attending physicians to round together on teaching services, including those in the ICUs.

- Teaching attending rounds are more formal case presentations performed at the bedside with a teaching faculty member, and they focus on one domain of performance. These can be independent of the attending work rounds or incorporated into them.

- Program directors' rounds involve the program director and residents meeting for an evaluation of trainees' oral presentation and medical reasoning skills and to conduct chart-stimulated recall exercises.

Multidisciplinary rounds can also be structured as a teaching opportunity for patient care. Multidisciplinary rounds bring together the medical disciplines involved in total patient care, along with supporting hospital services such as pathology, radiology, nutrition, and pharmacy. This creates an opportunity for clinical specialties that normally have no direct patient interaction to be involved in patient care.

Pediatric residency programs have completed research on inpatient family-centered care that incorporates a multidisciplinary concept and family involvement. Healthcare providers participating in this model of patient care report increased levels of satisfaction because they are able to participate in timely patient care discussions. Patients' families also report higher levels of satisfaction because they have more input into the patient care given. Additionally, family-centered care models are associated with a clearer understanding of patients' treatment plans,[8] and an improved working relationship among all healthcare providers.[9]

Sign-out and morning report

The sign-out activity is another excellent opportunity for teaching patient care. Historically, morning report (MR) has served the following purposes:

- Education

- Evaluation of residents and services

- Adverse event reporting

- Discussions of nonmedical issues

- Forum for social interactions (Stiles article)

MR is an example of an existing system that can provide multiple teaching experiences for patient care. During MR, faculty members evaluate residents' ability to work through case-based presentations, assess junior residents' basic knowledge and patient care skills and senior residents' decision-making processes, and expand specific cases beyond patient care to include aspects of systems-based practice.

Stiles et al. developed a morning report modification that most primary care residency programs use. Originally designed as a night float handoff process for residents to discuss consults and new admissions, the exercise has evolved into a learning experience on continuity of care. Residents give patient information in an evidence-based format and review relevant radiology reports and appropriate literature.[10]

A subsequent article by Stiles describes the further development and refinement of this post-night float MR process. Residents lead the activity, and they are responsible for presenting the cases, gathering the data, and managing the discussion.

Banks presents an effective way to introduce evidence-based medicine into patient care practices. He invited a librarian to MR who performed an online literature search of the topic presented during MR. The results of the search were disseminated at the end of the case presentation. The results of his study showed that the inclusion of the literature search resulted in a shortened length of stay and lower hospital charges when compared with the study controls.[11]

SBAR and patient safety techniques

As previously stated, patient safety is directly related to patient care. Because The Joint Commission has increased its scrutiny of patient safety, many hospitals are implementing systemwide patient safety measures. There are ample opportunities to adapt current techniques and tools used for patient safety and incorporate them into resident training.

One such tool is SBAR, which stands for situation background assessment recommendation. SBAR provides a framework for communicating important points of information, and it can be used in all patient-related communications. It promotes patient care and safety, as the information necessary to making medically appropriate decisions is transferred effectively and efficiently between caregivers. Training in SBAR may consist of a video, reading material, role playing, and a short assessment tool.

Self-reflection/assessment

Resident self-reflection or self-assessment represents another opportunity for meeting the patient care competency. These assessments or self-reflections can focus on the following:

- An individual patient that the resident has cared for and his or her reflection on the care of that patient

- Patient care rendered by someone other than the resident but witnessed by the resident

- Observational writings of the impact of team management on patient care

Branch describes the use of critical incident reports, which are short narrative accounts describing an event that influenced the resident's professional development.[12]

Ambulatory care

Outpatient care represents much of the care delivered worldwide. Educators should not overlook the ambulatory care learning experience when developing a competency-based curriculum. Ferenchick et al. outline the opportunities for evaluating patient care in the ambulatory care setting.[13] They describe a basic three-step process that includes planning, teaching, and reflection. The authors describe strategies for resident learning, including:

- Orienting learners to patients

- Asking learners to present their cases in the exam room

- Using the one-minute preceptor model for giving feedback, described in Chapter 2

- Reflecting on one's teaching to improve effective teaching scripts

The ambulatory care setting offers residents an opportunity to experience patient care in an outpatient situation. This experience will mirror much of their own practice after they complete their training. It is an excellent setting for preceptors to observe residents as they care for patients and provide timely feedback.[13]

Assessment Strategies for Patient Care

As you can imagine, the methods of evaluating resident competence in patient care are as varied as the opportunities for teaching and learning patient care. The ACGME suggests the following list of best methods:

- Standardized patients

- Patient survey

- Global rating

- 360-degree global rating

- Checklist

- Objective structural clinical examination

- Chart-stimulated recall

- Record review

- Simulations and models

- Procedure or case logs

- Portfolios

- Mock orals

Consider the following example which describes one program's methods for teaching, assessing, and evaluating patient care.

In the Southern Illinois University skills lab activity mentioned in the "Teaching strategies" section, Dunnington et al. developed procedure certification programs for the technical and invasive procedure subcompetency. These programs prepare residents for real patient cases. To become certified in laparoscopic cholecystectomies, for example, residents must complete:

- A CD-ROM program that provides an overview of the procedure

- Twenty repetitions of four skills in the laparoscopic box trainer

- Three levels of difficulty on the minimally invasive surgical virtual reality trainer

- Two laparoscopic cholecystectomies using a torso trainer with a porcine liver/gallbladder segment[6]

While performing the laparoscopic cholecystectomies, residents use a performance checklist and the final procedure is videotaped for later review.

The certification program includes evaluation of residents' skills lab activities. Residents cannot perform their first procedure in the operating room until they complete all of the steps for a specific procedure and achieve certification.[6] Educational leaders can reproduce this type of certification program for other surgical or bedside procedures. Medical educators can use this model to teach procedures and to ascertain whether a resident is competent to perform the procedure before treating a live patient.

360-degree evaluations

The 360-degree global evaluation is arguably the most comprehensive evaluation tool for patient care because it incorporates the observations of everyone involved in the healthcare team: faculty members, the patient, nursing staff members, allied health professionals, and resident team members. Faculty members can evaluate residents in the patient care competency using the standard formal method of completing evaluation forms, or they can hold global assessment forums in which the attending physicians and nursing staff evaluate residents through discussions that are recorded and transcribed. The following are examples of the various types of evaluations that can be utilized as part of a 360-degree evaluation.

Patient satisfaction questionnaire

Many programs have adopted a 10-item patient satisfaction questionnaire developed by the American Board of Internal Medicine (ABIM) to assess resident competency in patient care. This questionnaire can also be applied to residents training in other specialties. Ask patients seen by the resident to complete the survey as soon as the appointment or encounter concludes. Some programs have included a picture of the resident to make certain that patients evaluate the residents who treated them.[6]

Ancillary staff evaluations

The nursing staff can complete evaluations of residents' patient care skills and interactions with patients/families. They can comment on effective and ineffective behaviors the resident demonstrated during those interactions. Nurses can also evaluate the ability of the resident to work with the nursing staff and to manage the complexities of the healthcare system.

Programs that include hospital services personnel on patient teams—such as pharmacy, discharge planning, and nutrition—can also be included in the evaluation processes.

Peer evaluations

Some of the most valuable sources for 360-degree evaluations are resident peer evaluations. The University of Buffalo – State University of New York (UB – SUNY) Department of Surgery uses an Internet-based peer evaluation form that junior residents use to rate senior residents. The evaluation focuses on the senior residents' administrative and team management skills and is completed at the end of each rotation. The development of these skills by senior residents is invaluable for effective patient care. Periodically, the senior residents receive the results of these evaluations, and they discuss the evaluations with their mentors during one-on-one meetings. The senior residents meet with the program director and evaluate the junior residents. Rather than completing evaluation forms, the senior residents and program director discuss the junior residents' performance. The program director then gives feedback to the junior residents. All peer evaluation results are reviewed four to six months out of phase. This maintains confidentiality, and encourages honest, objective comments.

Patient care exam

Educators may use patient assessment and management exams to evaluate residents' progress in meeting patient care, medical knowledge, interpersonal and communication skills, and professionalism competencies. This exam uses standardized patient encounters.

A potential variant of the standardized patient involves the formalized use of the "interesting patient" in the emergency department (ED). All of the learners in the ED examine patients with unique clinical findings or presentations. Assuming the patient is willing, that time permits, and that the learners are unaware of the patient's condition, learners can examine and report on the case and be evaluated on their performance.

This process has limitations. The patient is not trained to present in a standardized fashion, and he or she is not a trained educator for the particular disease process. Furthermore, ethical questions are raised in this scenario, such as undue pressure on a patient to participate or the possibility of a breach of confidentiality.[14]

Logbooks

The ADASP Working Group encourages trainees to maintain a logbook detailing complicated cases they managed. They also suggest that residents and fellows keep their presentations and projects. Programs can use these records to document residents' growth and performance year over year. By the end of training, programs can use these documents as evidence of competence and readiness to practice independently.[4]

Checklist evaluations

Use a checklist evaluation in informal rounding situations or in formal assessment situations. During rounds, the faculty member directly observes the resident performing his or her clinical duties. Using a checklist of items or behaviors that the program director determines are critical, the faculty member indicates whether the resident demonstrated those behaviors or items. The items or behaviors are directly observed during a real clinical scenario with all parameters of the delivery of care visible.[14]

A more formal use of a checklist in an assessment situation, developed by the ABIM, is the mini-Clinical Evaluation Exercise (mini-CEX). The mini-CEX is a focused, time-limited, scheduled faculty observation of residents in patient care situations.

The process takes 20–25 minutes to complete and can offer residents feedback by multiple faculty members over a broad range of clinical situations. The structured clinical observation is a similar construct, consisting of limited, structured observations of pediatric residents while performing clinical duties.

As observations take place over an extended period, they will become more comprehensive, giving a better global picture of the resident's performance of patient care. Immediate feedback, both positive and constructive, should follow observation and evaluation.

Observers should also discuss strategies of remediation or correction with residents. The results of the more formal assessment can be used as targets for improvement during the more informal rounding experience.

Mock oral examinations

The mock oral examination process is a more formal method for evaluating the decision-making processes in representative case scenarios of patient care

activities. Typical case conferences or morbidity and mortality conferences often use this process in a more informal manner.

Portfolios

The resident portfolio may be a repository for the written results of resident work efforts, such as self-reflections and evaluations, case studies, patient care logs, procedural logs, presentations, and quality improvement projects. A portfolio can be used as a mechanism for tracking growth in the competencies, with the goal being a mastery of the competencies by a specific time within the training period. Components that may show competency in patient care include:

- Invasive procedure/case logs

- Monthly faculty evaluations

- Direct faculty observation and evaluation of invasive procedures, including obtaining consent, confirming the site, conducting a timeout, and advising patients regarding adverse events or outcomes

- 360-degree evaluations

- Safety training courses

Record review

The Emergency Medicine Consensus Group lists record review as one method of evaluating patient care. This method involves the retrospective review of patient records to assess documentation, resource utilization, and overall patient care by inference from the document.

     A Practical Guide to Teaching and Assessing the ACGME Core Competencies, Second Edition

Coding, billing, and medical–legal feedback can also be extracted. Peers, supervisors, or a computer program can perform these reviews, and medical records or quality improvement personnel can initially screen the charts for review. Use a checklist or standard for the review to minimize subjective judgments and inconsistency between reviewers.

Because there is a proliferation of computerized informatics systems for emergency medicine that have sophisticated chart and documentation analysis capabilities, this process is more efficient and less burdensome for training programs than manual reviews. This assessment tool also may be used to quantify aspects of patient care, such as number of patients seen per shift or number of procedures performed.[14]

Procedural logs/case logs

Although procedural logs/case logs can serve as documentation for the procedures performed, they do not clearly indicate competence in patient care by themselves. However, training programs may establish a threshold of procedures that residents must learn and perform. After learning and performing the specified number of procedures, a faculty member directly observes and assesses the resident performing the procedure.

This assessment determines the resident's level of competency for the mastery of the procedure and for patient care. Educators may also develop threshold numbers for procedures performed as part of skills lab certification activities such as those created by Dunnington et al. and described previously in this chapter.[6]

As a final example, read "Integrating the Accreditation Council for Graduate Medical Education Core Competencies into the Model of the Clinical Practice of Emergency Medicine" by Dane M. Chapman, MD, PhD; Stephen Hayden, MD; et al. This was published in the *Annals of Emergency Medicine* 2004;43(6), p. 756–769.

This article focuses on how emergency medicine has incorporated the competencies into their curricula. The authors have created a model that focuses on various physician tasks and evaluates those activities in terms of levels of competency. The patient care core competency is embedded in all activities described.

Simulation

The use of simulation has become very popular in medical education. It provides residents a safe environment in which to learn technical skills and elements of patient care and patient safety. Use simulation for initial teaching and practice of procedures, testing and assessment opportunities, and remediation.

Simulation should mirror patient care situations and settings. The focus is to provide a learning environment for the resident that closely relates to an actual patient care activity. Incorporate simulation into other teaching and assessment activities including standardized patient encounters or objective structural clinical examinations.

Simulation-based training as a methodology or technique of teaching has several educationally positive attributes. It provides a safe and error-tolerant environment for teaching and practicing skills. Simulation also provides an opportunity for faculty members to give immediate feedback on performance while allowing the educator to focus on and be in control of specific content areas. It also provides a structured educational format that is consistent for all the learners.[15]

This methodology is the basis of the Simulation Module for Assessment of Resident Targeted Event Responses (SMARTER) approach, which utilizes simulation scenarios, along with their measurement tools, to capture resident performance and generate corrective feedback.[15] The SMARTER process consists of the following steps:

1. Select a specific subset of one of the ACGME core competencies.

2. Develop measurable and trainable objectives.

3. Determine a clinical scenario that can accommodate the objectives.

4. Define what skills, knowledge, and attitudes are needed for a good performance.

5. Determine what events in the scenario will allow the resident to display the skills, knowledge, and attitudes that have been defined. Provide technologies and participants as needed to create the scenario and events.

6. Define what responses will be used as objectively observable behaviors.

7. Develop assessment tools that will draw upon the events and skills, knowledge, and attitudes.

Simulation laboratories are typically designed to mirror a patient care environment, using commercially constructed manikins to simulate the patient. The manikin can be programmed to present certain symptoms that the resident would diagnose and treat, and to respond to the treatment. This type of setting also promotes the importance of team training activities.

For example, use a simulation activity to teach and assess trauma resuscitation. Nurses and trauma physicians, both attendings and residents, participate in team training sessions specific to their role and activities during trauma resuscitations.

A simulation session involving all team members follows the initial individual activities. Video tape these simulation sessions and review them with participants as a learning activity. The videotapes can also be used for assessment. A healthcare team training program called TeamSTEPPS has been developed by the Department of Defense that can be used for this activity.[16]

Many programs are developing curriculum that incorporate multiple simulation models, depending upon the competency or skill that is being taught.

Ophthalmology training programs are developing curriculum to assess competency in cataract surgery. They are using a combination of wet laboratories and computer simulation to enhance skills training prior to performing the procedure in the OR. Residents practice specific surgical skills on animals and cadavers in the wet lab and using computer simulation programs.

Faculty members can evaluate a resident's performance as he or she develops skills. When the targeted level of performance is achieved, the residents participate on a rotation during which they perform specific parts of the procedure. This facilitates continued deliberate performance and formative feedback.[17]

Conclusion

The clinical environment in which physician training takes place provides ample opportunity for patient encounters that require patient safety training. Using these encounters to develop a curriculum, resident activities, and methods of assessment that are focused on patient care will allow for the opportunity to assess not only patient care, but also the other five and interrelated ACGME competencies.

Innovative Approaches, Models, and Assessment Tools for Teaching and Assessing Patient Care

CONTENTS

     A Practical Guide to Teaching and Assessing the ACGME Core Competencies, **Second Edition**

Innovative Approaches
for Teaching
Patient Care

Link Core Competencies to National Patient Safety Goals

Every year, The Joint Commission releases its National Patient Safety Goals (NPSG). This begs the following questions: Can your residents name the NPSGs, and do they realize that many of the patient care protocols they follow daily are mandated by the goals?

All too often, hospital and GME administrators overlook teaching residents about NPSGs. Instead, they educate attending physicians, assuming the message will trickle down to the residents.

Everyone in the hospital should view residents as a critical part of the hospital's care delivery team. It's just as important to teach residents about the NPSGs as it is to educate nurses, attending physicians, and other healthcare providers, says Constance K. Haan, MD, MS, senior associate dean of educational affairs and designated institutional official at University of Florida College of Medicine–Jacksonville.

Resident education is critical for compliance with Joint Commission standards, says Bud Pate, REHS, vice president of The Greeley Company, a division of HCPro, Inc., in Marblehead, MA. "The NPSGs apply to all staff. There is no difference in expectation for residents than anyone else when it comes to complying with the goals," Pate says.

Additionally, by integrating training on NPSGs and the core competencies, GME programs gain another method for teaching the competencies, which is always nice to highlight during an ACGME site visit, and they

help trainees develop the mentality that patient safety comes first.

Embed NPSGs in the core competencies

Every NPSG aligns with one or more of the ACGME core competencies, says Haan. The accreditor lists detailed objectives, referred to as elements of performance, which hospitals need to meet in order to comply with the overarching goals. The elements of performance provide specific actions and activities. Most pertain to patient care, but you can link them to many of the competencies.

To build a culture of patient safety, medical educators must integrate the NPSGs into every aspect of residents' education and patient care responsibilities, says Chermain Cross, MBA, senior associate director of GME at Woodhull Medical Center in Brooklyn, NY.

Consider tying the NPSGs into the following four activities typically utilized to teach the core competencies:

- **Campuswide grand rounds.** At Haan's institution, residents must attend a campuswide grand rounds presentation that covers the NPSGs.

  "We made this a mandatory training because we wanted to send the message that patient safety is important," Haan says.

  Make the information stick by showing residents how NPSGs affect their daily patient care responsibilities. Haan distributes and posts online a handout that describes the goals and how residents apply them on a local level. For example, the handout describes what The Joint Commission (formerly JCAHO) expects hospitals to do to comply with NPSG.02.05.01, regarding handoffs. It then lists the facility's procedure for handoffs and outlines what happens if residents violate one of the policies or procedures. Following procedures is a component of the professionalism competency.

- **Joint Commission educational resources.** The Joint Commission frequently offers satellite video training on many NPSGs. Cross' institution treats these as town hall sessions and invites everyone—residents, attending physicians, and other healthcare staff members—to listen in.

  Whether the session covers eliminating healthcare-associated infections or improving medication reconciliation, Cross says the sessions fulfill two core competencies: medical knowledge and patient care.

  Residents' schedules make it difficult for them to participate in every session. The GME office should work with the office responsible for Joint Commission accreditation to present training during specific department meetings or grand rounds, which residents will most likely attend.

- **Quality improvement projects.** Encourage residents to develop quality improvement initiatives that will help the hospital meet the NPSGs.

"Being on the front line of care delivery, they're often the ones that see the error potential," Haan says. "They often have the best ideas for how to solve problems."

To develop successful quality improvement projects, residents must have an understanding of how the healthcare system works, which is an element of systems-based practice. Several NPSGs call on organizations to consider evidence-based practices—a component of practice-based learning and improvement—when developing processes and determining their effectiveness.

- **Hospital committees.** Most GME programs see resident participation on hospital committees as an ACGME institutional requirement and a way to meet the systems-based practice core competency. It's also a venue for exposing residents to patient safety initiatives. These committees routinely develop systemwide policies dictated by the NPSGs.

  Resident members learn and offer input as the committee reviews hospital systems and creates processes to ensure that they're in compliance.

It's never too soon to talk safety

Build a culture of patient safety among residents from day one at institutional or departmental orientation, says Tonia Chauvin, RN, quality management program coordinator at Leonard J. Chabert Medical Center in Houma, LA.

Developing a presentation on patient safety may seem daunting for GME leaders, so Chauvin recommends asking the quality department to speak to residents.

At Chauvin's institution, this partnership has resulted in a half-day training for the residents. Chauvin and representatives from the pharmacy and medical records departments explain the National Patient Safety Goals (NPSG) and the many policies and procedures residents must follow to maintain compliance with the goals.

"I am surprised at how many of the residents have never heard of the NPSGs. This is one of the many reasons why this orientation process is so important," Chauvin says.

The education department also presents storyboards to residents that depict scenarios and information on patient safety. Additionally, residents must pass a test after completing the orientation training. Other institutions introduce incoming residents to NPSGs even earlier.

"We use online modules, including one on the NPSGs, [that] they complete prior to their start date," says Cross, "By including this module, residents know right off the bat that we're serious about patient safety and complying with the Joint Commission standards."

Programs follow up on the modules with department-specific training on patient safety and quality of care during orientation.

Source: **Residency Program Alert,** *March 1, 2009.*

Models and Assessment Tools for Teaching and Assessing Patient Care

Figure 3.3	**Department of Surgery: PGY-1 Evaluation Form**

Demographic Information:
Evaluator
Resident name and PGY level
Hospital and rotation names
Dates of rotation
Evaluation requested date and completion date

Amount of contact time:
_____ No contact with resident _____ Frequent contact (3–4x/wk)
_____ Infrequent contact (1x/mo) _____ Daily regular contact
_____ Occasional contact (1–2x/wk)

Overall rating:
_____ Unsatisfactory performance
_____ Needs significant improvement
_____ Satisfactory performance

Please rate the resident on the following competencies. If "Skill decriment" or "Skills need significant improvement" are chosen, please explain.

Patient care	Insufficient contact to assess	Skill decrement to below level of training	Skills need significant improvement	Skills emerging	Skilled
Demonstrates good interviewing skills					
Obtains a complete history and physical exam					
Assimilates and synthesizes data					
Demonstrates manual dexterity appropriate for level of training					
Demonstrates ability to develop and execute patient care plans appropriate for level of training					

Interpersonal and communications skills	Insufficient contact to assess	Skill decrement to below level of training	Skills need significant improvement	Skills emerging	Skilled
Communicates effectively with attending and team					
Communicates effectively with other healthcare professionals					
Effectively documents practice activities appropriate to level of training					
Supervises and teaches students					

Figure 3.3	Department of Surgery: PGY-1 Evaluation Form (cont.)

Practice-based learning and improvement	Insufficient contact to assess	Skill decrement to below level of training	Skills need significant improvement	Skills emerging	Skilled
Demonstrates a desire to learn					
Reads, assimilates, and applies relevant literature					
Demonstrates the ability to learn from practice					
Critiques personal practice outcomes appropriate to level of training					
Demonstrates a recognition of the importance of lifelong learning in surgical practice					
Seeks and responds to feedback					
Is aware of strengths and limitations					

Professionalism	Insufficient contact to assess	Skill decrement to below level of training	Skills need significant improvement	Skills emerging	Skilled
Demonstrates a commitment to continuity of patient care					
Displays a sense of responsibility and respect to patients, families, staff, and peers					
Maintains a professional appearance					
Demonstrates cultural sensitivity					

Systems-based practice	Insufficient contact to assess	Skill decrement to below level of training	Skills need significant improvement	Skills emerging	Skilled
Demonstrates a knowledge of risk-benefit analysis appropriate to level of training					
Practices cost effective healthcare and resource allocation					

Medical knowledge and clinical skills	Insufficient contact to assess	Skill decrement to below level of training	Skills need significant improvement	Skills emerging	Skilled
Critically evaluates and demonstrates knowledge of pertinent scientific information					
Demonstrates appropriate clinical skills for level of development					
Applies knowledge appropriately					

Strengths: _____

_____

_____

Weaknesses: _____

_____

_____

     A Practical Guide to Teaching and Assessing the ACGME Core Competencies, Second Edition

Figure 3.4	**Department of Surgery: PGY-2 Evaluation Form**

Demographic Information:
Evaluator
Resident name and PGY level
Hospital and rotation names
Dates of rotation
Evaluation requested date and completion date

Amount of contact time:

_____ No contact with resident   _____ Frequent contact (3–4x/wk)

_____ Infrequent contact (1x/mo)   _____ Daily regular contact

_____ Occasional contact (1–2x/wk)

Overall rating:

_____ Unsatisfactory performance

_____ Needs significant improvement

_____ Satisfactory performance

Please rate the resident on the following competencies. If "Skill decriment" or "Skills need significant improvement" are chosen, please explain.

Patient care	Insufficient contact to assess	Skill decrement to below level of training	Skills need significant improvement	Skills emerging	Skilled
Demonstrates good interviewing skills					
Obtains a complete history and physical exam					
Demonstrates manual dexterity appropriate for level of training					
Demonstrates ability to develop and execute patient care plans appropriate for level of training					

Interpersonal and communications skills	Insufficient contact to assess	Skill decrement to below level of training	Skills need significant improvement	Skills emerging	Skilled
Communicates effectively with attending and team					
Communicates effectively with other healthcare professionals					
Effectively documents practice activities appropriate to level of training					
Supervises and teaches students					

Figure 3.4	Department of Surgery: PGY-2 Evaluation Form (cont.)

Practice-based learning and improvement	Insufficient contact to assess	Skill decrement to below level of training	Skills need significant improvement	Skills emerging	Skilled
Demonstrates a desire to learn					
Demonstrates the ability to learn from practice					
Critiques personal practice outcomes appropriate to level of training					
Demonstrates a recognition of the importance of lifelong learning in surgical practice					
Seeks and responds to feedback					
Reads, assimilates, and applies relevant literature					
Is aware of strengths and limitations					

Professionalism	Insufficient contact to assess	Skill decrement to below level of training	Skills need significant improvement	Skills emerging	Skilled
Demonstrates a commitment to continuity of patient care					
Displays a sense of responsibility and respect to patients, families, staff, and peers					
Maintains a professional appearance					
Demonstrates cultural sensitivity					

Systems-based practice	Insufficient contact to assess	Skill decrement to below level of training	Skills need significant improvement	Skills emerging	Skilled
Demonstrates a knowledge of risk-benefit analysis appropriate to level of training					
Practices cost effective healthcare and resource allocation					

Medical knowledge and clinical skills	Insufficient contact to assess	Skill decrement to below level of training	Skills need significant improvement	Skills emerging	Skilled
Critically evaluates and demonstrates knowledge of pertinent scientific information					
Demonstrates appropriate clinical skills for level of development					
Applies knowledge appropriately					

Strengths: _____   Weaknesses: _____

_____   _____

_____   _____

_____   _____

Figure 3.5	**Department of Surgery: PGY-3 Evaluation Form**

Demographic Information:
Evaluator
Resident name and PGY level
Hospital and rotation names
Dates of rotation
Evaluation requested date and completion date

Amount of contact time:

_____ No contact with resident   _____ Frequent contact (3–4x/wk)

_____ Infrequent contact (1x/mo)   _____ Daily regular contact

_____ Occasional contact (1–2x/wk)

Overall rating:

_____ Unsatisfactory performance

_____ Needs significant improvement

_____ Satisfactory performance

Please rate the resident on the following competencies. If "Skill decrement" or "Skills need significant improvement" are chosen, please explain.

Patient care	Insufficient contact to assess	Skill decrement to below level of training	Skills need significant improvement	Skills emerging	Skilled
Demonstrates good interviewing skills					
Obtains a complete history and physical exam					
Assimilates and synthesizes data					
Demonstrates manual dexterity appropriate for level of training					
Demonstrates ability to develop and execute patient care plans appropriate for level of training					

Interpersonal and communications skills	Insufficient contact to assess	Skill decrement to below level of training	Skills need significant improvement	Skills emerging	Skilled
Communicates effectively with attending and team					
Communicates effectively with other healthcare professionals					
Effectively documents practice activities appropriate to level of training					
Supervises and teaches students					

Figure 3.5	Department of Surgery: PGY-3 Evaluation Form (cont.)

Practice-based learning and improvement	Insufficient contact to assess	Skill decrement to below level of training	Skills need significant improvement	Skills emerging	Skilled
Demonstrates a desire to learn					
Demonstrates the ability to learn from practice					
Critiques personal practice outcomes appropriate to level of training					
Demonstrates a recognition of the importance of learning in surgical practice					
Seeks and responds to feedback					
Reads, assimilates, and applies relevant literature					
Is aware of strengths and limitations					
Demonstrates proficiency with relevant information technology					

Professionalism	Insufficient contact to assess	Skill decrement to below level of training	Skills need significant improvement	Skills emerging	Skilled
Demonstrates a commitment to continuity of patient care					
Displays a sense of responsibility and respect to patients, families, staff, and peers					
Maintains a professional appearance					
Demonstrates cultural sensitivity					
Demonstrates quality and timeliness in medical record keeping, documentation, and reports					

Systems-based practice	Insufficient contact to assess	Skill decrement to below level of training	Skills need significant improvement	Skills emerging	Skilled
Demonstrates a knowledge of risk-benefit analysis appropriate to level of training					
Practices cost effective healthcare and resource allocation					
Demonstrates an understanding of local population trends and resources					

Medical knowledge and clinical skills	Insufficient contact to assess	Skill decrement to below level of training	Skills need significant improvement	Skills emerging	Skilled
Critically evaluates and demonstrates knowledge of pertinent scientific information					
Demonstrates appropriate clinical skills for level of development					
Applies knowledge appropriately					
Clearly understands the scientific basis for patient complaints					

Strengths: _____   Weaknesses: _____

_____   _____

_____   _____

_____   _____

Figure 3.6	Department of Surgery: PGY-4 Evaluation Form

Demographic Information: Evaluator
Resident name and PGY level
Hospital and rotation names
Dates of rotation
Evaluation requested date and completion date

Amount of contact time: _____ No contact with resident   _____ Frequent contact (3–4x/wk)
_____ Infrequent contact (1x/mo)   _____ Daily regular contact
_____ Occasional contact (1–2x/wk)

Overall rating: _____ Unsatisfactory performance
_____ Needs significant improvement
_____ Satisfactory performance

Please rate the resident on the following competencies. If Skill decrement or Skills need significant improvement are chosen, please explain.

Patient care	Insufficient contact to assess	Skill decrement to below level of training	Skills need significant improvement	Skills emerging	Skilled
Demonstrates good interviewing skills					
Obtains a complete history and physical exam					
Assimilates and synthesizes data					
Demonstrates manual dexterity appropriate for level of training					
Demonstrates ability to develop and execute patient care plans appropriate for level of training					
Constructs a comprehensive differential diagnosis					

Interpersonal and communications skills	Insufficient contact to assess	Skill decrement to below level of training	Skills need significant improvement	Skills emerging	Skilled
Communicates effectively with attending and team					
Communicates effectively with other healthcare professionals					
Effectively documents practice activities appropriate to level of training					
Supervises and teaches students					
Counsels and educates family/patient regarding the nature of the illness or procedure					
Presents cases in a complete and organized fashion					

Figure
3.6

Department of Surgery: PGY-4 Evaluation Form (cont.)

Practice-based learning and improvement	Insufficient contact to assess	Skill decrement to below level of training	Skills need significant improvement	Skills emerging	Skilled
Demonstrates a desire to learn					
Demonstrates the ability to learn from practice					
Critiques personal practice outcomes appropriate to level of training					
Demonstrates a recognition of the importance of lifelong learning in surgical practice					
Seeks and responds to feedback					
Reads, assimilates, and applies relevant literature					
Is aware of strengths and limitations					
Demonstrates proficiency with relevant information technology					

Professionalism	Insufficient contact to assess	Skill decrement to below level of training	Skills need significant improvement	Skills emerging	Skilled
Demonstrates a commitment to continuity of patient care					
Displays a sense of responsibility and respect to patients, families, staff, and peers					
Maintains a professional appearance					
Demonstrates cultural sensitivity					
Demonstrates quality and timeliness in medical record keeping, documentation, and reports					
Ability to apply sound moral standards to decision-making					

Systems-based practice	Insufficient contact to assess	Skill decrement to below level of training	Skills need significant improvement	Skills emerging	Skilled
Demonstrates a knowledge of risk-benefit analysis appropriate to level of training					
Practices cost effective healthcare and resource allocation					
Demonstrates an understanding of local population trends and resources					
Recognizes the importance of the interdisciplinary team and uses contributions from others					
Appropriately participates in treatment/discharge planning including community resources					

Medical knowledge and clinical skills	Insufficient contact to assess	Skill decrement to below level of training	Skills need significant improvement	Skills emerging	Skilled
Critically evaluates and demonstrates knowledge of pertinent scientific information					
Demonstrates appropriate clinical skills for level of development					
Applies knowledge appropriately					
Clearly understands the scientific basis for patient complaints					

Strengths: _____

_____

_____

_____

Weaknesses: _____

_____

_____

_____

     A Practical Guide to Teaching and Assessing the ACGME Core Competencies, Second Edition

Figure 3.7	Department of Surgery: PGY-5 Evaluation Form

Demographic Information:

Evaluator

Resident name and PGY level

Hospital and rotation names

Dates of rotation

Evaluation requested date and completion date

Amount of contact time:

_____ No contact with resident _____ Frequent contact (3–4x/wk)

_____ Infrequent contact (1x/mo) _____ Daily regular contact

_____ Occasional contact (1–2x/wk)

Overall rating:

_____ Unsatisfactory performance

_____ Needs significant improvement

_____ Satisfactory performance

Please rate the resident on the following competencies. If "Skill decriment" or "Skills need significant improvement" are chosen, please explain.

Patient care	Insufficient contact to assess	Skill decrement to below level of training	Skills need significant improvement	Skills emerging	Skilled
Demonstrates good interviewing skills					
Obtains a complete history and physical exam					
Assimilates and synthesizes data					
Demonstrates manual dexterity appropriate for level of training					
Demonstrates ability to develop and execute patient care plans appropriate for level of training					
Develops rapport and therapeutic alliance					
Constructs a comprehensive differential diagnosis					
Formulates and implements a comprehensive treatment plan					

Interpersonal and communications skills	Insufficient contact to assess	Skill decrement to below level of training	Skills need significant improvement	Skills emerging	Skilled
Communicates effectively with attending and team					
Communicates effectively with other healthcare professionals					
Effectively documents practice activities appropriate to level of training					
Supervises and teaches students					
Counsels and educates family/patient regarding the nature of the illness or procedure					
Presents cases in a complete and organized fashion					

Figure 3.7	Department of Surgery: PGY-5 Evaluation Form (cont.)

Practice-based learning and improvement	Insufficient contact to assess	Skill decrement to below level of training	Skills need significant improvement	Skills emerging	Skilled
Demonstrates a desire to learn					
Demonstrates the ability to learn from practice					
Critiques personal practice outcomes appropriate to level of training					
Demonstrates a recognition of the importance of lifelong learning in surgical practice					
Seeks and responds to feedback					
Reads, assimilates, and applies relevant literature					
Is aware of strengths and limitations					
Demonstrates proficiency with relevant information technology					

Professionalism	Insufficient contact to assess	Skill decrement to below level of training	Skills need significant improvement	Skills emerging	Skilled
Demonstrates a commitment to continuity of patient care					
Displays a sense of responsibility and respect to patients, families, staff, and peers					
Maintains a professional appearance					
Demonstrates cultural sensitivity					
Demonstrates quality and timeliness in medical record keeping, documentation, and reports					
Ability to apply sound moral standards to decision-making					

Systems-based practice	Insufficient contact to assess	Skill decrement to below level of training	Skills need significant improvement	Skills emerging	Skilled
Demonstrates a knowledge of risk-benefit analysis appropriate to level of training					
Practices cost effective healthcare and resource allocation					
Demonstrates an understanding of local population trends and resources					
Recognizes the importance of the interdisciplinary team and uses contributions from others					
Appropriately participates in treatment/discharge planning including community resources					

Medical knowledge and clinical skills	Insufficient contact to assess	Skill decrement to below level of training	Skills need significant improvement	Skills emerging	Skilled
Critically evaluates and demonstrates knowledge of pertinent scientific information					
Demonstrates appropriate clinical skills for level of development					
Applies knowledge appropriately					
Clearly understands the scientific basis for patient complaints					

Strengths: _____   Weaknesses: _____

_____   _____

_____   _____

_____   _____

References

1. Recommendations for clinical skills curricula for undergraduate medical education. AAMC website. 2005. *https://services.aamc.org/publications/index. cfm?fuseaction=Product.displayForm&prd_id=141&prv_ id=165* (or *www.aamc.org/meded/clinicalskills*).

2. Outcome Project. ACGME website. *www.acgme.org/ Outcome/.* Accessed February 14, 2010.

3. Residency programs. Overview. Bridgeport Hospital Graduate Medical Education website. *www.bridgeporthospital.org/gme/residency.* Accessed January 18, 2007.

4. ADASP. Curriculum content and evaluation of resident competency in anatomic pathology: a proposal. *J Human Pathol.* 2003;08.009.

5. Crain B, Alston S, et al. Accreditation Council for Graduate Medical Education (ACGME) competencies in neuropathology training. *Am Assoc Neuropath.* 2005;64(4):273–279.

6. Dunnington G, Williams R. Addressing the new competencies for residents' surgical training. *Acad Med.* 2003;78(1):14–21.

7. Program Director Guide to the Common Program Requirements. ACGME website. *www.acgme.org.* Assessed February 14, 2010.

8. Rappaport DI, Cellucci MF, Leffler MG. Implementing family-centered rounds: pediatric residents' perceptions. *Clin Ped.* (Phila). 2010 April;49(3):228–234.

9. Rosen P, Stenger E, Bochkoris M, Hannon MJ, Kwoh CK. Family-centered multidisciplinary rounds enhance the team approach in pediatrics. *Pediatrics.* 2009 April:123:e603–e608.

10. Stiles B, Reece T, et al. General surgery morning report: a competency-based conference that enhances patient care and resident education. *Curr Surg.* 2006;63(6):385–390.

11. Banks D, Shi R, Timm D, Christopher K, Duggar D, Comegys M, McLarty J. Decreased hospital length of stay associated with presentation of cases at morning report with librarian support. *J Med Libr Assoc.* 2007 Oct;95(4):381–7.

12. Branch W. Use of critical incident reports in medical education. *J Gen Intern Med.* 2005;20(11):1063.

13. Ferenchick G, Simpson D, Blackman J, DaRosa D, Dunnington G. Strategies for efficient and effective teaching in the ambulatory care setting. *Acad Med.* 1997;72(4):277–280.

14. King R, Schiavone F, Counselman F, Panacek E. Patient care competency in emergency medicine graduate medical education: results of a consensus group on patient care. *Acad Emerg Med.* 2002;9(11):1227–1235.

15. Rosen M, Salas E, Silvestri S, Wu T, Lazzara E. A Measurement tool for simulation-based training in emergency medicine: the simulation module for assessment of resident targeted event responses (SMARTER) approach. *Sim Healthcare* 3:170-179, 2008.

16. Capella J, et all. Teamwork Training Improves the Clinical Care of Trauma Patients. Virginia Tech Carilion School of Medicine, Roanoke, VA. Presentation at Surgical Education Week April 20–24, 2010 San Antonio, Texas.

17. Oetting T. Surgical competency in residents. *Current Opinion in Ophthalmology.* 2009. 20:56–60.

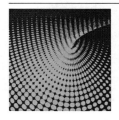

Practice-Based Learning and Improvement

F. Daniel Duffy, MD, MACP, FAACH

Introduction

Practice-based learning and improvement (PBLI) is the habit of advancing knowledge, attitudes, and skills through feedback and reflection on measures of practice and taking deliberate action to improve practice systems, including one's part in it. This complex competency integrates learning concepts and methods to advance professionals across the developmental stages of learning to practice. Residents and seasoned physicians learn how to deliver medical care by doing it, reflecting on it, and changing their ideas, habits, and systems to improve it. PBLI is the active interaction between individual professionals and a healthcare system designed to deliver medical care.

PBLI merges learning theory with methods of knowledge management (KM) and system improvement.

Through the practice of PBLI, individual professionals hone their skills in the other five competencies: medical knowledge, communications and interpersonal skills, professionalism, patient care, and systems-based practice. Much more than independent learning or self-study, PBLI entails guided KM, the use of scientific methods for making decisions, and active improvement of the system of practice while delivering actual care in a learning organization.

The process of PBLI describes the process of learning medicine from medical school and residency through continuing medical education. It is the central competence for medical educators, certifiers of professional competence, and individual professionals. This chapter describes my perspective on the practice of PBLI as the central competence for continuous professional development.

What Is PBLI?

Several themes describe the purpose of PBLI. The overarching theme of PBLI is reflection on one's work or "holding a mirror up to ourselves to document, assess, and improve our practice."[1] It is also the habit of lifelong learning,[2] with the aim of getting better in the practice of medicine.[3] It is the "experiential bridge between continuous learning and good patient care."[4] It is the habit of systematically monitoring our team's processes and outcomes of care and proactively making positive changes rather than reacting to changes enforced by others.[5]

The ACGME defined PBLI, and the American Board of Medical Specialists (ABMS), which certifies the competence of graduates of ACGME accredited residencies, immediately adopted it.

To meet the PBLI competency, physicians must examine, assess, and improve how they care for patients and investigate and absorb scientific evidence. There are six subcompetencies of PBLI. They are:

- Reflect and analyze practice experiences and conduct improvement activities using systematic methodology (system improvement)

- Examine, evaluate, and incorporate scientific evidence associated with patients' illnesses (KM)

- Gain and utilize patient population data (population health)

- Apply high-quality evidence obtained from the scientific method to make medical decisions (evidence-based medicine)

- Appraise clinical studies and other medical literature using knowledge of statistics and study designs (medical informatics)

- Teach students and other healthcare team members (healthcare education)

Developmental Stages in Professional Practice

We acquire competency to perform professional practice in a developmental process that requires competence in PBLI. More than simple education, this developmental process fundamentally changes our lives. PBLI for the purpose of professional development is a whole body experience extending far beyond cognitive learning. Dreyfus described how this process might occur in a model of progressing through five developmental stages: novice, advanced beginner, competent, proficient, and expert.[6]

In the novice stage, students are committed to becoming practitioners, but are presently unskilled; they are learning the terminology, core concepts, and rules of the practice; they are willing to watch and mimic practice. The students at this stage need a teacher, books, and formal courses. As we acquire new knowledge and skills throughout our professional careers, we return to the novice stage. Medical schools teach novice professionals during the first and second years of medical school. When residents begin to learn a new procedure, they are at the novice stage.

In the advanced beginner stage, nascent practitioners possess a working knowledge of practice terminology and concepts; they apply simple rules in order to perform the methods of the practice; they have little experience and rely on others for the outcome of their work. The advanced beginner stage learner needs a coach and lots of practice in solving simulated problems. The coach drills the developing practitioner, motivates repetition until skills are honed, and gives immediate corrective feedback on observations of the advanced beginner's practice. Medical schools and residency programs coach advanced beginner stage professionals during the third and fourth years of medical school and the first year of residency.

In the competence stage, developing practitioners experience actual practice and accept responsibility for the outcomes of their actions. They recognize common patterns but resort to reasoning and applying rules of thumb in making many decisions. During this phase, practitioners develop intuitive knowledge but doubt their competence, relying instead on analysis and reasoning. They experience the emotional highs of success and the lows of failure, and they begin to appreciate complexity and nuance in the practice. At this stage, the developing practitioner needs a facilitator who makes the practitioner take responsibility for his or her decisions in actual practice, encourages efficiency and pattern recognition, and provides corrective feedback. Residency and fellowship training programs work with professionals in the competent stage.

In the proficient stage, practitioners have much experience and practice efficiently with routine problems. They regularly recognize the patterns of problems in their discipline, act intuitively, and only occasionally resort to formal reasoning and analysis for difficult

problems. Practitioners may miss rare or unusual problems and dismiss observations that don't fit their experience or concepts.

During this stage, practitioners need a supervisor or mentor to prevent them from becoming too focused on efficiency and losing curiosity. The mentor helps them slow down, advises them to look up information, and guides them to reflect on and improve their practice. Continuing medical education programs and the medical specialty boards' maintenance of certification programs guide professionals in the proficient stage.

In the expert stage, practitioners have a great deal of experience, and they work with other experts or mentors. Practitioners in the expert stage enjoy complex or unusual problems, and they expand the concepts and methods of their practice to incorporate nuances and irregularities. Expert stage practitioners seek mentors who are also in the expert stage. Opinion leaders and experts in the profession work with each other and their protégées in the expert stage.

The experiential learning cycle

Professional development is learning that permanently changes one's life situation. This development results in the adoption of purposeful patterns of action and using specialized knowledge. The development occurs only through guided experience in practice and must be emotionally cemented by moral values of selfless service to meeting the needs of others. Medical educators guide professionals through the developmental stages, but the developing professional must be changed by real clinical experience in medical school, residency, and continuing medical education.

We guide practice-based learning by applying Klob's concept of experiential learning to construct a learning cycle of four connected processes:

1. Instruction and learning facts, abstract concepts, and a method for their scientific validation

2. Creating opportunities for concrete experiences in supervised professional practice that brings the abstract concepts to life

3. Providing feedback on directly observed or indirectly measured behavior to guide the learner's reflection on action and ascertain the generalized mental models, reasoning approach, and emotional and moral processes underlying the service commitment

4. Observing professional action in subsequent practice situations that demonstrates the assimilation of new cognitive, emotional, moral, and technical processes[7]

This experiential learning model emphasizes the relationship between acquiring explicit knowledge through memorizing terms, abstract facts, and concepts and acquiring tacit knowledge through reflecting on the here-and-now experience of solving clinical problems in real-life patients under real-time circumstances.

Where individual medical students or residents start in the learning cycle varies based on their learning preferences. For example, some prefer to begin with a concrete experience and then learn the terminology, facts, and concepts rationalizing it. Others acquire an understanding of the terminology and concepts before participating in a real experience. Another learner may prefer to reflect on the experience of others to learn patterns and only later have his or her own experiences. Regardless of personal preference, practice-based learning involves experience in all four processes: abstract concepts, practical experience, feedback for reflection, and performance in action.

Medical educators make an error when they rigidly structure learning to present facts and concepts first and later provide experience in practice. Instead, practice-based learning takes place during the use of explicit, but abstract, conceptual knowledge in real-life problem-solving. In this process, conceptual knowledge is transformed into tacit (intuitive) knowledge attached to a particular situation, and it is no longer the same knowledge as it was prior to being used.[8]

Active learning and constructing neural pathways

Understanding the neurobiological nature of learning makes the concept of PBLI not a unique competence for physicians, but rather the explanatory model for all learning. PBLI describes an approach that activates the neurobiological circuitry of our brains to select the new experiences we will keep and those we will discard. It is a whole-brain activity using the temporal lobe (memory), visual cortex (images), parietal lobe (motor), limbic system (emotions), and frontal lobe (judgment and motivation).

Learning through a lecture appears to be passive reception of spoken or graphic representations of facts, concepts, and ideas. If learning is occurring, an incredibly active process of knowledge-building is taking place within the brains of the listeners. During learning, both the teacher and the listener actively engage in shaping the neural networks of each other's brains. New information or perspectives on old information attach to activated neural networks, reinforce them, add nuances, or begin to reshape them in new ways. Learning takes place when learners are cognitively and, for skills development, physically involved in using the facts and emotionally involved and connected with the teacher and the experience.

Teaching for learning is emotionally engaging and immediately relevant to learners' past experiences. New information is not "absorbed" or merely "acquired," but rather is the active, energy-consuming neurologic process that creates new meaning within the learner's brain. The process is active cognitively, physically, and emotionally.

Realistic examples of concepts integrated with existing tasks stimulate more neural pathway development and more effective and efficient learning. Contrary as it may seem, it is the learner, not the teacher, who decides when and how knowledge residing in the learner's neural networks will be modified. New knowledge is almost always constructed through the personal interpretation of current personal experiences in the world, including interaction with a teacher, with past experiences.

Looked at from this neurologic perspective it now makes sense that learners (particularly learners in the proficiency stage) should participate in establishing learning goals and tasks, and have input into the methods of instruction and assessment that work best for them. However, learning a professional practice cannot be entirely learner-centered, especially at the early stages. Unfamiliarity with the complexity of real patient challenges and problems places learners at the advanced beginner and competent stages (residents) in a state of experience overload and emotional distress. This is not a bad thing as it provides the emotional experience necessary for learning some of the most important moral and ethical lessons of professional practice.

Teaching and learning during the competent stage of development compresses the time between performance and assessment of outcomes to an almost simultaneous event. Learning in this stage requires a coach as a teacher. A coach combines structured professional work with practice in problem-solving conferences, case discussions, and simulation drills. The patient care delivered by the residents drives the content of the curriculum; the developmental stage of the professional drives the method of teaching.

In the developmental approach to learning, teaching ceases to consist of teacher-selected lessons and becomes a fluid process of directly observing the learners' clinical work, actions, and decisions and their manual, cognitive, and emotional development in doing their jobs as new professionals. Then the work stops, and the teacher and learners engage in reflection on action. Together they practice skills in problem-solving, analyzing data, or practicing clinical skills in simulation settings. In this type of teaching, the attending physician:

- Gives corrective feedback

- Highlights problems of emerging relevance to the resident

- Structures rounding conversations around primary concepts

- Seeks and values the resident's point of view

- Adapts the curriculum of case discussions to address the resident's suppositions, work habits, clinical skills, and emotional responses in solving his or her patients' problems

Quality Improvement

The concept of PBLI evolved at a time of intense public scrutiny of the quality of medical care in the United States.[9, 10] Many problems with healthcare safety and quality were documented,[11, 12] and process improvement, such as the Six Sigma and Lean (Toyota) Production methods, adopted by other industries, was recommended as a pathway for improving the quality and safety of healthcare.[13] Once improvement science was introduced into medical care, the quality agenda shifted away from the idea that training doctors to do the right thing would yield excellent outcomes (professionalism). The new quality agenda recognized that quality of care is a system characteristic that develops through the deliberate application of quality measurement and improvement practices.[14]

Self-Assessment and Self-Directed Learning

Professional autonomy and responsibility for self-regulation lie at the heart of medical professionalism (separate competence). Medical education promotes these values by rigidly dividing physician education between the highly regulated, structured, and teacher-directed undergraduate medical education and graduate medical education (GME) and the almost completely unstructured and self-directed continuing medical education of the independently practicing professional. This divide overvalues the autonomy and independence of the practicing professional's competency in self-assessment of learning needs and self-directed learning.

Affirming the idea that professional values are sufficient to drive accurate self-assessment and self-directed learning, most medical specialty boards, until recently, certified diplomates to be "competent for life." Unfortunately, accumulating evidence does not support this claim. Choudhry's meta-analysis demonstrated that professional knowledge and competency decline with time after completing residency.[15] Moreover, Davis demonstrated that physicians, especially less competent ones, are particularly poor at accurate self-assessment of learning needs.[16] Training in PBLI and evaluation of performance in practice throughout a professional career has become the major goal for medical educators and licensing and certifying boards.[17]

The introduction of quality measurement, evaluation, and improvement in medical practice over the previous 15 years highlighted another problem in the value of physician autonomy. Quality improvement science has demonstrated that the quality of medical care depends on more than just the knowledge and skills of an individual professional. Equally important is the competency of the clinical microsystems (the frontline people and patients who work together with the common aim to deliver care), and how these microsystems are organized into a system of care.[18] Studies repeatedly demonstrate that physicians can correctly answer examination questions regarding medical knowledge, but they often fail to do what they "know" in actual practice.[12] A wealth of medical knowledge does not directly translate to high quality of care.

For these reasons, the medical specialty boards changed their certification from a single lifetime certification to time-limited certification earned at the end of formal training. Practitioners must maintain their certification via their boards' Maintenance of Certification (MOC) program over a lifetime of practice. MOC brings PBLI to life for practicing physicians. It engages participants in guided:

- Self-assessment of knowledge and clinical reasoning

- Reflection on feedback from patients and peers

- Examination of knowledge and clinical reasoning

- Reflection on and improvement in measures of actual practice

This multifaceted peer-guided assessment promotes continuous professional development and improvement in practice performance. More than 80% of the American Board of Internal Medicine (ABIM) board-certified physicians who have completed a cycle of MOC reported improvement in practice and benefit to patients from their guided self-assessment, study, and improvement activities.[19]

As a result of the success of the MOC program for life-long learning and continuous professional development, all boards under the ABMS are applying similar assessment and learning approaches to documenting professional development across the six competencies during residency and fellowship training. In the near future, we can expect that initial board certification will be based on evidence of participation in guided self-assessment, measurement, and improvement in quality of practice processes, and reflection and action on feedback received from patients and peers.

Content of PBLI

There are six task areas of PBLI competence. These tasks are loosely tied together within this new competency, and they are:

1. **System improvement** involves measuring performance in practice and redesigning care delivery processes and systems to improve care. Tightly linked to the competency of systems-based practice, this element of PBLI acknowledges that the quality of healthcare depends not solely on the knowledge and skills of a physician, but on the coordinated and standardized work of a team of staff members and professionals. This is a new concept for physician practice and education, and it may be the most important component of PBLI.

2. **KM** is the second element of PBLI competency. Traditionally, KM involved searching for published information in library collections and online databases, but KM has come to mean much more. It encompasses a broader perspective on the nature of medical knowledge (separate competency) as being more than the acquisition, assimilation, and analysis

of the scientifically based explicit knowledge published in the medical literature. It involves capturing and transmitting knowledge learned through practice. It is the essence of PBLI.

In the early 1990s, business professionals recognized that much of their knowledge either resided in the insights and experiences of their employees or was embedded in their organizational processes or practices. KM developed into a discipline comprising a range of strategies and practices used by individuals and organizations to identify and facilitate adoption of employees' insights and experiences. KM identified processes for capturing both tacit and explicit knowledge, and organizing, classifying, and storing it in such a way that it can be retrieved to solve problems, teach new employees, and improve outcomes.

Although KM originated in the business and information systems files, it is now spreading to other areas, such as public policy and clinical medicine through quality improvement and medical informatics, which are two other components of PBLI. In clinical medicine, KM explicitly identifies the process of practice-based learning by capturing the insights from everyday practice, and by understanding the exceptions clinicians make when protocols or the evidence doesn't apply to particular patient situations. KM captures the successes and failures of rapid-cycle tests of process changes aimed at improving care, thus linking to the system improvement component of PBLI.

Currently KM is largely an organizational activity (systems-based practice) that includes the management of individual practice knowledge. KM focuses on organizational objectives such as:

- Enhanced performance

- Competitive advantage

- Innovation

- Imparting lessons learned

- Continuous betterment of the organization

KM is the aspect of organizational learning that focuses on information as a professional asset of an organization and an individual. As an organizational process, KM encourages the storage, transition, and sharing of practice-based knowledge; therefore, it ties closely to the PBLI element of medical education (discussed shortly). KM becomes the essential tool to facilitate information and knowledge exchanges between individuals and groups in order to reduce redundancies in work.

3. **Population health** is the third element of PBLI. Population health is the analysis and assessment of health outcomes of a group of individuals (e.g., the population of patients seeking care from an individual practice), including how those outcomes are dispersed across the group.[20] The principles and practice

of public health underpin measurement of quality and system improvement. Population health seeks to step beyond the individual-level focus of clinical medicine and public health by addressing a broad range of factors that impact health on a population level, such as environment, social structure, and resource distribution. By incorporating principles of population health into the competency of PBLI, we bring an awareness of how the individual physician can help improve the health of an entire population, such as the community in which he or she practices. Population health also provides a framework in which a physician can reduce health disparities among different subgroups within a community or within the physician's own practice population.

This element of PBLI highlights the fact that environmental and social factors beyond the scope of the usual practice of the individual practitioner are often more important than medical care in improving overall health.

4. **Evidence-based medicine** (EBM) is the disciplined habit of PBLI wherein the physician applies the highest-quality evidence obtained from the scientific method to make medical decisions about different diagnostic or therapeutic strategies. This element involves:

    • Formulating a clinical question

    • Locating scientific evidence that may answer the question

    • Analyzing the veracity of the evidence in order to make a cogent judgment about actions to be taken

Science, engineering, and statistics comprise EBM. Residents should incorporate evidence, research, and published literature into their practice. Physicians are expected to base their decisions on scientific evidence.[21]

5. **Medical informatics** involves the use of systems to facilitate the acquisition, storage, and utilization of healthcare information. Physicians commonly use smartphones, computer software, and publications, such as practice or clinical guidelines. The practical elements of medical informatics for the clinician involve knowledge and skill in using an electronic health record, templates for systematically recording standardized data, embedded decision support tools, patient care registries, and health information exchanges. It also helps physicians understand the importance of standards in information management. Medical informatics provides powerful tools for KM, incorporating evidence-based medicine into decision support at the point of care, and connecting clinicians and patients with each other through electronic communication.

6. **Healthcare education** ties up the loose ends in this complex competence. It is a component of KM that entails the human dimensions of transferring knowledge and technical skill to novice and advanced beginner members of the healthcare team. It involves the training and

education needed to implement changes in care processes and to adapt new knowledge and techniques into the healthcare processes. This includes teaching junior members of the profession as well as engaging in collaborative learning with other professionals. This element highlights the importance of viewing the clinical microsystem as a learning organization. The tasks of this element include:

- Developing the knowledge and skills needed to create a safe environment for learning

- Achieving focus on quality of care for the curriculum

- Using the measurement of performance in practice as the source of information to drive learning from working in and changing the processes that deliver care

Healthcare education is not only about giving a good lecture. It is also about organizing and communicating information to others that stimulates them to create the knowledge and habits that make the microsystem work more effectively to achieve the highest quality of care.

Curriculum in PBLI

The curriculum for teaching and learning PBLI can be woven throughout the program's general curriculum. During each rotation, residents can read about the principles of PBLI. They can complete online courses, attend lectures and workshops, and participate in evidence-based medicine, quality improvement, and

information management activities that apply to the specific content and experiences of the rotation. Because PBLI is a relatively new competency, residency programs need to begin by conducting a knowledge and skills needs assessment of entering residents. Residents will most likely be at the novice stage with regard to most of the PBLI terminology, concepts, and methods.

The literature reporting educational innovations in teaching the concepts, skills, and attitudes that comprise the PBLI elements is growing rapidly. Here I will attempt to bring these individual experiences together into a coherent approach to incorporating PBLI competency training into a GME program.

The goal of PBLI is to help physicians establish the habit of PBLI into the routine activity of professional practice. This includes adopting new medical informatics tools and methods, and applying KM, systems improvement, evidence-based medicine, and population health to the continuous learning and practice improvement of the clinical microsystem of which the physician is a part.

Learning objectives and their measurement for evaluation

The second column of Figure 4.1 lists suggested learning objectives for each of the six elements of PBLI. Local experts should refine this list so that it reflects the local educational situation and rapid evolution of medical knowledge and practice innovations. Many PBLI learning objectives can be used during rotations through the multiple clinical microsystems that comprise the clinical learning experiences of the specialty. Although workshops are important venues for learning terminology, concepts, and methods, residents can

    A Practical Guide to Teaching and Assessing the ACGME Core Competencies, Second Edition

acquire the habit of PBLI only by applying these principles and practices during each clinical rotation and its microsystem. I have ordered the elements from the most basic to the most advanced elements of PBLI.

The third column of Figure 4.1 suggests assessment and evaluation tools that may be used to measure development of the habit of PBLI. Unfortunately, research indicates that few of these tools accurately measure the competence of PBLI.[22] Written tests of

knowledge and surveys of attitudes about confidence in being able to practice PBLI and the importance of PBLI to professional practice have been demonstrated to be effective measures of these elements of competence.[23] Global ratings and checklists are regularly suggested, although there are no data to prove that they are effective in measuring PBLI. A few programs have reported the use of the objective structured clinical examination using simulations to measure skills in PBLI.[24]

Figure 4.1	Learning Objectives and Evaluation Methods for PBLI	
PBLI element	**Learning objectives**	**Measurements for evaluation**
Medical informatics	• Use a personal laptop and PDA, EHR, and Learning Portfolio, • Describe the value and use of templates, decision support tools, and embedded reference materials for clinical decision-making, • Transmit electronically clinical information and communicate with consultants, patients, pharmacies, and other healthcare providers efficiently • Use MI tools to coordinate care	• Global rating of computer, PDA, EHR, and other MI use • Medical Record Review[1] • Checklist use of EHR embedded decision support reminders • Checklist use of EHR templates for recording standardized data • Checklist use of cell phone, e-mail, and other forms of electronic communication.
Knowledge management	• Use of PubMed or other online information databases to search for medical information • Use of SharePoint or other collaborative work programs • Use of Learning Portfolio for knowledge management • Select and evaluate learning activities needed to meet portfolio-guided learning goals • Use a system for tracking and storing the developing knowledge learned from practice • Write clinical policies and procedures, including process diagrams that implement practice-based knowledge in clinical practice	• Global performance rating • Written test of knowledge of the principles and practices of KM • Assessment of portfolio entries of reflection on action and self-assessment of learning needs • Learner rating of learning activity • Assessment of the residents' entries in knowledge management databases such as EndNotes • Checklist assessment of residents' use of practice-based knowledge generation, storage, and dissemination tools

Figure 4.1	**Learning Objectives and Evaluation Methods for PBLI (cont.)**

PBLI element	Learning objectives	Measurements for evaluation
System improvement	• Describe the structure, organization, roles, responsibilities, and processes of each clinical microsystem through which the resident rotates • Describe the relationship between the microsystem and the larger system of care, • Describe of the process for handoffs and transfers to and from the clinical microsystem, • Use of process diagram to describe the work flow of key processes in the microsystem • Use performance measures to chart the quality of microsystem processes and outcomes • Use patient and peer feedback to evaluate the patient experience of care provided by the microsystem • Use of microsystem control charts to track stability of care processes, • Perform PDSA rapid-cycle test of change during clinical rotation • Actively contribute to team meetings, • Use of microsystem process check-lists	• Global performance rating • Knowledge examination of the structure and process function of the microsystem • Knowledge examination of the terminology and processes used in structured quality improvement of clinical processes • Portfolio assessment of the outcomes of participation in QI rapid-cycle tests of change to improve performance measures in practice • Assessment of control charts of microsystem performance during the time period when the resident was a member of the microsystem
Evidence-based medicine	• Ask relevant clinical questions arising from performing patient care • Retrieve published evidence from the medical literature • Retrieve practice-based knowledge from local medical knowledge storage • Analyze the quality of scientific method used for evidence for clinical decisions • Uses of EBM statistical methods in clinical problem solving • Reference evidence to support clinical decisions in the EHR and during clinical conversations	• Global performance rating of use of EBM principles and practices • OSCE demonstrating use of EBM methods to solve simulated clinical problems • Written examination of knowledge of statistical terminology and concepts used in EBM • Peer and/or faculty rating using a checklist of skills performed in case conference using EBM practices • Portfolio assessment of entries documenting use of EBM in clinical work

| Figure 4.1 | **Learning Objectives and Evaluation Methods for PBLI (cont.)** |

PBLI element	Learning objectives	Measurements for evaluation
Population health	• Compare and contrast the characteristics of the patient population served by each microsystem in which the resident rotates • Describe the disparities in health outcomes by segment of the population, • Describe the social determinants of the problems managed by the microsystem, • Uses population statistics in clinical decision making • Uses an EMR registry or data warehouse to identify segments of the population with particular needs	• Global performance rating of use of principles of epidemiology and population health • Written examination of knowledge of statistical terminology and concepts used in population health • Written examination of knowledge of the social determinants of health and disease • Self-assessment of the outcome measures of care stratified for population characteristics in the microsystem in which the resident participates
Medical education	• Diagnose the developmental stage of staff, students and colleagues • Adjusts teaching and learning conversations to the developmental stage of students, colleagues and staff • Select teacher styles appropriate to learners' developmental stage, • Apply the concepts and methods described by the learning cycle in teaching • Provide and receive feedback on performance skillfully • Use objective measures of performance in providing feedback • Practice reflection on action and reflection in action • Develop graphical representations of mental models to guide the work performed in the clinical microsystem • Interact with teachers to receive guidance in progression through the developmental stages • Use electronic educational support tools (e.g., PowerPoint) to effectively communicate concepts and processes of care	• Global performance rating on medical education for self-directed learning and helping others learn • OSCE demonstrating skill in assessment of learning needs, giving feedback, teaching, coaching, and facilitation methods to help others learn • Written examination of knowledge of developmental stages, experiential learning cycle, and principles of feedback in learning • Peer and/or faculty rating on a checklist of teaching, coaching, facilitation, and mentoring skills • Team member rating of contributions to the team's learning during team meetings in the clinical microsystem • Portfolio assessment of entries documenting reflection on action in teaching and coaching • Portfolio assessment of self-assessment of learning needs and self-directed learning plan

1. Stephen R. Hayden, MD, Susan Dufel, MD, Richard Shin, MD. Definitions and Competencies for Practice-based Learning and Improvement. Academic Emergency Medicine November 2002, Vol. 9, No. 11 p. 1242–1248.

Teaching–learning methods

The literature on teaching methods for PBLI is growing. Most of the reports describe workshops, quality improvement projects, and the integration of PBLI practices into established learning activities in the residency.

Some programs have reported successful use of the ABIM's Practice Improvement Modules as an effective tool for teaching and learning quality improvement in practice. All of these methods are important beginnings. However, because PBLI is a habit, it becomes the basis for the entire curriculum and is experienced constantly by faculty members, residents, students, and staff members.

To accomplish this sort of integration, program directors might attend to four separate aspects of the teaching methods design:

1. Orientation to PBLI as a cultural habit of members of the residency program

2. Workshops for learning terminology, principles, and methods

3. Existing teaching–learning activities modified to encompass the elements of PBLI

4. Faculty development

Orientation

When a new class begins and at the beginning of each year, senior leaders in the program should explicitly describe how the clinical service and educational programs are inextricably bound through PBLI. This statement resolves the conflict between service and learning. Anchored by this philosophy, practice learning and knowledge generation occur continuously while providing our service.

Moreover, PBLI does not end with completion of the educational program, but continues throughout our professional careers. This restatement of philosophy and explicit description of how it is applied in practice cannot be repeated too often for everyone—residents, faculty members, and staff members.

Workshops for learning concepts

Learners in the novice stage of skills development will need teaching and training experiences to learn the terminology, principles, methods, and use of tools for PBLI.[25] Several programs demonstrated the value of teaching PBLI principles using a combination of reading assignments, online programs, and workshops.[26, 27] Residency programs have ample time set aside for conferences and large group meetings.

Dedicate some of these to advancing everyone from the novice to the advanced beginner stages in PBLI. Do not assume that medical school graduates are in the competent stage of PBLI. Additionally, the specific approaches used by the residency will need to be learned by everyone.

Workshops are designed to provide the learning experience needed to achieve the objectives shown in the table. Residents can learn the principles and terminology via readings and lectures/discussions.

However, hands-on workshops are the best way to teach the application of methods. PBLI uses many computer-based tools in medical informatics, quality improvement, KM, and evidence-based medicine. Everyone will need to be at least at the advanced beginner stage in order to use these tools to engage in PBLI.

Examples include electronic health records, PDAs (laptops), smartphones, e-mail, and the learning portfolio. Other tools for collaboration, KM, and quality improvement will be specific to the local setting. The theory behind these tools is not important, but ability in their use is.

Many of the microsystems residents experience in the program provide the opportunity for applying QI processes and team-based practices to improve care. The clinical policies and procedures used in these microsystems may not be well developed; therefore, they can be used to diagram care processes, identify redundant or workaround steps, and improve the quality of the care. Where they exist, programs may use these microsystem improvements as examples and encourage residents to help the Microsystems apply these tools for quality improvement, knowledge management, and evidence-based practice.

Incorporate PBLI practice into every rotation

Explicitly define the PBLI objectives for each rotation: All microsystems use medical informatics tools. Residents can apply evidence-based medicine principles to every clinical decision. KM, although a relatively new concept, is applied in different ways in different settings. The introduction of quality measures and system improvement practices within the microsystem

demonstrates how knowledge about practice is generated and managed. Medical education shifts from lectures, rounds, conferences, and reading to the dynamic process of team meetings and both individual and microsystem betterment through continuous quality improvement. The curriculum is driven by the need to solve patient problems and to continually improve the care we deliver.[28]

Teaching rounds (clinic attending): The content and process of the conversations between teacher and learner during teaching rounds, clinic, or a procedure should focus on the attending physician understanding the learner's thinking and making the appropriate corrections to errors in methods.

When the teacher focuses on the care delivered and sees the learner as a professional member of the team and microsystem delivering the care, the elements of PBLI come alive. Every attending physician activity is an opportunity to demonstrate the principles of medical education contained within PBLI. When you bring the learning portfolio into the clinical setting, it becomes a useful tool for tracking learning and demonstrating improvement.

Morning report, mortality and morbidity conferences, quality improvement conferences, and microsystem team meetings: Routinely scheduled conferences and meetings in the program and each microsystem provide ample opportunity for learning and practicing PBLI.

Focus these conferences on using medical informatics tools, generating and managing knowledge, and applying evidence-based medicine analysis for the scientific validity of knowledge and the generation of local knowledge through the process of system improvement. When the content of knowledge and practice is equally balanced with exploration and improvement of the processes, PBLI is in action in the program. However, this transition requires intensive faculty development.

A portfolio for PBLI is the tool for reflection on action and developing the objective measurement of the learning and outcome of the practice. The portfolio is a personal learning plan and record of progress in generating and organizing knowledge.

The use of learning portfolios is in its infancy in medical education; however, the experience is rapidly growing, and increasingly user-friendly Web-based tools will continue to be developed.[29, 30, 31, 32] Faculty assessment of the quality and contents of the portfolio provides evidence of PBLI and the basis for advancement through the residency.

Faculty development

Program directors select content and process experts in medical informatics, KM, evidence-based medicine, systems-improvement population health, and medical education to conduct the workshops for residents, new employees, and faculty members. The evaluation of faculty performance should include measurement, observation, and feedback on their application of the elements of PBLI in their teaching in individual professional development. This evaluation should become an essential component for faculty promotion and recognition.

In addition to faculty development in the application of PBLI principles, methods, and use of the tools that support it, faculty members should develop to the competent stage in medical education practice. This means applying the experiential learning cycle, diagnosing the developmental stage of learners, and selecting a teaching, coaching, facilitation, or mentoring approach best suited for the stage.

Faculty members will need to develop competent stage skills in giving feedback and stimulating reflection on action. Some faculty members must develop skills in performing assessments and evaluations of learners' achievement of the learning objectives for the rotation.

Conclusion

PBLI is the basis for all professional development and medical education. It is a habit of practice that involves interaction with professionals at more advanced developmental stages. PBLI distinguishes two types of medical knowledge: explicit scientific knowledge assessed and developed through evidence-based methods, and tacit knowledge that is generated through changes to systems to improve quality by measuring processes and outcomes of our work and using the measurement to design and test improvement ideas. Both forms of knowledge are essential to medical practice and both require active personal and organizational KM.

The computer and the Web are essential tools for managing information and knowledge and improving the efficiency and accuracy of coordinating and improving care across large and complex systems. The mastery of these tools for clinical practice is another component of PBLI. Underpinning evidence-based medicine and system improvement are the sciences of epidemiology and statistics derived from the field of population health. This approach expands our horizons beyond the individual patient and into the population and community from which the patient comes.

Lastly, the heart and soul of PBLI is medical education rooted in the practice of experiential learning guided by those who have advanced farther along the professional development scale. Self-assessment and self-motivated learning are channeled through more advanced guides and continuous feedback from patients, peers, and the public on how well we are meeting the needs we've committed our professional lives to serve.

PBLI is much more than a quality improvement project or analysis of published knowledge. It is a way of life that is essential for continuous professional development.

Innovative Approaches, Models, and Assessment Tools for Teaching and Assessing Practice-Based Learning and Improvement

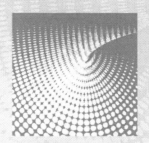

CONTENTS

A Practical Guide to Teaching and Assessing the ACGME Core Competencies, Second Edition

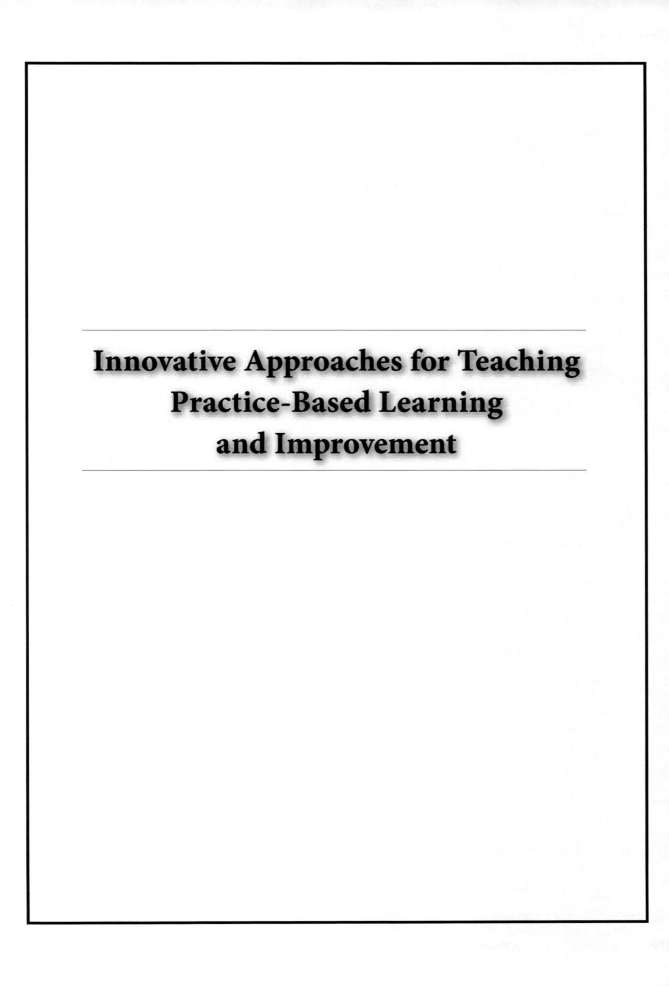

Innovative Approaches for Teaching Practice-Based Learning and Improvement

Four-Step Learning Activity to Meet the Practice-Based Learning and Improvement Competency

The new year is an introspective time as many set resolutions for the year ahead. Apply the same introspective spirit to your program by strengthening teaching efforts in the competency all about self-reflection—practice-based learning and improvement (PBLI).

PBLI can be simply summed up as a physician analyzing and improving his or her own practice behaviors. The goal is for program directors, coordinators, and faculty members to teach residents and fellows to become lifelong learners who constantly strive to improve their practice.

According to the ACGME, residents and fellows must meet the subcompetencies of PBLI:

- Identify strengths and areas that need improvement

- Set goals for improvement

- Evaluate their clinical practice

- Use feedback to improve their practice

- Find, evaluate, and assimilate medical information related to patients' problems

- Use information technology as a learning tool

- Teach the public and members of the healthcare team

Designing meaningful curricular activities that teach trainees to self-reflect, grow, and be lifelong learners is a challenge, says Alexandre Hageboutros, MD, director of the hematology/oncology fellowship program at Cooper University Hospital in Camden, NJ. To meet this challenge, Hageboutros developed a four-part learning exercise that provides a framework for self-reflection and improvement. By the end of the exercise, fellows will have hit upon each of the PBLI subcompetencies.

Map out the path to lifelong learning

Successful PBLI learning activities must be "consistent, repetitive, and get fellows into the habit of learning and acquiring knowledge through self-reflection," says Hageboutros.

The exercise Hageboutros developed repeats itself every month during the three-year fellowship program. By graduation, trainees have completed the cycle more than 30 times, he says. The cycle is composed of the following four steps:

1. Trainee meets with the program director to discuss his or her performance and identify areas of medical knowledge that need improvement

2. Trainee researches the identified subject

3. Trainee writes five multiple-choice questions about the subject and provides supporting evidence and a summary regarding each answer choice

4. Trainee teaches another colleague about the topic

Each step has built-in documentation, showing the ACGME that you taught fellows PBLI, says Vicki Kay, coordinator for the hematology/oncology fellowship program at Cooper University Hospital.

Get self-reflection on the calendar

Residents and fellows often don't take time to reflect on their experiences. That's why one-on-one meetings with the program director are vital to this process. If trainees know they will be expected to discuss their performance, they will have to sit down and think about it, Hageboutros says. During the meeting, discuss the following with residents or fellows:

- **Trainee's observations.** Ask trainees what challenged them since the last meeting and discuss those experiences, Hageboutros says.

- **Feedback.** Share advice on how trainees should handle similar situations in the future. Additionally, pass along any feedback you've received from attending physicians during the past month or rotation.

- **Areas needing improvement.** Discuss with trainees the areas in which they need to improve in any of the six competencies. Then help trainees identify an area of medical knowledge they're uncomfortable with, Hageboutros says, adding that trainees should spend the next month researching that subject.

Note: Because the cycle repeats itself, you should also dedicate part of the meeting to discussing the topics of study from the previous month's assignment.

The meetings sound time-intensive, but Hageboutros says keeping them focused makes them manageable. "Encounters are probably only 15–20 minutes," he says. "If you have a lot of fellows, divide them among other division members. It doesn't have to be just the program director who meets with them."

The regularly scheduled meetings serve as the documentation needed to show the ACGME that these teaching sessions occurred, Kay says. Along with monthly evaluations, the evidence is on the calendar.

Research and appraise information

After the meeting, trainees research the area of medical knowledge identified and write five board-style multiple-choice questions related to the topic.

Throughout these parts of the exercise, trainees engage in several aspects of PBLI. They learn how to use information technology to find, evaluate, and assimilate medical information.

Give trainees guidelines for how to structure the multiple-choice questions. Ask residents or fellows to provide explanations as to why each answer given is correct or incorrect. Require trainees to cite each source used in developing the questions and answers so you can ensure that they are using the most appropriate and reliable resources.

At the end of the month, the fellows e-mail their questions to Hageboutros and all of the other fellows. The other trainees can test their knowledge and learn a little about the topic as well.

Tip: Compile all of the questions trainees send you to create a board study guide.

The e-mails are the next step for ACGME documentation. A site visitor can flip through a folder with the fellows' e-mails and see that you're meeting both the PBLI and medical knowledge competencies, Kay explains. In fact, a site visitor commended Hageboutros for this exercise during the program's last review.

Become the teacher

The final step is for the fellow or resident to give an informal verbal presentation on the subject to a nurse or other member of the healthcare team.

In addition to meeting the teaching component of PBLI, this step ensures that trainees truly grasp the information they've been researching. To teach a subject, trainees must really understand and have inherent knowledge of the topic. "If the fellows are motivated learners, they will come up with their own questions, learn the subject, and teach it," Hageboutros says.

Pull it off with a team effort

Although this exercise is easy to implement, pulling it off is a team effort, Hageboutros and Kay say.

As the coordinator, Kay is responsible for setting all of the meetings between the fellows and Hageboutros. She also sends notifications to the fellows each month reminding them of the upcoming meetings.

"The fellows are doing this exercise in addition to all of their other clinical and educational responsibilities, so it's a good idea to give them a heads up when the questions are going to be due," Kay explains.

Hageboutros and Kay say feedback regarding the exercise is positive. Graduates tell them they apply the habits learned in this exercise daily in their practice.

"This drill is still a part of how they're continuing to learn and improve themselves," Hageboutros says.

Source: Residency Program Alert, published by HCPro, Inc., January 2010.

Develop a Curriculum for a Resident Teacher Training Program

Starting any project from scratch can be a daunting task. It's always easier if you have a template to work from, and the same holds true for developing a resident-as-teacher training course for your residency program.

The number of teaching templates and tools—specifically those created for GME—has boomed since the introduction of the practice-based learning and improvement competency, which specifically states that residents must be able to teach others.

"You don't have to reinvent the wheel. There are materials available to make it easier and [they] won't be that difficult to implement," says Elizabeth Morrison, MD, MSED, director for faculty development at Eisenhower Medical Center in Rancho Mirage, CA.

Excel with the BEST curriculum

One good place to start your search for resources is The Residents' Teaching Skills website that Morrison developed in conjunction with the GME section of the Association of American Medical Colleges. Access the site at *www.residentteachers.com*.

The site offers a curriculum called Bringing Education & Service Together (BEST). The program covers 10 topics and comes with a faculty guide for each subject. There's also a complete instructor's manual available for a fee.

The website also offers the following tools:

- Video triggers

- Clinical Teaching Perception Inventory* (CPTI), discussed below

- Objective Structured Teaching Examination (OSTE)

Tip: Consider adopting some of these curricula into faculty development seminars. Many of the same theories apply, says Morrison.

Assess your residents

Gauge your residents' teaching skills and perceptions before starting any training program, says Morrison. Ask residents to log in to The Residents' Teaching Skills website and complete the CPTI before and after the training to determine whether the lessons improved their skills.

"It basically helps the person measure his or her own comfort level with teaching," explains Morrison. The results identify the strengths and weaknesses in residents' teaching skills.

You can also use an OSTE to evaluate residents before and after training, says Morrison. Although an OSTE is a robust evaluation method, it can be time-consuming and expensive. You can request OSTE cases and rating skills on The Residents' Teaching Skills website.

    A Practical Guide to Teaching and Assessing the ACGME Core Competencies, Second Edition

Teaching on the spot

Many teachable moments occur on the wards or during rounds, when a senior resident only has one minute to convey a lesson to a junior resident or medical student. That's why many curricula include lessons regarding the one-minute preceptor.

This is a five-step process, and each step is a micro-skill of teaching. "Somebody presents a case to you, and then you have five things you do to have a meaningful teaching interaction," says Lisa Coplit, MD, director for the Institute of Medical Education at Mount Sinai School of Medicine in New York City.

To illustrate the five steps, consider the following example. A medical student goes to a senior resident with a patient care question. Rather than telling the student how to handle the situation, the resident employs the following five steps:

1. **Obtain a commitment from the learner.** This step engages the student in the patient's treatment and forces him or her to think about and make a decision about the patient's condition. Engage the student by asking questions such as, "What do you think is going on with the patient?"

2. **Ask the learner about supporting evidence.** Ask about how the learner came to his or her conclusion and get details about the student's thought process, says Coplit. Ask the student, "Why do you think that?"

3. **Teach a general rule.** "You want to teach one or two clinical pearls. Keep it short. You don't have to teach everything in one sitting," says Coplit.

4. **Emphasize what the learner did well.** Give the learner positive feedback, highlighting what he or she did well. Being specific helps learners easily identify correct behaviors, explains Coplit.

5. **Provide feedback about errors.** In a constructive manner, say what the student did incorrectly or should have done differently. Explain what he or she can do in the future to improve.

Leading the pack

Residents need to learn how to supervise a team. Junior residents often see their senior counterparts juggling several responsibilities and want to be ready to do the same, so add leadership training to your curriculum.

As an icebreaker to the leadership session, consider having residents complete a leadership inventory that measures their leadership skills and gives insights into how they work with others.

The results can prompt residents to think about things such as why they have trouble working with one personality but no problems working with another personality.

With these teaching strategies in mind, you can instruct residents on being better teachers. "Once you plant that seed that 'you are a teacher now' that tends to be an eye-opening experience [for residents]," says Morrison. "I've seen it help them take pride in their work."

Lights, camera, action!

Training residents to be better teachers works best when lessons are interactive, says Morrison. Many programs enhance their training with role-playing. The following are a few of Morrison's tips:

- Divide residents into small groups. Give them a scenario and topic for which they will have to practice teaching for about 10 minutes. Then give the group time to provide the teacher with feedback.

- Base training scenarios on real-life situations you have experienced with former residents.

- Use the term "practice teaching" with residents rather than "role-playing." Some have negative associations with the term "role-playing."

Source: **Residency Program Alert,** *published by HCPro, Inc., June 2008.*

Models and Assessment Tools for Teaching and Assessing Practice-Based Learning and Improvement

| Figure 4.2 | **Presenter Self-Reflection and Improvement Plan** |

Presenter's Name: _____ **Presentation Date:** _____ **Topic:** _____

What do you feel went well with this presentation?

Note to resident/fellow: Please take a moment and review the feedback forms that audience members completed before you continue. If you have an opportunity to watch a videotape of yourself, please do so before continuing.

From your own self-reflection and the feedback of your peers/mentors, what specific <u>areas</u> <u>for</u> <u>improvement</u> do you feel are most outstanding?

1:

2:

3:

What do you plan to <u>do better or differently</u> next time you present?

1:

2:

3:

This evaluation was reviewed with the resident/fellow:

Resident/fellow signature: _____

Reviewer: _____ Date: _____

Note to resident/fellow: Please include the following **documentation** and place in your portfolio folder:

a) All **rating forms** from this presentation

b) Your signed **self-reflection** and learning plan document (this document)

c) Copies of your **handouts** or other presentation materials

Source: Ruth H. Nawotniak, MS, C-TAGME, general surgery coordinator, University of Buffalo.

| Figure 4.3 | **Presenter Evaluation Rubric** |

Presentation Evaluation Rubric

Presenter Name: _____ Presentation Date: _____ Topic: _____

Directions: The purpose of this scoring rubric is to provide presenters with helpful, constructive feedback for professional development. Check the box below the description that most closely matches your observation.

Competency	1 Beginning	2 Developing	3 Accomplished	4 Exemplary
Medical Knowledge	❑ Presentation exhibited significant errors or omissions in medical facts.	❑ Some errors in medical knowledge were apparent, some pertinent concepts were not included.	❑ The important medical issues (both superficial and complex) were identified and correctly explained in the presentation.	❑ Superficial and complex issues were identified and subtle nuances of the medical issues were explained insightfully.
Communication Skills	❑ Presenter was difficult for learners to understand, language was unclear or inappropriate, nonverbal behaviors were distracting or unprofessional.	❑ Appeared to make a conscious effort to engage learners, but there were still distracting or unprofessional elements.	❑ Presenter used clear speech, understandable language, and a professional delivery style. Learners were clearly interested and engaged.	❑ This presenter displayed an exceptional level of communication skills and near flawless delivery. This effort sets a benchmark for quality. Learners were at the highest level of interest and engagement.
Use of Appropriate Supporting Materials	❑ No appropriate handouts or visual aids were used. Learners were left confused and ill-prepared to apply this material.	❑ Handouts or visual aids were incomplete, poorly prepared, may not have been linked to content, or exhibited errors in grammar or spelling. Learners were left desiring more information.	❑ Handouts or visual aids were effectively used to support this presentation. The quality of these tools was professional and appropriate. Learners were able to leave with a full complement of useful and relevant information.	❑ The quality, appropriateness, and professionalism of the handouts or visual aids for this presentation were of the highest standard. Learners were able to leave with a professional-quality set of materials that clearly supported all of the learning objectives of the presentation.

    A Practical Guide to Teaching and Assessing the ACGME Core Competencies, Second Edition

Figure 4.3		**Presenter Evaluation Rubric (cont.)**		

Competency	1 Beginning	2 Developing	3 Accomplished	4 Exemplary
Basis in sound, relevant medical research	❏ Research cited in this presentation was dated, incorrect, or lacking. Learners were left without key information or provided with misinformation.	❏ Research was used in this presentation, but could have been enhanced by additional citations or a more thorough analysis. Learners were left without all the most important information supporting this topic.	❏ Research used in support of this presentation was relevant, timely, and effectively synthesized. Learners were exposed to the key, relevant information and research surrounding this topic.	❏ Research drew on an exceptional body of scholarship and made conclusions that went well beyond the obvious. Learners were given a clear and precise overview of the essential research grounding for this topic.
Evidence of preparation	❏ Presentation appeared to have little planning or focus. Evidence of "last minute" preparation. Learners were left confused or frustrated.	❏ Presentation had a discernable direction and plan, but could benefit from more planning or thought. Learners had to make an effort to follow the "flow" of this presentation.	❏ Presentation was planned, flowed at an appropriate pace, exhibited a clear focus and evidenced preparation. Learners were taken through a presentation with a clear set of objectives and a precise plan for instruction.	❏ Presentation was nearly flawless. Speaker was extremely well prepared. Learners were completely clear on the agenda, supporting arguments, and conclusions.

Comments:

What were three things that you felt were effective, interesting, or especially worthwhile about this presentation?

  1:

  2:

  3:

Everyone can become a better speaker and presenter with feedback and practice. You can help today's speaker by providing a few ideas for improving this skill:

  1:

  2:

  3:

What general comments and feedback do you have about this presentation?

Note to resident: Please include the following documentation and place in your portfolio folder:

  a) All rating forms from this presentation

  b) Your signed self reflection and learning plan document

  c) Copies of your handouts or other presentation materials

Source: Ruth Nawotniak, MS C-TAGME, general surgery coordinator, University of Buffalo.

| Figure 4.4 | **Sample Journal Club Presentation Evaluation** |

Date: _____

Resident: _____

Faculty advisor: _____

Title of article: _____

_____

_____

Scoring scale

1 – Needs improvement

2 – Below average

3 – Average

4 – Above average

5 – Superior

Evaluation

Presentation clear and concise	1	2	3	4	5
Defined the research question	1	2	3	4	5
Explained the materials and methods	1	2	3	4	5
Reviewed pertinent results	1	2	3	4	5
Discussed the strengths and weaknesses of the study	1	2	3	4	5
Offered an opinion about applicability to patient care	1	2	3	4	5
Presentation included review criteria from checklist	1	2	3	4	5

_____

Faculty advisor signature

Source: Department of Obstetrics and Gynecology, Carolinas Medical Center.

      A Practical Guide to Teaching and Assessing the ACGME Core Competencies, Second Edition

| Figure 4.4 | **Resident Self-Reflection Evaluation of Journal Club Presentation** |

Date: _____

Resident: _____

Faculty advisor: _____

Title of article: _____
_____
_____

1. Name a new research concept you learned by reviewing this article.

2. How would improve the design of this study?

3. Do you believe the results of this study will change your clinical management of patients with this problem? How?

4. If the outcomes of this study will not change your clinical practice, what study would you like to have conducted to answer this particular clinical question?

_____

Resident signature

Source: Department of Obstetrics and Gynecology, Carolinas Medical Center.

References

1. Ziegelstein RC, Fiebach NH. "The Mirror" and "The Village": a new method for teaching practice-based learning and improvement and systems-based practice. *Acad Med.* 2004;79:83–88.

2. Surdyk P, Olsen G. The challenge of the outcome project ACGME

3. Gordon P, Tomasa L, Kerwin J. ACGME Outcomes Project: selling our expertise. *Fam Med.* 2004;36:164–167.

4. Mazmanian, PE. Practice-based learning and improvement. *J Contin Educ Health Prof.* 2003;23:53.

5. Lynch DC, Swing SR, Horowitz SD, Holt K, Messer JV. Assessing practice-based learning and improvement. *Teach Learn Med.* 2004;16:85–92.

6. Dreyfus SE. The five-stage model of adult skill acquisition. *Bull Sci Technol Soc.* 2004;24:177–181.

7. Kolb D. *Experiential Learning: Experience as the Source of Learning and Development.* Englewood Cliffs, NJ: Prentice Hall PTR; 1984.

8. Eraut M. *Developing Professional Knowledge and Competence.* Bristol, PA: The Falmer Press; 1994.

9. National Healthcare Quality Report 2005. ARHQ website. *www.ahrq.gov/qual/nhqr05/nhqr05.htm.* Accessed September 4, 2007.

10. Blumenthal D. The role of physicians in the future of quality management. *NEJM.* 1996;335:1328–1331.

11. Institute of Medicine. *To Err is Human: Building a Safer Healthcare System.* Washington, DC: The National Academies Press; 2000.

12. McGlynn EA, Asch SM, Adams J, et al. The quality of health care delivered to adults in the United States. *NEJM.* 2003;348:2635–2645.

13. Committee on Quality of Health Care in America, Institute of Medicine. *Crossing the Quality Chasm: A New Health System for the 21st Century.* Washington, DC: National Academies Press; 2004.

14. Berwick DM, James B, Coye MJ. The connections between measurement and reporting. *Med Care.* 2002;41(suppl):I30–I38.

15. Choudhry N, Fletcher R, Soumerai S. Systematic review: the relationship between clinical experience and quality of health care. *Annals Int Med.* 2005;142: 260–273.

16. Davis DA, Mazmanian PE, Fordis M, Van Harrison R, Thorpe KE, Perrie L. Accuracy of physician self-assessment compared with observed measures of competence: a systematic review. *JAMA.* 2006;296: 1094–1102.

17. Duffy FD, Holmboe ES. Self-assessment in lifelong learning and improving performance in practice: physician know thyself. *JAMA.* 2006;296(9):1137–1139.

18. Nelson EC, Godfrey MM, Batalden PB, et al. Clinical microsystems, part 1. The building blocks of health systems. *Jt Comm J Qual Patient Saf.* 2008;34(7): 367–378.

19. Holmboe ES, Lynn L, Duffy FD. Improving the quality of care via maintenance of certification and the web: an early status report. *Pers Biol Med.* 2008;51(1);71–83.

20. Kindig D, Stoddart G. What is population health? *Am J Public Health.* 2003;93(3):380.

21. Sackett DL, Rosenberg WM, Gary JA, Haynes RB, Richardson WS. Evidence based medicine: what it is and what it isn't. *BMJ.* 1996;13:312(7023)71–72.

22. Laurie SJ, Mooney CJ, Lyness JM. Measurement of the general competencies of the Accreditation Council for Graduate Medical Education: a systematic review. *Acad Med.* 2009;84(3):301–309.

23. Lyman JA, Schorling J, Nadkarni M, May N, Scully K, Voss J. Development of a web-based resident profiling tool to support training in practice-based learning and improvement. *J Gen Intern Med.* 2008;23(4):485–488.

24. Verkey P, Natt N, Lesinck T, Downing S, Yudkowsky R. Validity evidence for an OSCE to assess competency in systems-based practice and practice-based learning and improvement: a preliminary investigation. *Acad Med.* 2008;83(8):775–790.

25. Ogrinc G, Headrick LA, Morrison LJ, Foster T. Teaching and assessing resident competence in practice-based learning and improvement. *J Gen Intern Med.* 2004; 19:496–500.

26. Tomolo AM, Lawrence RH, Aron DC. A case study of translating ACGME practice-based learning and improvement requirements into reality: systems quality improvement projects as the key component to a comprehensive curriculum. *Postgrad Med J.* 2009; 85(1008):530–537.

27. Huntington JT, Dycus P, Hix C, et al. A standardized curriculum to introduce novice health professional students to practice-based learning and improvement: a multi-institutional pilot study. *Qual Manag Health Care.* 2009;18(3):174–181.

28. Morrison LJ, Headrick LA. Teaching residents about practice-based learning and improvement. *Jt Comm J Qual Patient Saf.* 2008;34(8):453–459.

29. Carraccio C, Englander R. Evaluation Portfolio for the Association of Pediatric Program Directors (APPD). APPD website. *www.appd.org.*

30. O'Sullivan PS, Cogbill KK, McClain T, Reckase MD, Clardy JA. Portfolios as a novel approach for residency evaluation. *Acad Psych.* 2002;26:173–179.

31. Pinsky LD, Fryer-Edwards K. Diving for PERLS: working and performance portfolios for evaluation and reflection on learning. *J Gen Intern Med.* 2004;19:582–587.

32. Driessen EW, Van Tartwijk J, Overeem K, Vermunt JD. van der Vleuten CPE. Conditions for successful reflective use of portfolios in undergraduate medical education. *Med Educ.* 2005;39:1230–1235.

CHAPTER 5

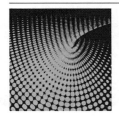

Systems-Based Practice

Ruth H. Nawotniak, MS, C-TAGME

Introduction

One of the most challenging and interesting of the six core competencies is systems-based practice. A major obstacle for many medical educators regarding this competency is in understanding its purpose and definition. Once you understand what the competency is all about, a wealth of opportunities for documenting the learning process toward competency will present themselves.

Definitions and ACGME Expectations

The competency of systems-based practice can be defined as being aware of how to use the healthcare system to provide relevant services for quality patient care that are cost-effective and that enhance patient safety. According to Davison, Cadavid, and Spear, systems-based practice encompasses how the business aspects of practicing medicine affect how the healthcare team cares for patients.[1]

In general, the ACGME's statements of competency are broad. Then they take each competency and break it down into subcompetencies, or focus points, which are inherent within the broad statement. Programs may find that developing learning situations that teach and assess a specific component is easier than trying to address the broad competency.

Consider the descriptions of the following five subcompetencies of systems-based practice:

- Residents comprehend how the healthcare system affects their practice and how their patient care practices affect healthcare practitioners, organizations, and society

- Residents comprehend how practice and delivery systems differ, including strategies for restraining costs and allotting resources

- Residents maintain high-quality patient care while watching costs and resource use

- Residents champion quality patient care and help patients manage the complex healthcare system

- Residents understand how to work collaboratively with other members of the healthcare team to evaluate, coordinate, and advance healthcare, and know how this affects healthcare system performance[1]

Why Teach and Assess Systems-Based Practice?

Physicians are expected to provide the best and safest care for their patients. In doing so, medical educators must teach physicians-in-training to recognize system components, evaluate the effectiveness of these systems and resources, and, when appropriate, effect change.[2] This means residents must:

- Cultivate empathy and compassion

- Be aware of the obstacles patients and their families experience

- Understand the social determinants of health

- Recognize how they can serve patients

- Realize the benefits of active learning[3]

Wang and Vozenilek state, "The provisions of this core competency require that residents understand the relationship of their individual medical practice to the context of the health care system as a whole."[4]

Appropriate methods of assessment for this competency are still being developed. It can be argued that this competency, along with the competency of practice-based learning and improvement, are not fully developed until the physician has been in practice, and therefore, residents cannot be adequately assessed at the physician-in-training level. Systems-based practice education fosters an understanding of the competency, recognition of the complexities of providing quality patient care, and appreciation of the impact that the healthcare system as a whole will have upon the physician's individual practice.

Lee et al. suggest thinking of the definition and sub-competencies of systems-based practice as constantly evolving because the system is always changing. Physicians must dedicate themselves to lifelong learning in order to evolve with the system and constantly improve their practice and the system.[5]

Building a Curriculum

A curriculum usually results from the identification of an educational need and the decision to meet that need. It includes goals and objectives, educational activities, and an assessment process. The assessment process provides the feedback for continual improvement.

With a competency-based education model, educators set specific objectives that learners must become proficient in and attain. It shifts our focus away from process-oriented measures of education (e.g., how many procedures a resident completed) to outcome-oriented measures (how well the resident completed the procedure).[6]

In developing a curriculum for systems-based practice, we can first break down the "systems" that are involved in healthcare delivery. The list of items for consideration can be grouped by theme:

- **Healthcare services:** in-hospital services and systems, such as imaging and lab studies; prescribing medications; patient safety concerns, including communication and resident handoff procedures; and discharge planning, including end-of-life care, home healthcare services, rehabilitation services, therapy services, nursing home services, and assisted living services

- **Healthcare needs:** medications, equipment, transportation, and nutrition

- **Patient-related concerns:** economics and ethnic makeup of the community served, living will requirements, and patient–family relationships and responsibility issues

- **The cost of doing business:** insurance providers, physician contracts, coding, and office expenses such as equipment and personnel

Use these groups of systems as a guide to the breadth and depth of material from which you can draw when developing teaching points.

The ACGME website (*www.acgme.org*) offers examples and programs to help educators develop curricula and assessment methods for all the competencies. You can find these in two locations using the side menubar. The first is under the Outcome Project tab. Here you will find several subtopics, including:

- **Assessment:** provides a toolbox of assessment methods as well as examples from the field

- **Implementation:** includes an extensive list of resources and a section called RSVP— Recognizing Success Via imPlementation— that lists assessment and evaluation activities residency programs are currently utilizing

The second resource is under the Review Committees tab. The top item is All RC Notable Practices. This page includes a collection of activities from various clinical specialties that the ACGME has found worthy to share with the field. Numerous best practices are described from both surgical and nonsurgical specialties.

Regarding curriculum development for systems-based practice in particular, the ACGME suggests basing the curriculum not on the broad competency statement, but rather on the subcompetencies that are relevant for the rotation and educational experience you have chosen.[7] The goal is for residents to realize that they are part of a larger healthcare system and that they must know about these systems in order to become an advocate for quality care for their patients.

Specific Teaching Strategies for Systems-Based Practice

In 2009, the ACGME launched the *Journal of Graduate Medical Education*. The inaugural issue, published in September 2009, focused on articles regarding systems-based practice. It is an excellent collection of recent literature on teaching and assessment strategies. You can access it by going to *www.acgme.org* and clicking on the Journal Grad Med Ed tab.

Davison, Cadavid, and Spear's article "System-Based Practice: Education in Plastic Surgery" provides a comprehensive example of how to use competency-based education to teach systems-based practice.[1] They state that training program leaders must establish objectives for the residency program and for individual residents.

Program objectives include determining appropriate activities and providing adequate support for the activities. This support should come in the form of resources, evaluation tools, and faculty feedback that ensure that residents met their objectives. Establish individual resident objectives, including completing, documenting, and evaluating the activities required. Residents can use self-study activities such as required reading, as well as video and online instructional programs to examine the risks involved with patient care. Use didactic lectures, small group discussions, and grand rounds presentations in conjunction with, or independent of, self-study programs.

An article by Dunnington and Williams, "Addressing the New Competencies for Residents' Surgical Training," discusses activities developed at their institution for teaching the competencies, including systems-based practice.[8] See the authors' recommendations in Figure 5.1.

Figure 5.1		SIU Competency Recommendations	

ACGME Competency	Sub-Competency	Method for Fostering Learning of This Competency	Measurement Instrument
Systems-based practice		Residents complete a 12-month service on one of the hospital quality improvement/patient safety committees during the second year of residency	Residents maintain a log book that records the issues that were discussed during their service on the committee and indicate how they will practice differently as a result of this experience
		Resident to design and complete one project during tenure as a resident that deals with a healthcare systems issue; this project may be stimulated by committee experience, morbidity and mortality conference, or patient care experiences	Resident to prepare project report and present during grand rounds at the end of the second year; the project report is to identify the problem, describe a solution to the problem, discuss the merits of the solution, and anticipate new problems that the solution may produce

Residents to work in teams on two of these projects |
| | | Resident submits a practice-based improvement form for his or her cases presented at M & M; The form guides the resident to describe the complication and its active and latent causes, and prompts the resident to indicate system changes and personal practice changes that could avert such errors in the future or mitigate their effects. | Practice-based improvement form |
| **Patient care** | Communication with patients and significant others | Core curriculum
Universal issues curriculum
Feedback from attendings, patients, and significant others | SIU clinical performance and professional behavior (CPPB) scale
ABIM patient satisfaction questionnaire
Notable resident performance reports for clinically effective and ineffective behaviors |

Figure
5.1

SIU Competency Recommendations (cont.)

ACGME Competency	Sub-Competency	Method for Fostering Learning of This Competency	Measurement Instrument
Patient care (cont.)	Data collection	Surgical grand rounds Core curriculum Self-directed learning Feedback from attendings	SIU CPPB scale
	Diagnostic and therapeutic interventions	Surgical grand rounds Core curriculum Self-directed learning Feedback from attendings	SIU CPPB scale
	Patient management	Surgical grand rounds Core curriculum Self-directed learning Feedback from attendings	SIU CPPB scale
	Patient counseling and education	Core curriculum Self-directed learning Feedback from attendings and patients	SIU CPPB scale Patient assessment and management examination
	Technical skills	Performance in the OR and clinic	Sentinal-case mapping rating forms, SIU CPPB scale
		Surgical skills lab curriculum with procedure certification (PGY I-III)	Surgical skills lab procedure certification
	Prevention and health maintenance	Core curriculum Self-directed learning Feedback from attendings	Patient assessment and management examination SIU CPPB scale
	Working with other health-care professionals	OR and clinic experience Feedback from attendings and other healthcare professionals	
	General patient care	Surgical grand rounds OR and clinic experience Feedback from attendings Core curriculum Self-directed learning	Patient assessment and management examination SIU CPPB Scale

Figure 5.1	SIU Competency Recommendations (cont.)

ACGME Competency	Sub-Competency	Method for Fostering Learning of This Competency	Measurement Instrument
Medical knowledge		Surgical grand rounds Self-directed learning Core curriculum Preparation for ABSITE	American Board of Surgery In-Training Examination (ABSITE) SIU CPPB Scale
Practice-based learning and improvement	Information technology use	Self-directed learning Feedback from attendings	Skill will be evidenced through journal club activities and through project described under systems-based practice
	Critical appraisal of literature	Preparation for and participation in journal club Preparation for patient care	Residents complete and submit structured clinical appraisals of articles as part of their journal club responsibilities.
	Facilitate learning of students and other healthcare professionals	Residents as teachers workshop	End-of-clerkship teaching evaluation
Interpersonal and communication skills		Self-directed learning Feedback from healthcare professionals Core curriculum Practice with patients Feedback from patients Practice in OR and clinic	SIU professional behavior instrument SIU CPPB scale ABIM patient satisfaction questionnaire Patient assessment and management examination SIU CPPB scale
Professionalism		Practice in OR and clinic Feedback from patients and other healthcare professionals Surgical ethics curriculum Universal issues Curriculum Practice with patients	ABIM patient satisfaction questionnaire Patient assessment and management examination.

Adapted from: Dunnington, Gary L MD; Williams, Reed G, PhD. Addressing the New Competencies for Residents' Surgical Training. Academic Medicine Vol 78(1) January 2003, p. 14–21.

The authors of these two articles utilize many small group discussion formats to teach residents about systems-based practice. Small group discussions are ideal for facilitating interaction between residents and the faculty or other appropriate hospital personnel.

The ability to capture and use immediate or recent resident experiences in a hands-on learning situation has tremendous educational value. Small group discussions allow the maximum opportunity for individual contributions to the discussion. The authors also offer a method of objective and subjective evaluations to assess the learning activity.

The following are examples of potential opportunities for small group discussions:

- Morbidity and mortality (M&M) conferences

- Discharge planning sessions

- Patient relations sessions

- Quality improvement/patient safety committee

- Risk management/root-cause analysis committee

- Hospital outreach programs[1]

M&M conferences

Most programs have M&M conferences built into their schedules. In some programs they are called M&M conferences; in others, they are called risk management or quality assurance conferences. Regardless of the title, residents discuss patient care outcomes, focusing on death or complications during this conference.

Because M&M conferences are already established in most programs, they are ideal for expanding into many educational areas. M&M conferences may be one of the most robust activities in which educators can teach systems-based practice. The impact of the healthcare delivery system on patient outcomes is the focus of the conference. Use M&M conferences as an opportunity to choose timely cases and apply the systems-based practice subcompetencies to the discussion. There are many teaching strategies for managing M&M educational opportunities:

- Presentations by residents with a systems-based practice focus

- Discussions with the healthcare providers involved in a patient case

- Presentation by hospital administrative personnel on policies and procedures

A more complete learning activity involves taking the initial discussion of a specific case at M&M, and following up with multiple discussions with various members of the healthcare team. The intent of this activity is for the resident and the team to identify ways to improve the healthcare delivery system.

Rosenfeld's article describes how an analysis of contributing healthcare system problems can augment typical case presentations. This analysis expanded the discussion to include patient safety issues, communication problems, ethical concerns, and cultural issues.[9]

Residents can document this process by placing a copy of their presentation in their portfolio. They can also keep a log of their cases and then analyze a system problem that affected one or two of those cases. The resident can discuss these with the program director during file reviews, or in a small group session specifically scheduled for this purpose.

The following are further examples of projects residents can complete and discuss at M&M conferences:

- Residents discuss the correct coding for procedures done during the case. This exercise teaches current procedural terminology (CPT) descriptors and the use of modifiers, as well as the impact that coding has on the billable and reimbursable costs involved with the procedure performed.

- Residents examine the timing of events—such as when an order was given and when it was carried out, or when a consult was requested and when the consult occurred—and the impact the timing may have had on the patient outcome.

- Residents analyze the impact of multiple medications, dosage, and timing.

Each of these examples can be modified to apply to real-time patient encounters.

Discharge planning sessions

Partnering the resident with other healthcare managers and providers to assess a patient's needs outside the hospital familiarizes the resident with the agencies and healthcare providers involved in the post-hospital phase of the patient's care. In this setting, the resident experiences firsthand how the patient's environmental,

economic, and social circumstances can impact care. The resident gains a greater understanding of the complexity of the healthcare system. As trainees learn of the various options for executing their patients' treatment plans, they can factor patients' environmental and socioeconomic situations into their treatment decisions.

Establish small group sessions with the resident, utilization nurse, or social worker on a regular basis to discuss the discharge process for one of the resident's patients. Address the following questions during this session:

- Is the patient being discharged to home or to a healthcare facility?

- Which discharge planning, coordination, and outside healthcare provider systems will the patient require? What impact will these services have upon the economic welfare of the patient?

- What are all the options?

Another facet of this session would be a discussion of the paperwork trail and legal responsibilities as well as resource allocation.[1]

The resident can also use a pre- and post-audit process to document learning activities that involved meetings with other healthcare workers. Before an activity takes place, the resident completes a grid that shows the demographics of the patient, a short statement explaining why he or she was in the hospital and what occurred there, a short description of the treatment plan going forward, and a short discharge note. Ten days after the discharge planning session, the resident completes the grid for another patient.

Review the grid during a small group discussion or a faculty/resident discussion, looking for a more detailed discharge note on the post-activity grid. The more detailed note should indicate the resident's increased awareness of what is involved in his or her patient's post-hospital care.

Expand this documentation activity to include a study of the cost of at-home follow-up care, including an analysis of the cost of medications, both short and long term.

Patient relations sessions

Small group discussions with hospital-based patient advocacy or patient relations personnel should focus on the support structure, or lack thereof, for patients; cultural or ethnical communication issues; patients' rights and privacy issues; and patient-directed activities such as do-not-resuscitate or living will guidelines. Although issues of professionalism are important here, discussions of these items make residents aware of the support and services that are available and/or necessary to the patient after his or her hospital stay.[1] Residents will learn to facilitate these support services for their patients.

Quality improvement/ patient safety committee

Assign residents to sit as members of patient safety/ quality committees, or schedule independent discussion groups between residents and hospital patient safety or quality improvement personnel. By attending these meetings, residents have the opportunity to participate in discussions to develop system improvements

that enhance patient safety. By witnessing the impact system modifications can have on patient safety, residents begin to have a better understanding of how the system functions as a whole and contributes to patient care. They will also see how improvements ultimately affect the cost of healthcare to the post-hospital patient.[1]

Risk management/root-cause analysis committee

Including residents on risk management committees or asking the risk management attorney or hospital administrator to speak with residents provides a learning experience regarding the legal aspects of practicing medicine.[1] These meetings usually take place after an adverse outcome occurs regarding patient care. The discussion of the adverse outcome can highlight the impact that documentation can have on legal activities. By discussing recent events, educators and other experts can emphasize the importance of properly executed patient consent forms, time and date stamps with signatures, and supporting documentation for patient treatment plans in patients.

Assess residents' knowledge by creating and administering a pre- and post-assessment questionnaire. This type of assessment can also demonstrate how exposure to various healthcare systems affected the resident's patient care practices over time.

Use attendance records, meeting agendas, or a checklist of healthcare system topics addressed as documentation for small group sessions and committees.

Hospital outreach programs

Many hospitals already have outreach programs that facilitate delivery of care to the underserved. These programs address the balance between the fiscal and medical missions of hospitals. Resident involvement in these programs or participation in in-service training sessions focused on these programs also teaches residents about systems-based practice.

Small group venues give the resident the opportunity to interact with other healthcare providers within the hospital system. Residents can then apply new knowledge and understanding of systems-based practice directly to the care of their patients when partnering with other service providers such as RNs, LPNs, discharge planners, and so on. Residents can use this knowledge and understanding to help and teach patients to navigate through a complex healthcare delivery system.

Possible assessment methods for these sessions include keeping a log listing the systems involved with cases, using a checklist for cases discussed during the small group sessions that incorporates the various systems available for patient care, or producing a write-up of an assigned case showing the incorporation of the various systems in the management of a patient's care. Sign-in sheets or minutes provide documentation of resident participation in training sessions, meetings, or small group discussions.

Formal didactic lectures

Davison, Cadavid, and Spear also emphasize the need for formal didactic lectures to disseminate general knowledge to larger groups. Most training programs already have a grand rounds schedule, which usually focuses on formal presentations given by residents, faculty members, and invited speakers. Grand rounds topics typically are clinically oriented, but they can also include topics that provide additional educational benefits and meet some of the requirements for education in the six competencies. All of the didactic lectures discussed in the following sections include systems-based practice concepts and can easily fit into a grand rounds concept and schedule. If the lectures are scheduled on a rotating basis throughout the total training period, structure the topics in a manner that fosters continuous discussion and understanding by the resident. Document resident attendance at these formal lectures using sign-in sheets. Document residents' participation and work by keeping copies of their presentations in their portfolios.

Lee, Beaver, and Greenlee designate specific grand rounds in their lecture schedule that focus on systems-based content. The residents receive notification in advance so that they can select one of their cases for presentation that has systems-based practice applications.[5] Some of the topics to focus on include system practices, utilization of hospital resources and/or personnel, pharmacology practices, and lab/test ordering as they applied to the patient's care.

The hospital experience

This presentation covers the patient experience, from patient registration (including confirmation of benefits, insurance verification, preauthorization, preoperative processes, and documentation required for insurance companies) to the patient diagnosis and medical treatment plan, surgical booking, and postoperative treatment, to billing issues including payment options, reconciliation of billing to payments, explanation of benefits, and patient deductibles.[1] By covering the entire patient experience, residents have the opportunity to view the system (its strengths and inefficiencies) from the patient's perspective.

The hospital experience presentation can also include a description of prescription and lab test ordering that can affect not just patient expenditures, but also hospital expenditures on behalf of patient care. Residents learn what these tests cost both the patient and the hospital. Eglander et al. launched an institutional cost-reduction systems-based practice activity that targeted laboratory fees. Residents, as primary users of the laboratory resources, were engaged in the process, identified the issues, created the solutions, and implemented the new system design.[10]

Healthcare structure

This presentation can cover the gamut of healthcare regulations and delivery systems, from HMOs to Stark laws and acts of Congress, such as the Health Insurance Portability and Accountability Act. This is a crucial topic because it helps the resident understand the effect that societal issues have on the larger system of medicine and how that will affect their practice once they complete their training.[1]

Current procedural terminology (CPT)

This is an essential presentation because it gives residents a basic understanding of how and why CPT codes are used in billing, and how this helps provide cost-effective healthcare. Petrey, Allen, and Thorwarth

emphasize that, "The reimbursement and economic arena will significantly affect daily practice, relationships with other specialties, and compensation."[11] Couple this discussion with a presentation on the International Classification of Diseases, 9th Revision, Coding, which is used for diagnosis and in writing orders, including those for tests.[1]

A limited literature search showed that programs use a combination of either didactic presentation on aspects of coding, or small group instructional sessions and a review of resident documentation. Training programs recruited personnel experienced in coding guidelines to teach the sessions. Residents received instruction on the use of appropriate procedure and diagnostic codes that accurately reflected the patient care activity that was performed.

Petrey, Allen, and Thorwarth discuss the opportunity for training programs to provide education on how residents' daily practice can affect their future reimbursement. Topics or training activities include developing appropriate dictation and coding techniques, understanding reporting guidelines, and increasing the awareness of the multidisciplinary approach and interdependence of physicians in the treatment of patients. A presentation on the current reimbursement and economic climate rounds out the learning experience.[11]

Pre- and post-resident coding activity reviews are commonly used as an assessment tool, with the goal being a decrease in coding errors and an increase in more appropriate dictations.

Evaluation and management codes

Pair a lecture on evaluation and management codes with the lecture on coding just described. During this presentation, discuss what residents should document for evaluation and management codes and how billing differs for time and documentation, as well as what systems are involved during a physical review.[1]

Governance

The purpose of a lecture on governance is to acquaint residents with the roles of several national agencies and how they impact the delivery of care. Ask a hospital administrator to present on this topic. Include the following national agencies in the presentation:

- The Joint Commission

- Centers for Medicare & Medicaid Services

- ACGME

- Occupational Safety and Health Administration

Consider expanding this presentation to include a discussion of the complexities of healthcare in the United States, healthcare reform, and perhaps comparisons with healthcare systems used in other countries. Leave time to discuss how the current system could be improved.[1]

Job search

It is interesting to note that Davison, Cadavid, and Spear also include the job search process in their examples of how to teach systems-based practice. This topic affects how the resident will provide quality care to his or her patient. Discuss the following topics in didactic sessions:

- Differences in medical practices and delivery systems

- Academic versus private/institutional practices

- Surgeon-to-patient ratios

- The uninsured ratios of different communities and their economic impact on healthcare delivery[1]

Patient safety

Patient safety is at the heart of medical education. It, alone, can be a topic for major discussion as it transcends all the competencies. However, aspects of patient safety can easily be added to the list offered by Davison, Cadavid, and Spear. Tailor presentations about patient safety issues to your training program.

Derive these presentations from small group sessions on risk management and root-cause analysis. These presentations can also serve as an initial introduction to a topic, from which small discussion groups are developed. One example of an objective presentation could focus on how larger patient safety issues—such as communication issues during the handoff between resident teams and attending physicians, chart notations, or labeling the patient for a surgical procedure—come out of an analysis of individual incidents to show that the system as a whole may contribute to medical error.

Consider taking a larger patient safety issue—such as the process involved from the time a patient presents in the emergency department to when a consult is called—and develop a project that would improve the system practice that is already in place.

These didactic sessions give residents the opportunity to see the larger picture of healthcare delivery and how what they do in practice can impact that delivery.

Recent literature shows that many residency programs are utilizing teaching strategies that go beyond didactic lectures, small group discussions, and meetings. More multidisciplinary activities are being designed, as well as self-learning Web-based programs. Also, many medical educators now recognize that residents have little or no training in practice management, and more programs are developing activities in that area.

Mock court

One interesting teaching strategy for forensic pathology is listed in Nine's article. Nine conducts an annual mock court held by the law students at the University of New Mexico. During this multidisciplinary activity, pathology fellows play the role of the expert witness, and the law students play the prosecutors and defense attorneys. According to Nine, this activity helps forensic pathologists foster relationships with the legal community.[12]

Web-based educational materials

Time constraints and duty hour regulations have led to the development of Web-based educational materials. The Risk Management Foundation and the Kaiser Family Foundation are just two groups that have developed materials to educate residents on the structure of the healthcare system in the United States.

Achieving Competence Today is another program, which was designed by Peters, Kimura, Ladden, March, and Moore. This particular program consists of a four-week course during which residents participate in activities that examine how money flows through the complex healthcare system. In their article, "A Self-Instructional Model to Teach Systems-based Practice and Practice-based Learning and Improvement," Peters et al. explain that during this program, residents detect a problem in their institution's system, pinpoint a patient case that illustrates the issue, and employ tools or solutions to resolve the issue. The exercise broadens residents' understanding of the system and provides a framework for identifying and acting on areas needing improvement.[13]

Clinical Health Economics System Simulation (CHESS), a computerized team-based quasi-competitive simulator, was developed by Voss, Nadkarni, and Schectman to teach the principles and everyday use of health economics. CHESS is a scenario-based program that simulates treatment costs to patients and society as well as physician reimbursement in a spreadsheet database. Using three differing reimbursement models, teams of residents view scenarios and select from two or three treatment options. Each option is medically justifiable but has different potential cost implications. As treatment options are changed or modified, CHESS displays physician reimbursement and patient and societal costs.[14]

The Surgical Council on Resident Education is developing a national curriculum for general surgery training. It has created a password-protected interactive website that presents more than 200 case-based scenarios, lectures, and procedural video clips along with a robust resource of radiological imaging.[15]

Patient care across sites and transitions of care

Thomas describes an approach for meeting the systems-based practice competency for internal medicine residents with particular focus on the geriatric experience. Residents participate in one of two opportunities. The first option is for the resident to follow one of his or her ambulatory or hospital patients once the patient moves to a subacute or long-term care facility. The second option involves the resident providing care for a hospitalized patient who is usually treated at home or in a nursing home. In each option, the resident sees the patient in the hospital and outside settings. These opportunities give the resident a greater understanding of how transitions between hospitals and outside sites occur, how the transition affects the patient, and how continuity of care is preserved. Residents also gain insights regarding the type of care given at these other facilities.[16]

Practice management program

Jones developed a three-part surgical practice management program for residents. The first part includes a series of monthly lectures presented by hospital administrative staff members that covers topics such as negotiating a contract, managed care, and marketing a practice. The second part consists of education on documentation and coding. The institution's coding and compliance manager meets with residents and uses a combination of lectures and chart review to discuss how and when certain codes and modifiers can be used. The third part is an interactive activity in the clinic setting. At the end of a patient encounter, the resident presents the chart to the coder who will discuss the level of service coded. In this setting, a discussion takes place regarding the use of appropriate evaluation and management service codes and modifiers.[17]

Systems-based practice rotations

Turley, Roach, and Marx developed a unique teaching strategy for systems-based practice. They created a five-day rotation that focuses on the economic and business elements of the healthcare system. The curriculum, assessment tests, evaluations, and results are presented in their article, "Systems Survivor: A Program for House Staff in Systems-Based Practice."[18]

The ACGME offers an excellent overview of the Outcome Project and the development of a competency-based curriculum. This is presented in a downloadable five-module series called "Educating Physicians for the 21st Century." You can find these modules on the ACGME website, *www.acgme.org*, by clicking on the Outcome Project tab on the left sidebar.[19] In the "Introduction to Competency Based Education" module, designed by B. Joyce, PhD.

Joyce suggests opening the discussion of systems-based practice with a series of questions that guide the faculty to define the competency as it applies to their particular program. She also suggests utilizing staff and hospital personnel and services already available to teach residents the concepts of practicing cost-effective healthcare and patient safety issues.

Joyce expands upon this idea in the module, "Practical Implementation of the Competencies." She divides the teaching of systems-based practice into three areas:

- Knowledge of the healthcare system

- Knowledge of practice management issues

- Patient advocacy and safety

She comments on the use of the following activities, some of which were put to use by both Davison, Cadavid, and Spear and Dunnington and Williams in the articles previously mentioned:

- Discussions during clinical teaching times

- Multidisciplinary team rounds

- Patient safety projects, such as root-cause analysis

- M&M conferences and discussions of error or "near-miss" occurrences

- Didactic lectures

- Reviewing and critiquing mock financials based upon their own patients

- Using an actual patient bill to analyze the impact of their decisions on the patient and/or the system

- Analyzing prescription patterns from pharmacy printouts as opportunities for teaching systems-based practice

Even though this list is quite extensive, it is by no means limiting or mandatory. Each program is encouraged to explore other activities and opportunities for educational experiences that may present themselves within the program's own unique setting.

Specific Assessment Strategies for Systems-Based Practice

The ACGME provides several grids that list the competencies and their subcompetencies along with a multitude of assessment methods. For example, in Appendix A, Assessment System Grid, in the Power-Point module "Developing an Assessment Method," Joyce offers the following for assessment of systems-based practice:

- A Clinical Performance Rating tool completed by faculty members who have set behavioral anchors and agree on what those anchors mean

- Focused observation by the faculty who have agreed on the criteria for rating the resident

- Portfolio review by the program director, which contains work effort products produced by the resident showing growth in the understanding of systems-based practice

A second grid in the Implementation section of the Outcome Project suggests the following, in order of preference, as the best methods of evaluation:

- Use the following instruments and tools to enhance residents' understanding of the interaction between their practices and the larger system:

  - 360-degree global rating

  - Objective structured clinical examination (OSCE)

  - Portfolios

- The following assessments measure residents' knowledge of practice and delivery systems:

    - Multiple-choice question (MCQ) exam

    - Chart-stimulated recall

    - Portfolios

    - OSCE

- The following measure how well residents practice cost-effective care with:

    - Checklist

    - 360-degree global rating

    - Record review

- The following instruments evaluate residents' ability to advocate for patients within the healthcare system:

    - 360-degree global rating, patient survey

    - OSCE

    - Portfolios

    - Checklist

Again, these methods are just guidelines for discussion and development. The choice of assessment methods has to fit the program and the opportunities that are available for teaching the competency of systems-based practice.

The assessment tools used by Davison, Cadavid, and Spear suggest two possible assessment methods:

- **360-degree evaluation:** Ask members of the healthcare team who regularly advocate for the patient, such as discharge planning nurses, to evaluate how well residents supported the patient.

- **Pre- and post-tests:** Use these tests to measure the progress of a resident throughout the training period. Utilize a pre-test at the incoming resident level, and administer post-tests mid-cycle and at the end of the training. This provides a longitudinal assessment to monitor the growth of understanding.[1]

Dunnington and Williams use a year-long project for second-year residents. These trainees sit on the hospital committee for quality improvement and patient safety. They keep a record of the issues discussed and results of changes implemented. The residents are then divided into teams of two, and each team chooses a project from those discussions that would apply to one of their patients. This project, when completed, is given as a presentation, and the presentation is placed in the resident's portfolio.[8]

Other assessment tools

Other options for assessment tools include:

- Focused observations focused on systems-based practice: Ask faculty members to monitor the development of the resident in applying the concepts of systems-based practice to the management of his or her patients.

- Short personal reflections written by residents at intervals throughout their training program: The faculty and program director should review the reflections and give feedback to the resident. Some possible topics include:

  - A review of a resident's overall management of a patient with regard to imaging and lab utilization

  - The choice of medications used by the resident in treating a specific patient, showing options, cost concerns, health impact, and reasons for his or her ultimate choice

  - The healthcare systems that one of the residents' discharged patients will need access to

Although time-consuming, consider assigning the resident a patient to shadow. This activity allows the resident to see what the patient must do to navigate through his or her healthcare experience, from office visit, to hospital stay, to discharge and post-hospital care. The resident could create a journal of the activities and systems needed by the patient, including those that were available and those that were not.

Another activity option is to schedule a session with the billing department and the coder, to see how a patient's procedure and/or care were coded and how it affected both the billing and the costs of healthcare. Document both of these activities by asking the resident to complete a case write-up, a personal reflection, or a formal presentation.

Jones, who developed the surgical practice management activity described, evaluated residents quarterly via a chart audit that focused on a specific battery of evaluation and management service codes. The compliance rate was pre-established, and a pre-set number of charts were randomly chosen. Residents were evaluated on an individual basis, as well as a total group.[17]

It is interesting to note that the literature indicates that medical educators are using OSCEs and standardized patients as both simulation activities and evaluation assessment tools.[20, 21]

Much of the recent literature discusses direct observation, checklists, and self-reflections as evaluation methodologies. Lurie and his colleagues performed a search on Medline and ERIC for articles on either qualitative or quantitative data on assessment activities for the competencies since 1999. Their article on the results of this search provides interesting insight into the reliability and validity of preliminary studies.[2]

Faculty Development

Use the ACGME presentation series mentioned earlier, "Educating Physicians for the 21st Century," as a tutorial to train faculty on competency-based education, curriculum development, and evaluation processes. It is an excellent tool for establishing a solid foundation in understanding the educational concepts that underlie the competencies.

However, the competency of systems-based practice requires a broad understanding of the complexities of the healthcare system, including providing cost-effective medicine without compromising the quality of patient care. Many of the recent articles on systems-based practice discuss the fact that there are few faculty members who are trained or expert in the subcompetency areas. This has both positive and negative implications.

On the positive side, this forces training programs to utilize the expertise of other hospital and/or healthcare personnel, creating a multidisciplinary environment. On the negative side, it is more difficult to find faculty mentors for case presentations and/or independent study projects.

Suggested faculty development activities include:

- Encouraging the faculty to participate along with the residents in the systems-based practice activities

- Including presentations by hospital administrative personnel in departmental meetings with time for discussion built in

- Planning an educational retreat whose focus is systems-based practice

- Developing a "Suggested Reading" list on systems-based practice and distributing it to the faculty

Conclusion

In developing curriculum and assessment tools for systems-based practice, it is clear that there is a wealth of material and experiences to draw upon. The good news is that most of this is already available within the structure of the hospital systems in which residents train. A review of the ACGME comments and guidelines, as well as a review of the articles referenced in this chapter, shows that competency in systems-based practice is most successful in an interactive setting that monitors growth, understanding, and habit in the application of the concepts and knowledge of healthcare delivery systems and their impact on the economics of providing patient care and safety.

As managers of graduate medical education training programs, it is important to note that adherence to the ACGME's requirements, including creating a curriculum and measurable outcomes for the six competencies, is mandatory for continued accreditation.

For systems-based practice, the ACGME is looking for measurable outcomes that indicate that residents are attentive to the role the healthcare system plays in their practice and how to use resources within the system to provide the highest quality care.

It is clear from this that, whatever measurement tools you choose to develop to assess this competence, they will need to show the following: that the resident is knowledgeable regarding the healthcare systems that relate to the patient; that the resident shows growth in the utilization of those systems; and that the resident possesses an understanding of cost-effective care and patient safety issues.

Limited Literature Search

There has been an explosion of literature on systems-based practice since 2005. Here is a partial list of articles, some of which have been cited in this chapter, as well as articles that will describe in detail some best practices from the field, both for teaching and for assessment strategies.

Allen, et al. Teaching systems-based practice to residents by using independent study projects. *Acad Med.* 2005;80:125–128.

Nine, et al. Integrating the Accreditation Council for Graduate Medical Education general competencies into forensic pathology fellowship training. *Am J Forensic Med Pathol.* 2005;26(4)334–339.

Reich LM, David RA. Comprehensive Educational Performance Improvement (CEPI): an innovative, competency-based assessment tool. *Mt Sinai J Med.* 2005;72(5)300–306.

Rosenfeld JC. Using the morbidity and mortality conference to teach and assess the ACGME general competencies. *Curr Surg.* 2005;62:664–669.

Voss, et al. The Clinical Health Economics System Simulation (CHESS): a teaching tool for systems- and practice-based learning. *Acad Med.* 2005;80:129–124.

As-Sanie S, Zolnoun D, Wechter ME, Lamvu G, Tu F, Steege J. Teaching residents coding and documentation: effectiveness of a problem-oriented approach. *Am J Obstet Gynecol.* 2005;193(5):1790–1793.

Englander R, Agostinucci W, Zalneraiti E, Carraccio C. Teaching residents systems-based practice through a hospital cost-reduction program: a "win-win" situation. *Teach Learn Med.* 2006;18(2):150–152.

Swick, et al. Assessing the ACGME competencies in psychiatry training programs. *Acad Psych.* 2006;30:330–351.

Zenni, et al. A walk in the patients' shoes: a step toward competency development in systems-based practice. *Ambul Ped.* 2006;6:54–57.

Kerfoot, et al. Web-based education in systems-based practice. *Arch Int Med.* 2007;167:361–366.

Lee AG, Beaver HA, Greenlee E, et al. Teaching and assessing systems-based competency in ophthalmology residency training programs. *Surv Ophthalmol.* 2007;52:680–689.

Leenstra, et al. Validation of a method for assessing resident physicians' quality improvement proposals. *J Gen Intern Med.* 2007;22:1330–1334.

Limited Literature Search (cont.)

Turley C, Roach R, Marx M. Systems survivor: a program for house staff in systems-based practice. *Teach Learn Med.* 2007;19(2):128–138.

Hobgood, et al. Outcome assessment in emergency medicine – a beginning: results of the Council of Emergency Medicine Residency Directors (CORD) Emergency Medicine Consensus Workgroup on Outcome Assessment. *Acad Emerg Med.* 2008;15:267–277.

Jones K, Lebron RA, Mangram A, Dunn E. Practice management education during surgical residency. *Am J Surg.* 2008;196:878–882.

Oyler, et al. Teaching internal medicine residents quality improvement techniques using the ABIM's Practice Improvement Modules. *J Gen Intern Med.* 2008;23(7):927–230.

Peters AS, Kimura J, Ladden MJD, March E, Moore GT. A self-instructional model to teach systems-based practice and practice-based learning and improvement. *J Gen Intern Med.* 2008;237:931–936.

Sehgal, et al. A multidisciplinary team training program: the Triad for Optimal Patient Safety (TOPS) experience. *J Gen Intern Med.* 2008;23(12):2053–2057.

Carter KA, Dawson BC, Brewer K, Lawson L. RVU ready? Preparing emergency medicine resident physicians in documentation for an incentive-based work environment. *Acad Emerg Med.* 2009;16(5): 423–428. [ePub 2009 Mar 24]

Petrey WB, Allen B Jr, Thorwarth WT Jr. Radiology coding, reimbursement, and economics: a practical playbook for housestaff. *J Am Coll Radiol.* 2009;6(9):643–648.

Innovative Approaches, Models, and Assessment Tools for Teaching and Assessing Systems-Based Practice

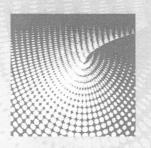

CONTENTS

     A Practical Guide to Teaching and Assessing the ACGME Core Competencies, Second Edition

Innovative Approaches
for Teaching
Systems-Based Practice

Ready, Set, Go: A Relay Race Model for Teaching Systems-Based Practice

If there's one competency that stumps medical educators more than any other, it's systems-based practice, says Stephanie Ward, MD, MPH, assistant professor of medicine and public health at Temple University School of Medicine (TUSM) in Philadelphia.

"A lot of us weren't actually trained in systems-based practice," says Ward.

It's no wonder that program directors often struggle to figure out how to teach, assess, and document residents' progress toward competency in this area.

Freshen up your systems-based practice curriculum by borrowing some of your colleagues' ideas for teaching this competency.

Many programs meet the systems-based practice competency standard by requiring residents to participate in quality improvement (QI) projects. However, this learning experience can fall flat if residents lack commitment and time to carry out the project, says Lawrence Ward, MD, MHP, FACP, associate program director of the internal medicine residency program at TUSM.

For example, many programs require residents to complete a QI project during one of their four-week rotations. In Ward's program, this barely gave residents enough time to develop an idea, perform a root-cause analysis, or implement and evaluate meaningful solutions.

To eliminate the time issue and better engage residents in QI projects, Lawrence Ward, Stephanie Ward, and other faculty members decided to implement an innovative relay race model.

Teams of first- and third-year residents work on one aspect of a QI project, which is integrated with their annual ambulatory block. At the end of the rotation, they pass the baton to the next group, which builds on the work of the previous group to complete the next step.

By the end, four groups have dedicated one month each to the project, advancing it along the way. The four-month process breaks down as follows:

- **Month 1:** The first group identifies the scope of the problem and collects the initial data

- **Month 2:** The second group performs a root-cause analysis to find out what's causing the problem and tries to address it objectively

- **Month 3:** The third group synthesizes the data, performs literature searches to determine how others have addressed the problem, and begins to identify potential solutions

- **Month 4:** The fourth group fills in any remaining holes and finalizes the implementation strategy

Residents transition the work to the next group during a presentation outlining what they've done and potential next steps. Faculty members oversee each project, thereby preserving continuity from one group to the next.

To help residents hit the ground running, the faculty leader also determines the issue residents will tackle. "By introducing the topic, faculty provide the residents with a little bit of background," says Stephanie Ward. Faculty members choose subjects they're already interested in, which reinforces their commitment to mentoring trainees. Past topics examined with this model include physician-industry relations, transition of care, obesity management, and smoking cessation.

Although faculty members are the drivers behind the project, it doesn't take much of their time. The key for faculty is to trust the residents, let them run the show, and fill in holes when needed, says Lawrence Ward.

One successful project looked at how physicians in the clinic managed chronic pain. As a result of the residents' project, program leadership determined there were insufficient policies and education on the subject. Now, clear practice guidelines and educational programs are in place, and physicians and patients are more satisfied with how chronic pain is handled.

No matter what part of the project trainees work on, by the end of the rotation, residents have hands-on experience in quality improvement and a better grasp of systems-based practice, Stephanie Ward says.

Source: Competency connection. **Residency Program Alert,** *July 1, 2009.*

A Tool for Enhancing Morbidity and Mortality Conferences

Morbidity and mortality conferences (MMC) are a staple of resident education and are required by the ACGME. But many MMCs are not designed to effectively teach systems-based practice and improve patient care, says Sean Berenholtz, MD, MHS, associate professor in the Department of Anesthesia/Critical Care Medicine and Surgery at The Johns Hopkins University School of Medicine in Baltimore.

To ensure that residents learn from the medical errors presented, the following needs to occur during MMCs:

- All staff members involved in an incident must give their input

- Caregivers must use a structured framework to probe all aspects of a case

- Leadership must assign responsibility for follow-up on recommendations

Berenholtz integrated this methodology into MMCs by requiring anesthesiology fellows to complete QI projects using the learning from a defect (LFD) tool, which was introduced in an article "A practical tool to learn from defects in patient care," published in the February 2006 *Joint Commission Journal on Quality and Patient Safety.*

Think of the LFD tool as a mini version of a root-cause analysis. Healthcare providers involved in adverse events fill out a one-page form, which asks them to consider system defects rather than individual errors,

Berenholtz says. The LFD tool has three components to give providers a systems perspective:

- Section 1 asks for an objective description of the event

- Section 2 instructs the person to identify factors from a list that may have led to the event, such as training, education, technology, or task- or team-related issues

- Section 3 asks for specific strategies to prevent the system failure from happening again

Fellows must complete one or two LFD projects selected from the clinical or operational adverse events they experienced, or events presented at MMCs or logged into the institution's Web-based error reporting system during their fellowship.

Fellows form an interdisciplinary team to complete the LFD tool. They also select faculty mentors to guide them through the project. Because faculty members may not have the knowledge or interest in leading these projects, allow fellows to look outside your program for mentors with expertise in QI, Berenholtz suggests.

The LFD projects have resulted in several successful initiatives, Berenholtz says. For example, one fellow's project examined an event in which a nasoduodenal feeding tube (NDT) went into the patient's bronchus and caused serious injury. The LFD tool revealed that several systems issues—including patient, task, and training factors—played a role in the event. The fellow convened an interdisciplinary group to form a protocol for NDT placement addressing the identified issues, which has been rolled out throughout the healthcare organization.

Although the LFD tool is typically used to assess issues that have already occurred, you can use it to prospectively prevent errors, Berenholtz says.

Use a modified version of the LFD tool as a survey to find out what potential system defects exist and distribute it to all healthcare givers.

"Frontline providers are the eyes and ears. They know how harm is going to occur because they know what they do every single day to defend against patient harm," says Berenholtz.

Since implementing these projects, fellows' evaluations of their educations have indicated that they feel more comfortable with systems-based practice and QI.

Source: Competency connection. **Residency Program Alert,** *July 1, 2009.*

Two for One: A Systems-Based Approach to Teaching Communication Skills

Everyone loves a two-for-one deal, so why not take that approach with the competencies by integrating systems-based practice into learning activities that focus on one of the other five competencies.

Besides hitting two competencies at once, you create an enriching educational experience for residents, says Paula M. Termuhlen, MD, FACS, general surgery program director, associate professor of surgery, and chief of the Division of Surgical Oncology at Wright State University (WSU) in Dayton, OH.

Termuhlen takes a systems-based approach to tackling a difficult interpersonal and communication skills topic: delivering bad news.

Termuhlen coordinates a three-hour workshop for all WSU first-year residents facilitated by educators from several specialties.

"I've had palliative care nurses present, hospice physicians, nephrologists, neurologists, pediatricians, and critical care doctors. That's the systems-based practice piece—it's a multidisciplinary event," Termuhlen says.

Bringing together physicians and trainees from various disciplines helps break down incorrect assumptions residents may have made about colleagues in other specialties.

"There's this sense of, 'Well, you guys don't do that,' or 'You don't have to break bad news or have these conversations.' It's very eye-opening for them to see that the OB/GYN, surgery, and family medicine residents have to do it," Termuhlen says.

Including hospice and palliative care nurses in the training is valuable because they can represent the patient or family's side of the story for the residents. Although the multidisciplinary nature of the activity makes it successful, boost the effectiveness by ensuring that you have facilitators from the specialties largely represented in the audience. A surgeon speaking to family medicine residents alone isn't as credible as a surgeon copresenting with a family medicine physician.

By the end of the workshop, residents have a broader understanding of what it takes to break bad news successfully and feel more comfortable doing so, says Termuhlen.

Source: Competency connection. **Residency Program Alert,** *July 1, 2009.*

Prepare Residents for the Real World with Practice Management Training

With graduation right around the corner, program directors and faculty members feel confident that graduates are ready to practice independently. But are you as confident that they are equally as prepared to practice the business of medicine?

Although you may have taught yourself the business ropes, the trial-by-fire method no longer works for this generation of physicians. From reimbursement to quality measures, the healthcare system is too complex for residents to leave the program without training. Set your residents up for success by developing a structured practice management curriculum.

The case for practice management training

Addressing practice management is important for two reasons. First, it eases the transition from the nurturing residency program to the everyone-fend-for-yourself real world, says David Kolva, MD, associate professor of family medicine at St. Joseph's Hospital Health Center in Syracuse, NY. Formal management training increases residents' chances for successfully gaining and maintaining employment, Kolva says.

The second reason is simply that the ACGME says so. Practice management training falls under the systems-based practice competency.

Educating residents on the business of medicine helps them better understand and navigate the healthcare

system. Additionally, some RRCs, such as family medicine, have more specific rules for leadership and management training.

How to bring the real world to the classroom

Creating a practice management curriculum is difficult for faculty and program directors because there are few frameworks to draw from. Luckily, there are several places you can turn to for ideas on what this training should entail:

- **Alumni.** Consider conducting postgraduation surveys. Ask alumni specific questions about what aspects of practice management they felt unprepared to handle when they entered practice, says Christina L. Wichman, DO, assistant professor of psychiatry at the Medical College of Wisconsin in Milwaukee.

  When surveying graduates, ask what kind of practices they joined after leaving the residency program. The answers can help you focus your teaching efforts on topics that will be most relevant to your residents in the future. For example, in the early 2000s, the curriculum in Kolva's program focused on opening and running a practice. In 2004, Kolva surveyed graduates from the previous five years (a total of 60 residents) and discovered only two had opened their own practice.

  "Most of the recent graduates are joining larger, established practices," Kolva says. "Spending a day or two talking about office layout or cash flow projections didn't make much sense because the vast majority are going to be employees, not employers."

- **Family Medicine Digital Resource Library.** The family medicine RRC requires residents to log 100 hours of leadership and management training. As a result, the family medicine field is further along than most other specialties in developing teaching tools, Kolva says. Other specialties can use the resources developed by family medicine educators as a starting point for designing practice management curricula.

- Many family medicine educators have made their curricula, lectures, activities, and evaluations available to all at no expense via the Society of Teachers in Family Medicine's database, Family Medicine Digital Resources Library (*www.fmdrl.org*).

- American College of Medical Practice Executives (ACMPE) and Medical Group Management Association (MGMA). The mission of these professional organizations is to provide education on the business and management aspects of being a physician, says Wichman.

ACMPE and MGMA outline eight domains of practice management knowledge for physicians. Wichman uses these domains as the framework for her psychiatry program's business curriculum:

- Financial management

- Human resources management

- Planning and marketing

- Information management

- Risk management

- Governance and organizational dynamics

- Business and clinical operations

- Professional responsibility

"These domains are general enough that they can be utilized for other specialties," Wichman says.

Find the time to talk business

Senior residents in Kolva's and Wichman's programs participate in practice management training. Although some educators believe the training should be longitudinal over the course of the program, Kolva says in his experience, first- and second-year residents do not perceive the information as relevant.

"When residents start their senior year, they're thinking about their future and how they're going to make a living," Kolva says. "A lot of them know where they're going to go next, so we can talk about that in the series, which makes it more relevant."

Consider offering the training during rotations that closely resemble real-world practices. "Our third-year residents run their outpatient clinics, which is like running their own practice. That seemed like the ideal time to incorporate some of these practice management skills," Wichman says.

Tip: Because there is so much that you must teach residents, it's easy to push practice management skills to the backburner. The best way to ensure that the topic gets the attention it deserves is to find champions for business education. The best advocates are faculty who have a background or interest in business or who ran their own practices for several years, Kolva says.

Options for structuring the training

There are several ways you can structure your curriculum. Kolva's program consists of the following:

- 20 interactive didactic lectures given throughout the final year of training.

- One-on-one instruction with Kolva during the residents' dermatology rotation. "I specifically introduce them to the concepts of pay for performance, patient-centered medical home, individual financial productivity, and benchmarking," he says.

- Service projects.

Wichman's curriculum spans 32 weeks. She spends four weeks teaching each of the ACMPE's and MGMA's eight domains. The four weeks of instruction on each domain include:

- **Week 1:** Residents attend a one-hour lecture on a domain given by an expert in the area, such as an attorney. "We ask them to keep things pretty broad. We knew that we weren't going to be able to provide the residents with everything they needed to know about the topic in one hour, but we wanted them to have enough information to be able to ask the right questions in the future," Wichman says.

- **Week 2:** Wichman or another faculty member leads a discussion regarding the domain. The

facilitator answers residents' questions and introduces other aspects of the domain.

- **Week 3:** Residents work on projects that tie the domain into their practice. "We do not meet specifically, but we are available if they have questions," Wichman says.

- **Week 4:** The group reconvenes, and residents present their findings.

Elements of a successful program

Although Kolva's and Wichman's programs are structured differently, they have many of the following similarities that make the training valuable to residents:

- **Protected time.** The programs allocate dedicated time for the didactic lectures. Freedom from clinical responsibilities helps ensure that residents attend the conferences. Reserving this time underscores the importance of the subject.

- **Outside speakers.** Local experts are identified to give presentations. When residents face these issues in practice, they will most likely have to go to experts in other disciplines for guidance. Kolva and Wichman solicit internal and external experts.

- "We wanted to give the residents exposure to the different individuals who would support them in their practice," Wichman says.

- For example, a person from the hospital's billing office presents a session on coding, and someone from the IT department discusses electronic medical records.

- "We have a certified financial planner who works with a lot of the physicians in the community do two sessions on personal finance and office finance," Kolva says.

- A healthcare lawyer presents on malpractice and malpractice risk management, he adds.

- **Projects.** The projects give residents hands-on application of what they are learning. It also teaches them the steps they need to take to solve problems in their own practice.

Kolva's residents pick a clinical or business problem that they see in the family medicine center to work on between November and April.

"We do a formal workbook study of how they research the issue, utilizing the plan-do-check-act model," he explains. For example, one of the residents looked at the problem of domestic abuse and found that physicians often do not address the issue or give victims enough resources. As a result, the hospital installed information-dispensing systems in the elevators and women's restrooms. Similarly, Wichman encourages residents to pick projects that will be practical and meaningful to their future practice. Residents complete one project per module, which they work on for about a week. Residents complete eight projects by the end of the curriculum. For example, a resident pursuing a child psychiatry fellowship developed a FAQ sheet describing legal and ethical issues associated with parents' involvement in their child's psychiatric care.

Measuring outcomes

Determining whether your practice management educational efforts were successful is difficult. Although "nobody has really developed a good outcomes-based evaluation," Kolva tries to frame questions in such a way that he can determine whether alumni retained key teaching points and whether the seminar series or service projects changed their behavior or helped them during an activity in their practice.

Observing graduates' behavior during practice can be an indication of whether the material stuck. For example, to determine whether the lecture on disability insurance sunk in, Kolva asks respondents whether they have their own long-term disability policy. However, evaluating the effectiveness of some topics may be more difficult. Respondents can't tell you whether the malpractice lectures helped them because most haven't been subject to a lawsuit. Instead, think of creative ways to measure those outcomes.

"We ask, 'In your current practice, is there an emphasis on medical malpractice risk management?' and 'What are the things the practice does in that regard?' " Kolva says, adding that any graduate can report this information.

Although Kolva is still gathering survey data, personal discussions with graduates and initial survey results indicate that the graduates find practice management education valuable.

Source: **Residency Program Alert,** *published by HCPro, Inc., May 2010.*

Models and Assessment Tools
for Teaching and Assessing
Systems-Based Practice

Figure 5.2	**Nurse Leader/Care Coordinator Evaluation of Resident**

BRIDGEPORT HOSPITAL
Internal Medicine Residency Program
Nurse Leader/Care Coordinator Evaluation of Resident

Resident Name:

The resident named above has recently rotated on your unit/service. We hope you will be able to answer the following questions about him or her and provide some brief narrative comments. Feedback will be provided to the resident only in summary form; your name will not be used in discussions with the resident even if you do provide your signature at the bottom, which is optional.

For each of the following statements, please indicate whether you agree or disagree by checking the appropriate box on the 1-5 scale below the statement:

Interpersonal and Communication Skills:

1) The resident communicated respectfully and effectively with patients and their families about all issues and particularly about pain management and other palliative care issues.

Strongly Disagree	Disagree	Neutral	Agree	Strongly Agree
1	2	3	4	5

2) The resident communicates respectfully and effectively with nursing staff and nursing leadership.

Strongly Disagree	Disagree	Neutral	Agree	Strongly Agree
1	2	3	4	5

Systems-Based Practice:

3) The resident participated effectively as a member of the multidisciplinary team.

Strongly Disagree	Disagree	Neutral	Agree	Strongly Agree
1	2	3	4	5

4) The resident demonstrated understanding and respect for the role and opinions of multidisciplinary team members.

Strongly Disagree	Disagree	Neutral	Agree	Strongly Agree
1	2	3	4	5

Overall

5) I would enjoy working with this resident again.

Strongly Disagree	Disagree	Neutral	Agree	Strongly Agree
1	2	3	4	5

6) I would be happy to have this resident participate in the care of a member of my family.

Strongly Disagree	Disagree	Neutral	Agree	Strongly Agree
1	2	3	4	5

Please provide a few comments about the residents' particular strengths and/or areas for improvement in the space below. Written comments often add a lot to the check-box answers.

Source: Bridgeport Hospital website: www.bridgeporthospital.org/gme/residency. Reprinted with permission.

| Figure 5.3 | **Evaluation of Resident's Performance in Discharge Planning** |

Trainee's Name: _____ **Date:** _____

1–3 Unsatisfactory; 4–6 Satisfactory (4 = marginal); 7–9 Superior

Please grade the resident or intern on the following components of performance:

1. **The resident was punctual for meetings.**

    1   2   3   4   5   6   7   8   9

2. **The resident treated discharge planners with courtesy and as fellow professionals.**

    1   2   3   4   5   6   7   8   9

3. **The resident demonstrated understanding of the full range of discharge planning resources.**

    1   2   3   4   5   6   7   8   9

4. **The resident contributed information from the medical assessment and history (regarding ADLs, etc.) allowing comprehensive consideration of discharge planning options (i.e., the discharge planner didn't have to do the background work).**

    1   2   3   4   5   6   7   8   9

5. **The resident faithfully carried out responsibilities (i.e., the plan discussed during rounds) associated with discharge planning and actual discharge.**

    1   2   3   4   5   6   7   8   9

6. **Would you want this resident to be involved in the discharge planning of a loved one?**

    Definitely not   Yes, with continued development   Definitely, ready

COMMENTS:

Source: Bridgeport Hospital website: www.bridgeporthospital.org/gme/residency. Reprinted with permission.

References

1. Davison, SP, Cadavid JD, Spear SL. Systems-based practice: education in plastic surgery. *Plast Reconstr Surg.* 2007;119(1):410–415.

2. Dyne PL, Strauss RW, Rinnert S. Systems-based practice: the sixth core competency. *Acad Emerg Med.* 2002;9:1270–1277.

3. Zenni EA, Ravago L, Ewart C, et al. A walk in the patients' shoes: a step toward competency development in systems-based practice. *Ambul Ped.* 2006;6(1):54–57.

4. Wang EE, Vozenilek JA. Addressing the systems-based practice core competency: a simulation-based curriculum. *Acad Emerg Med.* 2005;12:1191.

5. Lee AG, Beaver HA, Greenlee E, et al. Teaching and assessing systems-based competency in ophthalmology residency training programs. *Surv Ophthalmol.* 2007;52:680–689.

6. Joyce B. Introduction to competency-based education – facilitator's guide. ACGME April 2006. Presentation, Slide 3.

7. ACGME Curriculum Template.

8. Dunnington GL, Williams RG. Addressing the new competencies for residents' surgical training. *Acad Med.* 2003;78(1):14–21.

9. Rosenfeld JC. Using the morbidity and mortality conference to teach and assess the ACGME general competencies. *Curr Surg.* 2005;62:6.

10. Englander R, Agostinucci W, Zalneraiti E, Carraccio C. Teaching residents systems-based practice through a hospital cost-reduction program: a "win-win" situation. *Teach Learn Med.* 2006;18(2):150–152.

11. Petrey WB, Allen B Jr, Thorwarth WT Jr. Radiology coding, reimbursement, and economics: a practical playbook for housestaff. *J Am Coll Radiol.* 2009;6(9): 643–648.

12. Nine J, Zumwalt R. Integrating the Accreditation Council for Graduate Medical Education general competencies into forensic pathology fellowship training. *Am J Forensic Med Pathol.* 2005;26(4):334–339.

13. Peters AS, Kimura J, Ladden MJD, March E, Moore GT. A self-instructional model to teach systems-based practice and practice-based learning and improvement. *J Gen Intern Med.* 2008;237:931–936.

14. Voss J, Nadkarni M, Schectman J. The Clinical Health Economics System Simulation (CHESS): a teaching tool for systems- and practice-based learning. *Acad Med.* 2005;80(2):129–134.[abstract] (accessed –date- PMID number last)

15. The American Board of Surgery website. *www.absurgery.org.* ABS News Summer/Fall 2009. Accessed April 7, 2010.

16. Thomas DC, Leipzig RM, Smith LG, Dunn K, Sullivan G, Callahan E. Improving geriatrics training in internal medicine residency programs: best practices and sustainable solutions. *Annals Int Med.* 2003;139:628–634.

17. Jones K, Lebron RA, Mangram A, Dunn E. Practice management education during surgical residency. *Am J Surg.* 2008;196:878–882.

18. Turley C, Roach R, Marx M. Systems survivor: a program for house staff in systems-based practice. *Teach Learn Med.* 2007;19(2):128–138.

19. Outcome Project. ACGME website. *www.acgme.org/ outcome/.* Accessed January 28, 2010.

20. Kligler B, Koithan M. Competency-based evaluation tools for integrative medicine training in family medicine residency: a pilot study. *BMC Med Educ.* 2007;7:7.

21. Varkey P, Natt N. Validity evidence for an OSCE to assess competency in systems-based practice and practice-based learning and improvement: a preliminary investigation. *Acad Med.* 2008;83(8):775–780.

22. Lurie S, Mooney C, Lyness J. Measurement of the general competencies of the Accreditation Council for Graduate Medical Education: a systematic review. *Acad Med.* 2009;84(3):301–309.

CHAPTER 6

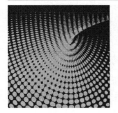

Professionalism

Elizabeth A. Rider, MSW, MD, FAAP

The most important problem for the future of professionalism is neither economic nor structural but cultural and ideological. The most important problem is its soul.

—Eliot Freidson, PhD[1]

Introduction

Physicians, patients, and society would agree that professionalism is valuable, important, and essential to medicine, and that unprofessional behavior is unacceptable. Yet requirements for teaching and assessing professionalism present medical educators with many challenges. Professionalism has been hard to define, and even harder to assess.

Interest in improving professionalism curricula in residency programs and medical schools has existed for several decades. Since the 1980s, the medical profession has demonstrated a sustained commitment to advancing professionalism.

Medical regulatory and accrediting organizations worldwide require physician competency in professionalism, and a number of these organizations have developed

initiatives to define and measure professionalism. The emphasis on professionalism at all levels of training is reflected in guidelines for medical schools (the Liaison Committee on Medical Education [LCME],[2] Association of American Medical Colleges [AAMC],[3] Institute for International Medical Education,[4] and General Medical Council[5]) and graduate and postgraduate certification standards (ACGME,[6] United States Medical Licensing Examination,[7] Royal College of Physicians and Surgeons of Canada,[8] Confederation of Postgraduate Medical Education Councils in Australia,[9] General Medical Council, UK,[10] Educational Commission for Foreign Medical Graduates,[11] and American Board of Medical Specialties [ABMS]). In 1999, the ACGME endorsed professionalism as one of six general competencies postgraduate residents should demonstrate. The ABMS, the Federation of State Medical Boards,[12] and The Joint Commission[13] have adopted the same competencies for practicing physicians.

Various professional societies[14, 15] have addressed the need to examine and promote professionalism in medicine. The American Board of Internal Medicine has been a leader in this realm, beginning with its Project Humanism in the 1980s and continuing with its focus on Project Professionalism in the 1990s and the development of a Physician Charter[16] in medical professionalism in collaboration with the American College of Physicians, the American Society of Internal Medicine, and the European Federation of Internal Medicine. The Physician Charter has been adopted by the ACGME, all specialties of the ABMS, and physician organizations throughout the world.[17]

Professionalism in healthcare: How are we doing?

"YOU ARE IN THIS PROFESSION AS A CALLING, NOT AS A BUSINESS; AS A CALLING WHICH EXACTS FROM YOU AT EVERY TURN SELF-SACRIFICE, DEVOTION, LOVE AND TENDERNESS TO YOUR FELLOW MEN. ONCE YOU GET DOWN TO A PURELY BUSINESS LEVEL, YOUR INFLUENCE IS GONE AND THE TRUE LIGHT OF YOUR LIFE IS DIMMED. YOU MUST WORK IN THE MISSIONARY SPIRIT, WITH A BREADTH OF CHARITY THAT RAISES YOU FAR ABOVE THE PETTY JEALOUSIES OF LIFE."

—SIR WILLIAM OSLER, MD[18]

Problems exist with the professional and ethical behavior of physicians and other healthcare professionals. Ludmerer[19] notes an increase in public concerns that physicians are impersonal, self-serving, and sometimes dishonest. The media often report professional transgressions by physicians. Studies show that many patient complaints about physicians involve unprofessional

behavior, and that patients are more likely to sue physicians they perceive as behaving unprofessionally.[20] However, we know that a small number of physicians generate a disproportionate number of complaints.[20]

How will we develop our learners as professionals, and identify and remediate the few whose impaired professionalism ultimately erodes the trust the public has in physicians? Consideration of the threats to professionalism is important in determining issues facing learners and physicians today.

The stakes are high. Regarding society's expectations of physicians, Jordan J. Cohen, MD,[21] President Emeritus of the AAMC, notes:

"Failing to deliver on these expectation, that is, falling short on the responsibilities of professionalism will surely result in a withdrawal of the tremendous advantages that now accompany our profession's status."

Threats to professionalism in medicine

"PHYSICIANS ARE JUMPY, LIVING WITH ... THIRD- PARTY PRESSURES ON WHAT THEY DO OR DO NOT DO, AND WITH THE CURRENT CONVENTIONAL WISDOM THAT PATIENT CARE IS SOME SORT OF IMPERSONAL COMMODITY TO BE BARTERED AT THE CHEAPEST PRICE IN THE MARKETPLACE."

—MALCOLM S. M. WATTS, MD[22]

Medicine faces myriad threats to professionalism. As a profession, medicine is under extraordinary scrutiny resulting from changes in working patterns, increased public concerns and expectations, loss of control over the medical marketplace (which is now largely controlled by the corporate sector and the state), and subsequent market forces that have led to commercialism and the corporate transformation of medicine.[23]

Howland notes that physicians are more often employed by or dependent on organizations with "… a business ethic that is indifferent and occasionally hostile to the values and behaviors of professionalism."[(p. 639) 24] Lundberg concurs: "The fundamental purpose of a business is to make money. … On the other hand, the fundamental purpose of a profession is to provide a service that reflects commitment to a worthy cause that transcends self-interest."[(p. 1541) 25]

Hafferty, Cohen,[26] and others describe the enemies of professionalism as commercialism and self-interest. Hafferty notes:

> *Today, physicians who transform biomedical discoveries into marketable products and then bring those products to Wall Street are the new heroes of academic medicine. Faculty are urged (with salary and pay raises on the line) to adopt a more entrepreneurial orientation toward their work.*[27]

Commercialism continues to thrive within clinical and research medicine, although efforts for transparency and disclosure of conflicts of interest are beginning to gain ground. Even with organized medicine's work to enhance and reinvigorate medical professionalism, only recently has there been more focus on professionalism by state medical boards.[28] Much work remains.

> *If medical students are to internalize the "true meanings" of professionalism, then organized medicine will need to rid the streets (as best as possible) of these commercial enticements, for this is where our students go (and learn) after classes end and after their teachers have retired for the evening.*[27]

Part of medicine's social contract is its promise to police itself in the public interest.[29] Hafferty recommends that organized medicine implement a meaningful and public system of peer review—with attention to commercialism and self-interest—so that the public will know that professionalism remains sacrosanct.[27]

Why teach professionalism?

> "MEDICINE IS A MORAL COMMUNITY, THE PRACTICE
> OF MEDICINE A MORAL UNDERTAKING, AND
> PROFESSIONALISM IS A MORAL COMMITMENT."
> —FREDERIC HAFFERTY, PHD[30]

All levels of medical education need to give attention to teaching and promoting professionalism. Professionalism is not sufficiently learned during medical school and residency training, though many programs are working to improve in this area.

Numerous reasons exist for developing a strong curriculum in professionalism. First, professionalism forms the basis of a social contract between medicine and society. Additional reasons to teach and assess professionalism include the association of professionalism in physicians with improved medical outcomes and of unprofessional behavior with adverse medical outcomes, ethical issues that affect the moral development of physicians, and patient and societal expectations. As noted earlier in this chapter, accreditation organizations require professionalism training throughout medical education.

Professionalism as a social contract

"Professionalism has come to serve as the basis of medicine's social contract."

—Sylvia R. Cruess, MD[31]

Cruess and Cruess[32] assert that professional status is not an intrinsic right but is granted by society. The continuation of professional status depends on the public's belief that professionals are trustworthy, and professionals must meet the obligations expected by society in order to remain trustworthy.[32] Stern and Papadakis note:

"What is at stake is nothing less than the privilege of autonomy in our interactions with patients, self-regulation, public esteem, and a rewarding and well-compensated career."[33]

Trust between the physician and the patient is primary, and healing is put at risk without this trust. The social contract functions only if both sides, physician and society, have reasonable expectations of each other. Figure 6.1 presents the expectations of medicine and society in the social contract.

Figure 6.1	The Social Contract Between Medicine and Society
Society's Expectations of Medicine	**Medicine's Expectations of Society**
• Services of the healer	• Trust
• Assured competence	• Autonomy
• Altruistic service	• Self-regulation
• Morality and integrity	• Value-driven and adequately funded healthcare system
• Accountability	• Participation in public policy
• Transparency	• Shared (patients and society) responsibility for health
• Source of objective advice	• Monopoly
• Promotion of the public good	• Status and rewards
	– Non-financial: respect and status
	– Financial

Source: Cruess SR. Professionalism and medicine's social contract with society. Clin Orthop Relat Res. 2006;449: 170–176. Reprinted with permission.

Medical educators and others involved in medical training must ensure that future physicians understand the social contract, and are equipped to fulfill their responsibility of trustworthiness and to uphold the primacy of the patient's welfare.

Professionalism and outcomes

Studies demonstrate an association between physician excellence and professionalism.[34] Trust is a component of professionalism, and patients are more likely to adhere to treatment recommendations when they trust their physician.[35] Studies show that patients who perceive their physicians as behaving professionally are more satisfied and are more likely to remain with and recommend their physicians to others.[36]

Papadakis and colleagues[37] found that physicians who were disciplined by state medical licensing boards were three times more likely to have shown unprofessional behavior in medical school than those with no such disciplinary actions. The strongest association occurred with those described as irresponsible or as having diminished ability to improve their behavior. The authors stressed the importance of identifying students who display unprofessional behavior, and the risk that un-professional behavior may persist over decades. Stern and colleagues[38] found that medical students who were unable to perceive their weaknesses and who lacked thoroughness during the first two years of medical school were more likely to show unprofessional be-havior during the clinical years. More recently, Papadakis and colleagues,[39] in a study of 66,000 internists, found that low professionalism ratings during residency re-sulted in significantly greater risk for future state licen-sing board actions. These studies provide empirical evidence for focusing on professionalism as a core competency in medical education.

Public concern about medical ethics has led many medical schools to increase their formal teaching of ethics, a significant component of professionalism. Hicks and colleagues[40] studied 108 medical students and found that nearly half had felt pressure to act unethically and 61% had witnessed a clinical teacher acting unethically. The medical students encountered three types of situations:

- Conflict between the priorities of medical education and patient care

- Responsibility exceeding a student's abilities

- Perception of involvement in patient care thought to be substandard

Notably, the ethical problems encountered were rarely discussed or resolved with clinical teachers. This study underscores the importance not only of teaching professionalism, but also of developing robust faculty development programs for this competency.

Definitions of Professionalism

> "CHARACTER IS DOING WHAT'S
> RIGHT WHEN NOBODY IS LOOKING."
> —JC WATTS, CONGRESSMAN, 1996

Medical professionalism has proven difficult to define. There is no consensus on a universal definition of professionalism in medicine, yet many similarities exist among conceptual frameworks and descriptions.

In addition to the social contract between medicine and society, Cruess and Cruess[41] propose that the physician fills two roles in society: those of healer and professional. They identify attributes of both the healer and professional roles, and the attributes common to both (see Figure 6.2). Cruess and Cruess recommend that faculty members direct careful attention to the teaching of both roles: "… great care must be taken to include all aspects of both roles as the definition dictates not only what is taught but also what will be evaluated."[(p. 14) 41] They also note that society needs the services of the healer, and that the professionalism taught must provide a moral foundation for future physicians whose duty is to make certain that "… both the role and the values of the healer survive."[(p. 14) 41]

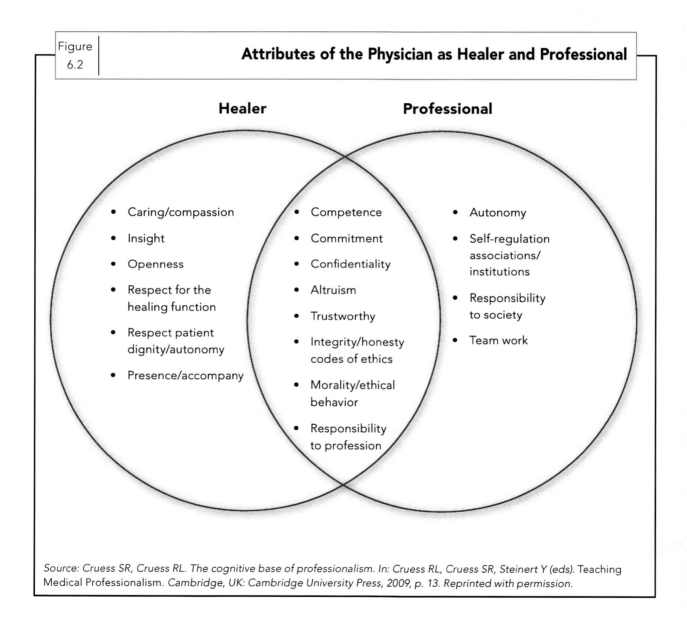

| Figure 6.2 | **Attributes of the Physician as Healer and Professional** |

Healer

- Caring/compassion
- Insight
- Openness
- Respect for the healing function
- Respect patient dignity/autonomy
- Presence/accompany

- Competence
- Commitment
- Confidentiality
- Altruism
- Trustworthy
- Integrity/honesty codes of ethics
- Morality/ethical behavior
- Responsibility to profession

Professional

- Autonomy
- Self-regulation associations/ institutions
- Responsibility to society
- Team work

Source: Cruess SR, Cruess RL. The cognitive base of professionalism. In: Cruess RL, Cruess SR, Steinert Y (eds). Teaching Medical Professionalism. Cambridge, UK: Cambridge University Press, 2009, p. 13. Reprinted with permission.

Various organizations have put forth definitions of professionalism (see Figure 6.3). Inui[42] notes that definitions of professionalism provide descriptions of how a virtuous physician would act. He advises medical educators to choose a definition and take it seriously, and to consider how learners can come to understand and exemplify these qualities.

| Figure 6.3 | **Selected Definitions of Professionalism** |

ACGME Definition of Professionalism [43]

Residents must demonstrate a commitment to carrying out professional responsibilities and an adherence to ethical principles. Residents are expected to demonstrate:

1. Compassion, integrity, and respect for others

2. Responsiveness to patient needs that supersedes self-interest

3. Respect for patient privacy and autonomy

4. Accountability to patients, society, and the profession

5. Sensitivity and responsiveness to a diverse patient population, including but not limited to diversity in gender, age, culture, race, religion, disabilities, and sexual orientation

A Physician Charter (ABIM, ACP, EFIM)[16]

Fundamental principles:

- Principle of primacy of patient welfare

- Principle of patient autonomy

- Principle of social justice

The charter outlines 10 professional responsibilities, which include a commitment to:

1. Professional competence

2. Honesty with patients

3. Patient confidentiality

4. Maintaining appropriate relations with patients

5. Improving quality of care

6. Improving access to care

Figure
6.3

Selected Definitions of Professionalism (cont.)

7. Just distribution of finite resources

8. Scientific knowledge

9. Maintaining trust by managing conflicts of interest

10. Professional responsibilities

The duties of a doctor registered with the General Medical Council, UK[44]

Patients must be able to trust doctors with their lives and health. To justify that trust you must show respect for human life and you must:

- Make the care of your patient your first concern

- Protect and promote the health of patients and the public

- Provide a good standard of practice and care

  - Keep your professional knowledge and skills up to date

  - Recognize and work within the limits of your competence

  - Work with colleagues in the ways that best serve patients' interests

- Treat patients as individuals and respect their dignity

  - Treat patients politely and considerately

  - Respect patients' right to confidentiality

- Work in partnership with patients

  - Listen to patients and respond to their concerns and preferences

  - Give patients the information they want or need in a way they can understand

  - Respect patients' right to reach decisions with you about their treatment and care

  - Support patients in caring for themselves to improve and maintain their health

- Be honest and open and act with integrity

  - Act without delay if you have good reason to believe that you or a colleague may be putting patients at risk

| Figure 6.3 | **Selected Definitions of Professionalism (cont.)** |

   – Never discriminate unfairly against patients or colleagues

   – Never abuse your patients' trust in you or the public's trust in the profession

You are personally accountable for your professional practice and must always be prepared to justify your decisions and actions.

Professionalism in Pediatrics: Statement of Principles
Policy Statement: American Academy of Pediatrics[45]

Core professional principles and values that pediatricians and pediatric subspecialists, including trainees, should embrace and that provide an ethical foundation for quality healthcare for children and their families:

Principles

- Honesty and integrity

- Reliability and responsibility

- Respect for others

- Compassion/empathy

- Self-improvement

- Self-awareness/knowledge of limits

- Communication and collaboration

- Altruism and advocacy

Values

- Responsibilities to patients and families

- Responsibilities to other health professionals and healthcare and support services providers

- Responsibilities to communities

- Responsibilities to the profession

What constitutes unprofessional behavior?

Papadakis and colleagues[37] found that the types of unprofessional behavior most strongly associated with disciplinary action by state medical boards were severe irresponsibility and significantly diminished capacity for self-improvement. Examples of unprofessional behavior abound. Duff[46] cites the following:

- Intellectual or personal dishonesty

- Arrogance and disrespectfulness

- Prejudice

- Abrasive interactions with patients and coworkers

- Lack of accountability for medical errors and administrative oversights, including when "… the student or physician fails to demonstrate sufficient personal investment in the patient's outcome"

- Fiscal irresponsibility, including ordering clinically unnecessary tests and accepting kickbacks

- Lack of sustained commitment to self-learning

- Lack of due diligence

- Personal excesses, including substance abuse and high-risk behavior

- Sexual misconduct

Building a Curriculum for Professionalism

> "HEALING IS THE MANDATE OF MEDICINE, AND PROFESSIONALISM IS HOW IT IS ORGANIZED."
> —SYLVIA CRUESS, MD[47]

The complexity of professionalism in medicine presents a challenge to educators seeking to teach and evaluate this competency. We know that physicians do not acquire professionalism via their upbringing, osmosis, academic coursework, one or two workshops during training, or other short-lived interventions. Instead, medical educators and leaders must explicitly define, clarify, teach, and model the values and capacities we expect physicians to learn and exhibit, and faculty role models must have a thorough knowledge of professionalism.

Designing curricula for professionalism requires attention to its various components, including the knowledge base of professionalism (i.e., the social contract and roles and attributes of both the healer and the professional), presented previously; the moral and ethical development of learners and faculty members; authenticity; and the learning environment, including the hidden curriculum (HC) and organizational culture.

Professionalism and moral reasoning

Moral reasoning and judgment are essential components of professional behavior, and they apply to both the awareness of moral issues and the demonstration of appropriate moral actions in medical education and clinical care.[48] Bebeau[49] found that education in the health professions did not promote moral judgment, but that the addition of ethics instruction increased moral reasoning and judgment. Self and Baldwin[50] documented a significant positive relationship between levels of moral reasoning and measures of clinical excellence in medical students, residents, and practicing physicians. In a study of malpractice claims against orthopedic surgeons, Baldwin and colleagues[51] discovered that orthopedists in the low-claims group had significantly higher levels of moral reasoning than orthopedists in the high-claims group.

It appears that medical education may profoundly influence moral development. Feudtner and colleagues[52] describe the "ethical erosion" reported by medical students. Patenaude et al.[53] presented striking results from their study: Entering medical students used higher-stage moral reasoning orientations than the same students at the end of their third year. Residents also fail to make age-expected growth in moral reasoning abilities during their training.[54]

A disconnect exists between the professed values of medicine and the actual practice that learners observe, making it hard for them to determine what values to learn, and resulting in increased stress, burnout, isolation, loss of empathy,[55, 56] ethical erosion,[52] and a stunting of moral development.[57] According to Rabow and colleagues, "When physicians are distanced from themselves and from such values as honesty and altruism, patient safety may suffer."[(p. 312) 58]

It appears that socialization into medical culture comes at a high price. Consequently, those involved in medical education must work to promote the moral development of their learners.

The moral and ethical development of learners and faculty

"MEDICINE, AFTER ALL, IS A MORAL PROFESSION."
—WILLIAM BRANCH, JR., MD[57]

Professionalism and the moral and ethical development of learners and faculty are inextricably entwined. Most learners are in their early adulthood, a time of significant moral development and attitudinal change.[59] Moral development is a lifelong task, and faculty members also continue to develop morally.

Burack and colleagues[60] studied attending physicians' responses to residents' and medical students' problematic behaviors on the wards—that is, showing disrespect for patients, cutting corners, and exhibiting outright hostility or rudeness. They found that attending physicians did not respond to problematic behaviors in any observable way and they let the majority of incidents pass without comment. In a minority of cases when attending physicians did respond, their feedback was subtle and often misinterpreted or unnoticed by learners.

Regarding Burack and colleagues' findings, Branch[57] notes that attending physicians' responses may play down the moral aspects of the trainees' behavior. He draws an association between the learners' dilemma (maintaining caring attitudes versus suppressing their moral principles to function on the clinical team) and faculty members failing to respond to the poor ethical behavior of their learners. Any curriculum for professionalism requires attention to the moral development of both learners and faculty.

Professionalism and authenticity

Coulehan draws a distinction between professional etiquette and professional virtue, noting "… if we focus on the former and pay only lip service to the latter, we have nothing but window dressing."[61] Hafferty concurs, and asserts that being a physician and "taking on the identity of a true professional" involves more than knowledge, skills, and outward behavior.[30]

> "There is a meaningful (and measurable) differ- ence between being a professional and acting professionally. … [W]e must attend to such incon- sistencies between the inner self and outward appearance, sending a message that authenticity is a matter of great concern."[30]

Boudreau and colleagues emphasize that for effective healing, "… it is not only what the healer 'does' that is important, but also who the healer 'is.' "(p. 7) [62]

Value orientations and commitment to learning, excellence, and genuinely caring behavior and practices remain primary.

Educating for professionalism: The hidden curriculum and organizational culture

> "No matter how much we write about professionalism's importance, or plan its inclusion into undergraduate or postgraduate curricula, it is the day-to-day experience of working within a clinical environment that will be most influential in its development."
> —Sean Hilton, MD, FRCGP[63]

Attention to the learning environment, including the HC and organizational culture, is essential to the teaching and learning of professionalism. The social and organizational environments of training institu- tions have a profound influence on professional identity formation. To improve professionalism education, we need to bring the formal curriculum and its moral, ethical, and humane values into alignment with the HC so that the HC consistently models these values. (For more on these issues, please see Chapters 1 and 7.)

The hidden curriculum and the culture of learning

> "… outside the courses lies the 'hidden curriculum,' the students' exposure to what we actually do in our day-to-day work with patients and one another—not what we say should be done when we stand behind podiums in lecture halls."
> —Thomas Inui, ScM, MD[42]

The HC, described as "… the unofficial rules for survival and advancement,"[64] results in pressure to conform and a focus on pleasing superiors, sometimes at the patient's expense.

> "The physician's attitudes, mindset, moral stance, and the hour-by-hour decisions about how to use one's time—all these and many other matters, even including how and what and how much to feel, are observed by the student and imitated assiduously."
> —Melvin Konner, MD[65]

Role modeling has the most powerful influence on learners' understanding of professionalism.[42] Negative role modeling experienced during clinical training undermines the attitudinal messages of the formal curriculum. Learners internalize and perpetuate attitudes and behaviors of their role models,[66] and they feel caught between their moral principles and the pressures to suppress their moral principles to fit in with team members.[57]

The culture of medical education can erode learners' idealism and social consciousness. Coulehan and Williams[67] describe socializing phenomena that make it difficult to be a caring physician, including the development of detachment, a sense of entitlement, and a nonreflective professional practice. The authors note that, although medical education in the United States promotes a commitment to traditional values of doctoring—empathy, altruism, and others—a tacit belief exists that physicians best care for patients as "objects of technical services (medical care)."[67]

Coulehan describes three styles of professional identity that can manifest in young physicians as a result of conflicts between explicit and tacit values and the formal and hidden curricula:[68]

1. A technical professional identity in which physicians practice medicine according to the hospital culture, discard traditional values, and narrow their responsibility to the technical arena

2. A nonreflective professional identity in which physicians believe they exemplify traditional professional virtues yet act in ways that are in conflict with those virtues, and contribute to problems in healthcare (e.g., poor physician–patient communication and others)

3. A compassionate and responsive professional identity in which young physicians have overcome the conflict between explicit and tacit socialization[68]

Coulehan believes that a large percentage of graduates manifest a nonreflective professional identity.[68]

Reisman[64] describes learners' natural instincts against the HC as a "gift" that can remind faculty members to encourage students to:

*   Share their experiences

*   Teach that what they observe might not always be the correct way to behave

*   Affirm the learner's caring for, and desire to protect, the patient

Organizational approaches to fostering professionalism

"UNDER PRESENT CIRCUMSTANCES, STUDENTS BECOME CYNICAL ABOUT THE PROFESSION OF MEDICINE—INDEED, MAY SEE CYNICISM AS INTRINSIC TO MEDICINE—BECAUSE THEY SEE US 'SAY ONE THING AND DO ANOTHER.' ... ADDITIONAL COURSES ON 'MEDICAL PROFESSIONALISM' ARE UNLIKELY TO FUNDAMENTALLY ALTER THIS REGRETTABLE CIRCUMSTANCE. INSTEAD, WE WILL ACTUALLY HAVE TO CHANGE OUR BEHAVIORS, OUR INSTITUTIONS, AND OURSELVES."
—THOMAS INUI, ScM, MD[(p. 4–5) 42]

Many believe that organizational change is a prerequisite to improving education for professionalism and for enhancing professionalism throughout healthcare institutions. How can we create institutionwide organizational change? First, professionalism needs to come up on the radar screen of institutional leaders and educators as an urgent focus, and then action for organizational change can follow.

To be effective, institution leaders and educators should design programs for systematic institutional implementation that guide and support professional development. Rider and Longmaid[69] note that interpersonal, communication, and management skills are critical for leaders of the change process, and that an awareness and understanding of systems issues and human factors increase the likelihood of success. They found that successful organizational change requires:

- Carefully planned and executed series of actions

- Effective communication on all levels

- Effective leadership

- An open process with stakeholder input

- Attention to institutional cultures

- Continuous involvement, input, and creation of the program by those most affected

Rider and Longmaid[69] propose steps that educators and organizational leaders can undertake to manage organizational and cultural change around institutional educational initiatives. Although their model was designed for residency program mergers, their guidelines

also are relevant for organizational change efforts to enhance professionalism. They are:

1. Lead with vision

2. Establish and reinforce communication links early to maximize collaboration

3. Challenge everyone in the organization to think about and own the process of change

4. Acknowledge and consider different cultures and identify shared values

5. Start with a clean slate and respect each other

6. Develop mechanisms for and solicit stakeholder input

7. Listen to and learn from each other

8. Maintain equity and fairness

9. Delegate and empower teams for action[69]

In his seminal paper, "A Flag in the Wind: Educating for Professionalism in Medicine," Inui[42] provides specific action agenda items for institutional change in order to promote professionalism education. He notes that not everything needs to change at once, and that small changes can lead to larger changes in the interconnected organizational network of academic healthcare institutions. The caveat, and necessary ingredient, is that institutional leaders facilitate and support change from the top. Chapter 1 presents additional strategies for organizational change, including appreciative inquiry and positive deviance.

Teaching Professionalism

Professionalism can be taught and learned.[14, 71, 72] In addition to teaching the knowledge or cognitive base[41] of professionalism—the roles and attributes of both the healer and the professional and the social contract between medicine and society—described previously in this chapter, we must focus on the learning environment and organizational culture as well as the moral and ethical development of learners and faculty. Teaching professionalism includes a careful focus on the learner–teacher relationship, the development and enhancement of reflection and self-awareness, and an understanding of professional boundaries. As teaching reflection is essential for the development of reflection in learners, specific strategies for teaching reflection are discussed, including role modeling, enhancing reflection through reflective feedback, developing mindfulness, narrative medicine and storytelling, and critical reflection groups.

The learner–teacher relationship

Just as the physician–patient relationship forms the foundation of healthcare, the learner–teacher relationship forms the basis for the overall learning experience. The way teachers treat learners affects how trainees interact with patients and colleagues, and the extent to which teachers can foster development and learning.

Relationships are a significant mediating factor in the HC. Studies show that the learner–teacher relationship not only affects students' motivation to learn and the actual learning that occurs, but also impacts the learner's social identification.[74] The learner–teacher relationship, as it affects identity formation, can have a powerful influence on learners' professional behaviors and choices.[75] Chapter 1 also discusses the learner–teacher relationship.

Teaching strategies for developing the reflective physician

We know that reflection and self-awareness are necessary for the development of professionalism.[33, 58, 77, 78, 79, 80] The ability to reflect enables physicians to develop insight into interactions with patients and colleagues, enhances critical thinking, and is one factor that separates professionals from technicians. Reflective skills are associated with the ability to develop insight into one's self and one's learning needs, to direct one's learning, and, ultimately, to ensure that the physician can practice well autonomously.

Reflection merits specific attention and inclusion in medical education curricula. Studies show that residents do not know instinctively how to engage in systematic self-reflection,[81] and that psychological growth occurs only when reflection is part of professional education.[82]

Teaching about and modeling reflection and self-awareness promotes caring among learners and faculty. Branch[83] notes that the ethics of caring include:

- Preserving empathy and compassion—that is, receptivity—in learners

- Teaching learners to take responsibility for patients

- Ensuring an educational environment that values these attributes

Learning opportunities for reflection can occur individually, in one-on-one learning situations with a trusted teacher, and in small groups. An essential component of curricula for promoting reflection is the selection and training of faculty who are respectful of learners' needs, personally self-aware, and able to reflect.

Role modeling and reflection

"HELP US TO LEARN ABOUT HEALTHY WAYS TO COPE WITH DIFFICULT PATIENTS, UNCERTAINTY, AND OTHER CHALLENGES OF PRACTICING MEDICINE BY SHARING WITH US YOUR OWN RESPONSES, QUESTIONS, AND DOUBTS. IF YOU HAVE THE COURAGE TO INITIATE CONVERSATIONS ABOUT THESE DIFFICULT SITUATIONS, YOU WILL CREATE A SAFE ATMOSPHERE IN WHICH ALL PARTIES WILL LEARN— NOT ONLY ABOUT MEDICINE AND SCIENCE, BUT ABOUT PATIENT CARE AND COMPASSION AS WELL."

—JODI SKILES, MEDICAL STUDENT[73]

Role modeling is often considered a primary strategy for teaching ethical and professional behavior, and it is at the heart of character formation.[84] Role modeling is a powerful teaching method for conveying the values, knowledge, and skills of the medical profession. Although individual attending physicians alone cannot change the cultural climate of the HC by serving as positive role models, they can affect the culture of their team and the team's attitude toward patients. Learners observe their teachers as role models—positive or negative—and role models teach by example 24/7.

Unfortunately, faculty can miss opportunities for positive role modeling, and they may sometimes serve as negative role models. Stern[85] observed interactions between teachers, residents, and patients and found that professional values such as caring, honesty, and accountability were barely discernible during teaching rounds. Additional professional values such as altruism, confidentiality, and "do no harm" were noticeably absent.

Role models are "… individuals admired for their ways of being and acting as professionals."[86] Studies show that learners identified as excellent role models faculty members who:

- Love their work and are enthusiastic

- Stress the importance of the physician–patient relationship

- Teach psychosocial skills

- Have clinical skills and teaching abilities that are seen as highly competent[87]

Learners identify negative role models as those who:

- Are dissatisfied with their careers

- Have inadequate interpersonal interactions with patients and others[88]

Cruess, Cruess, and Steinert[89] note that learning from role models involves both unconscious and conscious processes and occurs through observation and reflection. Understanding both unconscious and conscious aspects is vital. The authors note:

> *Active reflection on the process can convert an unconscious feeling into conscious thought that can be translated into principles and action. In an equally powerful process, observed behaviors are unconsciously incorporated into the belief patterns and behaviors of the student.*(p. 718) [89]

Figure 6.4 shows the mechanism by which the process of role modeling occurs.

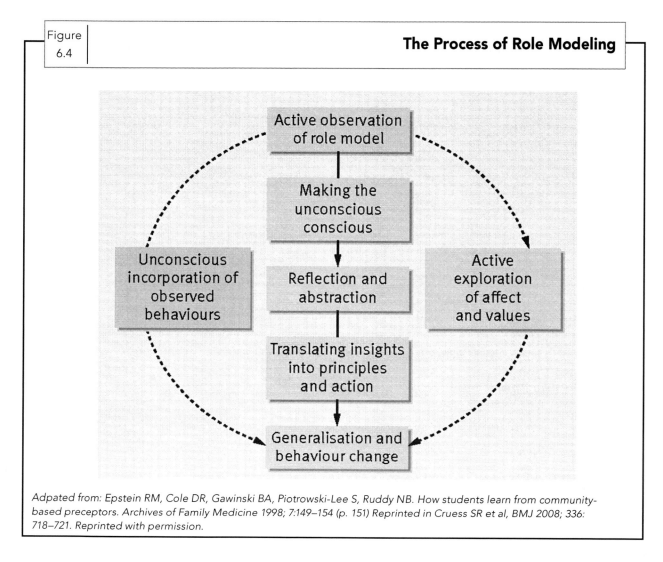

Figure 6.4 | **The Process of Role Modeling**

Adapted from: Epstein RM, Cole DR, Gawinski BA, Piotrowski-Lee S, Ruddy NB. How students learn from community-based preceptors. Archives of Family Medicine 1998; 7:149–154 (p. 151) Reprinted in Cruess SR et al, BMJ 2008; 336: 718–721. Reprinted with permission.

Branch and colleagues[90] recommend enhancing role modeling and teaching of the human dimensions of care by actively involving residents and students in reflection and introspection and by taking advantage of seminal events to create memorable learning opportunities. They suggest teachers develop active learning methods, guided by the following questions:

- How can I foster broad participation in this activity?

- How can I foster a safe environment for learners to share their own fears, concerns, and dilemmas?

- What opportunities exist for practice, feedback, and discussion?

- What opportunities for reflection exist during this activity?[90]

Role modeling alone is an insufficient teaching strategy unless it is combined with reflection on actions.[91] Follow-up discussion and reflection on experiences are necessary for the effective teaching of professionalism. Figure 6.5 lists suggestions for role modeling with reflection.

Figure 6.5	**Ground Rules for Role Modeling with Reflection**

1. Explicitly call attention to what you are role modeling.

2. Explain what you have done and why.

3. Treat learners with the respect with which you expect them to treat patients.

4. Ask learners to reflect on their observations and experiences. "How did that go for you?" "What did you learn?"

5. Articulate and teach values. For example, tell learners that you value caring for the patient and showing respect and compassion, and why.

6. Provide perspective. Place learners' observations/experiences in the broader context of patient care.

Reflective feedback: A strategy for teaching and enhancing reflection

Both feedback and reflection are essential components of medical education. Although medical educators recognize the value of giving effective feedback about professional behaviors,[92] such feedback is more often espoused than practiced.[93, 94, 95] Training programs use written evaluation instruments for residents, yet minimal time is spent giving ongoing, face-to-face feedback.[93] Positive feedback about good professional behaviors and attitudes draws attention to these positive actions and increases the likelihood that they will be repeated and will endure. Good feedback teaches not only what should occur, but also why it should occur, and teaching why certain behaviors are important gets back to the values of professionalism.[96]

Rider and Hinrichs[97] developed a reflective feedback model for faculty teaching communication skills and professionalism at Harvard Medical School. Rider further expanded the model for teaching and faculty development.[98] The goal of reflective feedback is to teach and enhance reflective skills, self-awareness, and reflective practice. Reflective feedback occurs when the clinical teacher actively facilitates and models a process of reflection in the setting of giving feedback.[97, 98]

Reflective feedback can provide a focus for teaching professionalism, interpersonal and communication skills, critical thinking, and skills for lifelong learning. Figure 6.6 presents a model and guidelines for reflective feedback. The phrases are not a script, but rather ideas to use to develop your own style. Faculty can use the model in brief or in extended discussions about interactions with patients, colleagues, and teams, and for learning specific skills and procedures.

| Figure 6.6 | **Guidelines for Reflective Feedback: What to Do When You Only Have Five Minutes** |

1. **Establish rapport** with the learner. Show interest, respect, and caring throughout your interactions.

2. **Ask about learning goals** before the observed interview or brief observation.

   - *"What are your learning goals for this interview / interaction / procedure?"*

   - *"Is there anything, specifically, that you would like to work on?"*

   - *"While I observe you, is there an area you would like me to pay particular attention to?"*

3. **Facilitate reflection:** Invite the learner to share their reflections. Stimulate curiosity. Facilitate the discussion to **keep reflection on an insightful level,** rather than a series of intellectual observations.

   - *"How did the interview (or interaction or procedure) go for you?"*

     - **Note:** This is different than asking, *"How do you think you did?"*

   - *"What stood out for you?"*

   - *"What were your impressions?"*

   - *"Was there anything that you were curious about?"*

   - Encourage the learner to delve deeper: *"Anything else?"*

   Ask the learner what he or she did well.

   - *"What did you feel good about?"*

   - *"What did you learn?"*

   Explore areas for improvement.

   - *"What might you do differently next time?"*

   - *"What do you think needs improvement?"*

4. **Model reflection:** After the learner has shared their reflections and thoughts, share yours.

   Validate positive behaviors: Teach why particular behaviors / skills / attitudes are important for communication with patients (or for performing a particular skill or procedure) and how they help to build the physician-patient relationship and the learner's skills. Be specific and use non-judgmental language.

Figure 6.6	**Guidelines for Reflective Feedback:** **What to Do When You Only Have Five Minutes (cont.)**

- *"After you validated the patient's emotions, she felt more connected with you and was able to share her concerns about ..."*

- *"I noticed that when you said X ..., the patient reacted Y ..."*

Help the learner explore feelings, motivations, nonverbal behaviors – and *why* they did or didn't do or say something.

- *"What was it like for you giving bad news?"*

- *"Say more about that."*

- *"Was there anything that made it hard or uncomfortable?"*

- *"When the patient said ... you replied ...: Do you remember why you said what you did?"*

- *"What do you think the patient is most concerned about?" "What did the patient want?"*

Suggest alternative strategies. Teach why they are useful.

- *"Sometimes the most helpful thing we can do for a patient is to just "be present," listen, and show that we care."*

- *"Here is a suggestion you can try."*

5. **Check for understanding.**

   - *"Why don't you summarize what we've talked about?"*

   - *"Let's review what we've talked about."*

6. **Make a follow-up plan.** What will the learner try or change in subsequent patient encounters?

   - *"What do you plan to try with the next patient?"*

   - *"With the next patient, consider asking at least two questions about their family / home life."*

   - *"You can try X approach and then we can talk about how it went."*

Source: © Elizabeth A. Rider, MSW, MD 2010. Used with permission.

Learning mindfulness

"ONE WAY OF DEFINING THE CHARACTER OF CLINICIANS IS TO EXAMINE THEIR MOMENT-TO-MOMENT ACTIONS DURING THE COURSE OF CLINICAL CARE. THESE SMALL ACTIONS, CUMULATIVELY, DESCRIBE THE CLINICIAN AS A PRACTITIONER AND MORAL AGENT."

—RONALD EPSTEIN, MD[99]

Teaching professionalism involves encouraging mindfulness in practice. Epstein[99] identifies habits of mind, including presence, self-awareness, attentiveness, and curiosity as key features of the mature professional and notes that the foundation of professional excellence is knowledge of and respect for the patient as a person with needs and values. Micro-ethical competence,

as he calls it, requires three factors: self-awareness, interpersonal skills, and the intention of healing.[100] Epstein notes that self-awareness and interpersonal skills can be taught but that intention of healing must be identified during the medical school admissions process and then nurtured and maintained.

Epstein recommends that clinical teachers cultivate mindfulness in learners in two ways: by asking them to observe their own thoughts and feelings when with a patient, and by using reflective questions to help learners discover their own answers.

Figure 6.7 provides examples of Epstein's reflective questions.[99]

| Figure 6.7 | **Habits of Self-Questioning: Reflective Questions** |

- How might my previous experience affect my actions with this patient?

- What am I assuming about this patient that might not be true?

- What surprised me about this patient? How did I respond?

- What interfered with my ability to observe, be attentive, or be respectful with this patient?

- How could I be more present with and available to this patient?

- Were there any points at which I wanted to end the visit prematurely?

- If there were relevant data that I ignored, what might they be?

- What would a trusted peer say about the way I managed this situation?

- Were there any points at which I felt judgmental about the patient—in a positive or negative way?

Source: Borrell-Carrio F, Epstein RM. Preventing errors in clinical practice: a call for self awareness. Annals of Family Medicine 2004; 4(2): 310–316. Reprinted with permission.

Narrative medicine and storytelling

"Culture consists of the matrix of stories, symbols, beliefs, attitudes, and patterns of behavior in which we find ourselves."
—Jack Coulehan, MD, MPH[68]

Charon[101] describes narrative competence as "the ability to acknowledge, absorb, interpret, and act on the stories and plights of others." Narrative competence develops from the learner's life experience, reflective practice, and positive role modeling.

Reflective writing, where learners reflect on their clinical and other experiences, is one method for increasing learners' awareness of their developing professional identities. Journaling (i.e., asking learners to keep a learning journal) allows learners to recognize their own personal journeys through medicine and helps them to connect what they learn to everyday practice.[102] Structured reflective writing with individualized faculty feedback can enhance teaching about reflective practice.[103]

Frankel states that the best way to teach professionalism is through storytelling.[104] Professionalism is embodied in the stories people tell about their day-to-day experience in medical settings, and stories illuminate the intersection of the formal and hidden curricula.[104] At the Indiana University School of Medicine, students write narratives about their professional experiences at intervals throughout their medical school experience, allowing students and faculty to track their professionalism developmentally.

Quaintance and colleagues[79] at the University of Missouri–Kansas City School of Medicine use an appreciative inquiry approach where students interview faculty members about their professionalism experiences, followed by reflecting on and writing about their teachers' stories. The authors found that this technique of storytelling seemed to deepen students' appreciation and understanding of professionalism.

As noted in Chapter 1, Reis and colleagues[105] recently developed a framework and guide, called the "Brown Educational Guide to Analysis of Narrative" (BEGAN), for crafting faculty feedback on medical students' reflective writing. Educators have also integrated the arts with medical education to enhance communication skills and self-reflection.[106, 107, 108]

Learning in reflection groups

How do we provide environments that promote reflection and the moral development of learners and faculty, both of which are essential for professionalism? Branch[57] proposes several educational interventions, including critical reflection by small groups of students and faculty, faculty role modeling and feedback, and faculty development. Critical reflection groups meet on a regular basis and provide a safe environment where learners can comfortably discuss values and reflect on ethical dilemmas and concerns. Faculty members with reputations for being good role models lead the groups.

The Healer's Art course,[109] a 15-hour elective course offered in 60 medical schools, helps students personally explore issues of meaning, shared core values, and professionalism in medicine. At the end of the course, students may write a personal mission statement about their highest professional values, giving them an opportunity to reflect on their concepts of professionalism.[110] The course includes a small group discussion during which learners can share personal experiences, critical incidents, and reflections. Evaluations have shown that the course validates and legitimizes the humanistic components of professionalism and creates a safe community for reflection and discussion.[58]

Professional boundaries

The establishment and maintenance of professional boundaries is an important aspect of professionalism that is not often explicitly taught.[111, 112, 113] Negotiating professional boundaries is a central developmental challenge for all physicians, especially for young trainees as they learn to become professionals.

Common boundary challenges encountered in clinical practice include self-disclosure, gift giving, personal questions, social invitations, and errands or other requests by supervisors.[113] Lapid and colleagues[114] studied psychiatry residents in six programs and found they perceived a need for more education on many topics relating to boundaries and relationships, including requests to work with inadequate supervision, mistreatment of medical students and residents, adequately caring for patients while adhering to work hour guidelines, sexual/romantic relationships between residents and medical students, resolving conflicts between attending physicians and trainees, responding to impaired colleagues, and writing prescriptions for friends and family members.

Gaufberg and colleagues[115] examined the perspectives of third-year medical students in negotiating several boundary challenges. They concluded that students' negotiation of professional boundaries was influenced by the HC and power differences, and recommended increasing awareness of these influences.

Gaufberg developed an interactive teaching session on professional boundaries for medical students and residents. The session uses trigger tape scenarios of common boundary challenges that help learners recognize professional boundary situations, explore boundary issues, and discuss and role-play problem-solving and communication strategies for managing boundary violations. A main theme is teaching the learner to ask: "What is in the best interests of the patient?"[113]

Davidson[116] designed a flexible course module to increase learners' self-awareness, motivation, and professional judgment abilities related to their professional boundaries. Objectives for learners include the ability to:

- Identify boundary violations and understand their impact

- Apply critical thinking skills to complex professional relationship situations

- Increase awareness of self and others, including personal boundary vulnerabilities

- Learn risk-minimizing strategies

Although developed for licensed social work professionals, the teaching concepts and strategies are relevant for enhancing the professionalism of residents, medical students, faculty, and other learners.

Comprehensive models for teaching professionalism

Some institutions have developed comprehensive and innovative models for teaching professionalism. The following section outlines two models.

Indiana University School of Medicine

The Indiana University School of Medicine (IUSM) implemented a new curriculum based on nine competencies, which include:

- Effective communication

- Basic clinical skills

- Using science to guide diagnosis, management, therapeutics, and prevention

- Lifelong learning

- Self-awareness, self-care, and personal growth

- The social and community contexts of healthcare

- Moral reasoning and ethical judgment

- Problem-solving

- Professionalism and role recognition[66]

All basic science and clinical courses address competencies related to professionalism. In conjunction with this new formal curriculum, IUSM has engaged in a multiyear culture change project to bring the formal and informal curricula into better alignment. The objective is to develop an organizational culture that reinforces the values of the new formal curriculum.

A central tenant of the IUSM organizational change strategy is to foster respectful relationships and partnership in all arenas of clinical care and the medical school environment. A new complexity theory, Complex Responsive Processes of Relating (CRPR),[117] guided this project. CRPR suggests that the patterns of relating that constitute an organization's culture must be continually reenacted. At any moment, anyone can enact different patterns. These small, local disturbances have the potential to amplify and spread, resulting in large-scale organizational change.

The IUSM organizational change project uses appreciative storytelling and reflection on action to promote greater mindfulness of exhibited values and to foster the widespread practice of reflecting on and discussing interactions as they occur. IUSM uses narrative extensively throughout the organization to bring attention to and reinforce community values and good work. IUSM faculty, staff members, and administrators are also invited to participate in faculty development programs in order to build personal awareness and relationship-centered capacity.

McGill University Faculty of Medicine

The undergraduate medical curriculum at McGill has three central themes: physicianship, the clinical method, and basic sciences and scientific knowledge.[41] Physicianship refers to the two simultaneous roles of the physician: healer and professional. The clinical method is the mechanism through which physicianship is enacted, and includes how the physician relates to patients and what he or she does in the context of patient care.

McGill has instituted integrated courses on physicianship that run longitudinally across all four years of medical school.[118] Educators introduce the roles of healer and professional on the first day of medical school and reinforce them throughout the curriculum. Additional elements of the curriculum include the social contract, communication skills, observation skills and listening, the healer role, and narrative writing about an example of professional or unprofessional behavior the student has observed. During the fourth year, students complete an eight-hour seminar series called "Professionalism, Medicine's Social Contract, and You."

McGill also established a mentorship program. Recognized mentors receive salary support and work with a group of six students throughout medical school. The mentors also supervise student portfolios on physicianship.

The graduate training program at McGill uses a similar approach. All residents in all specialties participate in a variety of activities that address components of professionalism. Second-year residents attend an annual half-day workshop, "Professionalism for Residents."

Residents also participate in cross-specialty and department-specific learning activities including small group discussion, grand rounds, lectures, retreats, and workshops.[119]

Snell[119] outlines the essential elements for teaching and learning professionalism at the resident level. These are taught through a variety of methods at McGill, and include learning the cognitive base and skills of professionalism, developing professional attitudes and fostering professional behaviors, evaluating professionalism, and faculty development.[119] McGill has instituted a comprehensive program of faculty development in professionalism,[120] described later in this chapter.

Assessment of Professionalism

"PROFESSIONALISM MUST REMAIN A TOPIC AND FOCUS FOR DEBATE AND DISCUSSION. THE SUREST ENEMY OF PROFESSIONALISM IS THE ASSERTION THAT WE HAVE DEVELOPED THE NECESSARY MEASUREMENT TOOLS AND LEARNING ENVIRONMENTS—AND THUS WE CAN CALL A HALT TO THE ARGUMENTS, DEBATES, AND DISCUSSIONS."
—FRED HAFFERTY, PHD[23]

The ACGME and other organizational requirements for competence in professionalism provide an impetus for training programs to teach and evaluate this competency in a more consistent and comprehensive manner throughout medical education. However, the evaluation of professionalism is complex and challenging. No consensus exists as to what to measure or how.

Arnold[121] reviewed the professionalism literature from the past 30 years to examine the state of the art of assessing professionalism. She found that although a wide array of assessment tools exist, their measurement properties need improvement. Veloski and colleagues[122] concur, noting that there are few well-documented studies of instruments that evaluate professionalism.

Wilkinson and colleagues[123] completed a review of assessment tools for professionalism in an attempt to match given tools to defined attributes of professionalism. They concluded that assessment of professionalism can occur with the use of multisource feedback, observed clinical encounters, patient opinions, simulations, and other methods. The authors found, however, that further development of measures is needed to assess important aspects of professionalism, including reflection/personal awareness, lifelong learning, advocacy, managing uncertainty, responding to audit results, and balancing one's availability to others with caring for oneself.[123]

Part of the difficulty in determining how to evaluate professionalism is that it is a complex construct, not a set of skills, behaviors, attitudes, or steps. Hafferty[30] recommends we keep three questions in mind:

1. How do we effectively define and assess something that is transmitted in a variety of learning environments through a wide range of both formal and informal, even tacit, educational practices?

2. How do we effectively assess something that may be conceived as both practice and identity?

3. How do we design a system of evaluation that assesses both the learners and their learning environments?[30]

How do we assess the physician's competence in professionalism?

"ENSURING THAT STUDENTS OF MEDICINE AT ALL LEVELS NOT ONLY ACQUIRE BUT CONSISTENTLY DEMONSTRATE THE ATTRIBUTES OF MEDICAL PROFESSIONALISM IS ARGUABLY THE MOST IMPORTANT TASK FACING MEDICAL EDUCATORS HERE AT THE BEGINNING OF THE TWENTY-FIRST CENTURY."
—JORDAN COHEN, MD[143]

Assessment should include both formative and summative evaluations. Formative evaluations assess learning needs, create learning opportunities, guide feedback and coaching, promote reflection, and shape values.[125] Summative evaluations generally judge competence in high-stakes evaluations for promotion, licensing, and certification, and thus require a high degree of psychometric reliability and validity. Evaluation serves various purposes, including:

- Rewarding excellent professional behavior

- Identifying learners with deficiencies in professionalism

- Dismissing the occasional learner who is unable to be professional

- Improving patient care

- Raising institutional awareness

- Identifying role models

- Providing a vocabulary for communicating about professionalism

- Ensuring continuous quality improvement of individuals or the system

Accordingly, methods for evaluating professionalism will vary based on the purpose of the evaluation.

Epstein and Hundert[126] recommend that a strong mentoring system accompany any assessment program. Without a good system for mentoring, feedback, and remediation, any assessment is weakened and possibly even undermined. They also note that a similar process of reflection, feedback, and remediation can occur at the institutional level to guide curricular change.

Lynch, Leach, and Surdyk[127] recommend a relationship-centered framework for identifying curricular content and assessment areas in professionalism. They suggest evaluating aspects of relationships in five levels: patient–physician, society–physician, healthcare system–physician, physician–physician, and physician–self.

Suggested methods for the evaluation of professionalism

"UNFORTUNATELY, PROFESSIONALISM REMAINS AMONG THE MOST DIFFICULT DOMAINS OF DOCTOR COMPETENCE TO ASSESS. ALTHOUGH MANY PROMISING APPROACHES ARE UNDER EVALUATION, NO SINGLE MEASURE OR SET OF MEASUREMENTS HAS YET PROVEN SUFFICIENTLY RELIABLE AND VALID TO MEET DEMANDING PSYCHOMETRIC CRITERIA."

—JORDAN COHEN, MD[26]

The most effective approach to evaluating professionalism is a program of longitudinal assessments that includes multiple assessment approaches; observations by faculty members, team members, peers, and patients; feedback with reflection; and mentoring. Methods of evaluation considered most desirable by the ACGME[128] for the professionalism competency include 360-degree evaluations, objective structured clinical examinations (OSCEs), and patient surveys.[129]

In addition, the ACGME Project Think Tank[130] recommends assessment of ethics knowledge using vignettes with multiple-choice and open-ended responses, as well as assessment of the learning environment through resident questionnaires.

Evaluation approaches to consider in designing a program to assess professionalism include the following:

- Direct observation by faculty, followed by feedback

- 360-degree and multirater evaluations

- Professionalism Mini-Evaluation Exercise (P-MEX)

- OSCE

- Assessment by peers

- Critical incident reports

- Comment cards

- Portfolios maintained by learners and used for self-reflection

- Use of case vignettes to assess ethics knowledge

- Assessment of the learning environment via resident questionnaires

Direct observation

Direct observation of students followed by constructive feedback from faculty and real or simulated patients is a powerful assessment tool, but a lack of faculty and simulated patient time and training in giving effective feedback can hamper these efforts. Rider and colleagues[131] designed a model program for a related competency, interpersonal and communication skills, with the goal of providing one-on-one observation and feedback for learners while conserving faculty time. Shrank and colleagues assert:

As the field of evaluating professionalism matures, there is little question that more direct observation and a more concerted effort toward honest assessment and feedback will move our profession closer to the ultimate goal of reliably evaluating students' professional qualities.[132]

360-degree evaluations

The use of 360-degree and multirater evaluations provides learners with multiple sources of feedback in the clinical setting. Evaluators may include patients, faculty, multidisciplinary team members, peers, and others. Kirk underscores the importance of 360-degree evaluations for assessing professionalism: "Attending physicians may feel comfortable judging a learner's knowledge and clinical decision-making ability, but they may not know how that person behaves in the middle of the night."[96] However, other authors[133]

caution about negative influences that may affect the quality of 360-degree assessments, including situational factors (e.g., amount of time spent with learners), characteristics of the rater (e.g., level of training, lack of interest), and factors relating to the specific assessment criteria. A large number of evaluations are necessary to provide a reliable measure of performance. Chapter 1 includes a unique use of 360-degree and multirater evaluations with gap analysis methodology, developed to promote learner self-insight and enhanced feedback from faculty.[134]

P-MEX

The Professionalism Mini-Evaluation Exercise (P-MEX),[135] developed at McGill University Faculty of Medicine and the University of Toronto Faculty of Medicine, is used for formative evaluation of professionalism in the clinical setting. The P-MEX uses the Mini-Clinical Examination Exercise (Mini-CEX) format, and is useful for promoting self-reflection and awareness of the importance of professionalism in daily encounters, identifying professionalism behaviors, and teaching about professionalism.

OSCEs

OSCEs have been shown to provide reliable and valid assessments of students' humanism, communication, and empathy. Although OSCEs can measure constructs related to professionalism (e.g., humanism, communication skills), these constructs are not professionalism itself. The psychometric reliability of OSCEs for professionalism and ethical behavior is considered too low for use in high-stakes examinations,[26] yet they may be useful for formative evaluation.

Assessment by peers

Assessment by peers may promote professionalism, teamwork, and communication, and peers may provide insight into a learner's interpersonal skills and professional behavior. Peer assessment also provides learners with the opportunity to gain skills in evaluation and feedback. Leach notes that peer assessment "offers the benefit of professional self-regulation and accountability."[136]

Critical incident reports

Critical incident reports refer to records of individuals' unprofessional behavior. These reports are used to report incidents of unprofessional behavior that are outside of usual norms. van Mook and colleagues[137] recommend that faculty also report minor incidents, without concern that these will lead to dismissal, so that faculty can implement remediation approaches. Repeated instances or patterns of unprofessional behavior identify learners with significant deficits necessitating formal action. Faculty and/or overview groups can consider whether learners are able to accept responsibility for their problems and whether remediation strategies are effective. If critical incidents of unprofessional behavior persist despite remediation attempts, learners may be dismissed.[137]

Comment cards

Various institutions use comment cards or forms to document both positive and constructive comments about the professionalism of learners and faculty. As part of its online Professional Development Portfolio, New York University School of Medicine implemented comment cards. Positive or negative written remarks can be posted to a student's portfolio. The person writing the comments is identified, and the card is automatically sent to the student, the faculty mentor, and the portfolio administrator.[138]

At the University of Maryland School of Medicine, exemplary comment forms and unprofessional behavior document forms are available for use at any time to report on the professionalism of residents, faculty, and students.[139] Comment cards were originally developed for internal medicine residents and subspecialty fellows by the ABIM as part of its Project Professionalism.[140]

Portfolios

Portfolios maintained by learners have attracted increasing interest, and some educators have designed them primarily for professionalism.[138, 141] The ACGME is developing a Web-based learning portfolio for residents to document, organize, and seek feedback on their experiences.[142] The portfolio promotes reflection, both by self-reflection and by sharing reflections chosen by the resident.[80, 143] Although portfolios are not specifically assessment instruments for reflection,[123] significant strengths of portfolios include their connection to reflection and a narrative-based approach to learning professionalism, their promotion of self-directed learning and lifelong learning skills, and their inherent valuing of the individuality and diversity of learners.

Case vignettes

Educators use case vignettes for both teaching and assessment at various levels of medical training. Learners identify the attributes and characteristics of professionalism, and discuss ethical and other aspects of the cases.[144]

The National Board of Medical Examiners (NBME) is developing an Assessment of Professional Behaviors program to assess behaviors that are essential for safe, effective, and ethical care. Its approach is the assessment of observable behaviors—one component of professionalism—in medical environments using a Web-based system to collect multisource feedback.

The NBME's pilot instrument contains 25 behavioral items, two narrative comment areas (one for praise/commendation and one to record behaviors needing improvement), one global assessment item, and two questions regarding the amount of contact the observer had with the learner.[145] At the time of this writing, the assessment is formative, designed to help learners gain insight into their strengths and their needs for further development regarding their professional behavior.[146]

Please see the last section of this chapter for specific assessment tools and forms for the following evaluation approaches: 360-degree/multirater evaluation, P-MEX, critical incident reports, comment cards, case vignettes, and assessment of the learning environment.

Assessing the professionalism of the learning environment

The learning environment, with its HC and organizational culture, plays a significant role in the development of professionalism in its learners. The LCME recently developed a new accreditation standard that requires ongoing evaluation of the learning environment and the development of strategies to enhance its positive influences and to mitigate its negative influences.[147] Chapters 1 and 7 provide further discussion on this topic.

Quaintance, Arnold, and Thompson[148] developed a unique assessment tool to measure the "professionalism climate" in clinical settings. Their Climate of Professionalism Survey is presented in the last section of this chapter. Please also refer to the C3[149] instrument in Chapter 1, which measures the patient-centeredness of the HC and other aspects of the learning environment.

Assessment of professionalism starts during the admissions process

Assessing professionalism ideally begins with the admissions process to medical school. Wagoner[150] recommends that medical schools consider recruiting competent, humanistic students with the potential for the highest levels of professionalism throughout their lives. Initial work on considering potential in professionalism as part of the admissions process to medical school has begun at IUSM.[104] Residency programs also can choose to use professionalism as an important factor in their recruitment and selection processes. Chapter 1 lists assessment methods for personal and interpersonal attributes used at the time of selection for medical school or residency.

The Importance of Faculty Development

> "WE MUST ACKNOWLEDGE … THAT THE MOST IMPORTANT, INDEED THE ONLY, THING WE HAVE TO OFFER OUR STUDENTS IS OURSELVES. EVERYTHING ELSE THEY CAN READ IN A BOOK."
> —DANIEL C. TOSTESON, MD[151]

Faculty members are often unprepared to teach and evaluate professionalism. They may be unable to articulate the attributes of the physician as a professional, and some may serve as ineffective or negative role models. Faculty development programs in professionalism must focus on individual faculty members and on the learning environments and organizational cultures in which learning occurs.

As noted previously in this chapter, Burack and colleagues[60] studied attending physicians' responses to residents' and medical students' problematic behaviors on the wards and found that attending physicians did not respond to problematic behaviors in any observable way, and they let the majority of incidents pass without comment. Bryden and colleagues[152] studied faculty members' experiences teaching and evaluating professionalism and found that faculty members' own lapses in professionalism and their failure to address these in their colleagues created the most significant obstacle to teaching professionalism. The authors note that "… faculty perceive themselves and their colleagues as colluding to create a culture in medical education of permissiveness and nonconfrontation around minor to moderate lapses in professionalism."[(p. 9) 152] The ramifications of such findings are considerable. These studies and others underscore the importance of developing strong faculty development programs for professionalism.

The Mayo Clinic created a professionalism covenant for use in all training programs.[153, 154] The covenant requires educators to "… exhibit the highest standard of personal and professional conduct and confidently expect the same from their learners."[154] The Mayo Clinic learner covenant stipulates that educators also will:

- Instill in learners the core value of professionalism that places the needs and welfare of the patient first, above all other considerations

- Mentor learners in integrity and professionalism

- Demonstrate genuine concern for every learner's success

- Respect learners as colleagues

- Provide an environment enriched by scholarship

- Encourage trainees to become lifelong learners[153, 154]

Viggiano and colleagues note that The Mayo Clinic's value-based culture of service, and its ongoing core focus on the primacy of patient welfare, provides its faculty and learners with "… both a moral compass to guide thought, actions, and reflective practice, and a yardstick to measure their success."[154]

Branch[57] recommends instituting large-scale faculty development programs that emphasize moral education, including its theoretical underpinnings and the importance of an approach that integrates compassion and caring into learners' work with patients. These programs include reflective discussion groups for faculty in which their own values and attitudes are explored.

Steinert and colleagues[120, 155] developed a comprehensive faculty development program to support teaching and evaluation of professionalism at the McGill University Faculty of Medicine. Their guiding principles include:

- Development of a common understanding of the definition, characteristics, and behaviors of professionalism

- Translation of content into practice by teaching and demonstrating professionalism in the clinical setting

- A focus on teaching professionalism

- Facilitation of experiential learning and self-reflection

Think tanks with educational leaders and invitational and facultywide workshops were part of the faculty development implementation at McGill. Faculty development programs were developed on the topics of teaching and evaluating professionalism and on specific learning strategies, including role modeling and reflection. Outcomes of McGill's faculty development initiative have included increased teaching of professionalism to residents and faculty, revitalization of the curriculum to include an emphasis on the physician as both a healer and a professional,[62] a renewed focus on the assessment of professionalism, and similar faculty development programs in other areas.[120]

Faculty involved in medical education must explicitly teach and model the capacities and values we expect physicians to learn; consequently, faculty development is an essential component of any professionalism curriculum. Faculty development should focus on change at both the individual and organizational levels in order to address the HC and the learning environment.

Take-Home Points: Principles to Consider for the Development of Programs to Teach and Assess Professionalism

1. Institutional support must come from the top:

   - Enlist active involvement and support from the dean, associate deans, department chairs, program and clerkship directors, and multidisciplinary leaders to fortify the message that professionalism is important and valued

   - Initiate programs to enhance professionalism across the institution

   - Request support from institutional leaders including allocation of teaching time, space, and financial resources

2. Select or adapt a definition of professionalism to use as a conceptual framework institution-wide for teaching, evaluation, and setting expectations.

3. Provide formal instruction in the knowledge base of professionalism:

   - Make explicit the idea that professional status is a privilege granted by society and can be changed if society chooses

   - Teach the nature of professionalism, its historical base, attributes, and values, and the social contract between medicine and society

   - Teach learners the attributes of the two simultaneous roles of the physician, healer and professional, and reinforce these throughout the curriculum

   - Ensure that faculty development programs provide faculty with the same understanding and conceptual framework for professionalism as that taught to learners

4. Design the curriculum to foster self-reflection and the moral development of learners and faculty members:

   - Provide developmentally appropriate experiences and the opportunity to reflect on those experiences.

   - Include structured opportunities, including one-on-one mentoring and small group learning, for learners to discuss professional issues in a safe environment.

   - Design learning opportunities to enhance moral reasoning, awareness of ethical issues, and appropriate moral actions

   - Use varied teaching methods to develop reflective capacity in learners and faculty. Implement:

Take-Home Points: Principles to Consider for the Development of Programs to Teach and Assess Professionalism (cont.)

– Attention to role modeling with reflection

– Reflective feedback as a strategy for facilitating and enhancing reflection

– Teaching of mindfulness

– The use of reflective writing, narratives, and storytelling

- Use critical reflection groups for learners with:

  – Regular small group meetings where learners can become comfortable discussing values, attitudes, feelings, and beliefs

  – Provision of a "safe" group environment whereby learners are free to reflect and to honestly share ethical dilemmas and issues

  – Faculty members who are positive role models to lead the groups

5. Create an education program in professionalism that spans the undergraduate and graduate curricula and residency programs across the institution:

  - Such a program should be longitudinal and ensure repeated opportunities to learn and reflect on professionalism

  - Implement varied educational approaches: Create teaching strategies to enhance reflection (noted earlier); utilize small group learning, seminar series, retreats, workshops, grand round presentations, and free-standing required courses; add professionalism-related content (ethics, moral reasoning, self-reflection, professional boundaries ,etc.) to new and existing courses; provide one-on-one mentoring and supervision; require involvement in community service and patient advocacy experiences; and others

6. Explicitly address the hidden curriculum and create ethical learning environments

  - Articulate, teach, and expect good values, demonstration of respect for patients and colleagues, and attitudes and behavior consistent with professionalism

  - Utilize discussion, writing narratives on professionalism, storytelling, and reflection to make the hidden curriculum explicit and to foster the development of professionalism

7. Identify teachers who can serve as good role models and who can create and maintain learning environments built on relationship, safety, trust, and respect:

Take-Home Points: Principles to Consider for the Development of Programs to Teach and Assess Professionalism (cont.)

- Understand the critical role of the learner–teacher relationship in the development and nurturing of professionalism in the learner

- Ensure that faculty know that the learner–teacher relationship sets the stage for the physician–patient relationship and for professional identity and behavior

- Remove poor role models from teaching roles; they are harmful to the development of professionalism and are associated with cynicism in learners

8. Provide formative and summative assessments of professionalism:

- Use multiple longitudinal evaluations with frequent observation and feedback, multiple assessment methods, and multiple observers/raters including faculty, team memebers, patients, and families

- Develop a mechanism for recording critical incidents and lapses in professionalism, and protocols for remediation and dismissal where necessary

- Provide positive feedback about good professional attitudes and behaviors to reinforce these and increase the likelihood that they will endure

- Evaluate professionalism during the admissions/selection process for medical school, residency, and fellowship programs

9. Faculty development is key:

- Develop a core group of teachers able to facilitate the teaching and learning of professionalism; involve as many faculty members as possible from all levels and specialties

- Teach faculty how to give feedback and teach reflection

- Increase faculty and resident awareness of their influence as role models 24/7

- Provide faculty with reflective discussion groups of their own as an arena for clarification of values and attitudes, self-reflection, and peer support for dealing with students and residents presenting poor professional attitudes or behavior

10. Appoint a designated professionalism curriculum director or group to ensure that teaching and assessing this competency is included where relevant and appropriate. Integrating professionalism into the ongoing training curriculum requires long-range planning and intent.

Adapted in part from 26, 57, 69, 98, 118.

Conclusion

"WHAT WE HAVE BEFORE US ARE SOME BREATHTAKING
OPPORTUNITIES DISGUISED AS INSOLUBLE PROBLEMS."
—JOHN W. GARDNER, 1965 SPEECH

Physicians must be professionally competent and capable in order to effectively practice medicine. Traditional medical education focuses on enhancing competence—knowledge, skills, and attitudes. Fraser and Greenhalgh[156] encourage educators to enable not just competence, but also capability—the extent to which individuals can adapt to change, generate new knowledge, and continue to improve performance.

Significant work remains. Medical institutions and organizations must act decisively to put the public interest—the welfare of our patients—first. The greatest challenge will be to create change to reinforce the values of professionalism in the organizational cultures and learning environments of our medical institutions. We must address the hidden curriculum, create ethical learning environments, attend to the moral and ethical development of our learners and faculty, develop self-reflective ability in our physicians, and pay constant attention to our role modeling. Faculty development remains essential.

Cohen states, "The physician professional is defined not only by what he or she must know and do, but most importantly by a profound sense of what the physician must be. Character, integrity, honor, moral fiber—these attributes are essential."[157] We can accomplish no less. Society, our patients, and our profession have much to gain.

Acknowledgments

I want to thank my colleagues who generously contributed their thoughts and ideas to this chapter: Karen Adams, MD; William Branch, MD; Jack Coulehan, MD, MPH; Dan Duffy, MD; Nehad El-Sawi, PhD; Ronald Epstein, MD; Rich Frankel, PhD; Elizabeth Gaufberg, MD, MPH; Paul Haidet, MD; Mariana Hewson, PhD; Peg Hinrichs, MEd; Tom Inui, ScM, MD; Adina Kalet, MD; H. Esterbrook Longmaid III, MD; Maxine Papadakis, MD; Kate Rider-Dobbins, BA, BSN; David Stern, MD; Tony Suchman, MD; and W. Wayne Weston, MD, CCFP, FCFP. A special thank you to Sylvia Cruess, MD, and Richard Cruess, MD, whose enthusiasm for this chapter and generosity were invaluable.

Innovative Approaches, Models, and Assessment Tools for Teaching and Assessing Professionalism

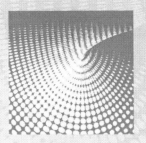

CONTENTS

Introduction

This section contains selected tools and forms for teaching and evaluating professionalism using various approaches: 360-degree/multirater evaluation, P-MEX, critical incident reports, comment cards, case vignettes, and assessment of the learning environment. Descriptions are provided for each tool. Most forms and tools are intended for teaching or formative evaluation, many continue to evolve, and none is considered a definitive product. Ideally, a form or tool is selected as part of an overall curriculum for teaching and assessing the professionalism competencies.

For all tools, please obtain permission from their authors before use. Some of the assessment tools come with a guide or additional educational materials, and these are available from the authors.

University of Oklahoma College of Medicine: 360-degree Professionalism Assessment Instrument

The 360-degree Professionalism Assessment Instrument was developed to evaluate medical students' and residents' strengths and weaknesses in the following areas of professionalism: honor and integrity, responsibility and accountability, leadership, altruism, caring, compassion and communication, excellence and scholarship, and respect.

The objectives are to identify learners with professionalism behaviors that meet or exceed expectations and learners with professionalism behaviors that are unacceptable or need improvement.[158] The institution distributes the form via an online survey website.

Figure 6.8	University of Oklahoma College of Medicine: Professionalism Assessment Instrument

Name of student:	Date of evaluation:	Name of evaluator:
Year of Student: MS1 MS2 MS3 MS4	Evaluator's Role: Peer, Resident, Faculty, Nurse, Patient, Self, Other	Evaluator's signature:

HONOR AND INTEGRITY Please choose one	UNACCEPTABLE 1	NEEDS IMPROVEMENT 2	MEETS EXPECTATIONS 3	SUPERIOR 4	CANNOT ASSESS
Consider the extent of trustworthiness in relation to interactions with peers, patients, faculty, and others.	Student considered untrustworthy, abandons responsibility; is known to lie and/or cheat; is arrogant.	Unsure if student can be trusted; reasons to believe may not always be honest.	Student always trustworthy; considered honest by most.	Student inspires trust from others, always honest, always handles confidential information discreetly.	Please mark if you cannot assess student in this area.

RESPONSIBILITY AND ACCOUNTABILITY Please choose one	UNACCEPTABLE 1	NEEDS IMPROVEMENT 2	MEETS EXPECTATIONS 3	SUPERIOR 4	CANNOT ASSESS
Consider the degree to which the student can be relied upon to take responsibility for accomplishing assigned tasks; accepts responsibility for errors; fulfills expectations of roles.	Student is regularly late; does not complete assignments or tasks on time; takes little or no responsibility for own mistakes; appearance often unprofessional (dress, hygiene).	Student is frequently late in arriving and/or completing assignments and tasks; often carries less than his or her share of team work; appearance often inappropriate.	Student is rarely late; absences seldom interfere with responsibilities; accepts appropriate share of team work; usually accepts responsibility for errors; appearance always appropriate to situation.	Student is consistently on time; always fulfills responsibilities and meets all deadlines; always accepts responsibility for errors; appearance always appropriate.	Please mark if you cannot assess student in this area.

LEADERSHIP Please choose one	UNACCEPTABLE 1	NEEDS IMPROVEMENT 2	MEETS EXPECTATIONS 3	SUPERIOR 4	CANNOT ASSESS
Consider the degree to which the student encourages a culture that facilitates professionalism; teaches others.	Student often blames others; competes destructively; is frequently the instigator of unprofessional behavior.	Student demonstrates some ability to be a leader but does not always encourage a culture of respect and compassion; not considered a role model.	Student often assumes leadership roles; constructively approaches conflict resolution, regularly assists peers and others.	Student is always in a leadership role; teaches and promotes professional development of others; serves as an example for others.	Please mark if you cannot assess student in this area.

ALTRUISM Please choose one	UNACCEPTABLE 1	NEEDS IMPROVEMENT 2	MEETS EXPECTATIONS 3	SUPERIOR 4	CANNOT ASSESS
Consider the degree to which a student puts others above him or herself.	Student exhibits greed or selfishness; never offers to help or assist others; criticizes others to make self look good.	Student occasionally puts others before self; will sometimes offer to help others.	Student exhibits unselfish concern for others; can usually be counted on to help when needed.	Student exhibits selflessness; regularly goes beyond what is required in order to help others.	Please mark if you cannot assess student in this area.

 A Practical Guide to Teaching and Assessing the ACGME Core Competencies, Second Edition

Figure 6.8	University of Oklahoma College of Medicine: Professionalism Assessment Instrument (cont.)				
CARING, COMPASSION, AND COMMUNICATION Please choose one	**UNACCEPTABLE 1**	**NEEDS IMPROVEMENT 2**	**MEETS EXPECTATIONS 3**	**SUPERIOR 4**	**CANNOT ASSESS**
Consider how the student treats and communicates with others (peers, faculty, staff, patients).	Student appears "heartless"; compassion is relative or selective depending on circumstances; ineffective communication skills.	Student needs to improve ability to demonstrate empathy toward patients, team members and others; trouble communicating effectively with others, often has difficulties with team members or staff.	Student always listens attentively to others; responds humanely in most situations; usually tolerant of differences; good communication skills, facilitates communication among team members.	Student always empathic toward others; is sensitive and perceptive; is tolerant of differences; always takes time to listen to others; excellent communication skills.	Please mark if you cannot assess student in this area.
EXCELLENCE AND SCHOLARSHIP Please choose one	**UNACCEPTABLE 1**	**NEEDS IMPROVEMENT 2**	**MEETS EXPECTATIONS 3**	**SUPERIOR 4**	**CANNOT ASSESS**
Consider the degree to which the student demonstrates competence and excellence in their learning and practice.	Student appears satisfied with minimally acceptable performance; known for taking shortcuts; often unprepared; wants to just "get by."	Student commitment to excellence is variable; puts limits on time and ability to achieve excellence; often settles for less than capable of accomplishing.	Student seeks additional knowledge and skills; consistent commitment to excellence; usually sets high expectations for self; usually intellectually curious and self-directed in learning; always fulfills educational assignments.	Student always prepared; takes initiative; always self-directed in seeking additional knowledge and skills; strives for excellence; sets lofty, but achievable goals.	Please mark if you cannot assess student in this area.
RESPECT Please choose one	**UNACCEPTABLE 1**	**NEEDS IMPROVEMENT 2**	**MEETS EXPECTATIONS 3**	**SUPERIOR 4**	**CANNOT ASSESS**
Consider the degree to which the student shows respect for peers, faculty, staff, and patients.	Student is often disrespectful others; intolerant of others attitudes or beliefs; treats people preferentially depending on position.	Student is sometimes disrespectful of others; can be intolerant of others beliefs and culture; seldom seeks to understand values and belief systems of patients and others.	Student is nonjudgmental; demonstrates balanced treatment of others; is typically respectful and tolerant; regularly seeks to understand values and belief systems of patients and others.	Student respects differences and always tries to be nonjudgmental; always tolerant of others; respectful toward those with more experience; always seeks to understand values and belief systems of patients and others.	Please mark if you cannot assess student in this area.
Comments:					

For additional information please contact: Sheila Crow, PhD, Director, Office of Educational Development & Support, University of Oklahoma College of Medicine. Sheila-crow@ouhsc.edu

Source: © University of Oklahoma College of Medicine. Reprinted with permission.

P-MEX: Professionalism Mini-Evaluation Exercise

The P-MEX is based on the Mini-CEX, a 15–30 minute direct observation assessment tool used to assess resident-patient interactions with real patients in clinical settings. Multiple evaluators assess residents in multiple encounters over time. While the Mini-CEX rates professionalism as a single global entity, the P-MEX was developed to evaluate specific characteristics of professionalism. McGill faculty members and residents identified 142 observable behaviors reflective of professionalism, and the authors distilled 24 behaviors for further evaluation. Four factors were found in an exploratory factor analysis: doctor–patient relationship skills, reflective skills, time management, and interprofessional relationship skills.[135] The P-MEX has good construct and content validity, and the use of 10 to 12 raters provides a reliability coefficient of 0.80.[14]

Developed at McGill University and University of Toronto Faculties of Medicine, the P-MEX has value as a formative tool, and has been used in various settings.

Figure 6.9	**P-MEX: Professionalism Mini-Evaluation Exercise**

Guidelines for using the P-MEX

The Professionalism Mini-Evaluation Exercise (P-MEX) focuses on the healing and professional behaviors that students/residents demonstrate in various settings during their daily professional activities. It is designed to be easily implemented and to encourage early feedback. It is to be used following an observation of a minimum of 15–20 minutes of a student/resident activity. This assessment will become part of the student's/resident's permanent record and is meant to encourage feedback.

Form and rating scale

For each encounter, each behavior should be categorized utilizing the following rating scale. Utilize the **N/A (not applicable)** category if the behaviour was **not observed** or if the category is **not applicable** to the setting.

Rating	Description of Behaviour
UNacceptable	Lapses of professional behaviour that are intentional, are likely to harm, and for which there are no mitigating circumstances.
BELow expectations	Lapses of professional behaviour that are unintentional, result in minimal to no harm, or for which there may be mitigating circumstances.
MET expectations	Demonstrated the performance expected for the level of the student/resident.
EXCeeded expectations	Exceptional performance, demonstrating the behaviours expected of an outstanding physician-to-be.
Critical Event	A clear breach of professional boundaries. Documentation of a critical event is sent directly to the appropriate authority for immediate action.

Please rate the student's/resident's performance during THIS encounter: **UN**acceptable, **BEL**ow expectations, **MET** expectations, **EXC**eeded expectations, **N**ot **A**pplicable.

Figure 6.9	**P-MEX: Professionalism Mini-Evaluation Exercise (cont.)**

Professionalism Mini-Evaluation Exercise

Evaluator: _____

Student/Resident: _____

Level: (please check)   ❑ 3rd yr   ❑ 4th yr   ❑ Res 1   ❑ Res 2   ❑ Res 3   ❑ Res 4   ❑ Res 5

Setting: ❑ Ward   ❑ Clinic   ❑ OR   ❑ ER   ❑ Classroom   ❑ Other _____

	N/A	UN	BEL	MET	EXC
Listened actively to patient					
Showed interest in patient as a person					
Recognized and met patient needs					
Extended him/herself to meet patient needs					
Ensured continuity of patient care					
Advocated on behalf of a patient					
Demonstrated awareness of own limitations					
Admitted errors/omissions					
Solicited feedback					
Accepted feedback					
Maintained appropriate boundaries					
Maintained composure in a difficult situation					
Maintained appropriate appearance					
Was on time					
Completed tasks in a reliable fashion					
Addressed own gaps in knowledge and/or skills					
Was available to colleagues					
Demonstrated respect for colleagues					
Avoided derogatory language					
Maintained patient confidentiality					
Used health resources appropriately					

▶ Please rate this student's/resident's overall professional performance during THIS encounter:
     ❑ **UN**acceptable   ❑ **MET** expectations   ❑ **BEL**ow expectations   ❑ **EXC**eeded expectations

▶ Did you observe a critical event?   ❑ No   ❑ Yes   (comment required)

Comments:

Evaluator's signature: _____

Student's/Resident's signature: _____   **Date and Time:** _____

Figure 6.9	**P-MEX: Professionalism Mini-Evaluation Exercise (cont.)**

Guidance for evaluators

Most students/residents will on most occasions "meet expectations." Some will demonstrate behaviours which exceed expectations on selected occasions. A few individuals will consistently demonstrate behaviours which exceed expectations.

Individuals may, at times, demonstrate behaviours which are "below expectations." It is extremely important to identify these occasions, because if they occur frequently, remedial action may be necessary. Behaviours classified as "unacceptable" will always require remedial action.

Evaluating behaviours

It is believed that the behaviours on the evaluation form are self-evident and that descriptors are not necessary. However, each behaviour observed must be placed in the context of the person, the situation, and the potential for harm caused by behaviours that deviate from the norm. For example, being late on a single occasion could either be acceptable, below expectations, or unacceptable depending upon the context. If the student/resident is late because they were giving patient care in an emergency situation it may be acceptable, while if they are late for frivolous reasons, it is not.

Developed by: R.L. Cruess, S.R. Cruess, Y. Steinert, McGill University and S. Ginsburg, J. Herold-McIlroy, University of Toronto. Used with permission.

University of California San Francisco School of Medicine: Physicianship Evaluation Forms

The University of California San Francisco School of Medicine uses critical incident reports to monitor students' professional behavior over the course of medical school and to report incidences of unprofessional behavior.[159] Course directors who identify students with lapses or deficiencies in professionalism submit a Physicianship Evaluation Form to the associate dean for student affairs. The dean then meets with the student for discussion and remediation.

If a student receives two or more forms during the first two years of medical school and one additional form during the third or fourth year, or if a student receives two or more forms in the third or fourth year, the student is placed on academic probation and his or her professionalism problem is described in the dean's recommendation letter for residency programs. The student can also be referred for review of his or her entire academic performance, and depending on the severity of the unprofessional behavior, can be dismissed from medical school, even if the student has passed all coursework. The Physicianship Evaluation Form used for first- and second-year medical students the Physicianship Evaluation Form for third- and fourth-year students are provided below.

Additional forms are available from:
www.medschool.ucsf.edu/professional_development/ professionalism/index.aspx.

<table>
<tr><td>Figure 6.10</td><td>**University of California, San Francisco School of Medicine: Physicanship Evaluation Form for First and Second Year Students**</td></tr>
</table>

UCSF SCHOOL OF MEDICINE

PHYSICIANSHIP EVALUATION FORM FOR FIRST AND SECOND YEAR STUDENTS

_____   _____
Student name (type or print legibly)   **Course (Dept. & Course No.)**

_____   _____
Course director   **Quarter, Year**

_____
Course director's signature

Date this form was discussed with the student _____

The student has exhibited one or more of the following behaviors that need improvement to meet expected standards of physicianship.

This student needs further education or assistance with the following: (circle)

1. **Reliability and responsibility**

    a.   Fulfilling responsibilities in a reliable manner.

    b.   Learning how to complete assigned tasks.

2. **Self improvement and adaptability**

    a.   Accepting constructive feedback

    b.   Recognizing limitations and seeking help

    c.   Being respectful of colleagues and patients

    d.   Incorporating feedback in order to make changes in behavior

    e.   Adapting to change

3. **Relationships with students, faculty, staff, and patients**

    a.   Establishing rapport

    b.   Being sensitive to the needs of patients

    c.   Establishing and maintaining appropriate boundaries in work and learning situations

    d.   Relating well to fellow students in a learning environment

    e.   Relating well to staff in a learning environment

    f.   Relating well to faculty in a learning environment

Figure 6.10	**University of California, San Francisco School of Medicine: Physicanship Evaluation Form for First and Second Year Students (cont.)**

4.   Upholding the Medical Student Statement of Principles

   a.   Maintaining honesty

   b.   Contributing to an atmosphere conducive to learning

   c.   Respecting the diversity of race, gender, religion, sexual orientation, age, disability or socioeconomic status

   d.   Resolving conflicts in a manner that respects the dignity of every person involved

   e.   Using professional language and being mindful of the environment

   f.   Protecting patient confidentiality

   g.   Dressing in a professional manner

Comments and Suggestions for Change:

_____

_____

_____

_____

_____

_____

This section is to be completed by the student.

I have read this evaluation and discussed it with my course director.

_____   _____

Student signature   Date

My comments are: (optional)

_____

_____

_____

From: Papadakis MA, Loeser H, Healy K. Early detection and evaluation of professionalism deficiencies in medical students: one school's approach. Academic Medicine 2001;76:1100–1106. Reprinted with permission.

| Figure 6.11 | **University of California, San Francisco School of Medicine: Physicanship Evaluation Form for Third and Fourth Year Students** |

UCSF SCHOOL OF MEDICINE
PHYSICIANSHIP EVALUATION FORM FOR THIRD AND FOURTH YEAR STUDENTS

_____
Student name (type or print legibly)

_____
Course (Dept. & Course No.)

_____
Site director

_____
Quarter, Block, and Year

_____
Site director's signature

_____
Location

Date this form was discussed with the student _____

A student with the pattern of the following behavior has not sufficiently demonstrated professional and personal attributes for meeting the standards of professionalism inherent in being a physician:

Circle the appropriate category. Comments are required.

1. **Unmet professional responsibility:**

   a. The student needs continual reminders in the fulfillment of responsibilities to patients or to other healthcare professionals.

   b. The student cannot be relied upon to complete tasks.

   c. The student misrepresents or falsifies actions and/or information.

   _____
   _____
   _____

2. **Lack of effort toward self improvement and adaptability:**

   a. The student is resistant or defensive in accepting criticism.

   b. The student remains unaware of his/her own inadequacies.

   c. The student resists considering or making changes.

   d. The student does not accept blame for failure, or responsibility for errors.

   e. The student is abusive or critical during times of stress.

   f. The student demonstrates arrogance.

   _____
   _____
   _____

| Figure 6.11 | **University of California, San Francisco School of Medicine: Physicanship Evaluation Forms for Third and Fourth Year Students (cont.)** |

3. **Diminished relationships with patients and families:**

    a. The student inadequately establishes rapport with patients or families.

    b. The student is often insensitive to the patients' or families' feelings, needs, or wishes.

    c. The student uses his/her professional position to engage in romantic or sexual relationships with patients or members of their families.

    d. The student lacks empathy.

    e. The student has inadequate personal commitment to honoring the wishes of the patients.

    _____
    _____
    _____

4. **Diminished relationships with members of the healthcare team:**

    a. The student does not function within a healthcare team.

    b. The student is insensitive to the needs, feelings, and wishes of the healthcare team members.

    _____
    _____
    _____

5. **Please comment on an appropriate plan of action to pursue when counseling the student**

    _____
    _____
    _____

This section is to be completed by the student.

6. I have read this evaluation and discussed it with the clerkship director.

    _____   _____
    Student signature   Date

7. **My comments are: (optional)**

    _____
    _____
    _____

From "Papadakis MA, Osborn EH, Cooke M, Healy K. A strategy for the detection and evaluation of unprofessional behavior in medical students. Academic Medicine. 1999;74:980–90." Reprinted with permission.

University of Toronto Faculty of Medicine: Clerkship Professionalism Evaluation Form

The University of Toronto Faculty of Medicine has developed a protocol for assessing professionalism of medical students. Preceptors and tutors complete online professionalism assessments for all students.

These forms are used for education on proper professional conduct. Medical education administrative staff members also can complete a form if they feel a student has professionalism issues. The school has a protocol in place for handling lapses of professionalism.

Additional information and forms are available online at *http://icarus.med.utoronto.ca/professionalism*.

	University of Toronto Faculty of Medicine: Clerkship Professionalism Evaluation Form
Figure 6.12	

Altruism

	Meets professional expectations	Observed 1 or 2 minor lapses of professional behaviour	Observed 1 major lapse or 3 or more minor lapses of professional behaviour	Was not in a position to observe professional/ unprofessional behaviour
Demonstrates sensitivity to patients' needs				
Takes time and effort to explain information to patients				
Takes time and effort to comfort the sick patient				
Listens sympathetically to patients' concerns				
Puts patients' interests before his/her own				
Shows respect for patients' confidentiality				

Duty: Reliability and Responsibility

	Meets professional expectations	Observed 1 or 2 minor lapses of professional behaviour	Observed 1 major lapse or 3 or more minor lapses of professional behaviour	Was not in a position to observe professional/ unprofessional behaviour
Completes assigned tasks fully and in a timely fashion				
Fulfills obligations undertaken				
Takes on appropriate share of team work				
Fulfills call duties				
Reports accurately and fully on patient care activities				
Always ensures transfer of responsibility for patient care				
Informs supervisor/team when mistakes occur				
Informs supervisor/team when faced with a conflict of interest				

Figure 6.12	University of Toronto Faculty of Medicine: Clerkship Professionalism Evaluation Form (cont.)

Excellence: Self Improvement and Adaptability

	Meets professional expectations	Observed 1 or 2 minor lapses of professional behaviour	Observed 1 major lapse or 3 or more minor lapses of professional behaviour	Was not in a position to observe professional/ unprofessional behaviour
Accepts constructive feedback				
Recognizes own limitations and seeks appropriate help				
Incorporates feedback to make changes in behaviour				
Adapts well to changing circumstances				
Reads up on patient cases				
Attends rounds, seminars, and other learning events				

Respect for Others: Relationships with Students, Faculty and Staff

	Meets professional expectations	Observed 1 or 2 minor lapses of professional behaviour	Observed 1 major lapse or 3 or more minor lapses of professional behaviour	Was not in a position to observe professional/ unprofessional behaviour
Establishes rapport with team members				
Maintains appropriate boundaries in work and learning situations				
Relates well to fellow students in a learning environment				
Relates well to faculty in a learning environment				
Relates well to other health care professionals in a learning environment				

Figure 6.12	**University of Toronto Faculty of Medicine: Clerkship Professionalism Evaluation Form (cont.)**

Honour and Integrity: Upholding Student and Professional Code of Condut

	Meets professional expectations	Observed 1 or 2 minor lapses of professional behaviour	Observed 1 major lapse or 3 or more minor lapses of professional behaviour	Was not in a position to observe professional/ unprofessional behaviour
Refers to self accurately with respect to qualifications				
Uses appropriate language in discussion with patients and colleagues				
Resolves conflicts in a manner that respects the dignity of those involved				
Behaves honestly				
Respects diversity of race, gender, religion, sexual orientation, age, disability, intelligence, and socio-economic status				
Maintains appropriate boundaries with patients				
Dresses in an appropriate professional manner (context specific)				

Critical event: Yes _____   No _____

Critical Comments (if there was a critical event, please document it here): _____

_____

_____

Areas of praise: _____

_____

Areas for improvement: _____

_____

Was this discussed with the student?   Yes _____ No _____

Source: © 2008 University of Toronto Faculty of Medicine. Reprinted with permission.

Professionalism Comment Cards

Institutions use comment cards to document both positive and negative comments about the professionalism of medical students, residents, and faculty. The American Board of Internal Medicine (ABIM) developed the Praise Card and Early Concern Note originally as a part of its Project Professionalism.[140]

The original ABIM cards, designed to provide information to the residency program director about the professional behavior and performance of residents and subspecialty fellows, were used by 40% of internal medicine residency programs, and also by subspecialty training programs. Initially printed double-sided on 3 x 5 cards,[140] the cards have been adapted and used online by various institutions and organizations.[14, 138, 139, 160]

The Professionalism Praise Card and the Professionalism Early Concern Note on the following pages focus specifically on professionalism competencies. These comment cards can be used for recognition, feedback, and documentation with learners at all levels.

Figure 6.13	**Professionalism Praise Card**

Professionalism Praise Card

Please complete and submit this form to _____ when you wish to praise the professional behavior and/or performance of a physician colleague. This information will be conveyed to the physician and noted in their file.

Name of physician: _____ **Date:** _____

My praise about the performance of this physician is based on his/her demonstration of exceptional ability in the following (please check):

❑ Altruism/responsiveness to patient needs that supersedes self-interest

❑ Honesty, integrity, and trustworthiness

❑ Caring and compassion

❑ Respect for patients' and families' privacy, autonomy, and dignity

❑ Respect for superiors, colleagues, peers, and others

❑ Respect for differences and diversity

❑ Ability to create and sustain therapeutic relationships with patients and families

❑ Places patient needs and welfare first

❑ Accountability to patients, society, and the medical profession

❑ Leadership of team and others

❑ Communication and collaboration

❑ Moral reasoning and ethical behavior

❑ Self-awareness/Recognizes own limitations

❑ Excellence and scholarship

❑ Self-improvement/Commitment to ongoing professional development

Comments:

Your name: _____ Institution/Department: _____

E-Mail: _____ Phone: _____

Source: © 2010 Elizabeth A. Rider, MSW, MD, FAAP
Adapted from:
1. ABIM. Project Professionalism. Philadelphia, PA: 2001.
2. ACGME. Program Director Guide to the Common Program Requirements. Chicago, IL: 2009.
3. University of Virginia School of Medicine. Praise Card and Early Concern Card. www.med-ed.virginia.edu

Figure 6.14	**Professionalism Early Concern Note**

Professionalism Early Concern Note

Please complete and submit this form to _____ when you have any concerns about the professional behavior and/or performance of a physician colleague. This information will be used constructively to help the physician.

Name of physician: _____ **Date:** _____

My concerns about the performance and/or professional behavior of this physician are based on:

❑ Critical incident   ❑ Gut-level reaction   ❑ Series of "red" flags

❑ Altruism/responsiveness to patient needs that supersedes self-interest

❑ Honesty, integrity, and trustworthiness

❑ Caring and compassion

❑ Respect for patients' and families' privacy, autonomy, and dignity

❑ Respect for superiors, colleagues, peers, and others

❑ Respect for differences and diversity

❑ Ability to create and sustain therapeutic relationships with patients and families

❑ Places patient needs and welfare first

❑ Accountability to patients, society, and the medical profession

❑ Leadership of team and others

❑ Communication and collaboration

❑ Moral reasoning and ethical behavior

❑ Self-awareness/Recognizes own limitations

❑ Excellence and scholarship

❑ Self-improvement/Commitment to ongoing professional development

Comments:

I have discussed my concerns with the physician   ____ Yes ____ No

I feel uncomfortable discussing my concerns with the physician   ____ Yes ____ No

Please call me about these concerns   ____ Yes ____ No

Your name: _____ **Institution/Department:** _____
E-Mail: _____ **Phone:** _____

Source: © 2010 Elizabeth A. Rider, MSW, MD, FAAP
Adapted from:
1. ABIM. Project Professionalism. Philadelphia, PA: 2001.
2. ACGME. Program Director Guide to the Common Program Requirements. Chicago, IL: 2009.
3. University of Virginia School of Medicine. Praise Card and Early Concern Card. www.med-ed.virginia.edu

McGill University Faculty of Medicine: Vignettes for Discussion and Worksheet for Vignettes on Professionalism

McGill has developed a series of case vignettes for residents, medical students, and basic science faculty, and for continuing professional development.[161] The accompanying Worksheet for Vignettes on Professionalism lists professionalism attributes and is a tool for facilitating discussion of the vignettes.[162]

Learners must determine which aspects of professionalism are present in a series of vignettes and discuss ethical and other issues regarding the cases. Residents identify aspects of professionalism raised in each case, and use this information to discuss their approach to the issues. Medical students and faculty discuss the attributes in small groups, using the worksheet as a guide. During the second year, educators present more sophisticated vignettes. In the third year, students prepare their own vignettes for discussion that describe positive or negative professional behavior they have personally experienced.[163]

Figure 6.15	**McGill University Faculty of Medicine: Vignettes for Discussion for Residents and Continuing Professional Development**

First identify the elements, characteristics, or attributes of professionalism raised by each of the following cases. You may then discuss solutions to the problem.

Case #1

Your daughter is scheduled to graduate from high school this afternoon. As you are preparing to sign out to a colleague, one of your long-time patients presents in the ER with chest pain. You enter the ER and a partner in your group practice is already there to evaluate the situation. You know that he is competent and conscientious, so you go to reassure your patient. He pleads with you to stay.

Case #2

A general hospital has asked all attending staff to work one weekend day and one night per month in the ER. A full-time attending physician refuses to work nights or weekends.

Case #3

An ER physician, seeing increased young people injured in car accidents caused by alcohol, organizes a series of visits to high schools in the community to present the problem and the effects of alcohol on students.

Case #4

You have become close friends with one of your colleagues and notice that at social events he frequently drinks excessively and he admits that he binges on weekends. You are on call with him and you notice alcohol on his breath.

Case #5

A long-time patient of yours requests a note from you documenting a nonexistent illness in order to recover cancellation penalties from the airlines on a nonrefundable ticket.

Case #6

Doctor Dell practices in a rural community. He has no training or experience in clinical trial methodology. A drug company offers him $100.00 for each patient he recruits from his practice to evaluate a medication in postmarketing surveillance.

From: McGill University Faculty of Medicine Undergraduate and Postgraduate Teaching Programs. Used with permission.

Figure 6.16	McGill University Faculty of Medicine: Worksheet for Vignettes on Professionalism					
Attributes of the Healer and the Professional		Case #1	Case #2	Case #3	Case #4	Case #5
Altruism	the unselfish regard for, or devotion to, the welfare of others; placing the needs of the patient before one's self interest.					
Autonomy	the freedom to make independent decisions in the care of patients and for the good of society.					
Caring and Compassion	a sympathetic consciousness of another's distress together with a desire to alleviate it.					
Commitment	being obligated or emotionally impelled to act in the best interest of the patient and society; a pledge given by way of the Hippocratic oath or its modern equivalent.					
Competence	to master and keep current the knowledge and skills relevant to medical practice, including communication.					
Confidentiality	to not disclose information given by patient and/or family without just cause.					
Insight	self-awareness; the ability to recognize and understand one's actions, motivations and emotions.					
Integrity and Honesty	uprightness, honesty, incorruptibility					
Morality and Ethical Conduct	to act for the public good; demonstrating behavior which is consistently right as opposed to wrong, conformity to the ideals of right human conduct in dealings with patients, colleagues, and society.					
Trustworthiness	worthy of trust, reliable					
Openness	willingness to hear, accept, and deal with the views of others without reserve or pretense.					

Figure 6.16	McGill University Faculty of Medicine: Worksheet for Vignettes on Professionalism (cont.)

Attributes of the Healer and the Professional		Case #1	Case #2	Case #3	Case #4	Case #5
Presence	to be fully present for a patient without distraction and to fully support and accompany the patient throughout care.					
Respect for the Healing Function	the ability to recognize, elicit and foster the power to heal inherent in each patient.					
Respect Patient Dignity and Autonomy	respects and ensures subjective well being and sense of worth in others and recognizes the patient's personal freedom of choice and right to participate fully in his/her care.					
Responsibility to the Profession	the commitment to maintain the integrity of the moral and collegial nature of the profession and to be accountable for one's own conduct to the profession					
Responsibility to Society	the obligation to use one's expertise for, and to be accountable to, society for those actions, both personal and of the profession, which relate to the public good.					
Self-Regulation	the privilege of setting the standards; being accountable for one's actions and conduct in medical practice, for the conduct of ones colleagues, and of the profession.					
Teamwork	the ability to recognize the expertise of others and to work with them in the patient's best interest.					

Copyright McGill University 2007. Used with permission.

University of Missouri— Kansas City School of Medicine

The Climate of Professionalism Survey, developed by faculty at the University of Missouri–Kansas City School of Medicine, measures the professionalism of a clinical setting. This survey was designed to report the extent to which student peers, residents, and faculty act professionally in a clinical environment, the extent to which faculty teach about professionalism in that environment, and faculty members' assessment of their own teaching about professionalism. The survey has demonstrated sound psychometrics with an alpha coefficient of 0.75 or higher. Positive correlations have been shown to exist between faculty's professionalism teaching and students' perceptions of professionalism behaviors.[148]

     A Practical Guide to Teaching and Assessing the ACGME Core Competencies, Second Edition

| Figure 6.17 | University of Missouri—Kansas City School of Medicine: Climate of Professionalism Survey |

Directions: Please rate the frequency that you have observed each group exhibiting each behavior during the past year.

Professionalism Behaviors	Medical Students				Residents				Faculty			
	Mostly	Often	Sometimes	Rarely	Mostly	Often	Sometimes	Rarely	Mostly	Often	Sometimes	Rarely
Show disrespect to patients, students, faculty, staff or other healthcare personnel												
Advocate for the well-being of patients, students, colleagues, the community and/or the medical profession												
Make selves look good at the expense of others												
Exceed expectations in patient care, class, conferences and/or rounds												
Finish their work and help others finish theirs												
Complain about professional obligations												
Lie to patients, professors, colleagues/peers or in the medical record												
Show respect and compassion toward patients, students, faculty, staff or other healthcare personnel												
Accurately and spontaneously report their own mistakes or uncertainties												
Ignore the unprofessional behavior of others												
Do just enough to get by in patient care, class, conferences and/or rounds												
Enjoy serving others												

The survey was developed by Louise E Arnold PhD, George S Thompson MD and Jennifer Quaintance, PhD at the University of Missouri-Kansas City School of Medicine and was funded in part by a grant from the Arnold P. Gold Foundation for Humanism in Medicine and by a Sarah Morrison Grant from UMKC-SOM. © 2008

For information contact: Jennifer Quaintance, PhD, (816) 235-1958, quaintancej@umkc.edu

Figure 6.17	**University of Missouri—Kansas City School of Medicine: Climate of Professionalism Survey (cont.)**

Directions: Please rate the frequency that most appropriately describes how your faculty supervisor/attending physician taught and modeled professional behavior over the past year.

Professionalism Teaching Behaviors	My Faculty Supervisor			
	Mostly	**Often**	**Sometimes**	**Rarely**
Acts professionally in relating to patients, students, colleagues, and staff				
Teaches about professionalism				
Discusses his/her own strivings toward professionalism and his/her own shortcomings productively and sensitively				
Creates an environment of warmth and mutual respect in relating with students				
Is a good role model of professionalism for me to emulate				
Sets clear expectations for students' professional behavior				
Enforces those expectations				
Explicitly describes the way a student should relate to a patient in a difficult situation				
After describing the way a student should relate to a patient in a difficult situation, demonstrates that behavior for students				
After the demonstration, asks students what they saw and solicits their comments				

The survey was developed by Louise E Arnold PhD, George S Thompson MD and Jennifer Quaintance, PhD at the University of Missouri-Kansas City School of Medicine and was funded in part by a grant from the Arnold P. Gold Foundation for Humanism in Medicine and by a Sarah Morrison Grant from UMKC-SOM. © 2008

For information contact: Jennifer Quaintance, PhD, (816) 235-1958, quaintancej@umkc.edu

Figure 6.17	University of Missouri—Kansas City School of Medicine: Climate of Professionalism Survey (cont.)

Directions: Please rate the frequency that most appropriately describes how you taught and modeled professional behavior over the past year.

Professionalism Teaching Behaviors Self-Assessment	Mostly	Often	Sometimes	Rarely
I aim to act professionally in relating to patients, students, colleagues, and staff				
I teach about professionalism				
I discuss my own strivings toward professionalism and my own shortcomings productively and sensitively				
I aim to create an environment of warmth and mutual respect in relating with students				
I am a good role model of professionalism for my students to emulate				
I set clear expectations for students' professional behavior				
I enforce those expectations				
I explicitly describe the way a student should relate to a patient in a difficult situation				
After I describe the way a student should relate to a patient in a difficult situation I explicitly demonstrate that behavior myself for students				
After the demonstration, I ask students what they saw and solicit their comments				

The survey was developed by Louise E Arnold PhD, George S Thompson MD and Jennifer Quaintance, PhD at the University of Missouri-Kansas City School of Medicine and was funded in part by a grant from the Arnold P. Gold Foundation for Humanism in Medicine and by a Sarah Morrison Grant from UMKC-SOM. © 2008

For information contact: Jennifer Quaintance, PhD, (816) 235-1958, quaintancej@umkc.edu

References

1. Freidson E. *Professionalism: The Third Logic*. Chicago, IL: University of Chicago Press; 2001.

2. Liaison Committee on Medical Education. *Functions and Structure of a Mmedical School.* Washington, DC: Liaison Committee on Medical Education; 1998.

3. Association of American Medical Colleges. *Medical School Objectives Project, Report III. Contemporary Issues in Medicine: Communication in Medicine.* Washington, DC: AAMC; 1999.

4. Institute for International Medical Education. Global minimum essential requirements in medical education. *Med Teach.* 2002;24:130–135.

5. General Medical Council. The new doctor: guidance on foundation training. September 2009. *www.gmc-uk.org/ New_Doctor09_FINAL.pdf_27493417.pdf.* Accessed March 14, 2010.

6. Accreditation Council for Graduate Medical Education. Common program requirements. ACGME Outcome Project website. *www.acgme.org/outcome/comp/ compCPRL.asp.* Accessed March 3, 2010.

7. Klass D, De Champlian A, Fletcher E, King A, Macmillan M. Development of a performance-based test of clinical skills for the United States Licensing Examination. *Fed Bull.* 1998;85:177–185.

8. Frank JR. The CanMEDS 2005 physician competency framework. Better standards. Better physicians. Better care. Ottawa: The Royal College of Physicians and Surgeons of Canada; 2005. *http://rcpsc.medical.org/ canmeds/CanMEDS2005/CanMEDS2005_e.pdf.* Accessed March 14, 2010.

9. Confederation of Postgraduate Medical Education Councils. Australian curriculum framework for junior doctors (version 2.2), 2009. Confederation of Post-graduate Medical Education Councils Web site. *www.cpmec.org.au/Page/acfjd-project.* Accessed March 14, 2010.

10. General Medical Council. Good medical practice. General Medical Council website. *www.gmc-uk.org/ guidance/good_medical_practice.asp.* Accessed March 14, 2010.

11. Whelan GP. Educational Commission for Foreign Medical Graduates: clinical skills assessment prototype. *Med Teach.* 1999;21:156–160.

12. Special Committee on Maintenance of Licensure. Draft report on maintenance of licensure. Federation of State Medical Boards, July 2008. *www.fsmb.org/pdf/Special_ Committee_MOL_Draft_Report_February2008.pdf.* Accessed March 21, 2010.

13. Sentinel Event Alert. Behaviors that undermine a cul-ture of safety. The Joint Commission, July 9, 2008. The Joint Commission website. *www.jointcommission.org/ SentinelEvents/SentinelEventAlert/sea_40.htm.* Accessed April 24, 2010.

14. American Board of Pediatrics and Association of Pediatric Program Directors. *Teaching and Assessing Professionalism: A Program Director's Guide.* Chapel Hill, NC: American Board of Pediatrics; 2008. *www.appd.org/professionalism.pdf* and *www.abp.org/ abpwebsite/publicat/professionalism.pdf.* Accessed April 20, 2010.

15. American Board of Internal Medicine. Advancing medical professionalism to improve healthcare. 2010. ABIM Foundation website. *www.abimfoundation.org/ Professionalism/About%20Professionalism.aspx.* Accessed April 25, 2010.

16. American Board of Internal Medicine Foundation, American College of Physicians Foundation, European Federation of Internal Medicine. Medical professional-ism in the new millennium: a physician charter. *Annals Int Med.* 2002;136:243–246. *www.abimfoundation.org/ Professionalism/~/media/Files/Physician%20Charter.ashx.* Accessed April 26, 2010.

17. American Board of Internal Medicine. Advancing medical professionalism to improve healthcare. Endorsements of the Charter. 2010. ABIM Foundation website. *www.abimfoundation.org/Professionalism/ Physician%20Charter/Endorsements%20of%20the%20 Charter.aspx.* Accessed April 25, 2010.

18. Osler W. The reserves of life. *St. Mary's Hosp Gaz.* 1907;13:95–98.

19. Ludmerer KM. Instilling professionalism in medical education. *JAMA.* 1999;282:881–882.

20. Hickson GB, Federspiel CF, Pichert JW, Miller CS, Gauld-Jaeger J, Bost P. Patient complaints and malpractice risk. *JAMA.* 2002;287(22):2951–2957.

21. Cohen JJ. Foreword. In: Stern DT, ed. *Measuring Medical Professionalism.* New York, NY: Oxford University Press; 2006, pp. v–viii.

22. Watts MSM. Of physicianship and patienthood. *West J Med.* 1986;145:237.

23. Hafferty F. The elephant in medical professionalism's kitchen. *Acad Med.* 2006;81:906–914.

24. Howland T. Medical education—professionalism [Letter]. *NEJM.* 2007;356:639.

25. Lundberg GD. The failure of organized health system reform—now what? Caveat aeger—let the patient beware. *JAMA.* 1995;273:1539–1541.

26. Cohen JJ. Professionalism in medical education, an American perspective: from evidence to accountability. *Med Educ.* 2006;40:607–617.

27. Hafferty F. Measuring professionalism: a commentary. In: Stern DT, ed. *Measuring Medical Professionalism.* New York, NY: Oxford University Press; 2006.

28. Special Committee on Maintenance of Licensure. Draft report on maintenance of licensure. Federation of State Medical Boards. July 2008. *www.fsmb.org/pdf/Special_Committee_MOL_Draft_Report_February2008.pdf.* Accessed March 21, 2010.

29. Cruess RJ, Cruess SR. Teaching medicine as a profession in the service of healing. *Acad Med.* 1997;72:941–952.

30. Hafferty FW. Professionalism—the next wave. *NEJM.* 2006;355:2151–2152.

31. Cruess SR. Professionalism and medicine's social contract with society. *Clin Orthop Relat Res.* 2006;449:170–176.

32. Cruess SR, Cruess RL. Professionalism must be taught. *BMJ.* 1997;315:1674–1677.

33. Stern DT, Papadakis M. The developing physician – becoming a professional. *NEJM.* 2006;355:1794–1799.

34. Baldwin DC, Bunch WH. Moral reasoning, professionalism, and the teaching of ethics to orthopedic surgeons. *Clin Orthop.* 2000;378:97–103.

35. Hall MA, Zheng B, Dugan E, et al. Measuring patients: trust in their primary care providers. *Med Care Res Rev.* 2002;59:293–318.

36. Hauck FR, Zyzanski SJ, Alemango SA, Medalie JH. Patient perceptions of humanism in physicians: effects on positive health behaviors. *Fam Med.* 1990;22:447–452.

37. Papadakis MA, Teherani A, Banach MA, et al. Disciplinary action by medical boards and prior behavior in medical school. *NEJM.* 2005;353:2673–2682.

38. Stern DT, Frohna AZ, Gruppen LD. The prediction of professional behavior. *Med Educ.* 2005;39:75–82.

39. Papadakis MA, Arnold GK, Blank LL, Holmboe ES, Lipner RS. Performance during internal medicine residency training and subsequent disciplinary action by state licensing boards. *Annals Int Med.* 2008;148:869–876.

40. Hicks LK, Lin Y, Robertson DW, Robinson DL, Woodrow SI. Understanding the clinical dilemmas that shape medical students' ethical development. *BMJ.* 2001;322:709–710.

41. Cruess SR, Cruess RL. The cognitive base of professionalism. In: Cruess RL, Cruess SR, Steinert Y, eds. *Teaching Medical Professionalism.* Cambridge, UK: Cambridge University Press; 2009:7–27.

42. Inui, TS. A Flag in the Wind: Educating for Professionalism in Medicine. Association of American Medical Colleges, Washington, DC, February 2003. Regenstrief Institute website. *www.regenstrief.org/bio/ professionalism.pdf/view*. Accessed April 26, 2010.

43. Accreditation Council for Graduate Medical Education. *Program Director Guide to the Common Program Requirements*. Chicago, IL: ACGME; 2009. ACGME website. *www.acgme.org/acWebsite/navPages/nav_ commonpr.asp*. Accessed April 27, 2010.

44. General Medical Council. Good medical practice: duties of a doctor. United Kingdom: GMC; 2006. General Medical Council website. *www.gmc-uk.org/guidance/ good_medical_practice/duties_of_a_doctor.asp*. Accessed April 27, 2010.

45. Committee on Bioethics, American Academy of Pediatrics. Policy Statement – Professionalism in pediatrics: statement of principles. *Pediatrics*. 2007;120;895–897.

46. Duff P. Teaching and assessing professionalism in medicine. *Am J Obstet Gynecol*. 2004;104:1362–1366.

47. Hutchinson T, McNamara H, Mount B, Lavery E. Teaching physicians the healer role: the McGill approach. The Physician as Healer and Professional, McGill Programs in Whole Person Care, May 3, 2008. Presentation. *www.afmc.ca/pdf/Healer-AFMC.pdf*. Accessed April 27, 2010.

48. Baldwin DC, Jr, Self DJ. The assessment of moral reasoning and professionalism in medical education and practice. In: Stern DT, ed. *Measuring Medical Professionalism*. New York, NY: Oxford University Press; 2006.

49. Bebeau MJ. The Defining Issues Test and the Four Component Model: contributions to professional education. *J Moral Educ*. 2002;31:271–295.

50. Self DJ, Baldwin DC Jr. Moral reasoning in medicine. In: Rest JR, Narvaez D, eds. *Moral Development in the Professions: Psychology and Applied Ethics*. Hillsdale, NJ: Lawrence Erlbaum Associates; 1994:147–162.

51. Baldwin DC Jr, Adamson TE, Sheehan JT, Self DJ, Oppenberg AA. Moral reasoning and malpractice: a pilot study of orthopedic surgeons. *Am J Orthop*. 1996;25:481–484.

52. Feudtner C, Christakis DA, Christakis NA. Do clinical clerks suffer ethical erosion? Students' perceptions of their ethical environment and personal development. *Acad Med*. 1994;69:670–679.

53. Patenaude J, Niyonsenga TY, Fafard D. Changes in the components of moral reasoning during students' medical education: a pilot study. *Med Educ*. 2003;37:822–829.

54. George JH. Moral development during residency training. In: Scherpbier AJJA, Van Der Vleuten CPM, Rethans JJ, Van Der Steeg AFW, eds. *Advances in Medical Education*. Dordrecht, Kluwer, Netherlands: Springer; 1997:747–748.

55. Newton BW, Barber L, Clardy J, Cleveland E, O'Sullivan P. Is there hardening of the heart during medical school? *Acad Med*. 2008;83:244–249.

56. Hojat M, Vergare MJ, Maxwell K, et al. The devil is in the third year: a longitudinal study of erosion of empathy in medical school. *Acad Med*. 2009;84:1182–1191.

57. Branch WT. Supporting the moral development of medical students. *J Gen Intern Med*. 2000;15:503–508.

58. Rabow MW, Remen RN, Parmelee DX, Inui TS. Professional formation: extending medicine's lineage of service into the next century. *Acad Med*. 2010;85:310–317.

59. Rest JR. Background: theory and research. In: Rest JR, Narvaez D, eds. *Moral Development in the Professions: Psychology and Applied Ethics*. Hillsdale, NJ: Lawrence Erlbaum Associates; 1994.

60. Burack JH, Irby DM, Carline JD, Root RK, Larson EB. Teaching compassion and respect: attending physicians' responses to problematic behaviors. *J Gen Intern Med*. 1999;14:49–55.

61. Jack Coulehan, MD, MPH, Stony Brook University School of Medicine, personal communication, 2007.

62. Boudreau JD, Cassell EJ, Fuks A. A healing curriculum. *Med Educ.* 2007;41:1193–1201.

63. Hilton S. Medical professionalism: how can we encourage it in our students? *Clin Teach.* 2004;1:69–73.

64. Reisman AB. Outing the hidden curriculum. *Hastings Center Report.* July–August 2006:9.

65. Konner M. *Becoming a Doctor: A Journey of Initiation in Medical School.* New York, NY: Penguin Group; 1988.

66. Suchman AL, Williamson PR, Litzelman DK, et al. Toward an informal curriculum that teaches professionalism: transforming the social environment of a medical school. *J Gen Intern Med.* 2004; 19:501–504.

67. Coulehan J, Williams PC. Professional ethics and social activism: where have we been? Where are we going? In: Wear D, Bickel J, eds. *Educating for Professionalism: Creating a Culture of Humanism in Medical Education.* Iowa City, IA: University of Iowa Press; 2000.

68. Coulehan J. Today's professionalism: engaging the mind but not the heart. *Acad Med.* 2005;80:892–898.

69. Rider EA, Longmaid HE. A model for merging residency programs during health care consolidations: a course for success. *Med Educ.* 2003;37:794–801.

70. Leach DC. Professional values and the workforce: what values do we want? 100th Anniversary of the AMA Council on Medical Education: Joint Educational Program of the Council on Medical Education and Section on Medical Schools, June 11–12, 2004. Unpublished presentation summary.

71. Accreditation Council for Graduate Medical Education. Advancing education in medical professionalism: an educational resource from the ACGME Outcome Project. Chicago, IL: ACGME, 2004. *www.acgme.org/ outcome/implement/Profm_resource.pdf.* Accessed April 20, 2010.

72. Mueller PS. Incorporating professionalism into medical education: the Mayo Clinic experience. *Keio J Med.* 2009;58(3):133–143.

73. Skiles J. Teaching professionalism: a medical student's opinion. *Clin Teach.* 2005;2:66–71.

74. Wortham S. The interdependence of social identification and learning. *Am Educ Res J.* 2004;41:715–750.

75. Haidet P, Stein HF. The role of the student–teacher relationship in the formation of physicians: the hidden curriculum as process. *J Gen Intern Med.* 2006;21(suppl):S16–S20.

76. Epstein RM. Mindful practice. *JAMA.* 1999;282:833–839.

77. Schon DA. *The Reflective Practitioner: How Professionals Think in Action.* New York, NY: Basic Books; 1983.

78. Mamede S, Schmidt HG. The structure of reflective practice in medicine. *Med Educ.* 2004;38:1302–1308.

79. Quaintance JL, Arnold L, Thompson GS. What students learn about professionalism from faculty stories: an "appreciative inquiry" approach. *Acad Med.* 2010; 85:118–123.

80. Leach DL. Resident formation – a journey to authenticity: designing a residency program that educes professionalism. In: Cruess RL, Cruess SR, Steinert Y, eds. *Teaching Medical Professionalism.* Cambridge, UK: Cambridge University Press; 2009:93–107.

81. Gordon MJ. Cutting the Gordian knot: a two-part approach to the evaluation and professional development of residents. *Acad Med.* 1997;72:876–880.

82. Sprinthall NA. Counseling and social role taking: promoting moral and ego development. In: Rest JR, Narvaez DF, eds. *Moral Development in the Professions: Psychology and Applied Ethics.* Hillsdale, NJ: Lawrence Erlbaum Associates; 1994:55–100.

83. Branch WT. The ethics of caring and medical education. *Acad Med.* 2000;75:127–132.

84. Kenny NP, Mann KV, MacLeod HM. Role modeling in physicians' professional formation: reconsidering an essential but untapped educational strategy. *Acad Med.* 2003;78:1203–1210.

85. Stern DT. Values on call: a method for assessing the teaching of professionalism. *Acad Med.* 1996;71(10 suppl):537–539.

86. Cote L, Leclere H. How clinical teachers perceive the doctor–patient relationship and themselves as role models. *Acad Med.* 2000;75:1117–1124.

87. Wright S, Kern D, Kolodner K, Howard D, Brancati F. Attributes of excellent attending-physician role models. *NEJM.* 1998;339:1986–1993.

88. Mutha S, Takayama JI, O'Neil EH. Insights into medical students' career choices based on third- and fourth-year students' focus-group discussions. *Acad Med.* 1997;72:635–640.

89. Cruess SR, Cruess RL, Steinert Y. Role modeling—making the most of a powerful teaching strategy. *BMJ.* 2008;336:718–721.

90. Branch WT, Jr, Kern D, Haidet P, et al. Teaching the human dimensions of care in clinical settings. *JAMA.* 2001;286:1067–1074.

91. Gracey CF, Haidet P, Branch WT, et al. Precepting humanism: strategies for fostering the human dimensions of care in ambulatory settings. *Acad Med.* 2005;80:21–28.

92. Longmaid HE, Rider EA. Feedback and performance improvement in clinical medical education. *JAMA.* 1995;274:1092.

93. Rider EA, Longmaid HE. Giving constructive feedback. *JAMA.* 1995;274:867.

94. Rider EA, Longmaid HE. Feedback in clinical medical education: guidelines for learners on receiving feedback. *JAMA.* 1995;274:938.

95. Rider EA, Longmaid HE. Guidelines for clinical teachers receiving feedback from learners. *JAMA.* 1995;274:996.

96. Kirk LM. Professionalism in medicine: definitions and considerations for teaching. *Proc Bayl Univ Med Cent.* 2007;20:13–16.

97. Rider EA, Hinrichs MM. Teaching communication skills: assessment and reflective feedback. MyCourses Web-based faculty development teaching module, Harvard Medical School, 2003. MyCourses website, *http://mycourses.med.harvard.edu*, and eCommons website, *http://ecommons.med.harvard.edu*. Accessed April 27, 2010.

98. Rider EA. Reflective feedback and teaching. Unpublished manuscript, 2009.

99. Epstein RM. Mindful practice and the tacit ethics of the moment. In: Kenny N, Shelton W, eds. Lost virtue: professional character development in medical education. *Adv in Bioethics.* 2006;10:115–144.

100. Schmidt S. Mindfulness and healing intention: concepts, practice, and research evaluation. *J Altern Complement Med.* 2004;10 (1 suppl):S7–S14.

101. Charon R. Narrative medicine: form, function, and ethics. *Annals Int Med.* 2001;134:83–87.

102. Hatem D, Rider EA. Sharing stories: narrative medicine in an evidence-based world. *Patient Educ Couns.* 2004;54:251–253.

103. Wald HS, Davis SW, Reis SP, Monroe AD, Borkan JM. Reflecting on reflections: enhancement of medical education curriculum with structured field notes and guided feedback. *Acad Med.* 2009;84(7):830–837.

104. Richard Frankel, PhD, Indiana University School of Medicine, personal communication, 2010.

105. Reis SP, Wald HS, Monroe AD, Borkan JM. Begin the BEGAN (The Brown Educational Guide to the Analysis of Narrative) – a framework for enhancing educational impact of faculty feedback to students' reflective writing. *Patient Educ Couns.* 2010 Jan 5. [Epub ahead of print]

106. Sklar D, Doezema D, McLaughlin S, Helitzer D. Teaching communications and professionalism through writing and humanities: reflections of ten years of experience. *Acad Emerg Med.* 2002;9:1360–1364.

107. Bertman S, Pretorius R. Webinar: Integrating the arts into medical education. Society for the Arts in Healthcare. Society for the Arts in Healthcare website. *www.thesah.org/template/page.cfm?page_id=582.* Accessed March 14, 2010.

108. The Literature, Arts & Medicine Database. New York University School of Medicine. New York University School of Medicine website. *http://litmed.med.nyu.edu.* Accessed March 14, 2010.

109. Remen RN, Rabow MW. The healer's art: professionalism, service and mission. *Med Educ.* 2005;39(1):1167–1168.

110. Rabow MW, Wrubel J, Remen RN. Promise of professionalism: personal mission statements among a national cohort of medical students. *Annals Fam Med.* 2009;7:336–342.

111. Gabbard GO, Nadelson C. Professional boundaries in the physician–patient relationship. *JAMA.* 1995;273(18):1445–1449.

112. Farber NJ, Novack DH, O'Brien MK. Love, boundaries and the patient–physician relationship. *Arch Int Med.* 1997;157(20):2291–2294.

113. Gaufberg E. Alarm and altruism: professional boundaries and the medical student. *Clin Teach.* 2006;3:206–209.

114. Lapid M, Moutier C, Dunn L, Hammond KG, Roberts LW. Professionalism and ethics education on relationships and boundaries: psychiatric residents' training preferences. *Acad Psych.* 2009;33(6):461–469.

115. Gaufberg E, Baumer N, Hinrichs M, Krupat E. Professional boundaries: the perspective of the third year medical student in negotiating three boundary challenges. *Teach Learn Med.* 2008;20(4):334–339.

116. Davidson JC. Professional relationship boundaries: a social work teaching module. *Soc Work Educ.* 2005;24(5):511–533.

117. Suchman AL. A new theoretical foundation for relationship-centered care: complex responsive processes of relating. *J Gen Intern Med.* 2006 Jan;21(suppl 1):S40–S44

118. Cruess RL. Teaching professionalism. *Clin Orthop Relat Res.* 2006;449:177–185.

119. Snell L. Teaching professionalism and fostering professional values during residency: the McGill Experience. In: Cruess RL, Cruess SR, Steinert Y, eds. *Teaching Medical Professionalism.* Cambridge, UK: Cambridge University Press; 2009:246–262.

120. Steinert Y. Faculty development for teaching and learning professionalism. In: Cruess RL, Cruess SR, Steinert Y, eds. *Teaching Medical Professionalism.* Cambridge, UK: Cambridge University Press; 2009:165–184.

121. Arnold L. Assessing professional behavior: yesterday, today, and tomorrow. *Acad Med.* 2002;77:502–515.

122. Veloski JJ, Fields SK, Boex JR, Blank LL. Measuring professionalism: a review of studies with instruments reported in the literature between 1982 and 2002. *Acad Med.* 2005;80:366–370.

123. Wilkinson TJ, Wade WB, Knock LD. A blueprint to assess professionalism: results of a systematic review. *Acad Med.* 2009;84(5):551–558.

124. Cohen JJ. Foreword. In: Stern DT, ed. *Measuring Medical Professionalism.* New York, NY: Oxford University Press; 2006.

125. Epstein RM. Assessment in medical education. *NEJM.* 2007;356:387–396.

126. Epstein RM, Hundert EM. Defining and assessing professional competence. *JAMA.* 2002;287:226–235.

127. Lynch DC, Leach DC, Surdyk PM. Assessing professionalism for accreditation. In: Stern DT, ed. *Measuring Medical Professionalism.* New York, NY: Oxford University Press; 2006.

128. Accreditation Council for Graduate Medical Education. Outcome Project: key considerations for selecting assessment instruments and implementing assessment systems. Chicago, IL: ACGME; 2001. ACGME Outcome Project website. *www.acgme.org/outcome/assess/keyConsider.asp.* Accessed April 27, 2010.

129. Accreditation Council for Graduate Medical Education. Toolbox of assessment methods. Version 1.1. Chicago, IL: ACGME; 2001. ACGME Outcome Project website. *www.acgme.org/outcome/assess/toolbox.asp.* Accessed April 27, 2010.

130. Accreditation Council for Graduate Medical Education. Outcome Project Think Tank. Chicago, IL: ACGME; 2001. ACGME Outcome Project website. *www.acgme.org/outcome/project/thinktank.asp.* Accessed April 27, 2010.

131. Rider EA, Lown BA, Hinrichs MM. Teaching communication skills. *Med Educ.* 2004;38:558–559.

132. Shrank WH, Reed VA, Jernstedt C. Fostering professionalism in medical education: a call for improved assessment and meaningful incentives. *J Gen Intern Med.* 2004;19:887–892.

133. Rees C, Shepherd M. The acceptability of 360-degree judgments as a method of assessing undergraduate medical students' personal and professional behaviours. *Med Educ.* 2005;39:49–57.

134. Calhoun AW, Rider EA, Meyer EC, Lamiani G, Truog RD. Assessment of communication skills and self-appraisal in the simulated environment: feasibility of multirater feedback with gap analysis. *Simul Healthc.* 2009;4(1):22–29.

135. Cruess R, McIlroy JH, Cruess S, Ginsburg S, Steinert Y. The Professionalism Mini-Evaluation Exercise: a preliminary investigation. *Acad Med.* 2006;81(suppl):S74–S78.

136. Leach DC. Competence is a habit. *JAMA.* 2002;287:243–244.

137. van Mook WN, Gorter SL, O'Sullivan H, Wass V, Schuwirth LW, van der Vleuten CP. Approaches to professional behaviour assessment: tools in the professionalism toolbox. *Eur J Intern Med* 2009;20(8):e153-7. Epub 2009 Sep 20.

138. Kalet AL, Sanger J, Chase J, et al. Promoting professionalism through an online professional development portfolio: successes, joys, and frustrations. *Acad Med.* 2007;82(11):1065–1072.

139. University of Maryland School of Medicine. The Professionalism Project: HELPERS-PRO. University of Maryland School of Medicine website. *http://medschool.umaryland.edu/professionalism/About.asp.* Accessed April 21, 2010.

140. American Board of Internal Medicine. *Project Professionalism.* ABIM Committee on Evaluation of Clinical Competence and Clinical Competence and Communications Programs. Philadelphia, PA: American Board of Internal Medicine; 2001. *www.abimfoundation. org/Resource%20Center/Bibliography/~/media/Files/ Resource%20Center/Project%20professionalism.ashx.* Accessed April 25, 2010.

141. Gordon J. Assessing students' personal and professional development using portfolios and interviews. *Med Educ.* 2003;37:335–340.

142. Accreditation Council for Graduate Medical Education. The ACGME Learning Portfolio: experience, reflect, learn, assess. Chicago, IL: ACGME; 2004. ACGME website. *www.acgme.org/acWebsite/portfolio/learn_ alp_welcome.asp.* Accessed April 20, 2010.

143. Driessen EW, van Tartwijk J, Overeem K, Vermunt JD, Van der Vleuten CPM. Conditions for reflective use of portfolios in undergraduate education. *Med Educ.* 2005;39:1230–1235.

144. Steinert Y. Educational theory and strategies for teaching and learning professionalism. In: Cruess RL, Cruess SR, Steinert Y, eds. *Teaching Medical Professionalism.* Cambridge, UK: Cambridge University Press; 2009:31–52.

145. National Board of Medical Examiners. Assessment of professional behaviors: 2009–2011 ABP Pilot for US residency and fellowship programs. Philadelphia, PA. *http://professionalbehaviors.nbme.org/2009Pilot.html.* Accessed April 24, 2010.

146. National Board of Medical Examiners. Assessment of professional behaviors. Philadelphia, PA. *http://professionalbehaviors.nbme.org/.* Accessed April 21, 2010.

147. Liaison Committee on Medical Education. New standard on the learning environment. Liaison Committee on Medical Education website. *www.lcme.org/standard.htm#learningenvironment.* Accessed February 2010.

148. Quaintance JL, Arnold L, Thompson GS. Development of an instrument to measure the climate of professionalism in a clinical teaching environment. *Acad Med.* 2008;83(10 suppl):S5–S8.

149. A61. Haidet P, Kelly PA, Chou C, et al. Characterizing the patient-centeredness of hidden curricula in medical schools: development and validation of a new measure. *Acad Med.* 2005;80:44–50.

150. Wagoner NE. Admission to medical school: selecting applicants with the potential for professionalism. In: Stern DT, ed. *Measuring Medical Professionalism.* New York, NY: Oxford University Press; 2006.

151. Tosteson DC. Learning in medicine. *NEJM.* 1979;301:690–694.

152. Bryden P, Ginsburg S, Kurabi B, Ahmed N. Professing professionalism: are we our own worst enemy? Faculty members' experiences of teaching and evaluating professionalism in medical education at one school. *Acad Med.* 2010 Jan 9. [Epub ahead of print]

153. Mayo Clinic College of Medicine. *Mayo Clinic Model of Education.* www.mayo.edu/pmts/mc5300-mc5399/mc5305-01.pdf. Accessed April 21, 2010.

154. Viggiano TR, Pawlina W, Lindor KD, Olsen KD, Cortese DA. Putting the needs of the patient first: Mayo Clinic's core value, institutional culture, and professionalism covenant. *Acad Med.* 2007;82(11):1089–1093.

155. Steinert Y, Cruess S, Cruess R, Snell L. Faculty development for teaching and evaluating professionalism: from programme design to curriculum change. *Med Educ.* 2005;39:127–136.

156. Fraser SW, Greenhalgh T. Complexity science. Coping with complexity: educating for capability. *BMJ.* 2001;323:799–803.

157. Cohen JJ. What new doctors must learn. *Med Gen Med.* 2006;8(1):45. National Center for Biotechnology Information website. *www.ncbi.nlm.nih.gov/pmc/articles/PMC1681993/.* Accessed April 27, 2010.

158. Crow S. 360-Degree Professionalism Assessment Instrument. MedEdPORTAL; 2006. Association of American Medical Colleges website. *http://services.aamc.org/30/mededportal/servlet/s/segment/mededportal/?subid=236.* Accessed April 25, 2010.

159. Papadakis MA, Loeser H, Healy K. Early detection and evaluation of professionalism deficiencies in medical students: one school's approach. *Acad Med.* 2001;76:1100–1106.

160. University of Virginia School of Medicine. Praise Card and Early Concern Card. The Listening Post. University of Virginia School of Medicine website. *www.med-ed.virginia.edu/forms/professionalismeval.cfm.* Accessed April 25, 2010.

161. McGill University Faculty of Medicine Undergraduate and Graduate Teaching Programs. Appendix C: The teaching of professionalism: vignettes for discussion. In: Cruess RL, Cruess SR, Steinert Y, eds. *Teaching Medical Professionalism.* Cambridge, UK: Cambridge University Press; 2009:287–290.

162. McGill University Faculty of Medicine Postgraduate Core Competencies Program: the resident as professional, 2007. Appendix E: Sample grid for use with discussion of vignettes. In: Cruess RL, Cruess SR, Steinert Y, eds. *Teaching Medical Professionalism.* Cambridge, UK: Cambridge University Press; 2009:292–293.

163. Sylvia Cruess, MD, and Richard Cruess, MD, McGill University Faculty of Medicine, personal communication, 2007 and 2010.

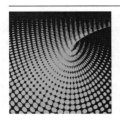

Competencies, Organizational Coherence, and the Hidden Curriculum of Medical Education

Frederic W. Hafferty, PhD

Introduction

From the outset it is important that we ask: "What does the hidden curriculum (HC) have to do with the six ACGME competencies?" The answer is "nothing" and "everything." Although the HC is not a competency per se, it has everything to do with how residency programs deliver a competency-based curriculum and, in turn, how residents master and internalize those competencies. Although the ACGME frames competencies at the individual level, and residents are expected to demonstrate the six core competencies at the level expected of a new practitioner, individuals are not the only social creatures against which we can layer the notion of competency. Organizations, such as medical schools and residency programs, can facilitate or impede residents' development based on issues of structural coherence. Thus, we legitimately can frame training sites and educational structures as competent, or not, in terms of what they seek to accomplish and

how they go about meeting those goals. In this chapter, in a manner somewhat different from the other chapters, we will approach issues of competence within a framework of "organizational competence."

On the following pages we will explore the history of the HC as a conceptual tool by using both definitions and metaphors to better understand the relationships that exist among the formal, informal, and hidden curricula of residency training. With this as our foundation, we will briefly review issues of assessment and the HC, and then examine how the medical education literature has used the HC to explore individual ACGME competencies. We then will examine how efforts to address some of the more pernicious effects of the HC have become institutionalized in educational policies. Here, too, we will examine the "ironies of success" as training in professionalism has moved from a largely tacit level to a formal curriculum as students begin to resist this shift. Within this context, we will examine both the Liaison

Committee on Medical Education's (LCME) newest (effective July 1, 2008) accreditation standard, MS-31-A, as well as how the HC plays a role in medical education reform in Canada. We close with some suggestions on how we might better think about and research the HC's role in developing a practical guide to both teaching and assessing the ACGME core competencies.

As a general introduction, and for the purposes of this chapter, the HC is a tool that medical educators can use to deconstruct and ultimately reconfigure the structure of residency training by placing competencies—their implementation, their attainment, and/or their assessment—within a systems context. This framing asks us not only to look at each of the six competencies as discrete educational entities, but also to examine each of them relative to the others. At its most fundamental level, the HC is a heuristic device allowing us to talk about the structural integrity of residency training and the degree to which what we say we are doing (the formal curriculum) is supported, reinforced, or countermanded by the various other pieces that go into our overall instructional milieu.

Any inquiry into the HC begins by asking about objectives/outcomes, in this case how a given program formally defines its competencies as objects of pedagogy (the formal curriculum). Then we push further and ask how the formal curriculum actually unfolds "on the shop floor" as experienced by residents. In particular, we are interested in how competencies are manifested within the social interactions and networks that make up the learning environments occupied by our trainees, including the phenomenon of role modeling (the informal curriculum), and how

the organizational culture (the HC) reflects the competencies or not.

Ultimately, the HC is a conceptual tool that allows us to view how a residency program responds to the dual challenges of internal integration (how things hang together) and external adaptation (how the program responds to exogenous environmental forces, such as policy changes or the funding of patient services). In the context of both types of challenges, issues such as faculty–student relations, faculty and resident burnout, or changes in duty hour regulation form an experiential backdrop against which competencies not only unfold, but also come to be defined and experienced by the participants themselves.

History, Definitions, and Metaphors

As noted in several of the other chapters, a core definition of the HC is rooted in the distinction between the formal curriculum—what a residency program says it is delivering to its students, including what the program includes in mission statements, formal operational policies, and ACGME accreditation filings—and what actually happens, including, but not limited to, what students experience when they are not being educated. In some instances what is represented is delivered, and all parties (faculty, students, and administration) agree that this is the case. In other instances the organization may believe it is delivering on its promises while students fail to recognize any such content. For example, it is entirely possible for a residency program to document that it delivers materials on systems-based practice, yet when queried, students see nothing of the sort. In a third iteration, it also is possible for an organization to believe it is providing students with, for example, a viable professionalism curriculum, and for students to point to such a curriculum, yet they also note the presence of other practices and/or forces that effectively neutralize what is being delivered. In other words, students see other things being "taught" within the general learning environment that undercut, countermand, or otherwise neutralize elements in the formal curriculum. Medical education is a complicated and complex process, and it is more than likely—in fact, it is a virtual certainty—that students will encounter instances where lessons taught in one setting, be they knowledge, skills, or values, are essentially retracted or muted within another setting.

Indeed, medical education is replete with stories about clashes between faculty where different role models and mentors struggle for student affections and attention by purporting to deliver the essence of what students need to know—often accompanied by demeaning comments about the "other side."

As a consequence, students often employ a chameleon type of socialization,[1, 2, 3] where they come to believe that the right way to know, do, or feel depends upon the setting (e.g., rotation, service, clinic) or the faculty member they happen to be working with at the time. This is not a very satisfactory or effective model of education, and it certainly is not a model of education that fits well with a discipline such as medicine that claims to be scientifically driven and scientifically grounded.

In short, the process of medical education (from undergraduate, through graduate, and on to continuing medical education) is replete with a cacophony of learning environments. Sometimes these learning environments speak the same language and reinforce the various lessons being taught, but all too often they do not.

The difficult task for educators is to maximize instances of concordance while minimizing discordance. This effort begins by recognizing that the formal curriculum is only one part of a much larger and more complicated process of learning. In the case of competencies, this also means not only looking within the competencies to make sure there is internal concordance, but also focusing across the competencies to make sure the interpersonal and communication skills that residents learn reinforce those within patient care.

Of course, all of this precludes a certain authenticity in a program's attempt to match objectives and practices and does not speak at all (as discussed shortly) to a related yet different issue of hidden agendas and double standards—including related issues where pedagogy is shaped on-the-fly or where efforts to tie educational practices to standards, such as accreditation review criteria, occur after the fact with the intent to game the system.

The Hidden Curriculum: A Brief History

The concept of an HC, including the notion that not all that a school teaches or that students learn takes place exclusively within the formal curriculum, is long-standing within educational circles. For example, more than 70 years ago the philosopher and educational reformer John Dewey argued for the importance of "collateral learning,"[4] and noted:

"Perhaps the greatest fallacy is the notion that a person learns only what he is studying at the time. Collateral learning ... may be, and often is, more important than the spelling lesson or lesson in geography or history."

—John Dewey, 1938

Early work by Jackson,[5] Apple,[6] Snyder,[7] and Cowell[8] extended this focus. Snyder's comparative examination of the learning environments at Massachusetts Institute of Technology (MIT) and Wellesley College are of particular interest here as he strove to show how student life revolved around discerning the space between expectations (formal) and requirements (hidden), and thus between what was actually expected of students as opposed to what they were formally required to do. As a psychiatrist, Snyder explored this space in terms of its impact on students' self-esteem and self-worth. Snyder was fascinated with the context of learning, something he defined as "the emotional and social surround of the formal curriculum."

For Snyder, the HC is ubiquitous within educational environments and the difference between the formal curriculum and the HC is manifested in the amount of dissonance experienced by students, along with feelings of scorn, hypocrisy, and cynicism. Snyder also saw students evincing a distinct element of "gamesmanship" in their responses to this dissonance as they learned to be both strategic and discrete and negotiated the space between formal versus "real" requirements. In addition to being the earliest and most detailed examination of the HC, Snyder's work is notable for several other reasons. First, it is a comparative analysis with Snyder casting his empirical and analytic lens on student life at two quite different educational institutions.

Second, Snyder uses an "ecological perspective" with an emphasis on complexity and on the interdependence of social actors and their surroundings.

As such, Snyder anticipates the current interest in applying the tools of complex science to medical education.[2] Third, Snyder identifies the covert student subculture as an important component of the HC and legitimates student experiences as a valuable source of information about teaching. Finally, Snyder is sensitive to and cognizant of the extenuating and outsider status of minority students when it comes to the HC. For Snyder, underrepresented minorities often lack the culturally based interpretive tools to discern a given school's HC, placing them at an even greater disadvantage as they attempt to understand and negotiate within what essentially is an alien organizational culture.

Since Snyder's groundbreaking work, there have been a formidable number of publications on the HC and education.[9, 10, 11, 12, 13, 14] The concept has evolved in terms of theoretical sophistication, with the leap into medical education widely tied to Hafferty and Franks' "The Hidden Curriculum, Ethics Teaching, and the Structure of Medical Education."[15] Even this attribution is somewhat misleading.

Twelve years earlier, Canadian sociologists Jack Haas and William Shaffir published a study on professional socialization ("Ritual Evaluation of Competence: The Hidden Curriculum of Professionalization in an Innovative Medical School Program") within an innovative curriculum (problem-based, community-focused, group-work, self-directed learning) at McMaster Medical School.[16] Although the authors cite both Jackson and Snyder, their actual use of the term hidden curriculum falls closer to Jackson's in that they do not define or develop the concept per se in their article. Instead, they briefly introduce the term as a conceptual hook, but without further explication. Like Snyder, the authors highlight issues of role playing and gamesmanship by pointing out how students adopt a ritualistic and self-protective "cloak of competence" in their interactions with faculty and patients.

Definitions

Building on Cowell's definition, "… that which the school teaches without, in general, intending or being aware that it is taught,"[(p. 98)] we can divide the learning environment of a medical school or residency program into three distinct but interrelated arenas: the formal, the informal, and the hidden curricula.[17] The formal curriculum is your intended and your stated curriculum. Others have used terms such as the "explicit curriculum" or the "curriculum on paper" (see Figure 7.1). Conversely, the informal curriculum is part of the learning that arises from (or is grounded in) the sporadic, happenstance, and idiosyncratic interactions among students or between faculty and students. The informal curriculum can happen anywhere (e.g., hallways, on-call rooms, elevators, the cafeteria, even classrooms), but the lessons, truisms, and learning pearls being advanced are not prescribed, nor are they found in a school's course catalogue, student handbook, class syllabus, or statements about learning objectives. In many respects, the informal curriculum is a curriculum on-the-fly, and although you cannot predict or preemptively control this kind of learning because it is so unpredictable and idiosyncratic, you can modify its impact.

The HC is neither formal nor idiosyncratic. It operates at the level of artifacts (pictures or award plaques hung on walls), within rituals such as White Coat or award ceremonies, and at the level of organizational structure and culture. The HC allows us to explore the learning that arises from being immersed in organizational culture. The HC is by no means an asocial form of learning. Although much of the HC can, and is, conveyed through the social relations and networks that exist among students and between students and faculty, the ability to differentiate between the informal curriculum and the HC allows us to better explore what medical schools and residency programs teach, even when we remove (superficially, at least) people from the equation. Thus, it is quite possible for an individual to learn much about a medical school or residency program simply by walking through the school and program and getting a "feel" for the building, its layout, and its contents. No words have to be spoken and no guide or interpreter needs to be employed.

For example, a school that has a predominant, large lecture hall and scant space devoted to smaller meeting rooms indicates to faculty and students alike the relative value (within that school) of didactic versus small group learning. Similarly, trainees are both obsessively willing and discerningly able to decode their curriculum schedule in terms of what the faculty or program considers most important in becoming a good physician. Yes, the content of such a schedule is formal (e.g., it is purposeful and explicit), but only the most naive administrator or faculty member would insist that this mapping of who, what, where, and when provides students with nothing more than a chronological road map. Similarly, students design their own relative value scale depending on whether a given learning experience is required or elective.

Meanwhile, faculty are just as adept at decoding their own learning environments when their school insists that faculty appointments within the clinician and/or educator tracts are just as valued as those in the research tract—except for the incidental fact that the latter comes with tenure while the former do not. Two final caveats are tied to the various ways in which the formal, informal, and hidden curricula have been characterized and labeled within the literatures of education and medical education. First, although they essentially mean the same thing, other terms besides "HC" appear in both literatures. When conducting a literature search on the HC and ACGME competencies, simply searching the term "hidden curriculum" will not be sufficient.

In fact, the HC literature (generically speaking) is replete with alternative phrasings and terms. Figure 7.1 contains some of these examples. Utilizing a simple dichotomy, Figure 7.1 differentiates between the formal and all other types of curricula.

This allows us to capture how different authors refer to the "formal," "stated," "intended," "paper," and "manifest" curricula. Correspondingly, we can see the substantial list of descriptors designed to capture the various kinds of teaching that take place within the other-than-formal curriculum. Of this list, one particular curriculum that bears notice is the "null curriculum," defined by Flinders and colleagues[18] as what gets taught in silence or what students learn by what is not said. In short, what a respected role model fails to do or say can have just as much impact as what he or she does do or say.

Figure 7.1	**Synonyms and Related Concepts of the HC**

- Formal

  - The curriculum on paper

  - The stated curriculum

  - The intended curriculum

  - The paper curriculum

  - The manifest curriculum

- The informal, hidden and other types of curriculum

  - The creditless curriculum

  - The curriculum in action

  - The experienced/experiential/ lived curriculum

  - The ideal/ideological curriculum

  - The institutional curriculum

  - The latent curriculum

  - The learned curriculum

  - The null curriculum

  - The operational curriculum

  - The operative curriculum

  - The perceived curriculum

  - The peripheral curriculum

  - The recommended curriculum

  - The shadow curriculum

  - The tacit curriculum

  - The taught curriculum

  - The tested curriculum

The second caveat involves the conceptual need to distinguish between "HC" and "hidden agendas." These two terms have been used as synonyms, yet they are very different sociological creatures. Returning to Snyder's reference to "gamesmanship" and Haas and Shaffir's references to how students attempt to wrap themselves in a "cloak of competence," both terms (along with related concepts by sociologists on role playing and passing) speak to the propensity of social actors to behave in a covert fashion as a consequence of discordant social structures.

Thus, although students may try to "game the system," they are doing so not out of some "hidden agenda," but rather as a response to structural conditions. Their intent is not to misdirect or deceive, and in these respects, the element of intentional deception is not part of the HC as a theoretical construct. Indeed, although many of the rules that govern the lives of faculty and students may be tacit and informal, they also are quite obvious to everyone in that community. The key difference is that these rules are not in the books. Indeed, their power may be tied to that relative invisibility. In short, although the HC and hidden agendas can, and often do, coexist, they are not the same thing.

Definitions at work

Educators have used the HC as a tool in class exercises to help students see aspects of their training environments that might otherwise be less than obvious to participants. Gaufberg and colleagues used such an exercise with their third-year medical students at Harvard.[19] For the activity, students wrote a two-page paper reflecting on a personal anecdote with the HC during a clerkship experience. The instructions defined the HC as follows, offered several examples (e.g., implicit survival rules within a particular work setting) and notes that the HC's influence can be positive, negative, or mixed.

"THE 'HIDDEN CURRICULUM' IS THE SET OF INFLUENCES ON ONE'S DEVELOPMENT AS A PHYSICIAN THAT IS NOT EXPLICITLY TAUGHT. IT IS TRANSMITTED THROUGH INTERPERSONAL INTERACTIONS ON THE WARDS OR IN OTHER CLINICAL SETTINGS, THROUGH POSITIVE OR NEGATIVE ROLE MODEL BEHAVIORS, AND THROUGH THE CULTURE AND HIERARCHY OF MEDICINE."

A related vehicle for exploring the HC comes from Dosani's request of his Canadian medical student peers to create a list of the "top ten things I learned in medical school but wasn't supposed to." Dosani, the president of McMaster Medical School's student council, polled the leaders of each of the 14 Canadian Federation of Medical School societies with the question: "If you could name one thing that you learned in medical school that you didn't think you were supposed to, what would that be?" He then compiled and categorized the results into a top 10 list.[20]

Although Dosani's question is not the only window into the HC (he could have asked an equally valid, yet different question, "If you could name one thing that you learned in medical school that you were supposed to know, but were not formally taught, what would that be?"), his approach is a valid and insightful window.

Types of responses included how textbooks and journals are a dated and inefficient way to acquire necessary clinical information, the relative value ranking (e.g., income, prestige) of various specialties, and various insider rules for how to circumvent the system to get what you want, such as a particular elective.

Metaphors

Because such a broad lexicon of terms has been developed to capture the informal side of the pedagogical coin (see Figure 7.1), it is sometimes quite useful to push definitions aside and think about the HC in terms of metaphors and/or similes. At its core, the formal, informal, null, hidden, and other curricula often operate in a complicated and interdependent dance of mutual influence and commonly proffered conclusions. Thus, the formal curriculum happens at one time or place (e.g., the classroom) while the informal exercises its influence at a different time or place (e.g., the ward), which often leads to simplistic and misleading conclusions.

For example, one frequently cited contrast in the medical education literature between the formal and the hidden curricula has students hearing one thing (e.g., about professionalism) in the classroom and then experiencing or seeing something different via role models on the wards or in clinic. On a surface level, this layering is quite apt. Where this example goes wrong is when faculty and/or residents conclude that the only thing that happens in the classroom is formal and the only thing that happens on the wards is hidden.

This simply is not the case. Classrooms involve a swirl of activities (after all, the null curriculum—what the teacher does not say—is an omnipresent companion to everything the teacher does say). The formal curriculum may dominate, but it is not the only teaching that takes place. Similarly, a great deal of formal instruction occurs on the wards as well.

So, what kind of metaphors are we talking about? A useful list is bounded only by one's imagination. One rather obvious metaphor is the iceberg—with its visible tip (e.g., the formal curriculum) dwarfed by a mass (e.g., the informal, hidden, etc.) lying directly below the surface. The iceberg metaphor appears even more fitting when we read in the medical education literature that the bulk of what students learn about professionalism takes place not within the formal curriculum but within the HC. Nonetheless, this visible/small versus hidden/large distinction is not always the case. There are occasions when most of what is going on largely unfolds within the domain of the explicit and formal, and with very little happening off-stage.[21] It all depends. However, it is not sociologically credible to insist that the only dimension of importance and relevance to the understanding of social action is that which takes place within the formal or explicit arenas of social life. This is never the case. How much takes place elsewhere depends on the circumstances, but there is always an elsewhere.

Assessment and the Hidden Curriculum

Although the bulk of writing on the HC is descriptive (e.g., this is the concept; here is what it looks like; here are some possible interventions) rather than empirical and analytical, there is a small but growing base of literature on assessment and the HC. Before looking at this literature, it is important to emphasize that investigating the HC poses particular methodological challenges for researchers. As noted at the end of the preceding section, much of what unfolds in the course of daily life, for a host of neurophysiological, psychological, and sociological reasons, remains relatively invisible to participants. Insiders' ability to optimally take in what happens around them is compromised to a degree, so it becomes difficult to evaluate the ability of the senses to pick up and process certain external stimuli, the influence of unconscious mental processes on decision-making, the taken-for-granted dimensions of everyday routines, or the tacit dimensions of group life, including organizational culture.

Thus, experts often point out that it is important to use culturally neutral (or naive) outsiders to study organizational culture. Their unfamiliarity with the ways of the group and their lack of preconceived notions about that group allows them a certain critical distance from those routines and normative practices that make up the bulk of everyday life and that are quite invisible to insiders. However, bringing in outsiders for the purpose of critical review often is expensive and may even disrupt the very processes they are being asked to examine.

With these qualifications in mind, there is a middle ground. Another important window into the HC comes via the experiences and reactions of initiates or recruits—and individuals who are cultural newcomers and in the process of moving from outsider to some kind of insider status.[22] Examples might include applicants to medical school, first-year students (actually, students in the first few months of school), beginning third-year students (particularly if there is a sharp delineation between their basic science and clinical training), third-year students as they transition from one clerkship to another (particularly if they are being trained within a block model), fourth-year students while interviewing at residencies, first-year residents

(again, particularly in the first month or two of residency), residents entering the job market, and residents just entering their first job. Faculty members face similar transitions as they move into academic life and make their way up the academic ladder. Both faculty and students experience a dual dynamic of moving away from (or even abandoning) an earlier identity or social status while concurrently moving into or adopting a new identity status.[23, 24, 25, 26] One window through which educators can view the volatility yet experiential invisibility of this process is when first-year medical students begin to bridle when they hear criticisms of medicine (practitioners, practices, etc.) and begin to experience them as a personal attack made by people who simply don't understand what is really going on.

Of additional interest here are recent shifts by younger physicians and trainees to draw sharp lines of demarcation between their personal and professional lives and maintain dual yet distinct identities, something that older physicians (tribal elders) see as evidence of a lack of commitment and/or buy-in by this latest generation of trainees.

The hidden nature of the HC and paradox of visibility presents a particular methodological challenge to assessing the HC. As students (or any newcomer, including faculty) move ever deeper into their new environments, they begin to recognize things that were once invisible, uninterpretable, or perhaps repulsive to rank outsiders. Thus, we encounter the window into the HC mentioned previously. However, these initiates are simultaneously enmeshed in a second transformational process during which many of these once-notable things quickly begin to disappear from view—as events, circumstances, or practices that would be noteworthy, disconcerting, or even outrageous to those outsiders transpose into things that are taken for granted, reasonable, or even natural and expected to insiders. What once would have been cause for concern ceases to be worthy of further consideration. The window now begins to close.

Edward Hundert, a physician–educator, conducted one of the earliest and most extensive research undertakings into the informal/HC while serving as dean of student affairs at Harvard Medical School. After securing consent forms from every intern and resident in a five-year general surgery residency program, Hundert asked students to carry tape recorders and record conversations in small group class discussions, in on-call rooms, during clinical rotations and meals, and even outside the hospital at their apartments. The effort generated hundreds of hours of tape recordings that were transcribed and analyzed for thematic content.[27, 28]

Among a range of findings, Hundert and his colleague, Darleen Douglas-Steele, concluded that students' professional and moral development took place more when faculty were not present, and that the informal curriculum was informal in name only—peer-influenced student learning was quite "rule-governed in tightly bound ways." Although these rules were not formally recorded (e.g., written down), they did form an unwritten code for students. Senior residents conveyed this code to junior trainees, leading to a practical ethics of conduct that shaped what students saw as "good, skillful, and right" on a given service. In light of these findings, Hundert concluded that medical education should shift its emphasis from teaching hospitals

to learning hospitals. Only two articles were ever published on these data, and it is my impression that only the data remain underexamined and underexplored. Other researchers have used focus groups,[29] semistructured one-on-one interviews,[30] case studies,[31] blogging,[32] direct observation,[33] critical incident reports,[34] narrative essays, and reflective writing, including writing on more general topics such as professionalism[35, 37] and palliative care.[38] Some studies have used multiple methods, such as direct observation and semistructured interviews.

Haidet and colleagues conducted a second notable study that introduces and attempts to validate a new measure, the C3, to capture patient-centeredness dimensions of the HC. The authors developed the C3 instrument, an Internet-based survey tool that captures three content areas with respect to the HC and patient-centered care:

- Role modeling

- Students' patient care experiences (e.g., student experiences)

- Perceived support for students' own patient-centered behaviors (e.g., support for student actions)

Students from 10 medical schools completed the survey. The authors found that schools with reputations for graduating students with well-developed patient-centered care skills scored significantly higher on the three content area scores than schools that did not have such a reputation. The authors argue that the C3 instrument also functions in a remedial capacity.

A low score on role modeling may call for a different intervention (e.g., faculty development) than a low score on support for student actions (e.g., a change in evaluation processes). More recently, the C3 has been used in a comparative analysis of patient-centeredness and the HC in medical schools in Saudi Arabia versus the United States.[40]

Finally, medical students have published articles that directly[41] and/or indirectly[42, 43, 44] comment on the HC of medical education. Somewhat ironically, the wave of formal coursework on professionalism that began to sweep through medical schools and residency programs in the 1990s is generating some frustration and cynicism among trainees. Students find themselves buffeted between the professionalism messages of the classroom and what they witness faculty members and others role-model on the wards and in clinics.

Prior to the advent of these formal professionalism modules, most trainees learned how to be a professional largely at a tacit level, and any inconsistencies and disjunctures in the learning process often were more invisible or opaque to participants. With the advent of formal professionalism coursework, however, these disjunctures became more evident. One of the unintended consequences of the formal professionalism curriculum is a growing awareness among educators that the role modeling students witness often contains decidedly unprofessional normative messages. Compounding this problem of divergent messages is students' perception of coursework that includes outdated and self-serving messages.[45] One observer team attributed this outdated material to faculty members' decidedly nostalgic (e.g., rooted in the past)

view of professionalism.[46] In addition to students' perception that faculty push their own professionalism agenda and the misanthropy students experienced when hearing faculty say one thing and seeing them do another, students also were sensitive to how medical education was rooted in an HC of structural dominance, power, and hierarchy. This left students feeling like they were inappropriately subject to the whims of faculty.[43, 44] Students are not alone in verbalizing these concerns. Medical leaders have also cited similar observations about hierarchy and abuses of power, particularly given medicine's penchant for preaching about collegiality and cooperation.[47]

Autobiographical accounts of medical training experience at the undergraduate and resident levels also contain details on medical education's HC. Although these authors do not use the term, these accounts are rich in details about the HC of medical training. Examples range from the early *Intern* by Doctor X[48] and the writings of surgeon William Nolan,[49, 50] through the more sardonic and quasifictional *The House of God*,[51] to the more contemporary narratives of Michael Collins[52, 53] and Danielle Ofri.[54]

This literature provides an experiential backdrop to research literature that formally links the HC to issues such as the loss of student idealism,[55] patient-centeredness,[56] empathy,[57, 58, 59] and humanism.[32] Other themes include the rise of trainee cynicism;[60] issues of ethical erosion,[61] student burnout,[62, 63, 64] student abuse, harassment, and mistreatment;[65] and the ethical dilemmas faced by students as they move through their training.[66] In turn, there is a more extensive literature on each of these and related topics, such as the unwillingness or inability of faculty to attend to problematic student behaviors, but where the HC is not invoked as a conceptual tool.[67]

In addition to the various methodologies used, particular groups of trainees have been examined using the HC as an analytic tool. For example, Wear and Skillicorn[68] examine the formal, informal, and hidden curricula of a psychiatry clerkship.

Similarly, Calabrese and colleagues appraise residents' views on the quality of psychotherapy training,[69] with other researchers studying residents' views of evidence-based psychiatry,[70, 71] psychiatric training in general,[72] pediatric residency training,[73, 74] primary care medicine,[75] orthopedic residents,[76, 77] OB/GYN clerkship training,[78] anesthesia,[79] and urology[80]—all from an HC perspective. There even have been some international comparisons such as Murakami and colleagues' examination of the HC in the United Kingdom and Japan.[81]

In conclusion, research on the HC has barely scratched the surface in trying to untangle the complexities of modern-day medical education. For the most part, researchers have gathered their data directly from trainees, with little attempt to plumb the other-than-surface aspects of medical training. In 2010, the Association of Faculties of Medicine of Canada (AFMC) released its "Future of Medical Education in Canada" report and identified the need to address the HC as one of its 10 key recommendations, as well as called for research on the HC.[82] We will explore this report in a later section of this chapter.

The Hidden Curriculum and Individual Competencies

As might be expected, the competency most often linked to the HC as a conceptual tool is professionalism. Medical professionals have used the HC as a conceptual scalpel to explore issues of professionalism since the early stages (1980s) of medicine's modern-day professionalism movement, both at the undergraduate medical education (UME) and graduate medical education (GME) levels. Although most of this literature focuses on undergraduate training, the basic issues addressed are similar to both levels. As we explore this topic, we will concentrate more on the competencies than whether a given article has a UME or GME focus.

Among the most widely cited HC-professionalism publications are Haidet and Stein's work on role models and the relational aspects of the HC,[83] Hilton and Slotnick's work on "proto-professionalism,"[84] Patenaude and colleagues' cohort study of changes in students' moral development during training,[85] Wear's examination of the professional development of medical education,[86] the informal aspects of mentoring between faculty and medical students,[87] the impact of the HC's effect on professional attitudes,[88] and the perceived adequacy of and satisfaction by medical students and house officers with professionalism training.[89] Other highly cited articles drawing upon hidden/informal curricula as a core analytic construct include Suchman and colleagues' look at the organizational transformation of the Indiana School of Medicine via an appreciative narrative/inquiry approach to relationship building,[90] and Wallace's examination of the shift in medical education from a teaching to a learning paradigm.[91] Additional articles on the Indiana experiment, which is one of the rare, if not the only, explicit efforts to change the organizational culture of medical education via hidden/informal curricula, include Cottingham and colleagues' overview of this effort,[92] a two-year assessment by Suchman and colleagues,[93] and Litzelman and Cottingham's five-year assessment of this project.[94] Here, too, we find Karnieli-Miller and colleagues' use of student critical incident narratives at Indiana to explore the hidden and informal curricula as an important adjunct to this literature.[37]

Perhaps reflecting the mutable and dynamic nature of professionalism, more contemporary publications have looked at the role of technology in reshaping the learning environment along with challenges to professionalism with the rise of e-learning.[95] Particular issues include student postings of patient and personal information to social networking sites along with the concomitant blurring of professional and personal identities.[96, 97]

Literature describing the application of the HC to the other five competencies is sparse. After professionalism, the two competencies most often linked to the HC are patient care, including issues such as ethical erosion, or related losses such as patient-centeredness, caring attitudes, and/or empathy,[57, 61, 98, 99] and interpersonal and communication skills.[39, 55, 100, 101, 102] Only one article covers systems-based practice and the HC. This study concludes that residents learn important information about systems-based practice both in the formal and informal curricula, and that these latter

lessons (learned in continuity clinic) both reinforce and undercut lessons taught within the formal curriculum.[33] Otherwise, it appears that the remaining two competencies—medical knowledge and practice-based learning and improvement—have yet to be explored using the HC as an analytic tool. However, as we will see in the following paragraph, competencies such as patient care and professionalism are broad enough to capture all kinds of educational issues that could be related to these remaining two areas.

Individual competencies aside, the medical education literature is rich with articles tying the HC to a variety of topics obviously related to the six ACGME competencies even if issues of accreditation or accreditation standards are not part of the analysis.

Examples include issues such as multiculturalism, cultural competency, and cross-cultural care;[103, 104, 105, 106, 107] end-of-life care;[108, 109, 110] medical ethics;[15, 111] conflict of interest and relations with industry;[112] evidence-based medicine;[70, 71] mindful practice, self-awareness, and relationship-centered care;[113] hospital specialists and clinical teaching;[114] humanism and bedside manner;[100, 115, 116, 117, 118] patient-centered care;[119] medical errors;[120] duty hours;[121] the impact of longitudinal training;[122, 123] and online learning.[124] At a more macro level, former Association of American Medical Colleges president, Jordan Cohen, also has written a thoughtful overview linking the HC to issues in GME in general.[125]

A study by Balmer and colleagues looks more inclusively at competencies and the HC, this time on a general pediatric inpatient service.[73] Their findings are of interest because of their methodology (observation plus interview) and their findings. Balmer found that competency-based goals are well supported within the implicit curriculum. However, although competency-based goals are well laid out within the explicit curriculum, residents did not recognize the formal curriculum as a source of teaching about these goals. Rather, residents exclusively relied on lessons learned within the implicit curriculum for meeting more than 90% of their competency objectives. Nonetheless, learning within the implicit curriculum was dominated by one particular competency: patient care.

Furthermore, the authors found that in spite of resident reliance on the implicit curriculum for their learning, the implicit curriculum was an extraordinarily messy learning environment—a conclusion echoed by long-time professionalism observer, David Stern.[126] Finally, Balmer and colleagues found that although the implicit curriculum was essential to resident learning, faculty did not recognize the implicit curriculum as a necessary part of their approach to medical education. In short, the authors found that resident learning was dominated by the HC, but that most of this learning is associated with a single competency (patient care). The program did not recognize the role of the HC in resident learning.

Finally, there is extensive literature on ethics and GME, but it does not include the informal and/or HC as part of the conceptual equation, although the link is obvious.[15] As such, materials from this general literature[127, 128] are not summarized as part of this chapter.

Formalizing the Hidden Curriculum: MS-31-A

The formal, informal, and hidden curricula are not static. They are dynamic and interdependent, and they and their relationships change over time. As aspects of the HC are uncovered, these once invisible influences can become the object of purposeful intervention and pass from the realm of the hidden to the formal. Conversely, aspects of the formal curriculum can become so taken for granted and/or ritualized that the initial rationales for why something that once was formally required can become lost and disappear from view.

As previously discussed, the HC has become formalized around issues of professionalism. Prior to the 1980s, the teaching of professionalism took place almost exclusively at a tacit and informal level. However, the rise of a professionalism movement, particularly within Western medicine, has resulted in the realization that students were being exposed to all sorts of unprofessional influences during their training, which led to the development of various formal professionalism curricula at both the medical school and residency levels (see the November 2007 issue of *Academic Medicine* for a long list of specific initiatives).

In turn, and in a somewhat ironic fashion, the development of these formal teaching programs brought into even sharper focus something that had long been hiding in plain sight[68]—the fact that medical practice behaviors and medical culture were indeed laced with unprofessional practices. However, as students were introduced to these formal professionalism offerings, they had to wrestle with a disjuncture between what they were being told in class and what they were encountering on the wards and in clinic. These disconnects not only resulted in a certain measure of cynicism about the professionalism they were being formally taught, but also resulted in a certain pushback by students as they began to question and even reject some of the traditionally bound professionalism precepts their teachers were presenting as core.[41, 43, 129]

However, professionalism is not the only place where the HC has been converted into a more formal part of the educational picture. As noted in the opening paragraphs of this chapter, although the HC is not a competency, at least in terms of ACGME framings, the LCME included the HC in its formal accreditation standards. The standard, MS-31-A (effective July 1, 2008), is labeled in medical education circles as the "learning environment standard" and it states:

> "MEDICAL SCHOOLS MUST ENSURE THAT THE LEARNING ENVIRONMENT FOR MEDICAL STUDENTS PROMOTES THE DEVELOPMENT OF EXPLICIT AND APPROPRIATE PROFESSIONAL ATTRIBUTES (ATTITUDES, BEHAVIORS, AND IDENTITY) IN THEIR MEDICAL STUDENTS."

In explicating this standard, the LCME notes:

> "THE LEARNING ENVIRONMENT INCLUDES FORMAL LEARNING ACTIVITIES AS WELL AS ATTITUDES, VALUES, AND INFORMAL 'LESSONS' CONVEYED BY INDIVIDUALS WITH WHOM THE STUDENT COMES INTO CONTACT."

Furthermore, the LCME expects that the school, including faculty, students, and residents, should frequently evaluate the learning environment with an eye toward detecting positive and negative factors that affect professionalism. The LCME also calls on the school to implement interventions to highlight positive influences and diminish negative ones.

In short, the LCME now holds medical schools responsible not only for what they teach (the formal curriculum) but also for the environments in which students learn (the informal and hidden curricula). Furthermore, and as a background note, during its early deliberations on what was then being referred to as the "hidden curriculum standard," the LCME requested a white paper ("Learning Environments & Medical Education: A Call to Action") from Hafferty and Franks linking the HC to the more neutral and inclusive nomenclature of learning environments.

It is too early to tell how medical schools will respond to this new standard, and how schools will demonstrate that they are taking responsibility for more than what faculty members teach. At the same time, it is worth noting that the values and informal lessons acquired by students during training involve much more than what is identified within MS-31-A as issues of "professional attributes." Students learn all kinds of things during training that are not, in and of themselves, professional issues.

For example, during their basic science coursework students not only learn factual knowledge about disease etiology, pathology, and treatment, but also more tacit messages about the very nature of science itself. In fact, the science medical students learn is not the same science graduate students learn, even when the same faculty member teaches their respective courses. The science presented in medical education is neither a watered-down version of graduate student science nor a condensed-but-otherwise-unchanged version. Rather, it is a fundamentally different representation of science. The science graduate students learn is riddled with uncertainties, ambiguities, and probabilistic knowledge. The science medical students learn is a science of facts. Perhaps this is one reason physicians have such a hard time accepting the place of science (at least as they understand it) within the messiness of clinical practice.

Competencies, the Hidden Curriculum, and Canadian Medical Education

In January 2010, the AFMC published a major report, "The Future of Medical Education in Canada: A Collective Vision for MD Education."[82] In this report, the AFMC outlined a vision of the future physician and a system of medical education designed to produce that physician. To this end, the AFMC identified 10 key recommendations, including one that calls on educators to address the HC. In addition, the AFMC identified five "enabling recommendations" to facilitate implementing its core 10. All 10 recommendations and five enabling recommendations were built around a foundational value (for both medical education and medical practice) of social responsibility. The report targets UME with future reports addressing GME and then continuing medical education. The report placed its findings and recommendations within the context of several other Canadian, U.K., U.S., European, and World Health Organization reports about medical education and its need to be more competency-focused.

In its recommendation to address the HC, the AFMC highlighted several issues relevant to our discussion in this chapter. It linked the HC to the formal curriculum, identified the HC as "pervasive and complex," framed the HC within both organizational structure and culture, and tied the HC to the broader value system of medical education.

More specifically, the report tied the concept of the HC to the process of physician socialization and to the practices of self-reflection and self-analysis. The report specified how the HC is tied to issues of power and hierarchy and to the "existing reward and recognition systems," and how the HC can influence student career and workforce decisions, with family medicine receiving special mention as a negative example. The report identified the HC as originating within forces both internal and external to medical education, including other healthcare disciplines, and to broader societal factors. The report specified that the HC can include elements that are positive in nature, but stated that the HC's impact is "counter-productive to learning." The report stressed mentoring (student–student and faculty–student), along with issues of interprofessional education.

In a subtler fashion, the report noted that addressing issues of the HC must occur at a system level (across the learning continuum), involve multiple learning venues (in terms of multiple medical schools and other health profession training programs), and be ongoing (the HC never disappears), and that both learners and teachers must work together to "identify and acknowledge the hidden curriculum." The AFMC's overall goal was to make the HC explicit and to better align it with the formal curriculum. The report's final recommendation called for more research on the presence and effects of the HC.

Several points are worth expanding on in light of the AFMC's report and its recommendations. First, and with respect to how best to align the formal and hidden curricula, the goal should never be to treat the HC as a servant to or facilitator of the formal curriculum. In other words, reform that seeks to address the HC should not uncritically identify the HC as the deviant or defective side of the educational coin, and thus to bring the HC into alignment with the formal curriculum. This point is subtle, yet important.

Although it is necessary to examine the formal and hidden curricula relative to each other, and although a person's ultimate objective may be to minimize his or her cross- or countervailing effects, the HC may not always be at fault. Some disconnects may point to flaws within the formal curriculum, rather than the other way around. Stated somewhat differently, evidence that the formal and hidden curricula are in conflict or otherwise working at cross-purposes does not unequivocally lead to the conclusion that remediation must come by changing aspects of the HC. Perhaps the classroom is "out of whack"? As noted by Castellani and Hafferty,[130] the professionalism being advanced by organized medicine, and around which most of the formal coursework in professionalism has been structured, is decidedly nostalgic in its conception of what it means to be a professional. Although principles such as professionalism obviously need to be grounded in some sense of tradition, those traditions need to be responsive to contemporary changes in the broader

socioeconomic and political environment. For example, the AFMC report calls for a "civic professionalism," a professionalism that reflects a spirit of collective community, societal and global responsibilities, and a "spirit of collaboration" across the health occupations. This rendering is quite different from a professionalism that centralizes the values of altruism, practice autonomy, and responsibility to individual patients. However, the AFMC's vision of professionalism (which almost reads like a Phase II or post professionalism) may not be the professionalism medical schools or medical associations are advancing.

It is, however, a form of professionalism that could be endorsed by health systems or by other health occupations given its calls for greater teamwork and a spirit of interprofessional relations. Given the pace and complexity of change within medicine and between medicine and society, there is always the likelihood that at least certain aspects of a school's formal curriculum may be out of sync with the needs of medical practice and/or foundational goals such as social responsibility and accountability.

Although the usual mantra about students hearing one thing in the classroom and seeing another in the clinic may indeed reflect an important source of evidence about disconnects, it would be a mistake to unilaterally identify the classroom as being the source of good/correct messages while the clinic is a source of bad/incorrect teachings. As a consequence, one needs to not preemptively focus remedial attentions on one side of the formal–hidden teaching equation than the other. Although possibly farfetched, it is conceivable that students may first encounter the AFMC's "social responsibility and accountability" version of professionalism in the clinic, far in advance of what they had been hearing in the classroom.

A second nugget lies in the notion of the HC as counterproductive to learning. Technically, this is never the case. The HC is all about learning. It is (often, but not always) just a different type and source of learning than what unfolds within the formal curriculum. It may involve learning that is unintended, is counterproductive, or at a minimum, falls outside the kinds of framings formally called for by faculty and/or administration, but it is learning nonetheless. In one of the first articles about the HC and medical education, the point was not that students lacked instruction in medical ethics prior to the widespread advent of medical and bioethics courses in the 1970s and 1980s.[15]

Rather, the argument was that merely adding more formal ethics teaching to what students had been learning about what it meant to practice ethically would accomplish little in producing more ethically attuned physicians. The same is true for professionalism courses in the 1990s.

Lectures on becoming a professional have long been a part of medical education. What is at issue here is not the learning, but the content of that learning and that what is being learned about professionalism, be it inside or outside the classroom, may be far removed from the precepts of professionalism being advanced today in documents such as the Physician's Charter or the AFMC Report.

A third and final important point lies in contrasting how the AFMC report, the LCME, and the ACGME handle the HC. To reiterate, the LCME (MS-31-A) requires that:

"Medical schools must ensure that the learning environment for medical students promotes the development of explicit and appropriate professional attributes (attitudes, behaviors, and identity) in their medical students."

As we examine the text, it is clear that the focus is on professionalism and professional attributes and not on medical education. In contrast, the AFMC's framing of the HC is more expansive. It remains to be seen how medical schools will respond to the requirement that makes them responsible for learning environments that apply to "professional attributes."

However, the LCME does not define "professionalism and professional attributes," so these attributes could come to mean all aspects of competence, from knowledge and skills through attitudes and values, and including such broad aspects of medical practice as quality of care and patient safety.

Finally, and technically speaking, there are no counterparts to MS-31-A within the ACGME's core competencies or its accompanying text. In short, the ACGME does not recognize the HC within its accreditation materials. The goal of transparency requires the qualification that the AFMC's focus on the HC targets undergraduate education. Whether this focus survives to the forthcoming report on GME and continuing medical education remains to be seen.

Conclusion

As noted at the outset of this chapter, although the HC is not a competency per se, the ability of residency programs to align both their formal and informal/hidden curricula is critical if competency goals are to be met. It makes no sense—and creates considerable pedagogical chaos and student cynicism otherwise—if programs invest major resources to embed the six ACGME competencies within their formal curricula, and yet steadfastly ignore what their residents are experiencing as they move through the various phases and sites of training. An almost universal theme within the HC literature exists that indicates considerable learning takes place with the informal and hidden curricula. However, residency programs often fail to acknowledge (operationally) that the HC is present.[73]

So, how does one begin to address residency learning from an HC perspective? If actions do, in fact, speak louder than words, and both public beliefs and pedagogical theory say they do, being attuned to the distance and difference between what we say and what we do must become a centerpiece of residency training. This is easier said than done, but it must be done.

A first step, and assuming that the concept may be somewhat new to faculty, is to compile a brief reading list on the HC. One example of six core articles would include Hafferty and Franks' article on the HC and ethics education[15] along with a follow-up article by Hafferty on moving beyond reforming the formal curriculum as the sole seat of change;[17] two articles by Haidet and colleagues on the HC and patient-centeredness[39] and the relational aspects of learning and the HC as a process;[83]

and two excellent articles by Delese Wear, including her recent study on the HC and psychiatry residency training with Skillicorn,[68] and her earlier examination of the HC and white coat ceremonies.[131] A number of other studies have been reviewed in this chapter, but these six articles are a good place to start. Two good supplemental (and extended) resources are Benson Snyder's (*The Hidden Curriculum*) examination of the HC in under-graduate college education,[7] and Thomas Inui's powerful reflections (*A Flag in the Wind*) on medical training.[132]

Next, calibrate and then reconcile what currently is going on within your formal curriculum and how that curriculum is being assessed, in terms of both traditional practices, such as student performance ratings (e.g., grading and related assessments) and general faculty oversight via medical education offices or faculty-led education committees. Any gap between what the program says is important (its formal curriculum) and what it actually evaluates (what it holds people accountable for) is the first place trainees look to see if their program really means what it says.

Medical education is a high-stakes, high-stress environment, and trainees are exquisitely attuned to what they are really being held accountable for as opposed to what the program says (formally) they are being held accountable for. And this attentiveness to the actual versus the stated should not come as a surprise to faculty. Students have been so attuned to exactly this critical difference for generations, and they have been learning to do so long before they arrived at the gates of medical schools and residency training programs. Asking faculty if something "is going to be on the test" or demanding that faculty be explicit about "what we are really supposed to take away" are time-honored questions by both undergraduate and resident students alike.

Similarly, residency leadership should pay attention to and identify what faculty see as the disconnects between what the program says it does with respect to the six ACGME competencies and what really takes place during day-to-day residency operations. If the only time faculty hear about the competencies is during orientation or when everyone meets to compile accreditation documents (faculty are directed to figure out how to prove the program is meeting its accreditation requirements), there is a disconnect between what we say and what we do. Under such circumstances of general indifference or "gamesmanship", faculty become indifferent to and/or cynical about what is supposed to be core to their educational efforts. Several studies on the HC have highlighted the importance of faculty development in narrowing the space between the formal and the informal/hidden curricula.[43, 79, 129] Before anything else, faculty need to be on board. Faculty need to know what the HC is; how it affects training; and what they can do to minimize its negative effects and maximize its positives. At a minimum, programs need to invest in faculty development around issues of the HC.

A third step might involve targeting one of the six competencies—a test case, so to speak—and making a concerted effort to examine both the formal curriculum (what is being taught) and what students are learning in terms of that competency. This is not a simple matter. One cannot simply identify the formal curriculum and then quiz/test residents on the basis of those competencies. Yes, such a summative review is a necessary part of an overall assessment program, but it is only one part. The issue here is not the attainment of a competency as much as it is what residents are learning about patient care, about medical knowledge, and about practice-based learning as they evolve into independent practitioners. The program may say that A, B, and C are key aspects of systems-based practice, but what if residents say they have learned A, D, and E about systems-based practice, and D is antithetical to B, and E is something altogether different from C? How do you find this out? You certainly do not ask preconceived or leading questions (e.g., "What have you learned about A?" or "You're learning A, aren't you?"). Instead, employ open-ended inquiries such as "What have you learned about systems-based practice?" or perhaps the even more inclusive "What are you learning about the six core competencies?" Furthermore, observe, perhaps using anthropological or sociologically informed field methods.

Again, this is easier said than done. In many instances, junior program faculty are not all that removed from their own residency training, yet what often happens is as soon as they take on the faculty mantle, their memories are wiped clean of all the unofficial things they learned. This is indeed an unfortunate loss of cultural memory.

A fourth step, and an extension of the test case explored in the preceding step, is to take the lessons learned about systems-based practice, for example, and apply them to the remaining five competencies.

A fifth and even more complicated integrative step is to then take all six competencies and begin the task of ensuring that what is being taught and learned with respect to each one is not only internally consistent across learning environments, but also consistent across the competencies.

None of this is easy. None of this is straightforward. And none of this is inexpensive, particularly in terms of faculty time. Yet the cost of doing nothing is high in regard to both the length and complexity of residency training and in terms of the increasingly complex practice environment into which residents much venture forth. Critics have long argued that undergraduate medical students are not adequately prepared to enter residency and that residents are not adequately prepared to enter practice.

This should not be the case, and part of addressing these inadequacies must lie in the amount of counter-vailing information, skills, and values students are forced to learn as they pass through the host of learning environments they encounter in their training—learning environments which, by the way, many trainees characterize as extraordinarily stressful, demeaning, and laden with wasteful tasks and scut work.

In the old days, we predicated much of our beliefs in the adequacy of student preparation around seat time. Given enough time in class and given enough time on the wards, we assumed that students would be sufficiently exposed to everything they needed to know to practice good medicine. This is no longer a safe assumption, if only for the recent reduction in duty hours.

Learning to be a good physician is a lifelong and complex process. It therefore needs to be approached at a systems level.

References

1. Dalfen AK. Medical students as emotional chameleons. *Can Med Assoc J.* 1999;160:182–193.

2. Hafferty FW, Castellani B. The increasing complexities of professionalism. *Acad Med.* 2010;85:288–301.

3. Hafferty FW, Hafler JP. The hidden curriculum, structural disconnects, and the socialization of new professionals. In: Hafler JP, ed. *Exemplary Learning in the Workplace.* New York, NY: Springer; [in press].

4. Dewey J. *Experience and Education.* New York, NY: Collier Books; 1938.

5. Jackson P. *Life in Classrooms.* New York, NY: Holt, Rinehard and Winston, Inc.; 1968.

6. Apple MW. The hidden curriculum and the nature of conflict. *Interchange.* 1971;2:27–40.

7. Snyder BR. *The Hidden Curriculum.* New York, NY: Alfred A. Knopf; 1971.

8. Cowell RN. The hidden curriculum: a theoretical framework and a pilot study [dissertation]. Cambridge, MA: Harvard Graduate School of Education; 1972.

9. Apple MW. The other side of the hidden curriculum: correspondence theories and the labor process. *Interchange.* 1980;11:5–22.

10. Gordon D. The concept of the hidden curriculum. *J Philos Educ.* 1982;16:187–198.

11. Bergenhenegouwen G. Hidden curriculum in the university. *Higher Educ.* 1987;16:535–543.

12. Anderson DJ. The hidden curriculum. *Am J Roentgenol.* 1992;159:21–22.

13. Gordon D. Hidden curriculum. In: Saha LJ, ed. *Encyclopedia of the Sociology of Education.* Oxford, UK: Pergamon; 1997:4884–4487.

14. Margolis E. *The Hidden Curriculum in Higher Education.* New York, NY: Routledge; 2001.

15. Hafferty FW, Franks R. The hidden curriculum, ethics teaching, and the structure of medical education. *Acad Med.* 1994;69:861–871.

16. Haas J, Shaffir W. Ritual evaluation of competence: the hidden curriculum of professionalization in an innovative medical school program. *Work Occup.* 1982;9:131–154.

17. Hafferty FW. Beyond curriculum reform: confronting medicine's hidden curriculum. *Acad Med.* 1998;73: 403–407.

18. Flinders DJ, Noddings N, Thornton SJ. The null curriculum: its theoretical basis and practical implications. *Curric Inq.* 1986;16:33–42.

19. Gaufberg E, Bell S, Batalden M. The hidden curriculum: what can we learn from third-year medical student narrative reflections? *Acad Med.* [in press].

20. Dosani N. The top ten things I learned in medical school (but wasn't supposed to). Paper presented at 2010 Canadian Conference on Medical Education; May 1–5, 2010, St. John's Newfoundland.

21. Goffman E. *The Presentation of Self in Everyday Life.* Garden City, NY: Doubleday; 1959.

22. Louis MR. Acculturation in the workplace: newcomers as lay ethnographers. In: Schneider B, ed. *Organizational Climate and Culture.* San Francisco, CA: Jossey-Bass; 1990:85–129.

23. Ashforth BE, Sluss DM, Harrison SH. Socialization in organizational contexts. *Int Rev Industr Org Psych.* 2007;22:1–70.

24. Hafferty FW. Professionalism and the socialization of medical students. In: Cruess RL, Cruess SR, Steinert Y, eds. *Teaching Medical Professionalism.* New York, NY: Cambridge University Press; 2008:53–70.

25. Sung AD, Collins ME, Smith AK, et al. Crying: experiences and attitudes of third-year medical students and interns. *Teach Learn Med.* 2009;21:180–187.

26. Turner V. Betwixt and between: the liminal period in rites of passage. In: Turner V, ed. *The Forest of Symbols: Aspects of Ndembu Ritual*. Ithaca, NY: Cornell University Press; 1970:93–111.

27. Hundert EM, Hafferty F, Christakis D. Characteristics of the informal curriculum and trainees' ethical choices. *Acad Med*. 1996;71:624–642.

28. Hundert EM, Douglas-Steele D, Bickel J. Context in medical education: the informal ethics curriculum. *Med Educ*. 1996;30:353–364.

29. Ginsburg S, Regehr G, Stern D, Lingard L. The anatomy of the professional lapse: bridging the gap between traditional frameworks and student perceptions. *Acad Med*. 2002;77:516–522.

30. Lempp H, Swale C. The hidden curriculum in undergraduate medical education: qualitative study of medical students' perceptions of teaching. *BMJ*. 2004;329:770–773.

31. Coulehan J, Williams PC. Vanquishing virtue: the impact of medical education. *Acad Med*. 2001;76:598–605.

32. Chretien K, Goldman E, Faselis C. The reflective writing class blog: using technology to promote reflection and professional development. *J Gen Intern Med*. 2008;23:2066–2070.

33. Balmer D. Learning about systems-based practice in the informal curriculum: a case study in an academic pediatric continuity clinic. *Ambul Ped*. 2007;7:214–219.

34. Branch WT Jr. Use of critical incident reports in medical education – a perspective. *J Gen Intern Med*. 2005;20:1063–1067.

35. Dyrbye LN, Harris I, Rohren CH. Early clinical experiences from students' perspectives: a qualitative study of narratives. *Acad Med*. 2007;82:979–988.

36. Rabow MW, Wrubel J, Remen RN. Promise of professionalism: personal mission statements among a national cohort of medical students. *Annals Fam Med*. 2009;7:336–342.

37. Karnieli-Miller O, Vu TR, Holtman MC, Clyman SG, Inui TS. Medical students' professionalism narratives: a window on the informal and hidden curriculum. *Acad Med*. 2010;85:124–133.

38. Olthuis G, Dekkers W. Medical education, palliative care and moral attitude: some objectives and future perspectives. *Med Educ*. 2003;37:928–933.

39. Haidet P, Kelly PA, Chou C. The communication, curriculum, and culture study group. Characterizing the patient-centeredness of hidden curricula in medical schools: development and validation of a new measure. *Acad Med*. 2005;80:44–50.

40. Al-Bawardy R, Blatt B, Al-Shohaib S, Simmens SJ. Cross-cultural comparison of the patient-centeredness of the hidden curriculum between a Saudi Arabian and 9 US medical schools. *Med Educ Online*. 2009;14:19.

41. Brainard AH, Brislen HC. Viewpoint: learning professionalism: a view from the trenches. *Acad Med*. 2007;82:1010–1014.

42. Christakis DA, Feudtner C. Ethics in a short white coat: the ethical dilemmas that medical students confront. *Acad Med*. 1993;68:249–254.

43. Leo T, Eagen K. Professionalism education: the medical student response. *Pers Biol Med*. 2008;51:508–516.

44. Reis DC. Who am I and why am I here? Professionalism research through the eyes of a medical student. *Acad Med*. 2008;83(10 suppl):S111–S112.

45. Hafferty FW. What medical students know about professionalism. *Mt Sinai J Med*. 2002;69:385–397.

46. Hafferty FW, Levinson D. Professionalism perspective: moving beyond nostalgia and motives: towards a complexity science view of medical professionalism. *Pers Biol Med*. 2008;51:599–614.

47. Kassebaum DG, Cutler ER. On the culture of student abuse in medical school. *Acad Med*. 1998;73:1149–1158.

48. Doctor X. *Intern*. New York, NY: Harper and Row; 1965.

49. Nolan WA. *The Making of a Surgeon*. New York, NY: Random House; 1970.

50. Nolan WA. *A Surgeon's World*. New York, NY: Random House; 1972.

51. Shem S. *The House of God*. New York, NY: Dell; 1978.

52. Collins MJ. *Hot Lights, Cold Steel: Life, Death and Sleepless Nights in a Surgeon's First Years*. New York, NY: St. Martin's Press; 2005.

53. Collins MJ. *Blue Collar, Blue Scrubs: The Making of a Surgeon*. New York, NY: St. Martin's Press; 2009.

54. Ofri D. *Singular Intimacies: Becoming a Physician at Bellevue*. Boston, MA: Beacon Press; 2003.

55. Woloschuk W, Harasym PH, Temple W. Undergraduate medical education: attitude change during medical school: a cohort study. *Med Educ*. 2004;38:522–534.

56. Christianson CE, McBride RB, Vari RC, Olson L, Wilson HD. From traditional to patient-centered learning: curriculum change as an intervention for changing institutional culture and promoting professionalism in undergraduate medical education. *Acad Med*. 2007;82: 1079–1088.

57. Crandall SJ, Marion GS. Commentary: identifying attitudes towards empathy: an essential feature of professionalism. *Acad Med*. 2009;84:1174–1176.

58. Cutler JL, Harding KJ, Mozian SA, et al. Discrediting the notion "working with 'crazies' will make you 'crazy'": addressing stigma and enhancing empathy in medical student education. *Adv Health Sci Educ*. 2009;14:487–502.

59. Hojat M, Vergare MJ, Maxwell K, et al. The devil is in the third year: a longitudinal study of erosion of empathy in medical school. *Acad Med*. 2009;84:1182–1191.

60. Testerman JK, Morton KR, Loo LK, Worthley JS, Lamberton HH. The natural history of cynicism in physicians. *Acad Med*. 1996;71(10 suppl):S43–S45.

61. Krupat E, Pelletier S, Alexander EK, Hirsh DA, Ogur B. Can changes in the principal clinical year prevent the erosion of students' patient-centered beliefs? *Acad Med*. 2009;84:582–586.

62. Eckenfels E. A socio-cultural framework for explaining perceptions of mistreatment and abuse in the professional socialization of future physicians. *Annals Behav Sci Med Educ*. 1997;4:11–18.

63. Dyrbye LN, Thomas MR, Huntington JL, et al. Personal life events and medical student burnout: a multicenter study. *Acad Med*. 2006;81:374–384.

64. Dyrbye LN, Thomas MR, Harper W, et al. The learning environment and medical student burnout: a multi-center study. *Med Educ*. 2009;43:274–282.

65. D'Eon MF, Lear N, Turner M, Jones C. Perils of the hidden curriculum revisited. *Med Teach*. 2007;29: 295–296.

66. Feudtner C, Christakis DA, Christakis NA. Do clinical clerks suffer ethical erosion? Students' perceptions of their clinical environment and personal development. *Acad Med*. 1994;69:670–679.

67. Burack JH, Irby DM, Carline JD, Root RK, Larson EB. Teaching compassion and respect: attending physicians' responses to problematic behaviors. *J Gen Intern Med*. 1999;14:49–55.

68. Wear D, Skillicorn J. Hidden in plain sight: the formal, informal, and hidden curricula of a psychiatry clerkship. *Acad Med*. 2009;84:451–458.

69. Calabrese C, Sciolla A, Zisook S, Bitner R, Tuttle J, Dunn LB. Psychiatric residents' views of quality of psychotherapy training and psychotherapy competencies: a multisite survey. *Acad Psych*. 2010;34:13–20.

70. Agrawal S, Szatmari P, Hanson M. Teaching evidence-based psychiatry: integrating and aligning the formal and hidden curricula. *Acad Psych*. 2008;32:470–474.

71. Coverdale JH, Weiss Roberts L, Louie AK. Teaching evidence-based psychiatry to residents and fellows: developing the curriculum. *Acad Psych*. 2008;32:453–457.

72. Agrawal S, Szatmari P, Hanson M. Integrating and aligning the formal and hidden curricula. *Acad Psych.* 2008;32:470–474.

73. Balmer DF, Master CL, Richards B, Giardino AP. Implicit versus explicit curricula in general pediatrics education: is there a convergence? *Pediatrics.* 2009;124:e347–354.

74. Lang CW, Smith PJ, Ross LF. Ethics and professionalism in the pediatric curriculum: a survey of pediatric program directors. *Pediatrics.* 2009;124:1143–1151.

75. Green AR, Betancourt JR, Park ER, Greer JA, Donahue EJ, Weissman JS. Providing culturally competent care: residents in HRSA Title VII funded residency programs feel better prepared. *Acad Med.* 2008;83:1071–1079.

76. Rowley BD, Baldwin DC Jr, Bay RC, Karpman RR. Professionalism and professional values in orthopedics. *Clin Orthop Relat Res.* 2000;387:90–96.

77. Pinney SJ, Mehta S, Pratt DD, et al. Orthopaedic surgeons as educators: applying the principles of adult education to teaching orthopaedic residents. *J Bone Joint Surg Am.* 2007;89:1385–1392.

78. Cohn FG, Shapiro J, Lie DA, Boker J, Stephens F, Leung LA. Interpreting values conflicts experienced by obstetrics-gynecology clerkship students using reflective writing. *Acad Med.* 2009;84:587–596.

79. Gaiser RR. The teaching of professionalism during residency: why it is failing and a suggestion to improve its success. *Anesth Analg.* 2009;108:948–954.

80. Joyner BD, Vemulakonda VM. Improving professionalism: making the implicit more explicit. *J Urol.* 2007;177:2287–2290.

81. Murakami M, Kawabata H, Maezawa M. The perception of the hidden curriculum on medical education: an exploratory study. *Asia Pac Fam Med.* 2009;8:9.

82. Association of Faculties of Medicine of Canada. *The Future of Medical Education in Canada: A Collective Vision.* Ottawa, Ontario, Canada: Association of Faculties of Medicine of Canada; 2010.

83. Haidet P, Stein HF. The role of the student–teacher relationship in the formation of physicians: the hidden curriculum as process. *J Gen Intern Med.* 2006;21 (1 suppl):S16–S20.

84. Hilton SR, Slotnick HB. Proto-professionalism: how professionalisation occurs across the continuum of medical education. *Med Educ.* 2005;39:58–65.

85. Patenaude J, Niyonsenga T, Fafard D. Changes in students' moral development in medical school: a cohort study. *Can Med Assoc J.* 2003;168:840–844.

86. Wear D. Professional development of medical students: problems and promises. *Acad Med.* 1997;72:1056–1062.

87. Rose GL, Rukstalis MR, Schuckit MA. Informal mentoring between faculty and medical students. *Acad Med.* 2005;80:344–348.

88. Martin J, Lloyd M, Singh S. Professional attitudes: can they be taught and assessed in medical education? *Clin Med.* 2002;2:217–222.

89. Barry D, Cyran E, Anderson RJ. Common issues in medical professionalism: room to grow. *Am J Med.* 2000;108:136–142.

90. Suchman AL, Williamson PR, Litzelman DK, et al. Toward an informal curriculum that teaches professionalism: transforming the social environment of a medical school. *J Gen Intern Med.* 2004;19:501–504.

91. Wallace AG. Educating tomorrow's doctors: the thing that really matters is that we care. *Acad Med.* 1997;72: 253–258.

92. Cottingham AH, Suchman AL, Litzelman DK, et al. Enhancing the informal curriculum of a medical school: a case study in organizational culture change. *J Gen Inter Med.* 2008;23:715–722.

93. Suchman AL, Williamson PR, Litzelman DK, Frankel RM, Mossbarger DL, Inui TS. Toward an informal curriculum that teaches professionalism: a two year progress report on cascading change at IUSM. *J Gen Intern Med.* 2005;20:39.